MW01626279

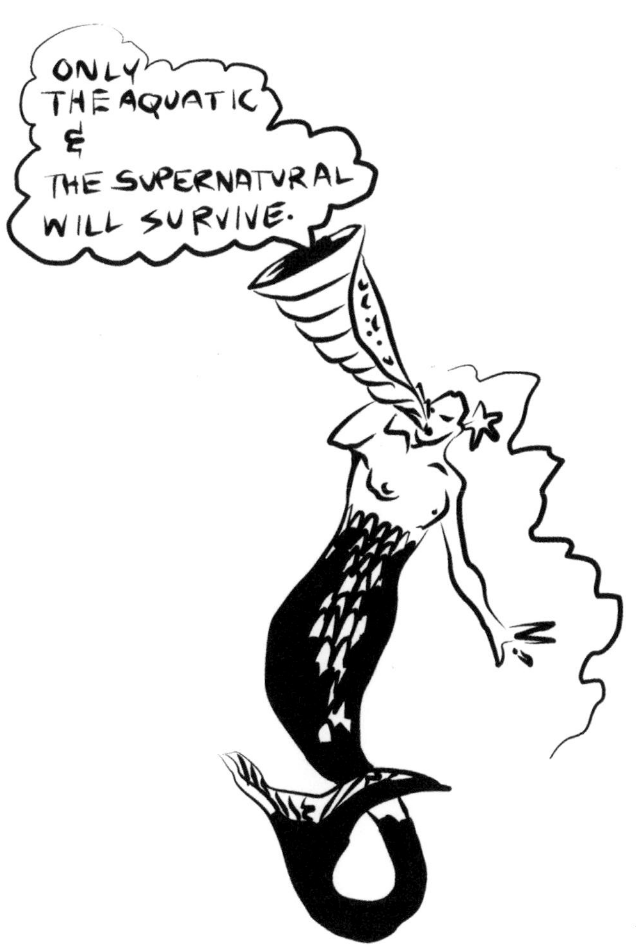
ONLY THE AQUATIC & THE SUPERNATURAL WILL SURVIVE.

MY BARBARIAN

Edited by Adrienne Edwards, Malik Gaines, Jade Gordon, and Alexandro Segade
with contributions by Joshua Chambers-Letson and Lia Gangitano

WHITNEY MUSEUM OF AMERICAN ART, NEW YORK
Distributed by Yale University Press, New Haven and London

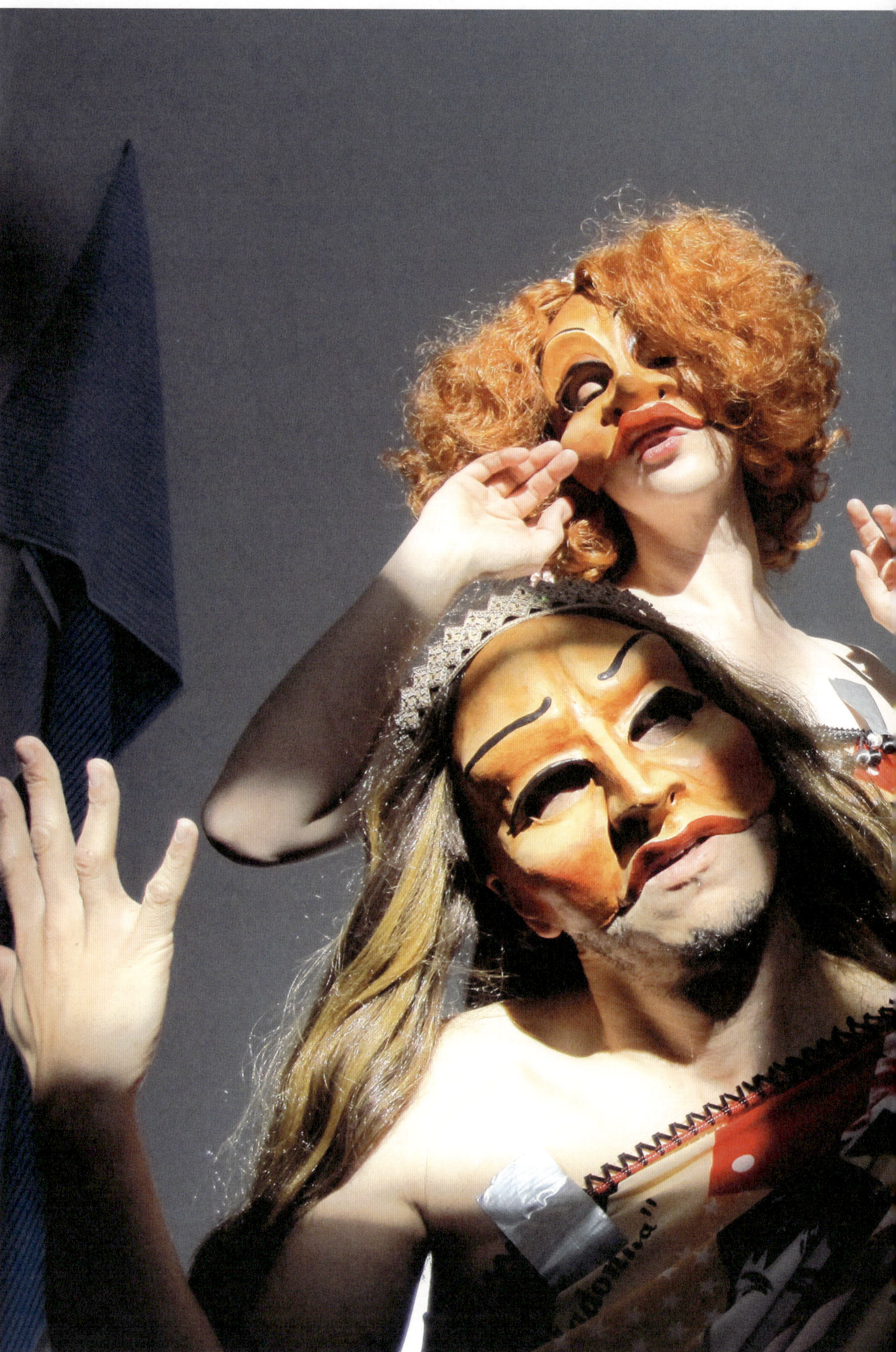

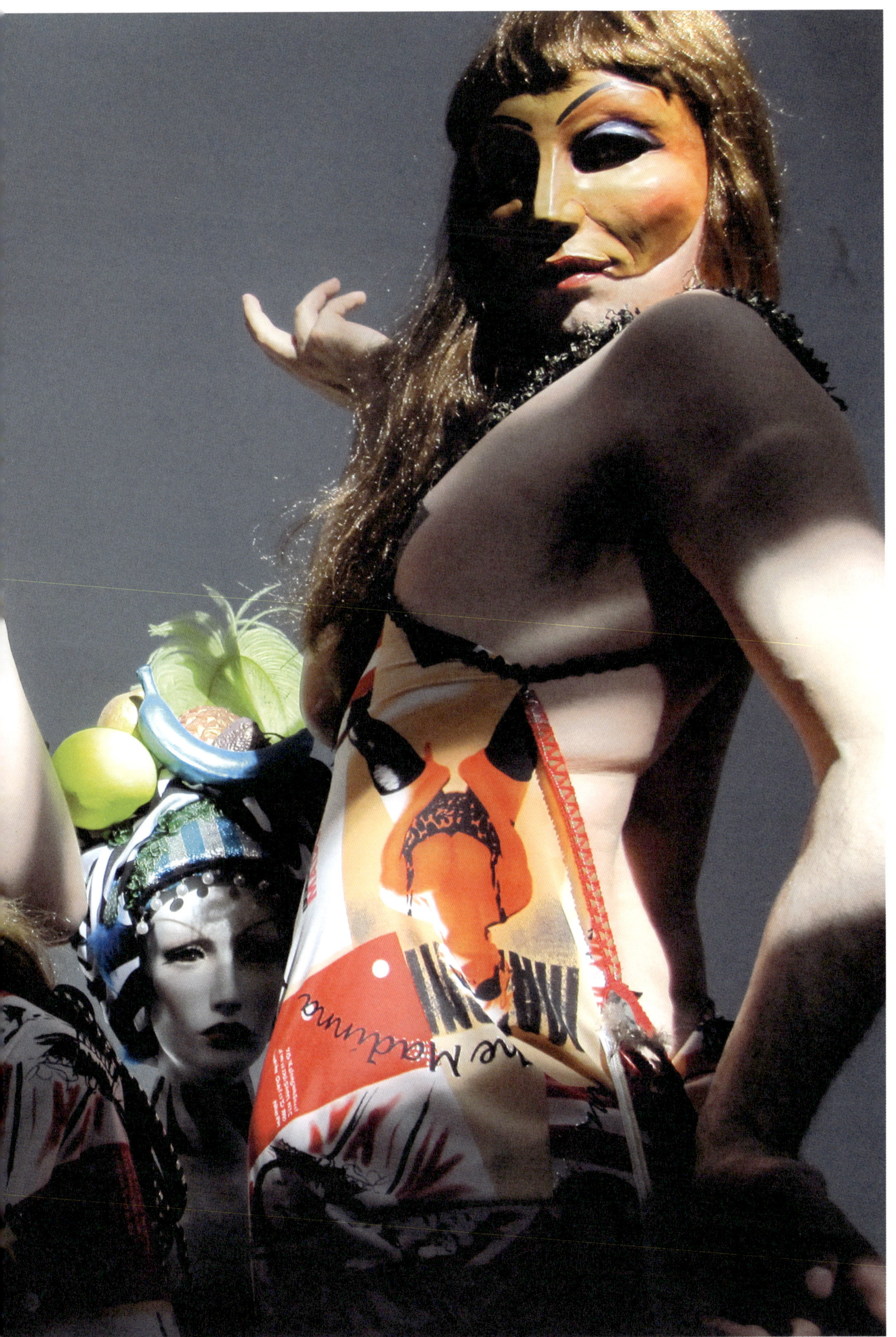

FOREWORD

Throughout its history, the Whitney Museum of American Art has often been a lightning rod. As a center for contemporary art and a home for living artists, it presents the art of our time—sometimes raw, at times inflammatory, and almost always challenging. The art of today does not simply reify and confirm but rather interrogates the norms of aesthetics, belief systems, and social conditions. This situation often puts the Museum in a complicated position, that of simultaneously being an establishment of "the system" and a vehicle for questioning "the system." One need only witness the tensions in museums and other cultural institutions today—from internal and external protests regarding the financial support of our organizations to the righteous calls for diversity and equity in terms of representation and compensation—to appreciate this reality.

The work of the brilliantly inventive collective My Barbarian (Malik Gaines, Jade Gordon, and Alexandro Segade) during the past twenty years brings these complications to the fore. In their performances—mash-ups and remixes of history and culture that draw on everything from Greek drama and the plays of Bertolt Brecht to the performances of Jack Smith, discos, and television dramas—the line between the presenting institution and the artist is diminished as is the line between art and life. When experiencing My Barbarian's works, viewers enter a netherworld, a place of raucous absurdity and alienation that is also strangely familiar, accessible, and even magnetic. One is simultaneously and inexorably drawn into their productions and repelled by them. My Barbarian holds up a cultural mirror that forces us to see ourselves, what we have created, what we have destroyed, the inequities and tragedies of life, history as fiction assembled and reassembled from a stew of facts and images along with the magical, supernatural, and spiritual rituals and traditions that make life bearable. The brilliance of My Barbarian lies in part in their ability to entertain, give pleasure, provide enjoyment, and offer catharsis while also confronting and compelling us to reexamine our motives, morals, means, goals, lives, and histories. Their performances, by turns slapstick, zany, haunting, and melancholic, are visceral experiences that set our teeth on edge, turn us on our ears, and raise our hair, reminding us that culture is malleable material used to relate narratives, reveal truths, and explain the way things are.

For My Barbarian, a museum is both a cordial and supportive host and an adversary to be investigated, admonished, and ridiculed (as particularly evidenced in the first episode for their 2015 video series *Double Agency*, "The Viewer and the Viewed"). They recognize the contradictions: the complicity of museums in making canons, creating stereotypes, establishing authority, and conferring power. They also recognize that their presence in and involvement with cultural institutions can make museums more vital and also places to question, undermine, and overturn hierarchies in the hope of realizing new paradigms of understanding. While My Barbarian's work is of profound seriousness, their playfulness and satirical sensibility is something to be admired. For it is through humor, making fun of themselves and everything we take for granted, that we, the audience, find new meanings.

My great gratitude goes to Adrienne Edwards, Engell Speyer Family Curator and Director of Curatorial Affairs, for recognizing the timeliness and even the urgency of organizing the exhibition *My Barbarian* at this moment. Working collaboratively, Adrienne and My Barbarian have realized an ambitious survey that assembles two decades of diverse and complex projects into a coherent whole that is far greater than the sum of its parts. My congratulations to Malik Gaines, Jade Gordon, and Alexandro Segade for creating a spectacle that reminds us of the fallibility, vulnerability, and wonder of life itself. Their persistent commitment to the demanding and time-consuming work of performance is to be lauded.

I am grateful to Nordstrom for sponsoring *My Barbarian* and recognizing the importance of performance at the Whitney. My thanks also go to Judy Hart Angelo; the John R. Eckel, Jr. Foundation; and the Whitney's National Committee for their generosity and commitment to the exhibition. The Marshall Weinberg Fund for Performance, endowed in honor of his parents, Anna and Harold Weinberg, provides crucial support for the performance program.

My Barbarian is already well known and greatly admired within the arts community; it is our hope that the exhibition, performances, and this volume will reach and be appreciated by a wider audience.

Adam D. Weinberg
Alice Pratt Brown Director

ARTISTS' ACKNOWLEDGMENTS

Malik Gaines, Jade Gordon, Alexandro Segade

The members of My Barbarian offer tremendous gratitude to Adrienne Edwards for shepherding this project so brilliantly and wisely, and with all of the humor the work requires. Much appreciation goes to Mia Matthias and to Reid Farrington, Seth Fogelman, Jacob Horn, Beth Huseman, Melanie Taylor, Raul Zbengheci, and everyone at the Whitney Museum. Thanks to Joseph Logan and Katy Nelson for designing this remarkable book, to editor Amanda Glesmann, and to Joshua Chambers-Letson and Lia Gangitano for their thoughtful essays. Thanks to Connor Kalista and Brian Aldous for their work on the exhibition.

We thank Susanne Vielmetter, Ariel Pittman, Matthew Lax, Caitlin Wade, Evelia Magallon, and David Bratton at Vielmetter Los Angeles for their support.

Thanks to our founding band members, Norwood Cheek, Dustin Ericksen, and Andy Ouchi; core musicians Scott Martin and Giles Miller; and others who have played music with us over the years, including Tiffany Anders, Aaron Buckley, Kelly Coats, Jonny Cragg, Anh Do, Jessica Espeleta, Paloma Griffin, Jimi Hey, Kim Humphries, Kathleen Kim, Tim Koh, Lynn Perko-Truell, Ethan Philbrick, Jonathan Silberman, Samita Sinha, Somi, Chuck Stolarek, Mazz Swift, and Amy Yao.

We are grateful to our community of collaborators and co-conspirators, including Scoli Acosta, Kelly Barrie, Patterson Beckwith, Roddy Bottum, Melissa Clemens, Rhys Ernst, Kim Fisher, Eve Fowler, Sherin Guirguis, Fritz Haeg, Karen Hallock, Gillian Haratani, Pearl C. Hsiung, Farrah Karapetian, Rosalie Knox, Daniel McDonald (Mended Veil), Matthew Monahan, Beth Murray, Jeff Ono, Isaac Resnikoff, Kathy Rivkin, Lara Schnitger, Will Schwartz, Anna Sew Hoy, J.J. Stratford, and Megan Whitmarsh.

We thank those who have performed with us, including: Robbie Acklen, Gaby Ader, Robin Anderson, Eleanor Antin, Isabel Aerenlund, Andreina Argonses, C. Bain, Morgan Bassichis, Ginger Brooks Takahashi, Nao Bustamante, Jibz Cameron, Moriah Carlson, Layla Childs, Vicente Colomar, Clary Creager, Elena di Gregorio, Charlotte Dobbs, Leilani Drakeford, Zackary Drucker, Adam Dugas, Lisa Lornetta Durbin, Mary Elizabeth Ellis, Talya Epstein, Maggie Finnegan, Sam Greenleaf Miller, Ariadne Greif, Miguel Gutierrez, Jan Hammer, John Hoobyar, Jasmine Hughes, Sandra Iyall, Obehi Janice, Stanya Kahn, Mary Kelly, Amirtha Kidambi, Zoe Leonard, Kate Lerner, Ian MacKinnon, Maliha Maslamani, Anthony P. McGlaun, Lucas Michael, Jennifer Moon, Paul Mpagi Sepuya, Joanne Nucho, Tavia Nyong'o, Artemis Pebdani, Will Rawls, Alia Raza, Earthen Ribbons, Sonya Robbins, Matana Roberts, Heber Rodriguez, Manuel Rodríguez, Dixie Salazar, Andrea Sofia Santizo, Justin Streichman, Jennifer Sullivan, Christine Sun Kim, Meir Tati, Christopher Preston Thompson, Hana van der Kolk, Larissa Velez-Jackson, Carlos Villanueva, Ingrid von Sydow, Kali Wilder, Jorell Williams, Alice Wu, members of Ballez (Katy Pyle, Charles Gowin, Deborah Lohse), Liūdni Slibinai (Dominykas Vaitiekūnas, Vaidas Kublinskas, and Aistė Lasytė), and Las Reina Chulas (Marisol Gasé, Cecilia Sotres, Ana Francis Mor, and Nora Huerta), and the participants in the *Post-Living Ante-Action Theater*.

We also acknowledge some of the many arts workers who have made our projects happen: Leah Abir, Ben Adair, Wayne Baerwaldt, Petrushka Bazin, Naomi Beckwith, Wenzel Bilger, Johanna Burton, Brande Bytheway, Amanda Cachia, Fabio Cavalucci, Travis Chamberlain, Bart De Lorenzo, Ann Demeester, Anne Ellegood, Anthony Elms, Alex Fialho, Lauri Firstenberg, Lia Gangitano, RoseLee Goldberg, Rita Gonzalez, Margo Handwerker, Geir Haraldseth, Macarena Hernández, Every Ocean Hughes, Ryan Inouye, Ana Janevski, Eungie Joo, Martha Joseph, Ruba Katrib, Anton Kern, Christine Y. Kim, Eric Kim, Thomas J. Lax, Glenn Ligon, George Lugg, Melissa McCalister, Kimberli Meyer, Lucas Michael, José Esteban Muñoz, Mark Murphy, Christina Natalicchio, Sarah O'Keefe, Tobias Ostrander, Javier Peres, Victoria Reis, Frank Smigiel, Aandrea Stang, Sara Stevenson, Matthew Thompson, Steve Turner, Asta Vaiciulyte, and Joe Wollen. Thanks to Jessica Bennett, Vilma Cruz, Daniel Leyva, Hiroshi McDonald Mori, Carolyn Murphy, Augie Robles, Isaac Silber, and Alex Zandi. A special thank-you goes to Robert Hickerson and Lekha Jandhyala.

Ian Marshall has provided decades of important support, as have our family members: Barbara Gaines, Charles Gaines, Victoria Gordon, Jackie Marshall, Roxana Landaverde, Joe Rosato, Eric Schaeffer, Irina Segade, Mateo Segade, and Gustavo Segade. Endless appreciation to Angelo, Gloria, and Oscar Marshall.

Finally, we'd like to thank each other for sticking with it, through laughter and tears. Said in the voice of a jaded actress with a cigarette in hand: "We've been in this business for twenty-one years . . ."

CURATOR'S ACKNOWLEDGMENTS

Adrienne Edwards

I offer my deepest thanks to My Barbarian. For more than three years, we have collectively delved into the complex ideas, surprising inspirations, and vital questions their work explores. This ambitious multi-format survey—exhibition, performance program, and catalogue—benefited tremendously from their generosity, patience, and attention to detail. Alex, Jade, and Malik: thank you for the opportunity to present your work and for sharing your treasure trove of an archive with the Whitney and our audiences.

Endless gratitude goes to Adam D. Weinberg, the Whitney's Alice Pratt Brown Director, who has made performance a pillar of his vision for this museum. I am also grateful to Scott Rothkopf, Senior Deputy Director and Nancy and Steve Crown Family Chief Curator, for recognizing this project's potential and for his abiding support.

A presentation of this range and complexity requires the expertise of staff throughout the Museum. My colleagues in the curatorial department generously shared their feedback and scholarship. Mia Matthias, curatorial assistant, has my heartfelt gratitude; without her partnership in organizing every aspect of this project, this ambitious undertaking could not have been realized. CJ Salapare provided crucial support as an intern.

This publication was made possible by the herculean efforts and generous support of colleagues within and beyond the Museum. Beth Huseman and Jacob Horn in the publications department expertly guided it to fruition with care, flexibility, and acute attention to detail. Great thanks are due to designers Joseph Logan and Katy Nelson, who have worked closely with us to create a book that is true to the aesthetics and themes of My Barbarian's work and captures the range and depth of their output. I am also grateful to Amanda Glesmann, who has been both a meticulous and patient editor. Joshua Chambers-Letson and Lia Gangitano, essential thought partners and longtime champions of the collective, have greatly enriched this volume with essays that thoughtfully contextualize My Barbarian's work.

I am grateful to Christy Putnam for her leadership throughout this process. The formidable exhibition design team, led by Melanie Taylor and supported by Jared Huggins, beautifully translated our wish for a "gallery as a theater" into reality, rendering an elaborate—and at times unwieldy—vision quite tangible. Thanks are due to Lindsey O'Connor, who was exhibition coordinator in the earlier stages of the project, and Seth Fogelman, who deftly wore two hats as both registrar and exhibition coordinator, handling complex logistics with grace, humor, and deep knowledge.

I salute the audiovisual team—this was a particularly complex and ambitious installation that required us all to think outside the box. Special thanks to Reid Farrington for his insight, guidance, and determination to bring My Barbarian's vision forward. Eva Von Schweinitz and Lucas Gonzalez handled the numerous projections and tech rehearsals with patience and understanding. Connor Kalista, video editor, and Brian Aldous, lighting designer, worked fluidly with us to meet the challenge of creating an immersive experience. Raul Zbengheci has expertly coordinated the in-person and digital programming essential to realizing the exhibition's performance program, working alongside Danielle Sheli Levy.

My appreciation also goes to the following individuals across the Museum and their teams: Morgan Arenson, Pamela Besnard, Danielle Bias, Anne Byrd, I.D. Aruede, Marilou Aquino, Wendy Barbee-Lowell, David Breslin, Andrew Cone, Larry DeBlasio, Jackie Foster, Jonathan Gorman, Hilary Greenbaum, Andy Hawkes, Megan Heuer, Nicholas S. Holmes, Gina Im, Sarah Isenberg, Eunice Lee, Jen Leventhal, Brianna O'Brien Lowndes, Carol Mancusi-Ungaro, Erin Manns, Chrissy Mellampe, Bridget Mendoza, Jane Panetta, Lindsay Pollock, Emma Quaytman, Londs Reuter, Joshua Rosenblatt and the team of art handlers in exhibitions and collection preparation, Amy Roth, Cris Scorza, Peter Scott, Dyeemah Simmons, and Barbi Spieler.

Our sincere gratitude goes to the lenders to the exhibition, who include Artist Pension Trust, Robert and Anne Conn, Carla Shen, and Beth Rudin DeWoody.

I am deeply thankful to Susanne Vielmetter for her incredibly generous support of this presentation and the documentation of this work. Thanks are also due to the team at Vielmetter Los Angeles, particularly Ariel Pittman and Matthew Lax. Anne Ellegood and Jamillah James of the Institute of Contemporary Art, Los Angeles, recognized the importance of the exhibition, and I am grateful for their partnership in sharing it with audiences in My Barbarian's hometown.

This exhibition, performance program, and publication are dedicated to the memory of my teacher José Esteban Muñoz.

ENTERTAINMENT SYSTEM: MY BARBARIAN'S TWENTY YEARS AT THE LIMITS OF POLITICAL CRITIQUE

Adrienne Edwards

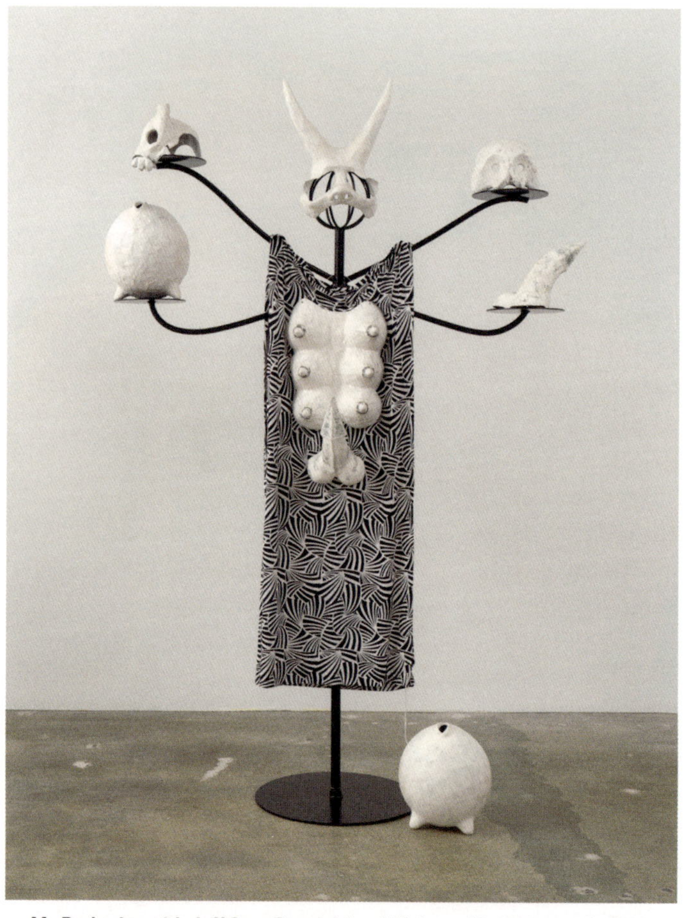

My Barbarian with Jeff Ono, *Standelabra 1 (4-Armed Bull Priestess)*, 2021. Steel, paint, papier-mâché, and spandex, stand: 48 × 15 × 69 in. (122 × 38.1 × 175.3 cm); base: 18¼ × 18¼ × 1¼ in. (46.4 × 46.4 × 3.8 cm). Collection of the artists, courtesy Vielmetter Los Angeles

For more than two decades, the members of My Barbarian—Malik Gaines (b. 1973), Jade Gordon (b. 1975), and Alexandro Segade (b. 1973), all born in California—have used performance to theatricalize the contours and entanglements of class, gender, race, and sexuality. Distinguished by their humorous and accessible style, the collective adapts a range of sources, including modern plays, historical texts, mythology, ritual, and media narratives, into structures for performances and related works across mediums. The resulting projects build on and reenvision the wide-ranging creative lineages that inform My Barbarian's work, such as queer and feminist theory, conceptualism, performance, institutional critique, social movements, pop culture, and political, musical, and community-based theater.

This catalogue was produced through a three-part close collaboration with the artists that also includes a twenty-year survey exhibition and a series of live performances at the Whitney Museum. Together these projects aim to illuminate My Barbarian's unique devotion to and deconstruction of theatrical formalisms and the influence of experimental queer, of color, and feminist artists of the 1960s to the 1980s, as well as the singular role the group has played in the evolution and presentation of performance in museums since the early aughts, when institutions began to give renewed attention to this interdisciplinary, ephemeral, embodied art form. The exhibition, drawing from their extensive archive, stages and contextualizes their work through performances for the camera, video documentation, music, sculptures, paintings, drawings, masks, textiles, costumes, and puppets. Concurrently, the performances reconceive iconic shows from My Barbarian's history in response to contemporary contexts and exemplify the array of theatrical styles and formal strategies the collective has explored.

It is not by accident that My Barbarian has returned again and again to classical Greek theater. Premiered at Participant Inc., New York, in November 2005 as part of the first Performa Biennial, *You Were Born Poor and Poor You Will Die*, a particularly crucial work for understanding the importance of the classics in their art, is structured in the style of a Dionysian play, although their take comingles mythology, occult rituals, biblical references, and economic oppression in a do-it-yourself, '70s California–style sing-along concert. It is deliciously wrong in every imaginable way, and that's the point. A uniquely My Barbarian mash-up of music, performance, lighting as scenography, visual art—including sculpture and textile banners—and costumes, here designed in collaboration with artist Jeff Ono, it is a ritual send-up of class conflict, marking a pivotal point in the collective's long-standing exploration of the effects of our economic system on American society. Indeed, in this work My Barbarian correlates human sacrifice with the violence of late capitalism. Their approach, campy and ambivalent, is far from virtuosic, at least as it concerns a demonstration of artistic perfection; it is actually intentionally quite the opposite. Rather, what they excel at is a total digestion of a seemingly unwieldy range of artistic, theatrical, theoretical, pop cultural, conceptual, social, economic, and political references, which arrive to us sprinkled with a bit of sugar and a dash of wildness to better make the medicine go down. In the midst of their raffish acts, serious discussion of the state of affairs is taking place, and real ethical work is literally in play.

Greek mythology is also present in the recurring figure of Cassandra, a woman who was cursed to tell true prophecies that are not believed. She is pivotal in *The Cassandra*, a 2013 element of *Broke People's Baroque Peoples' Theater* (2009–, hereafter *Broke/Baroque*), itself adapted from a 2009 staged performance developed for the group exhibition *Ecstatic Resistance*, organized by Every Ocean Hughes (formerly Emily Roysdon) at Grand Arts in Kansas City, Missouri. Dressed in white masks with flowing wigs and riotously colored and printed bounteous muumuus, their Cassandra (Wasserstein, played by Gordon) not only takes up Euripides's *The Trojan Women* and Aeschylus's *Agamemnon* but recasts these tales with the writing of lesbian feminist theater scholar Sue-Ellen Case—this is not "a mad woman tormented by death and destruction," as they quip in the *Broke/Baroque* video.[1] Shot in the parking lot of a Los Angeles studio with the backdrop of a barbed-wire-topped chain-link fence and a McDonald's McCafé billboard that has seen better days, the chorus wavers between feminist critique and shady reads. They literally have Cassandra's back, while Electra and Helen are bored in a "utopian theater enmeshed in globalism," and "their children and their children's children will all die of radiation poisoning."

Oracles figure prominently in *Broke/Baroque*, a piece with many variations in live performance, videos, and installation. In some versions the collective sings the core music of the project, while others feature opera singers, and another centers around a pantomime performed by Vicente Colomar, a Spanish actor trained in Golden Age theater, as "The Spirit of Wit and Economy." The recurring references to prediction

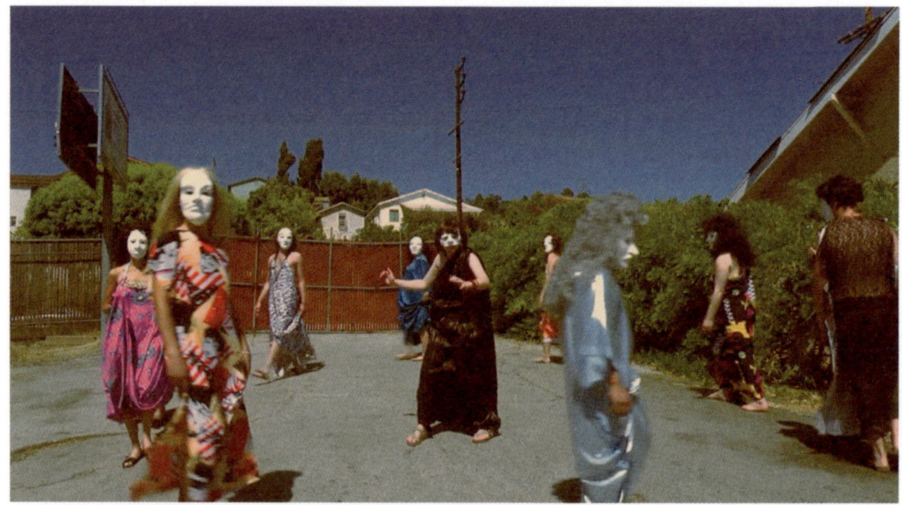

My Barbarian, *The Cassandra* (still), from *Broke People's Baroque Peoples' Theater*, 2013. HD video, color, sound, 10:49 min.

point to a long-standing interest in magic. However, My Barbarian is not simply invested in these themes but rather in the ways in which the function of allusion within Greek theater has possibilities for their own art.

A bridge between My Barbarian's early art band concerts at clubs in Los Angeles and their later fully elaborated performances, *Unicorns LA* and *Morgan Le Fay* (both 2004), in which they sing and dress up for rollicking rituals, are stylistically more akin to music videos. Indeed music, at times pop, at times operatic, at times punk, is the literal refrain or chorus across all of their works. *Unicorns LA* and *Morgan Le Fay* exemplify a proto-form for the collective that would evolve into a complete system of movements, references, and interrelations that illumine ceremonies as a systemic response in which social needs become individual/collective will, a dynamic within which the individual can do very little more than play.

In his essay "Political Poetics: A Social History of Drama," Brazilian theater innovator, theorist, and political activist Augusto Boal, an important influence for My Barbarian, sketches a history of the social function of Western theater that is productive in plotting our coordinates toward an understanding of such formal investments and detours within the collective's performances.[2] At the risk of reifying a genealogy that situates and by articulation here concretizes a history of theatrical evolution that seemingly always begins with Aristotle, this context for their art and creative choices must be acknowledged. For Boal, Aristotelian Greek theater's purpose was to convey specific information. Further, Marxian analysis necessitates that this information makes itself known through the social context in which it takes place and where the theatrical production is fostered and consumed, and in relation to the social class by whom it is ostensibly underwritten—which is to say, those with economic power. Boal's discussion of the latter puts a fine point on the role of this class in instrumentalizing theater (for our purposes) to convey their values, characterizing this as part of an arsenal of society-wide efforts to maintain and express power. Boal makes the distinction, however, that this strategy only concerns "dominant art," and notes that there are always modes of creativity that arise outside of this normative space and sensibility. It is in this outside zone where, millennia later, My Barbarian is situated.

Nevertheless, the Greek tragedies My Barbarian has drawn from, while performed in a democratic society for a broad public, are decidedly aristocratic in theme and were funded by the state and the wealthy with the aim of establishing an "ideal type of art," and with it a kind of status quo. Indeed, by the Middle Ages, theater "presented a static, stereotyped world, in which the generic and homogenous prevailed."[3] Boal describes the characters enacted in plays of this period (such as Lust, Sin, and Virtue) as abstractions of morals, spiritual beliefs, and social values with no basis in the real world.[4] The onset of early capitalism realized a style of theater concerned with modeling what Boal describes as "the methodic organization of life" in a totalizing effort toward maximizing commercial enterprise.[5] All things seemed ordered to leverage the very set of values or, more precisely, propaganda retained in American society today: the glory of individualism, freedom, and prosperity—possibly for all but in reality for the very few, with accumulated capital a sign of divine grace.[6] By the time of Shakespeare, there

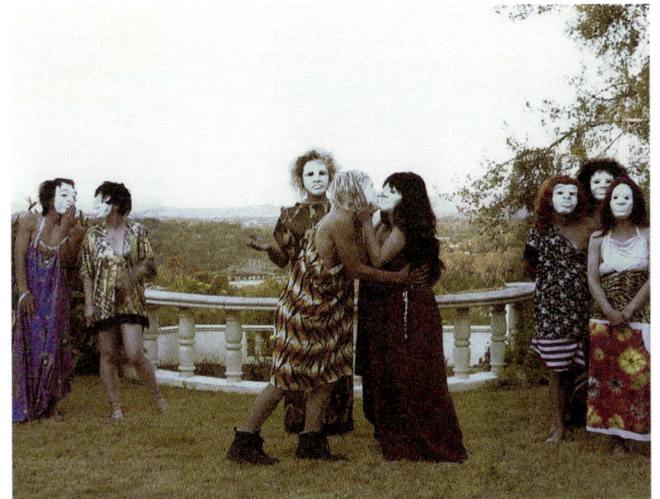

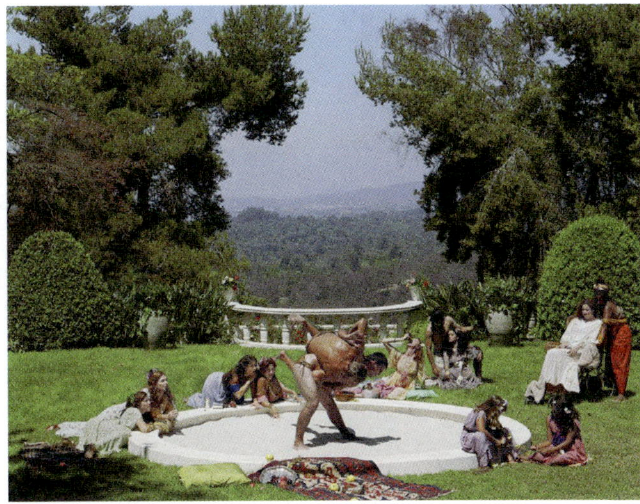

L: My Barbarian, *Shakuntala Du Bois* (stills), from *Broke People's Baroque Peoples' Theater*, 2012. HD video, color, sound, 30:14 min. R: Eleanor Antin, *A Hot Afternoon*, from *The Last Days of Pompeii*, 2001. Chromogenic print, 46⅝ × 58⅝ in. (118.4 × 148.9 cm)

had been a consolidation of this type of Renaissance character into those of intellectual acumen but few morals (who are, as Boal has it, "neutral like money"). He notes that Shakespearean themes follow the acquisition of power by someone with no right to it, some so-called extraordinary individual who has no demonstrable distinction or is, more precisely, mediocre. The purported values of Enlightenment are a poor shroud for war capital.[7]

Later, in the late eighteenth and early nineteenth centuries, German philosopher Georg Wilhelm Friedrich Hegel's philosophy of freedom explored theatrical characters who embodied ethical principles in a kind of everyday person (who then would without question have been described as "Man") playing out some conflict as a method that situates the meaning and culminates harmoniously.[8] Such a sensibility also informs realist theater, which positions the human as conditioned by their environment, an intense legibility full of clichés composed of triggers of the already familiar, essentially reproducing a normative reality.

My Barbarian works in opposition to such a style, resonating more closely with German playwright Bertolt Brecht's notion of epic theater and its quality of having an alienating effect or a process of defamiliarization that makes the experience of something familiar bizarre. This technique distances the audience from the action, instigating an overwhelming sense of detachment that forecloses the possibility of emotional fulfillment with the performance through staging devices such as captioning, projections, and performers breaking the fourth wall and revealing the artificiality of the context in which the play is taking place—the theater itself. Influenced by Marx, Brechtian theatrical sensibility, which is arguably on the spectrum of realism, was invested in understanding human behavior and the possibilities for resolving societal problems.

We can situate the sense of alienation in My Barbarian's art within and beyond an interest in Brechtian theater. While they share socialist foundations and materialist (formal) concerns for creating art that is inextricable from the times and the context in which it is made, their work is informed by the specificity of being California-born and -raised Gen Xers, or '70s babies, as I like to call our generation. California of the 1960s and '70s was the locus of a multitude of radical revolutionaries and experiments in reimagining what's possible in the social field, including the hippies, Black radicals, labor movements, gay liberation, and activists organizing for Chicano rights. This fostered an environment in which seemingly everything was questioned, up for grabs, and dismantled. We were born in the midst of utopian political and social upheaval and gained our consciousness in the dawn of its unraveling in Ronald Reagan's '80s, but the music was incredible, we had a freedom as latchkey kids that seems almost irresponsible today, and with limited television channels and barely emergent Atari games and Commodore computers we had to conjure up our own ways to play. And so when it came to working together, Segade, Gordon, and Gaines already well knew how to make do with minor things, with no tools other than writing and singing, bare necessities of a kind. And, of course, there was the fact that they are part of the generation that came into its sexual awakening knowing we could die from a night of fun. As '70s babies, coming of age was rife with anxiety, ambivalence, and irony—but it was also true that for us anything was on

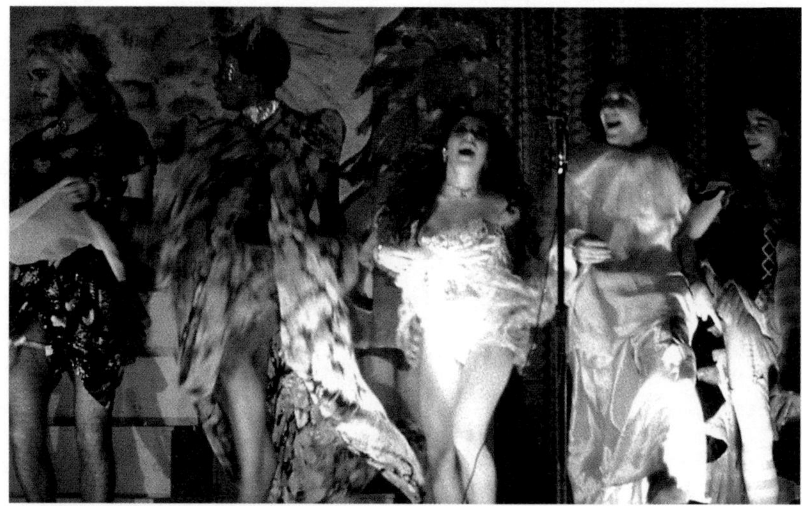

The Cockettes performing *Fairytale Extravaganza*, 1970. L–R: Tahara, Sylvester, Sweet Pam Tent, Raggedy Robin, Marquel Pettit

the table, and earnestness and authenticity were not part of our set of concerns.

My Barbarian's originary relationship to the radical creativity of queer, politically conscious artists of color of the '60s and '70s has influenced their theatrical approach for distinct reasons and in varying ways. They have spoken of their work taking "a queer attitude toward cheap materials" and "decorat[ing] itself in a hyper-feminine aestheticism to undermine class(y) distinctions of taste. A wealth of poverty, the chintzy is rich."[9] Their use of puppets, masks, and agit-prop, for instance, is informed in part by Bread and Puppet Theater's dramatic use of these elements to deeply engage in the civil rights and anti-war protest movements with ethically committed art. The Theater's take on medieval passion plays, the Bible, fairy tales, and other folkloric traditions of storytelling, and living and working within the means available, is present throughout My Barbarian's work.

Further, one can see how profoundly American wonder Jack Smith's feral performances have inspired them. This is particularly clear in aspects such as the deconstructed theatrical formalisms; characters that appear across plays; a decentered audience that is rather caught in the melee; political themes veiled in the parlance of pop culture and Hollywood fantasia; language appropriated from news headlines; a theatrical structure scaffolded by improvisation, coincidence, and assemblage; polyphony of live spoken lines, recorded sound effects, and music; and the rehearsal as performance itself.[10] During performances, Smith often read from a script, which was also dispersed to performers, as he directed live, at times with the effect of unmooring, if not undermining, the proceedings, and at others with a more ironic, easeful contrapuntal relation between elements and actors.[11] Titles such as *Unicorns LA*, *Broke People's Baroque Peoples' Theater*, and *Forest Brothers & Sisters* mirror Smith's own fantastically catty ones such as *Capitalism in Atlantis* and *Orchid Rot of Rented Lagoon*, to name but two performances that "queer and unsettle the subversive impact of American capitalism."[12]

Shakuntala Du Bois (2012) recalls a statement Smith made in relation to his work, "No one ever talks about the problems of daily life and so daily life becomes exotic," although My Barbarian's version is set in the California sun, not a gritty New York of the '70s, and has an updated soundtrack.[13] It shows the banality of a bourgeois woman trying to find life's purpose from the perch of her country estate. There are Valley Girl accents, a Sun God (the spirit of scheduling), and the chance to become a well-paid "consultant," and Gordon's character, Cassandra Wasserstein, has been framed by her grandmother, who's a sorceress and who hates her because she's an artist, and there's more . . . a wedding on a trashed tennis court and a Tibetan Buddhist chanting moment, all of it concluding with the Moon Goddess, played by Gaines, giving Shakuntala a massage while scatting in the style of pop singers Al Jarreau and George Benson. This is audacious, inappropriate world-making out of shards of history, styles, and scenes. For they knew "the social practice line item" of a museum's budget "wouldn't abolish prisons."[14]

My Barbarian's distinct irreverence can also be located in the influential shows of the Cockettes, a

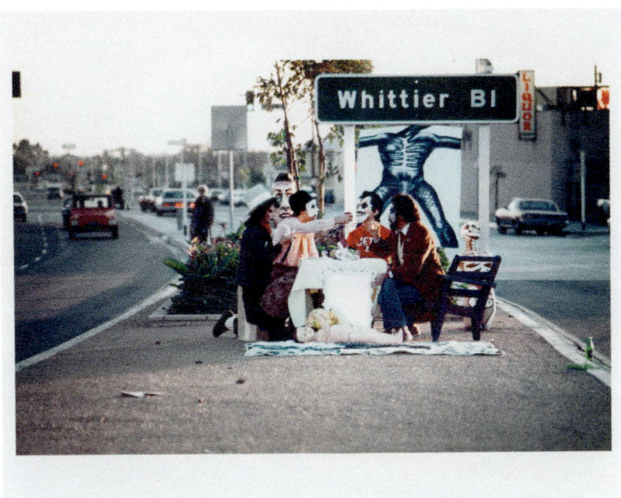

Asco, *First Supper (After a Major Riot)*, 1974, printed 2011. Chromogenic print, 16 × 20 in. (40.6 × 50.8 cm). Whitney Museum of American Art, New York; purchase with funds from the Photography Committee 2014.45

motley ensemble of glitter-bedazzled drag performers that coalesced in 1969 in San Francisco. In *Black Performance on the Outskirts of the Left: A History of the Impossible*, Gaines offers an insightful take on the Cockettes' use of "grotesque transformation and exaggerations [to] hold multiple meanings together, speaking in heteroglossic terms" that lends meaningful context here.[15] He locates the force of the troupe's work in its ambivalence, specifically in the function of critique in the carnivalesque, which according to philosopher Mikhail Bakhtin is an ungoverned forum for "the most extreme freedom and frankness of thought and speech," used by everyday folks "to explore their criticism, their deep distrust of official truth, and their highest hopes and aspirations."[16] The ambivalence toward both form and representations suggested here obviates majoritarian structures—and for both My Barbarian and the Cockettes this dazzling combination hippie and queer sensibility holds nothing sacred, often crossing lines such as performing in blackface (for the latter) or making acts about white slavery (for the former) that today would be unimaginable. Their shows and films tend toward melodrama, satire, and comic send-ups of Hollywood films and Broadway musicals.

Asco, composed of four Chicano artists in East Los Angeles who began collaborating in the late 1960s on public performances, media interventions, conceptual cinema, and performance murals, was also an important lodestar for My Barbarian.[17] Named after the expression "me da asco," which translates as "(your art) disgusts me," they created multifaceted work that was clear-eyed about the context in which they were situated: the larger art world and their local community, particularly the contested social spaces they could illuminate in order to undermine the different yet equally relevant conservatisms present in both realms.[18] Their work was a contrapuntal force that questioned and even undermined the iconography of the Chicano civil rights movement of 1965–75 even as they actively participated in it. Their murals reflected the range of ways violence manifested in their community: as "a cultural logic, an administrative tactic, a familial ritual, and a fact of everyday life."[19] It is Asco's particular approach to deconstruction of formalisms that I see in the work of My Barbarian. Namely, the ways in which they undermined the normativities of their Mexican American community and the desire for and tendency toward a certain representational legibility that was askance of their experimental imaginations to undermine such a desire. Theirs was a troubling presence—a style of deconstruction.[20]

Los Angeles–based artist Vaginal Davis also came up in the city's East Side punk scene, which over generations fostered artists like My Barbarian and Asco. Members of Asco were part of the emergence of experimental performance at gay bars such as Teddy Sandoval's Butch Gardens School of Fine Art.[21] More than the aforementioned artists, My Barbarian had a direct relationship with Davis. They saw her perform live many times, and even substitute hosted for her at her 2000s blues club Bricktops. Gordon acted in film projects with her, including Davis's own *The White To Be Angry* (1999) and a remake of Tennessee Williams's *Suddenly Last Summer* (2007) directed by John Aes-Nihil. Gaines curated Davis into

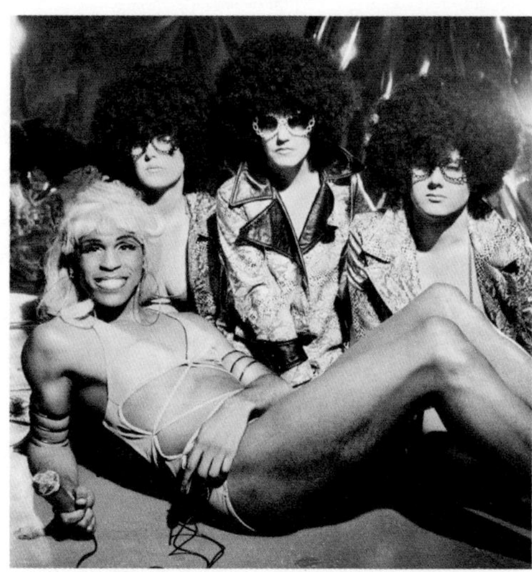

Vaginal Davis and the Afro Sisters, 1986

Fade: African American Artists in LA for the City of Los Angeles in 2004.

Davis did wild, socially critical shows at venues like Sucker with her Black soul Supremes–style back-up singers the Afro Sisters, and ¡Cholita!, a band of men and women in teen drag who sang Latin American pop songs and provisionally explored the contours of identity. In these performances, Davis needled the subterranean proclivities of American society concerning interracial relationships and queer desire through fierce representational strategies.

At its core, My Barbarian's work is a cultural and social critique of normative aesthetics, in this instance those of contemporary art in general. Their methods and techniques of "retroactive self-appropriation," as they named one 2010 work, enact what queer and Latinx theorist José Esteban Muñoz described as "identity-eroding effects."[22] Muñoz's formulation of disindentification allows for "a performative mode of tactical recognition that various minoritarian subjects employ in an effort to resist the oppressive and normalizing discourse of dominant ideology." He continues: "It is a reformatting of self within the social."[23] By resisting normative gender roles, playing with "types" or a range of ethnic cultural performances, and generally amalgamating irreconcilable references, the collective resists identifications, each artwork becoming a "site of self-fashioning and political formation" as bodies break from the restraints of representation, sometimes most compellingly, by operating precisely within them as an indexing of their limitations, as if for the record.[24] Their practice overall productively misrecognizes the referent such that the artists—and thus the spectators—are enabled to imagine something otherwise, and it is a tactical maneuver. If, for queer people of color and a woman, the task of experimenting is to situate oneself within the American social sphere, constructing contradictory subjectivities through performance provides an out from their strictures.

Then there is the question of the maternal, and the profound way in which the matter of artist genealogy shows up through the figures of feminist icons within conceptual art such as Eleanor Antin and Mary Kelly, whose influences are deeply embedded in My Barbarian's critical approach. They are also both referenced and present in specific works. For instance, the *Shakuntala Du Bois* video was shot in San Diego at the same location as Antin's *Roman* photograph series. Meanwhile, *Universal Declaration of Infantile Anxiety Situations Reflected in the Creative Impulse* has Kelly, Antin, and all three of their mothers in it; it is a video companion to *The Mother and Other Plays* (2013–14), a performance adaptation of Brecht's *The Mother*. Segade studied with Kelly and Andrea Fraser while a student at the University of California, Los Angeles, and Antin has been an informal mentor since 2008. Throughout My Barbarian's work, the presence of a multivalent white womanness prevails not only in the specific references but also as a noticeable affect accessible through their costume, tone, and thread of feminist thought. Indeed, all of their mothers are white. This unmistakable white maternal sensibility that I am trying to pinpoint in their perspective is akin to D.W. Winnicott's "good enough mother": the right amount of negligence and mordancy coupled with a finely calibrated modicum of care and attention.

My Barbarian's seriousness of play in engaging institutions, namely museums but also within academia, has been an important distinguishing factor in their work and extended through their multivalent engagement with the Whitney. Their style threads together some unlikely interlocutors, including camp, institutional critique, and politically conscious theater in pivotal works such as *Double Agency* (2015–19), the hilarious episodic spy thriller video series made at and about the Los Angeles County Museum of Art; *The Fourth Wall (Transparency)* (2009), an extravaganza contemplating the values of and possibility for intimacy and access at the Museum of Contemporary Art, Los Angeles; and the *Post-Living Ante-Action Theater* (PoLAAT) (2008–16), a massively scaled project initiated at the New Museum, New York, that was envisioned as a pedagogical workshop model based on Julian Beck and Judith Malina's The Living Theatre, Rainer Werner Fassbinder's antitheater, and Boal's Theater of the Oppressed that would grapple with the history of radical political theater and explore group building and the possibilities and limits of art-driven political critique. These performances allowed the collective to internalize the frame of the institution and develop ways of working with and against it, in, as Munõz describes, "a war of positions . . . predicated on the understanding that diverse sites of institutional and cultural antagonism must be engaged to enact transformative politics . . . the more multilayered and tactical war of positions represents better possibilities of resistance today, when discriminatory ideologies are less naked and more intricate."[25] This imperative, the animating force of My Barbarian's past twenty years of making, doing, and being in art, is "necessarily and inevitably contradictory"[26] and, much like the collective itself, finds strength in its multiplicity of various elements and perspectives, scaffolded by each other.

For José Esteban Muñoz

---

1 All quotes in this paragraph are from the 2013 video performance of *Broke People's Baroque Peoples' Theater*.

2 See Augusto Boal, "Political Poetics: A Social History of Drama," *Performing Arts Journal* 2, no. 1 (Spring 1977): 6–18.

3 Ibid., 7.

4 Ibid., 8.

5 Ibid., 9.

6 Ibid., 10.

7 See Sven Beckert, *Empire of Cotton: A Global History* (New York: Alfred A. Knopf, 2014), 38. War capitalism, on the one hand, "encompassed laws, institutions, and customs of the mother country, where state-enforced order ruled," and on the other hand, there existed within it an entirely different structure "characterized by imperial domination, the expropriation of vast territories, decimation of indigenous peoples, theft of their resources, enslavement, and the domination of vast tracts of land by private capitalists with little effective oversight by distant European states. . . . There, masters trumped states, violence defied the law, and bold physical coercion by private actors remade markets."

8 Boal, 14.

9 My Barbarian, "Broke People's Baroque Peoples' Theater," artist website, https://mybarbarian.com/Broke-People-s-Baroque-Peoples-Theater, accessed August 1, 2021.

10 J. Hoberman, "The Theater of Jack Smith," *The Drama Review: TDR* 23, no. 1 (March 1979): 5–6, 8.

11 Ibid., 7.

12 Ibid., 3.

13 Ibid., 12.

14 My Barbarian, conversation with the author, July 23, 2021.

15 Malik Gaines, *Black Performance on the Outskirts of the Left: A History of the Impossible* (New York: NYU Press, 2017), 141.

16 Ibid. See also Mikhail Bakhtin, *Rabelais and His World* (Bloomington: Indiana University Press, 1968), 296.

17 Chon A. Noriega, "'Your Art Disgusts Me': Early Asco 1971–75," *Afterall: A Journal of Art, Context and Enquiry* 19 (Autumn/Winter 2008): 109.

18 Ibid., 114.

19 Ibid., 115.

20 Ibid., 118.

21 Ibid., 119.

22 José Esteban Muñoz, "The White to Be Angry: Vaginal Davis's Terrorist Drag," *Social Text* 52/53 (Autumn–Winter 1997): 80.

23 Ibid., 83.

24 Ibid., 84.

25 Ibid., 100.

26 Stuart Hall, "Gramsci's Relevance for the Study of Race and Ethnicity," in *Stuart Hall: Critical Dialogues in Cultural Studies*, ed. Kuan-Hsing Chen and David Morley (New York: Routledge, 1996), 433.

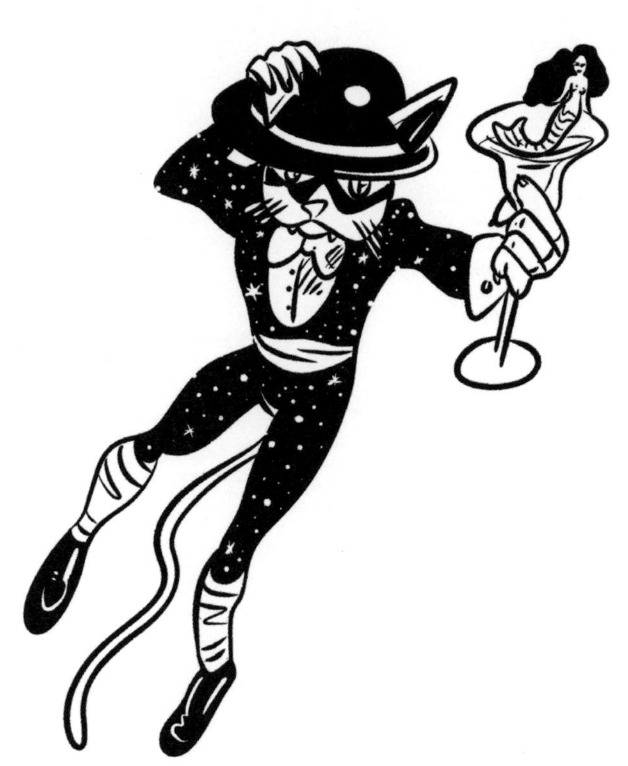

SHOWCORE

Alexandro Segade

I. Cult

"What kind of music does My Barbarian play?"
"Showcore."

Every band had a core, then. Ours was a hall of dressing room mirrors. Showcore wore secondhand Broadway T-shirts. Showcore lyrics were written in screenplay format. Showcore required multiple lead singers, accompanied by Malik's Rhodes, an electric piano we lugged from our Pasadena practice space to venues on Sunset Boulevard. Showcore got us onstage without having to rent the theater.

We each have a different explanation for the name My Barbarian. I thought it was a gay Saturday morning cartoon starring the sexy warrior Hot Blade. "My Barbarian" was also the title of our first number, an anthemic three-part harmony love song to the uncivilized (p. 140). "Ask the librarian/ Who never knew/ 'Bout My Barbarian." Also, "You don't wear underwear/ You tell the truth." Also, "I'm always fighting Christians." My Barbarian asserts an identification with, and a claiming of, the position of the other. In the early years, that described all the people who opposed, and were targeted by, the crusades of the post-9/11 Bush Era. Yes, My Barbarian was forged in Dungeons & Dragons role-play, exorcising our nerdy imaginations of toxic, intoxicating fantasies. But also: our band name opened up an ongoing conversation about what is inside and who is outside. My Barbarian first found a voice, in and out of tune, in showcore.

The members of My Barbarian each have a different origin story for our name. My version is that we borrowed it from the Doces Bárbaros, the 1970s Brazilian supergroup made up of musicians Gilberto Gil, Caetano Veloso, Maria Bethânia, and Gal Costa. We were all heavy into Os Mutantes and other late-1960s Tropicália music when we started out performing as an art band; we even covered Caetano Veloso and Gal Costa's song "Baby." —Jade

Malik, Jade, and I worked together on plays and short films before 2000, but it wasn't until that year, when we started performing as My Barbarian at Spaceland and the Silver Lake Lounge, that we found our audience. Our friends played with us, musicians including Tiffany Anders, Norwood Cheek, Anh Do, Dustin Erickson, Jimi Hey, Tim Koh, Scott Martin, Giles Miller, Andy Ouchi, and Amy Yao. We made costumes, props, and posters with artists Scoli Acosta, Patterson Beckwith, Pearl C. Hsiung, Rosalie Knox, Daniel MacDonald, Matthew Monahan, Jeff Ono, Anna Sew Hoy, and Lara Schnitger. We sought out the advice and blessings of informal mentors Bibbe Hansen, who had grown up in Fluxus, and Sean Carrillo, who had grown up in Asco, as well as Vaginal Davis, Ann Magnuson, and Imperial Teen, early influences who gave us early opportunities. The scene produced My Barbarian, and we aspired to cult status.

When I was still an aspiring actress and Alex was in film school, I co-starred in a few of his student films. In one of them, Alex's younger brother and I played juvenile delinquents. In another I was a campy redheaded Satanist hosting a dinner party. During the same era, Malik directed me in a low-budget play. —Jade

Showcore acted out. Our songs afforded us alter egos. We displaced our self-conscious displays of narcissism and exhibitionism onto: hard-luck chorus boys, bitter acting teachers, hapless drug dealers, chic police psychics, wry divorcées, grandiloquent ghosts, charming changelings, all kinds of witches. Genres boiled down to a catchy five minutes, a feat we called "hyper-narrative," accelerating the storytelling, embracing excess without attempting realism. My attitude at the time is expressed in the song "Off-Broadway," our showcoriest showstopper:

Start the show!
My sweat is fire exploding,
Want to take off my clothing,
But I'm shy.
Hello front row!
Ballet barre never ending,
Reaching over extending,
High!
Kick ball change 1, 2, 3
Re-arrange 2, 1, 3
Feel the pain 1, 2, 3
And sometimes I cry . . .

Malik, Jade, and I talked a lot about traumatic performance experiences we'd had in childhood. Showcore allowed us to reclaim our performing bodies while admitting we were hurt. We all had stories to tell—about the way it felt to be in a school play, to dislocate your arm onstage, to keep going because *Little Shop of Horrors* had one more number and you were in it.

I was always cast as a mouse in *Cinderella*. —Malik

II. Occult

Showcore is performed like a spell. There is respect for superstition among show people. Theater and ritual are intertwined. Showcore is a magic trick that doesn't try to fool you. You could call it camp—and we were interested in Susan Sontag, Jack Smith, and the Cockettes—but we thought of it as what Artaud calls a "true illusion."

Vinyl is magic. We collected records, the three of us, learning songs by Chico Buarque, Kate Bush, Nona Hendryx, Kander and Ebb, Dagmar Krause, Abbey Lincoln, Stevie Nicks, Laura Nyro, Buffy Sainte-Marie, Kurt Weill, and Stevie Wonder. We studied the arrangements of Amon Düül II, the B-52s, Boney M., Free Design, Kid Creole and the Coconuts, LaBelle, Os Mutantes, the Roches, Rotary Connection, Pentangle, and the Pointer Sisters. This music was better on a record player, especially in the afternoon, sun hitting the twisting art nouveau weed smoke, the cat bumping the needle. We watched movies on VHS too, low-budget musicals from the late 1970s and early '80s, Rocky Horror rip-offs and Bob Fosse bombs. Obsolete technologies gave this media the quality of a séance.

My husband and I owned a used vinyl record store in the Highland Park neighborhood of Los Angeles for a few years called Wombleton Records. We still have over fifty thousand LPs at home. Antiquated analog media looms large in the My Barbarian universe. —Jade

Even with dead-end day jobs, showcore became the stretch fabric of our lives, and we increasingly cohered around this sensibility, playing show tunes from shows that, as Nina Simone said, "hadn't been written . . . yet." *Purple Eyes* was our first attempt. Stringing our songs into a cabaret about zombies and the exploitative economics of tourism, it was performed first at Evidence Room Theater. Around that time, our CD *Cloven Soft-Shoe* (2005) was put out by KXLU deejays who liked what we were doing. Major indie labels were weirded out by us, and though that hurt our feelings we knew showcore wasn't *for* everyone, literally.

Our rehearsal space was a commons for an uncommon combination of subjectivities. Malik and I were a young Black and Latinx (to use a term that didn't exist yet) gay couple living in an anti-queer, pro-war, white supremacist country that hated everything about us. Bush's reelection was blamed on gay marriage, a victory for the Christianists. There was talk of California seceding. We were for it. My Barbarian was nothing if not separatist. "So what if our union destroys the state?/ Small price to pay for my soulmate," we sang. I say "we," but the three of us spoke from an entirely unified, non-singular position, performing our problems while enacting allyship for one another (before knowing that term either). Something else Jade, Malik, and I shared was a lack of economic resources, a constant struggle in the late-capitalist boom-and-bust art world. My Barbarian was a staging ground for alternate ways of being and making, a reversal of the economic logic we didn't understand anyway. My Barbarian rallied, communed, commiserated, reimagined, and rejected—not only the oppressive dominant culture but our own unexamined privilege and precarity as debt-ridden middle-class kids who wanted to be artists.

Common ground was where, and when, we came from, us three children of parents who met in 1970s California. We decided to write a show imagined as a double-sided album, *California Sweet & the 7 Pagan Rights* (2006), exploring our "Left Coast" lineage. The first side told the story of Josh Juarez, a radical theater dropout who takes a job on a cruise ship and gets killed, "execution-style," while running drugs in San Diego. Meanwhile, in Iraq, gay Marines dream of going back to Camp Pendleton. Our *Burning Flag* (2005/2021) prop was made for that scene. Composed with the mix-and-match mentality of counterculture, side two featured *Pagan Rights*, a fifteen-minute psychedelic ode to DIY spirituality. When asked to participate in the 2006 California Biennial at the Orange County Museum of Art, Newport Beach, we made *Pagan Rights* into a movie and installed it in a room with pillows on the floor and incense.

Pagan Rights was a response to our West Coast upbringing. Alex and Malik and I are all California natives. I was born in Sonoma County and grew up in Los Angeles, Malik is from the Central Valley, and Alex is from San Diego. All of our parents were hippies, activists, and/or artists. —Jade

We were adept at keeping these performances ultra-current. For an event organized by the artist Every Ocean Hughes, we opened our gay military number, "The Last Love in Iraq," with a cloaked incantation by the Iraq Study Group, mimicking a pointless governmental commission of the time. We chanted "corporate consultants" in eerie harmonies and then researched the topic by asking audience members, "What's your favorite thing about the Iraq war?" —Malik

Art spaces offered a way to experiment outside the limited setup of the nightclub. In galleries and museums we developed a performance strategy of reconsidering theater forms by setting them against the critical space of the white cube. Years before we'd heard of "Art and Objecthood," we sensed that *theatricality* was problematic in the modernist discourse informing these institutions. In true showcore form, we homed in on this problem and made it our act.

My Barbarian combined performance art strategies with traditions pulled from theater history. *Nightmarathon: Halloween Hextravaganza* (2002) was a durational site-specific penny dreadful at Fritz Haeg's Sundown Salon, Los Angeles, and *Medieval Morality* was an institutional critique folk play about freelancing, custom-made in versions at MAK Center's Schindler House, Los Angeles (2004), and Peres Projects, Berlin (2006). At the Roy and Edna Disney/CalArts Theater (REDCAT), Los Angeles, we presented *MB: The Mary Blair Story* (2004), a musical revue about the life of a visionary illustrator whose work disappeared into the backgrounds of classic Disney movies. *Squirrel Radio Action* (2005) was a radio play, commissioned by KPCC Southern California Public Radio, about rodent vectors for bubonic plague; their habitat shrinking, they passed the plague to humans, which they didn't want to do. It ends with a protest on the steps of Los Angeles City Hall, fuzzy ears attached to our hats, singing the names of every city council member, warning them, for all the good it did.

I again played a mouse in *Cinderella*, but owned it this time. —Malik

III. Cult

Pagan Rights got us to New York. We performed the two sides over two days on two floors at Participant Inc. That got us invited back to participate in the 2005 Performa Biennial. In our Boyle Heights studio we crafted a mystery play about class warfare, a rock opera about human sacrifice, titled *You Were Born Poor and Poor You Will Die*. *Pagan Rights* referenced mythology, but *Born Poor* was a myth: a plebeian novitiate is condemned by the High Priestess when he fails to pay a tithe, and the Bull God, never satisfied, destroys the city with a volcano. As the Priestess sings it, "The City State/ Requires blood to stay great/ Don't you know that's show biz, kid." Jeff Ono made masks, breastplates, and phalluses out of papier-mâché dollar bills, referencing ancient theater while materially embedded in late capitalism.

Music is My Barbarian's core: the call-and-response and counterpoint fostered by starting as a band is how we work. But the band itself ended with "Mythologic Mass," a set-list of songs from our self-made religion, played ecstatically, extra eyes stuck to our foreheads. I remember our last gig with the original line-up, at the Silver Lake Lounge. We were explosive, sweaty showcore brilliance that night. The audience moved to our beat as we sang about violently overthrowing the government and annexing Mars. We had fun. Fun is one way for a community to take care of itself. But showcore, with its internal illogic and deep-cut referentiality, was not infinitely scalable.

Out of the blue we asked performance curator RoseLee Goldberg to meet us on a trip to New York, which she did. After each video clip we showed her, she replied, "fun." —Malik

My Barbarian is a triad. Triangles are tight. Over six years into it, we wanted to find new audiences and collaborations, people who were not us. Increasingly interested in "performance art," we needed to better understand the context framing our work. In order to accomplish that, we broke up the band and deprogrammed showcore.

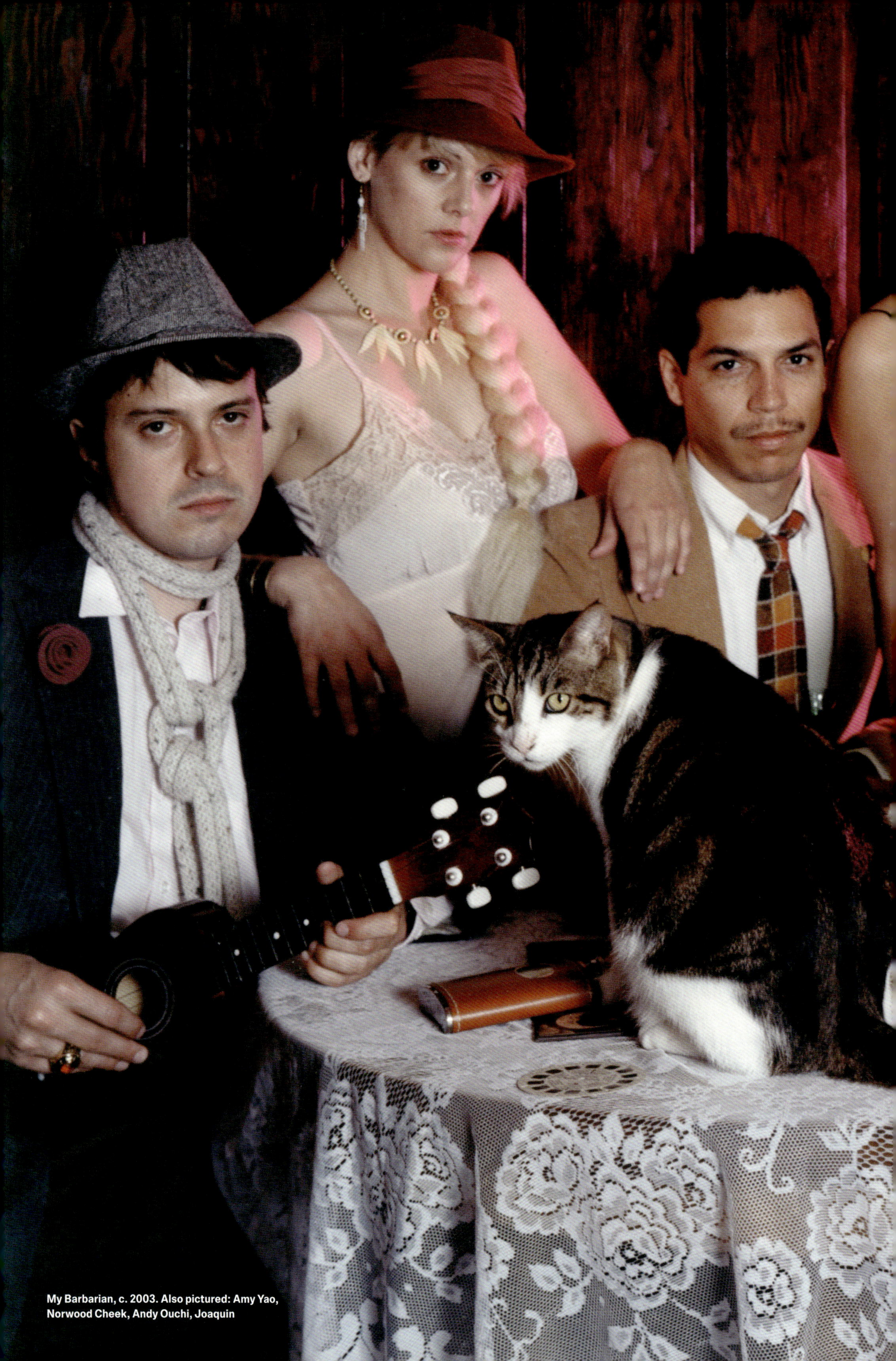

My Barbarian, c. 2003. Also pictured: Amy Yao, Norwood Cheek, Andy Ouchi, Joaquin

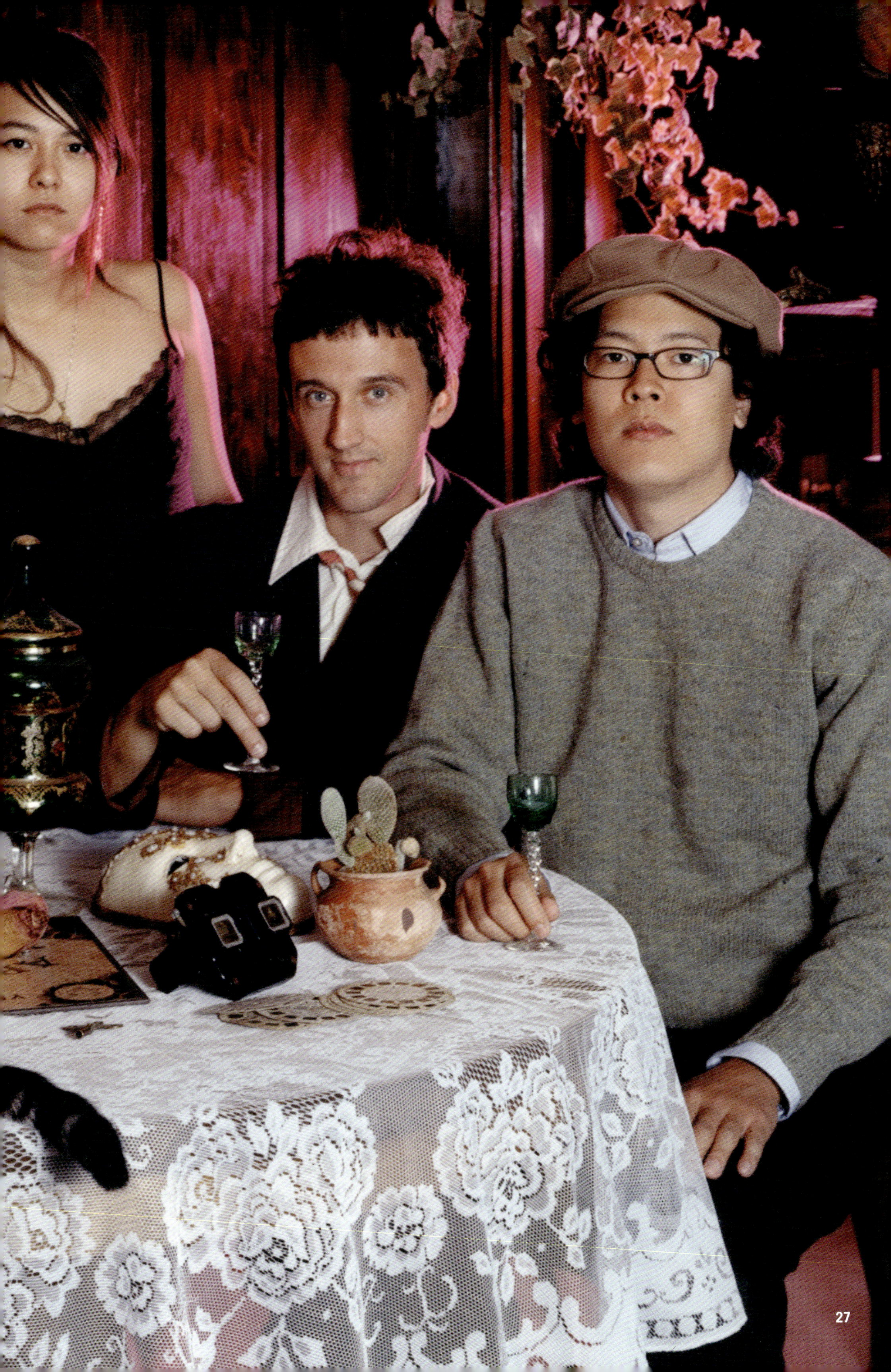

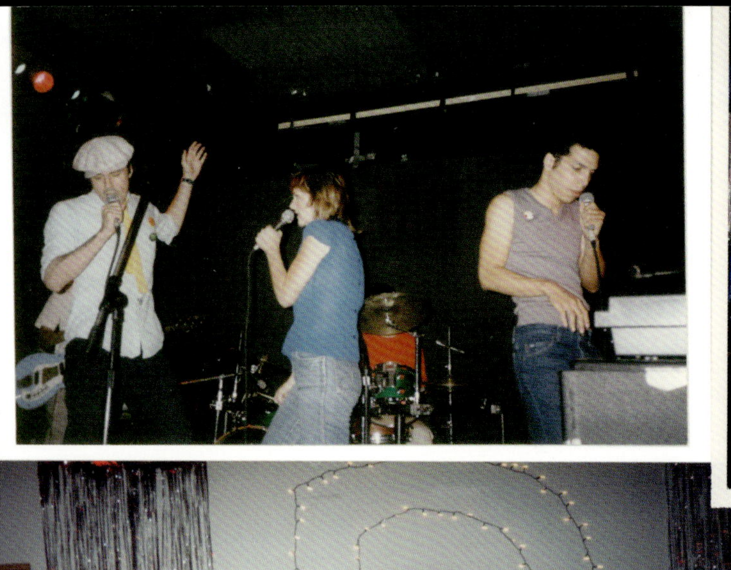
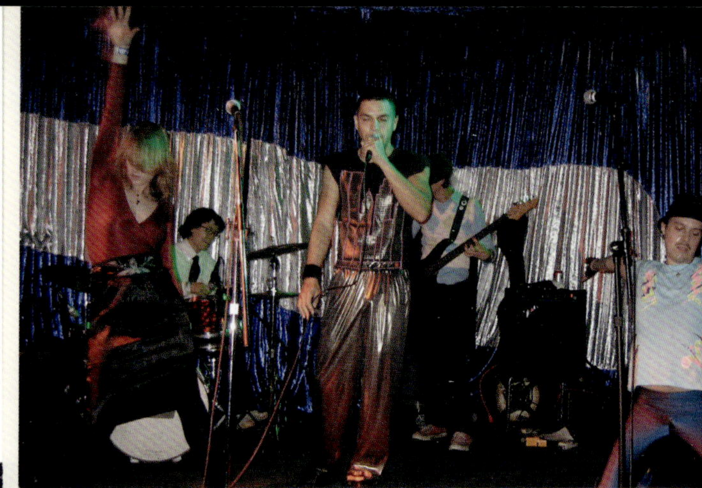
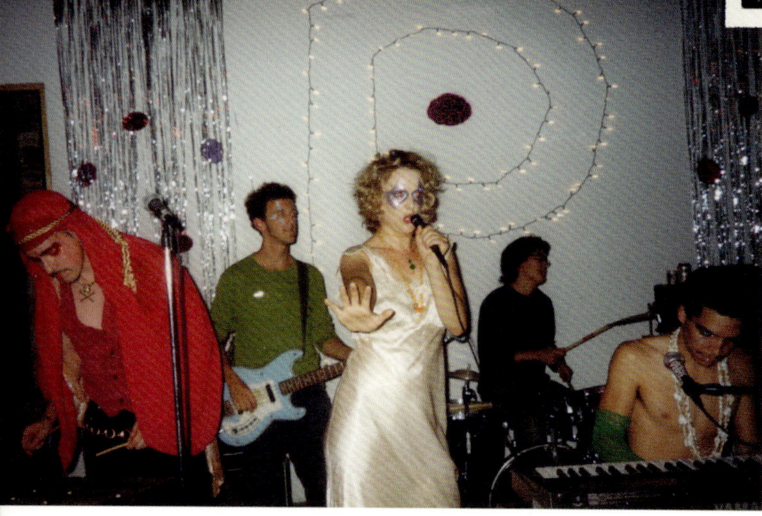
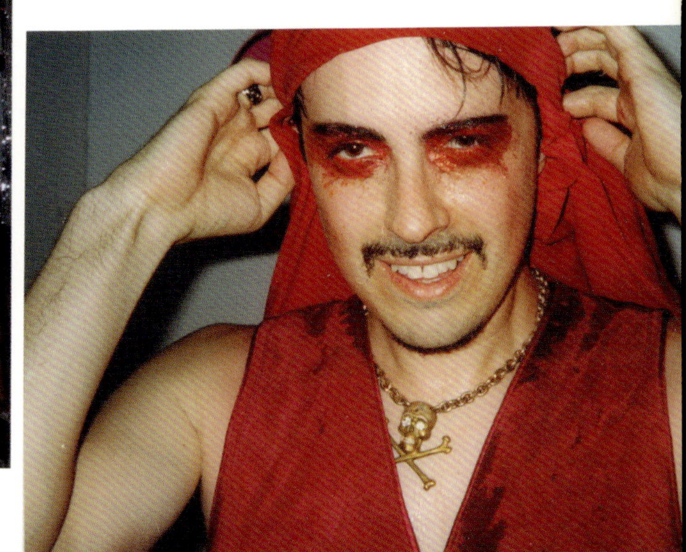
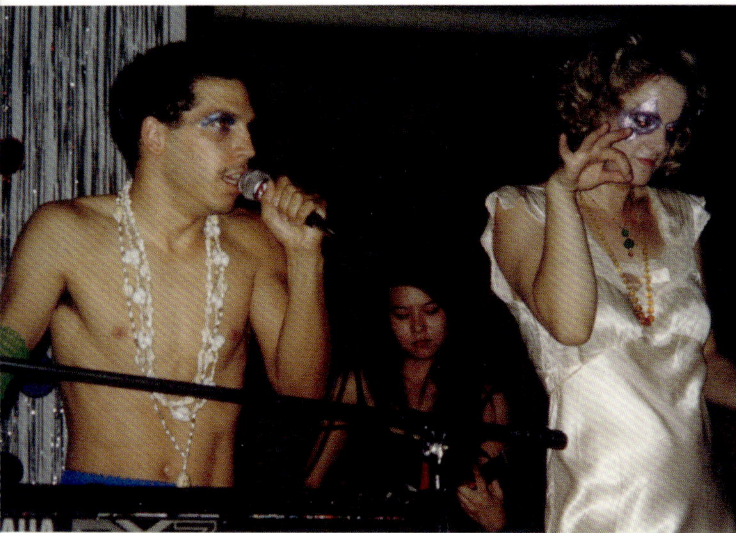
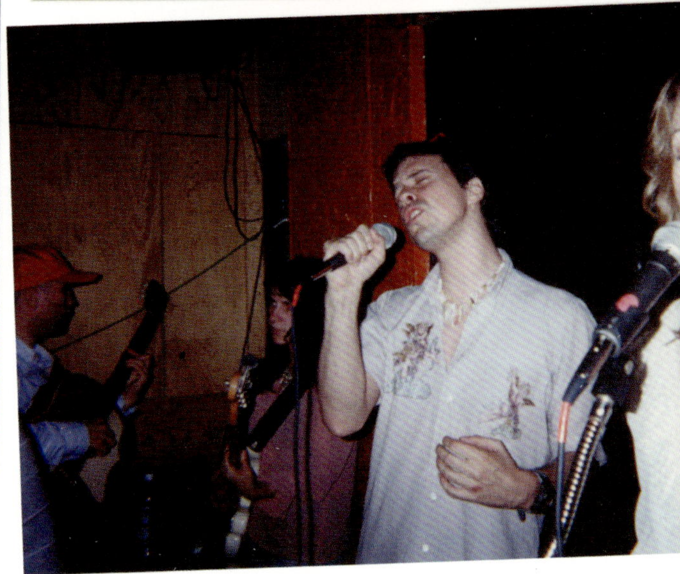
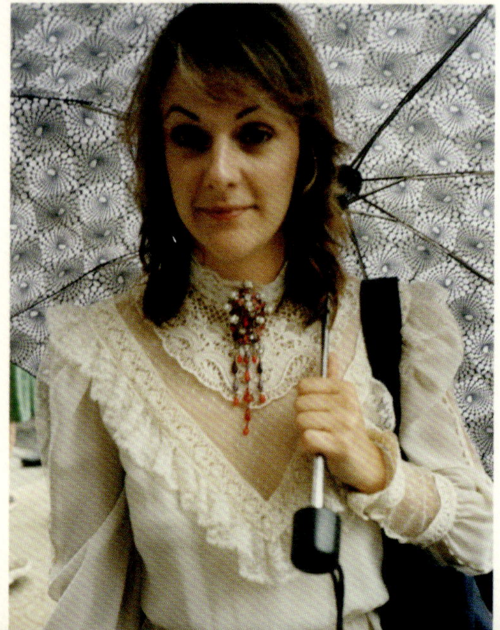
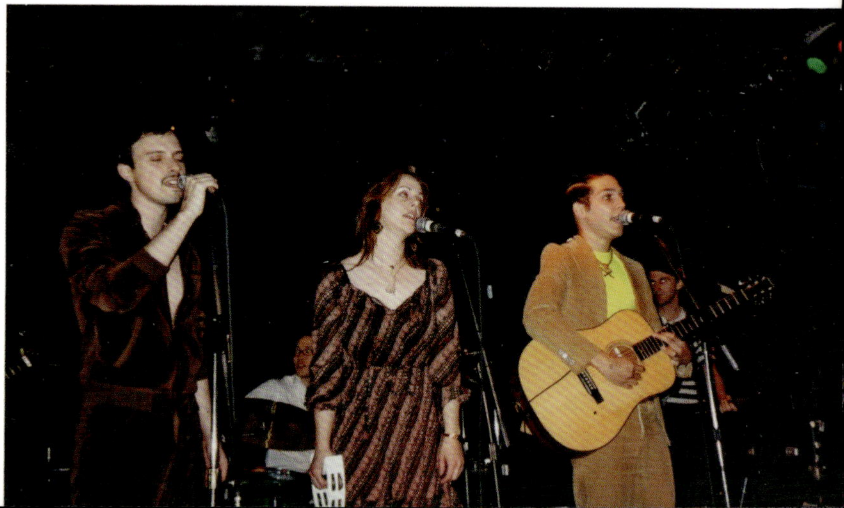

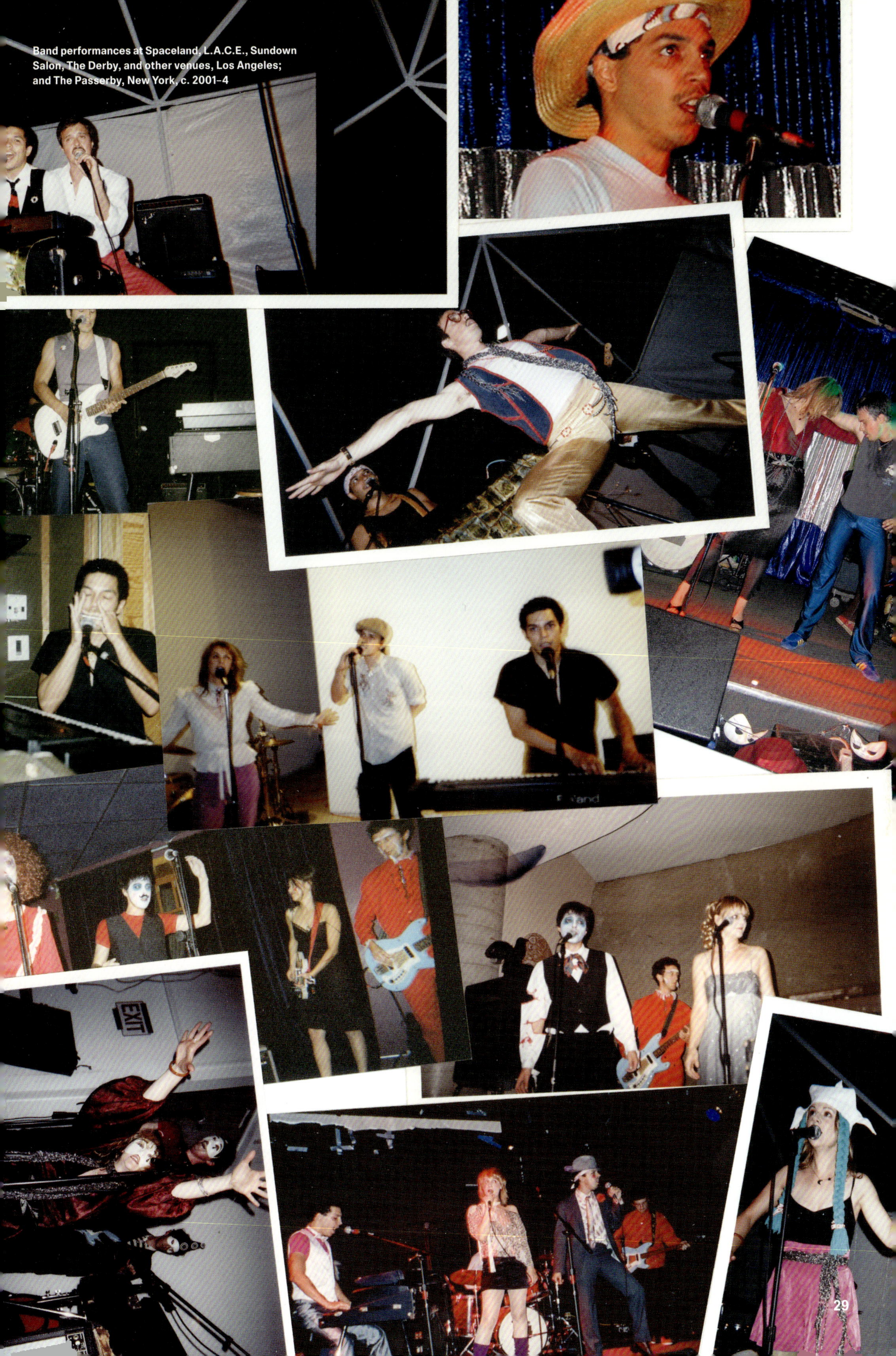

Band performances at Spaceland, L.A.C.E., Sundown Salon, The Derby, and other venues, Los Angeles; and The Passerby, New York, c. 2001–4

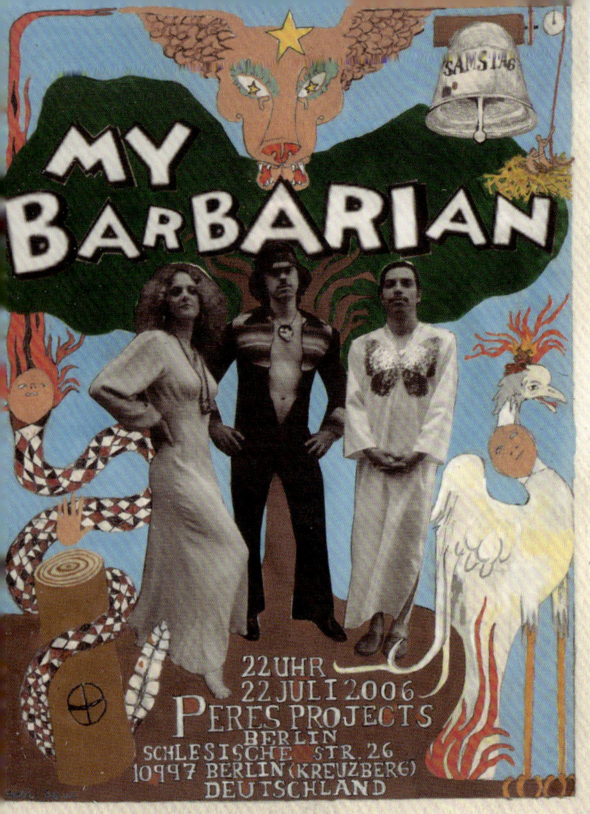

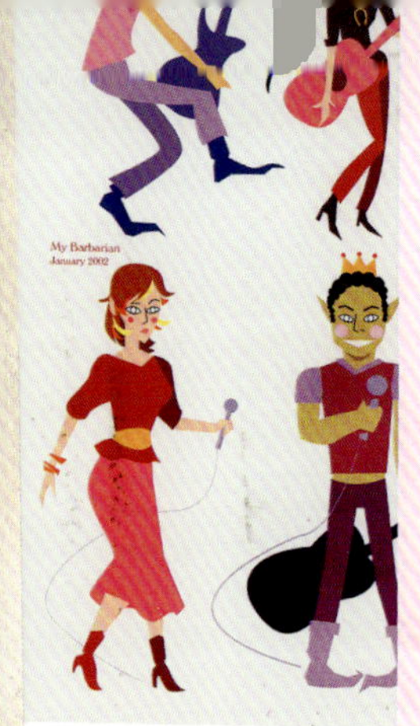

Thursday 1/22
11pm THE LOVEMAKERS (Oakland)
MY BARBARIAN (L.A.!) 10pm
KARAOKE PARTY (Tokyo) 9pm

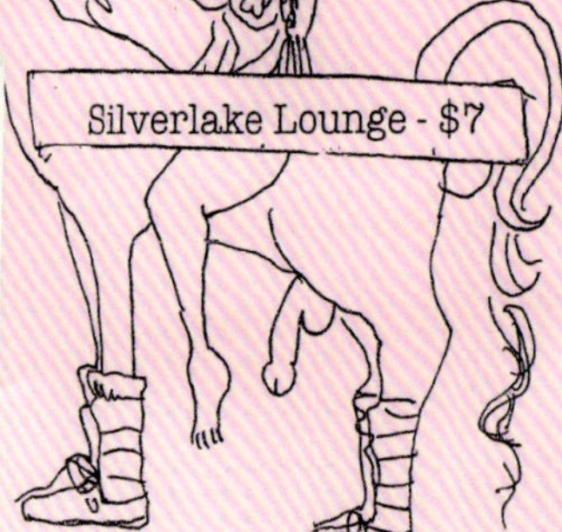

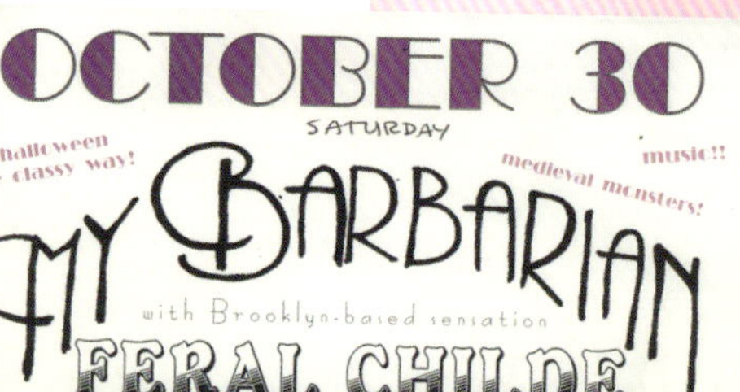

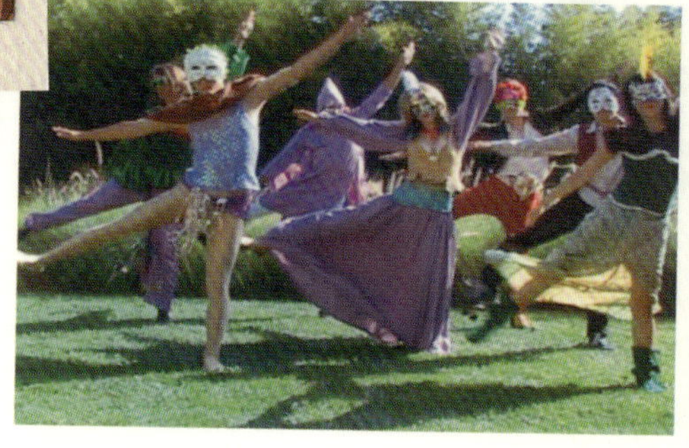

A HAPPENING
AT THE SCHINDLER HOUSE
fantasy!
dinges!
dancers!
séance!
2-6 PM $15.00

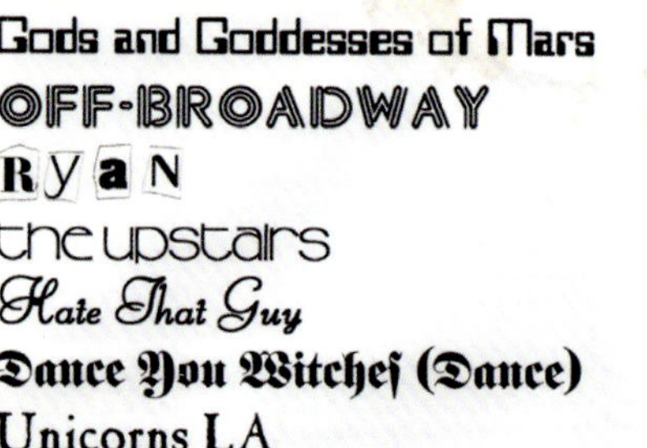

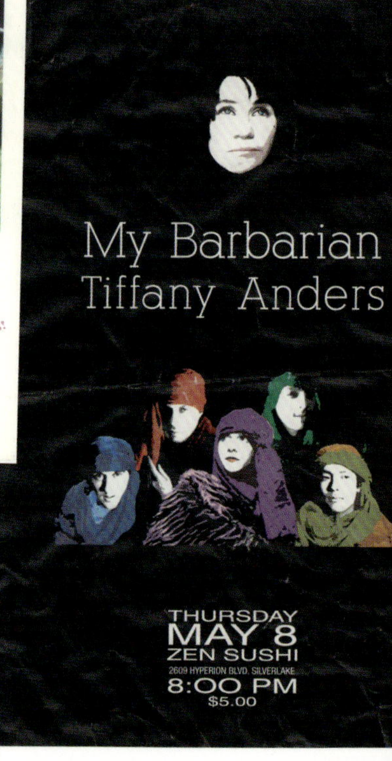

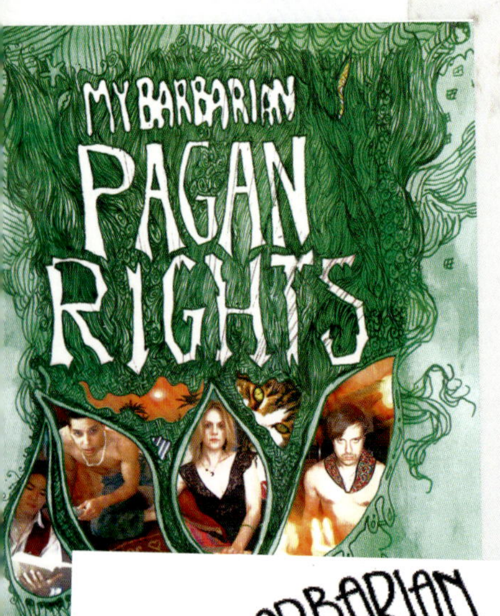

MY BARBARIAN
in
purple eyes
a musical fantasy
a night affair

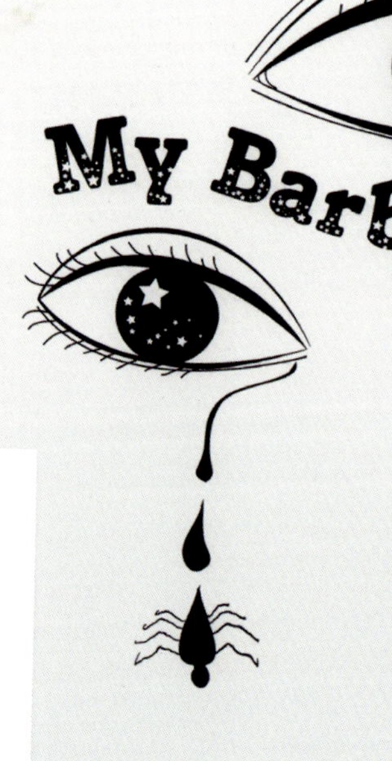

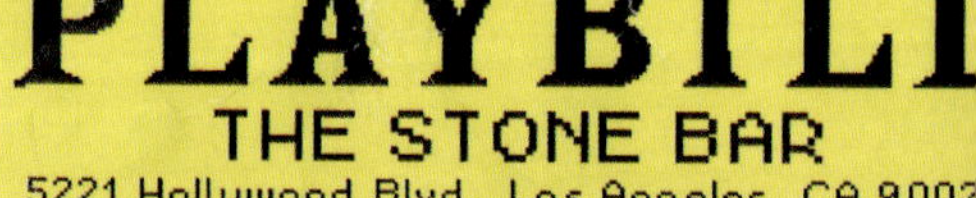

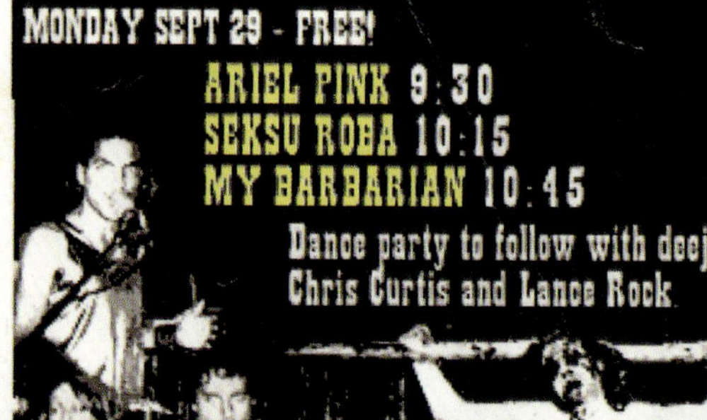

Performance flyers and posters, c. 2001-6

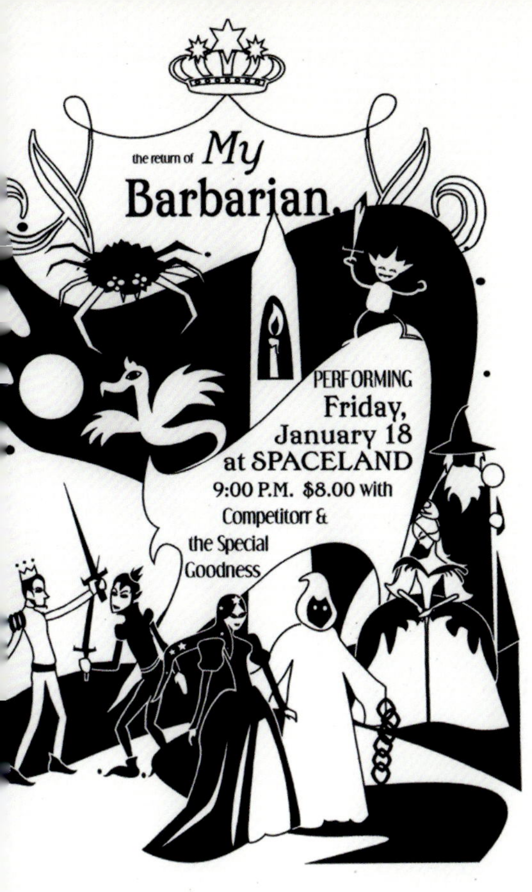

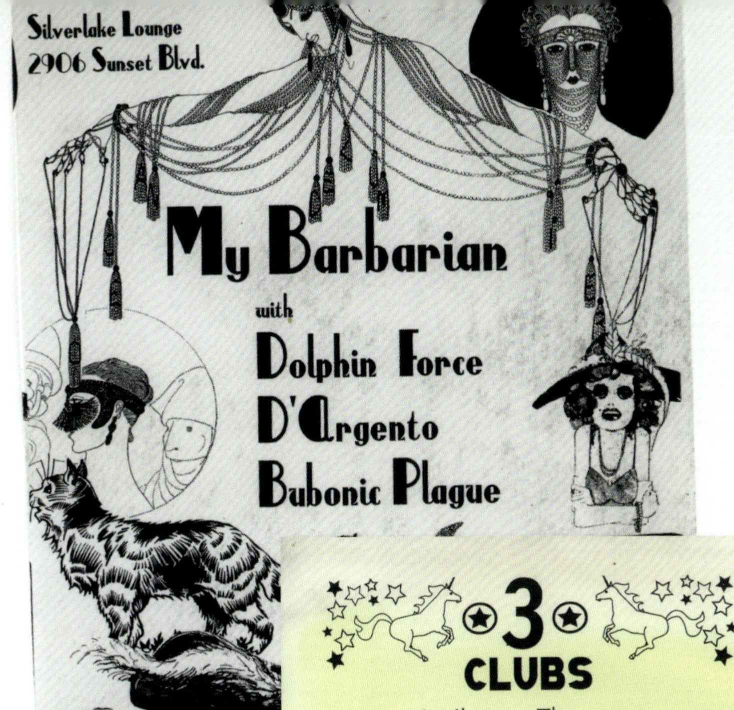

3 CLUBS
5 April 10:00 Thurs 2001
MY BARBARIAN
FREE SHOW
WITH DJ JIMI HEY

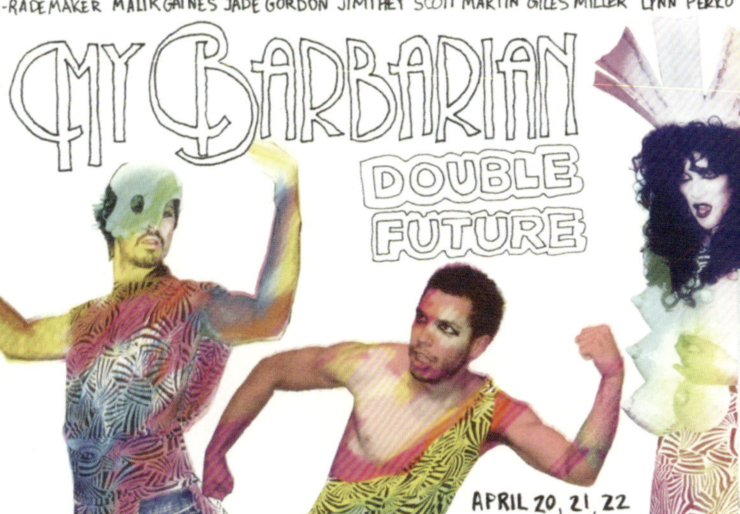

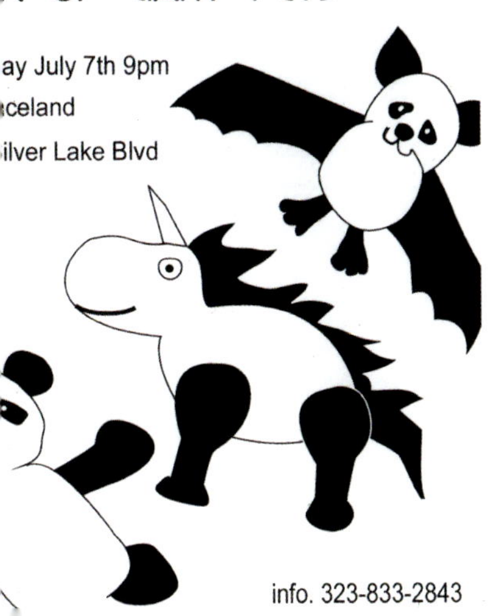

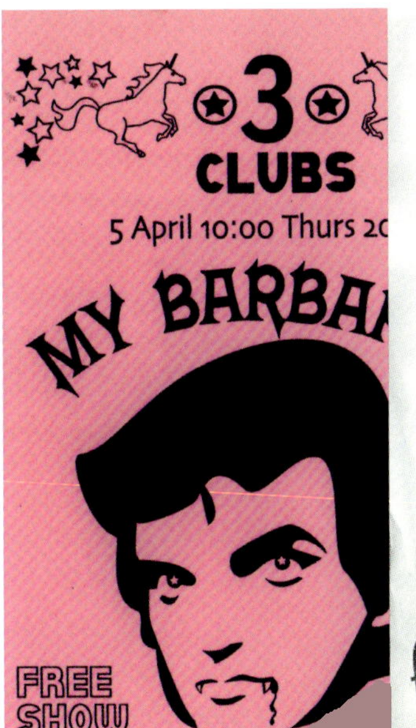

MY BARBARIAN

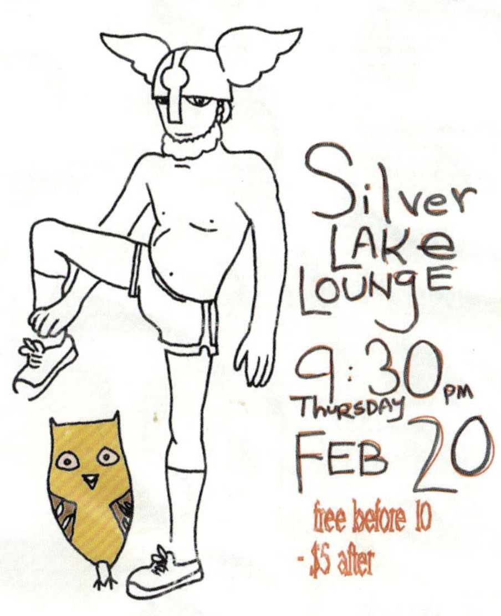

SQUIRREL RADIO ACTION

Scene 1 - The Forest

Narrator:
There's this story about the ground squirrels in Angeles Crest National forest. Every so often a bunch of them are found dead, and we here in the park take notice of the die-offs. The squirrels are disease vectors. The fleas on the squirrels carry the bacterium *Yersinia pestis*.

SQUIRREL SONG

We are the squirrels of the forest
We are carriers of bubonic plague
You are the people of the city
Heed our warning dire - why do you tempt fate
Homeless coyotes eat pets in Glendale
Deer on the 210 have no place to stay
Just as the forest grows smaller and smaller
So too the city collapses from its weight

Squirrel 1:
I've been a squirrel here all my life.

Squirrel 2:
All my life…too.

Squirrel 1:
We ground squirrels mostly just hang out in our burrows.

Squirrel 2:
We don't live in trees! Be sure to put that on the radio.

Squirrel 3:
I'm an 8 month-old squirrel. I'm in my prime.

Squirrel 4:
He's old. 6 months is like, the hottest age for squirrels.

Squirrel 1
You know it's like, we are really on the fringe of society, you know, in a national forest. And it's tough, fending for your self, practically at the bottom of the food chain…

FRI JUNE 24

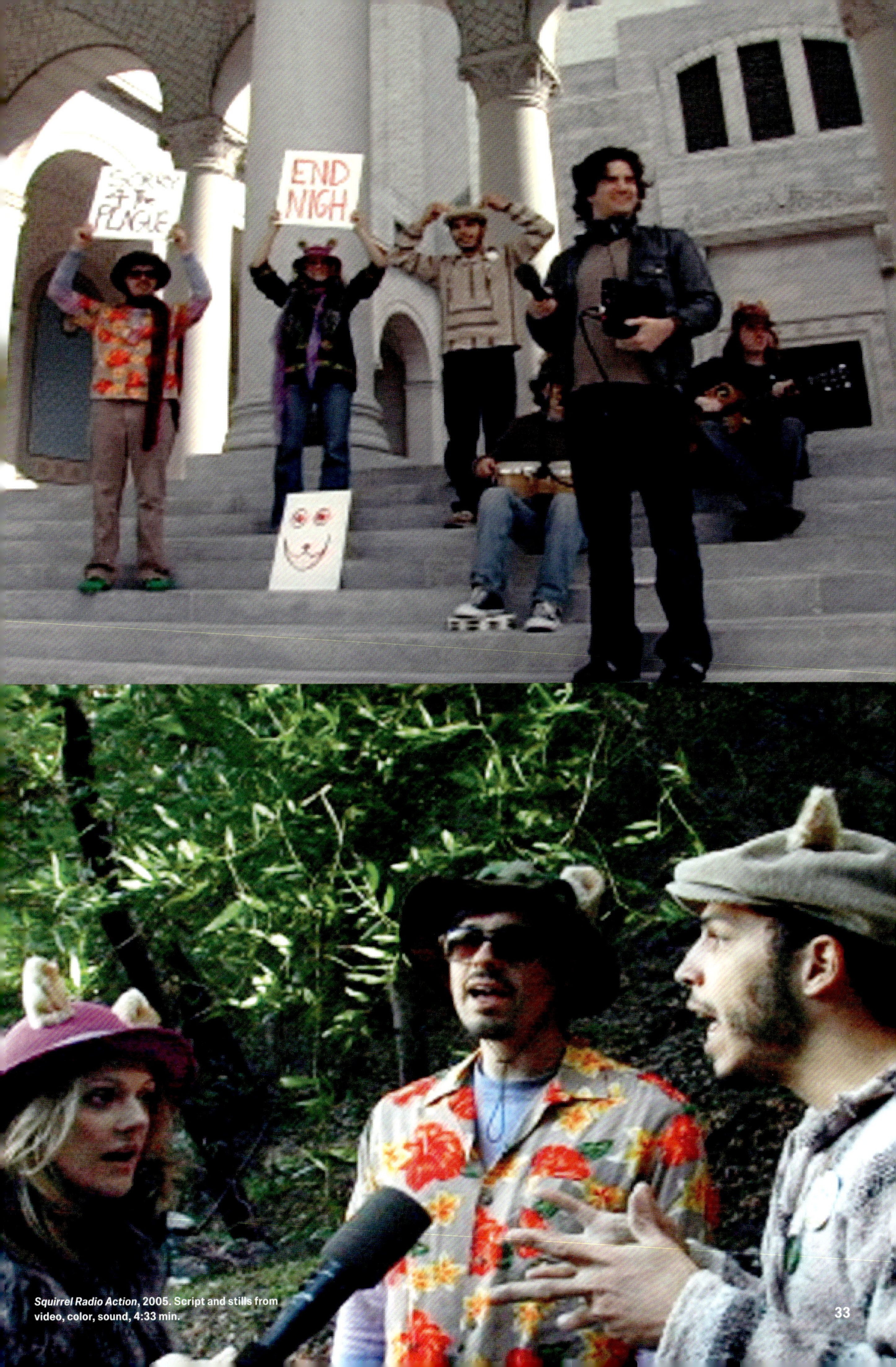

Squirrel Radio Action, 2005. Script and stills from video, color, sound, 4:33 min.

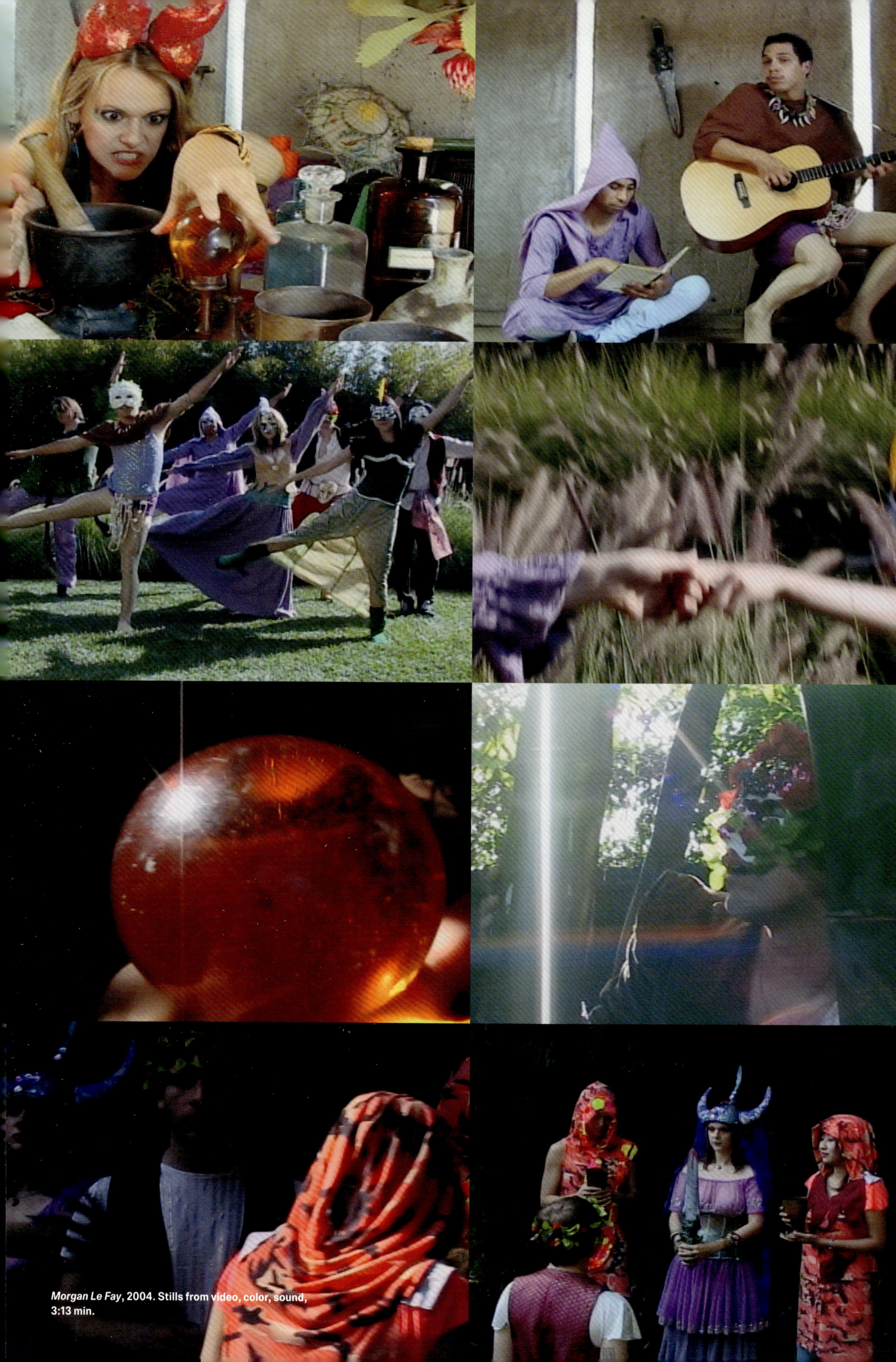

Morgan Le Fay, 2004. Stills from video, color, sound, 3:13 min.

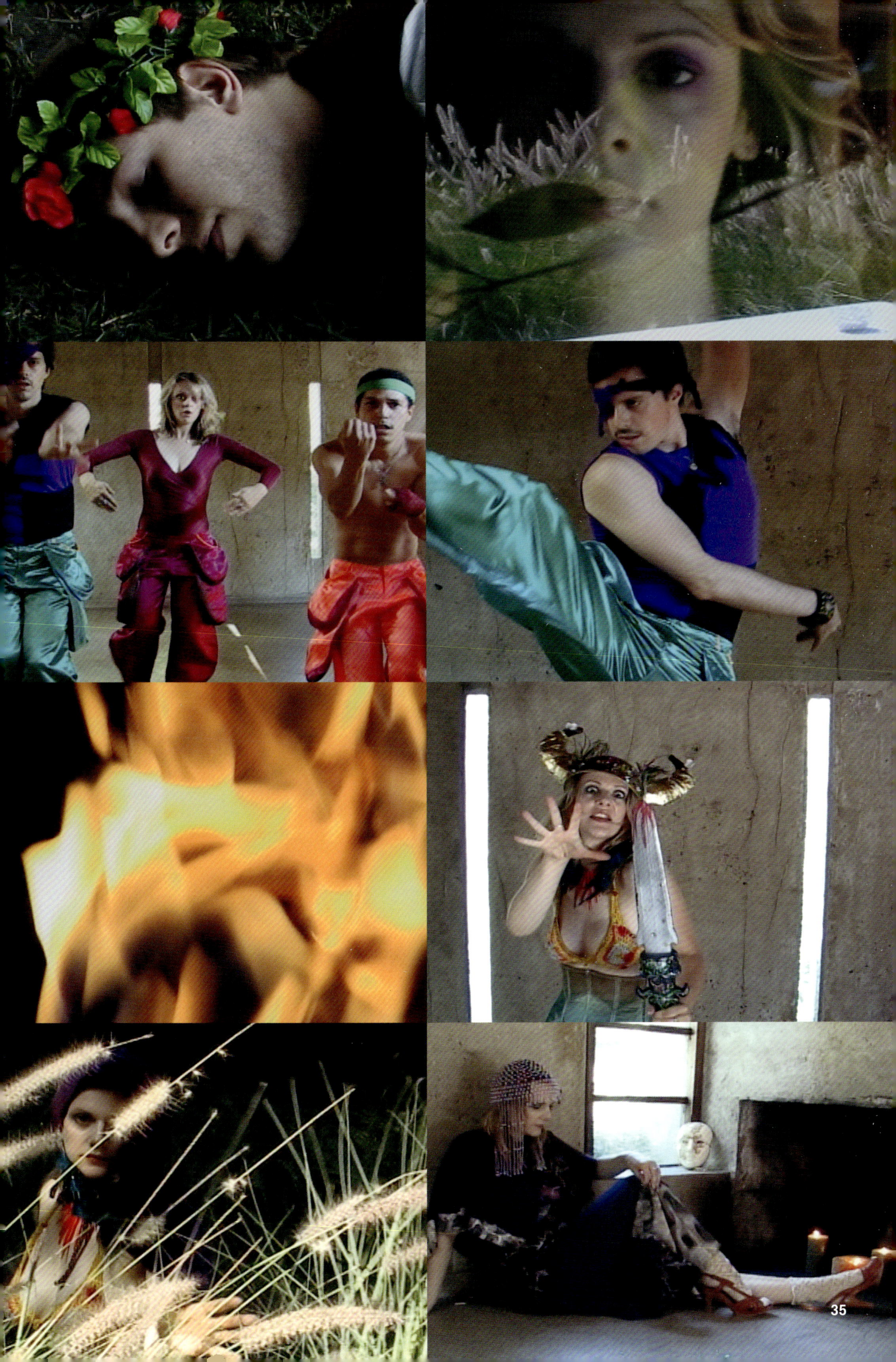

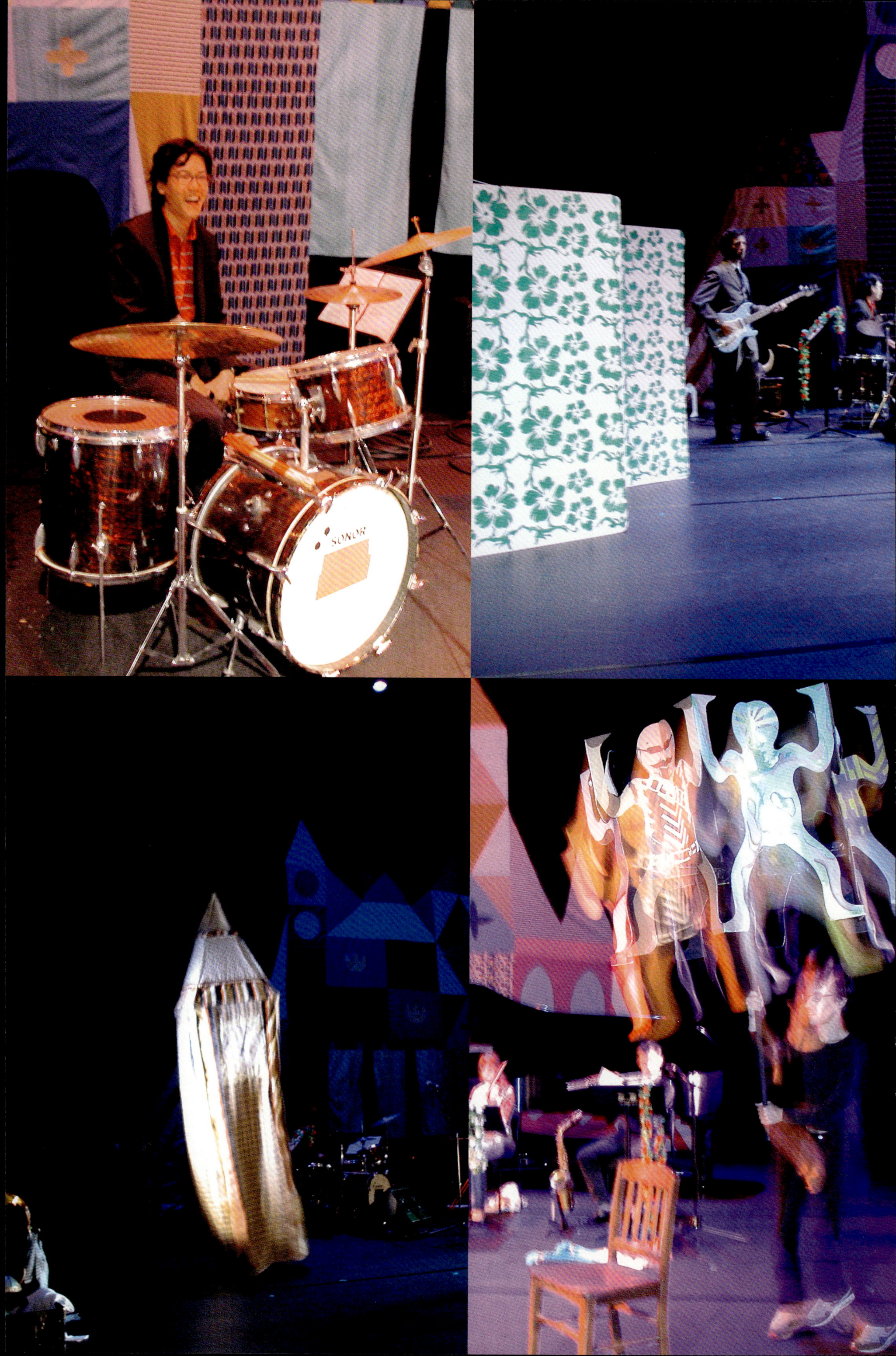
SONOR

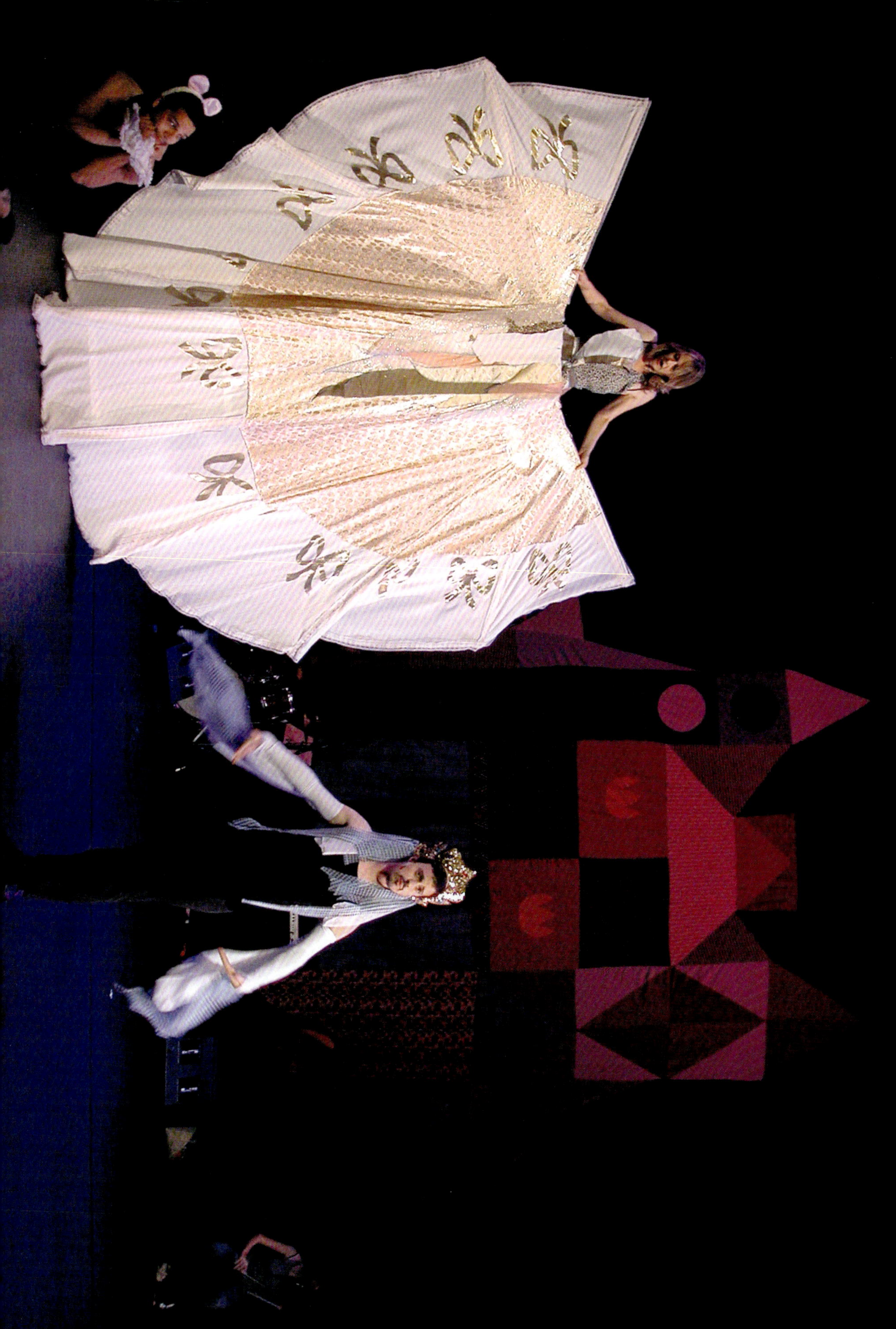

MB: The Mary Blair Story, 2004. Performance photographs, Roy and Edna Disney/CalArts Theater (REDCAT), Los Angeles

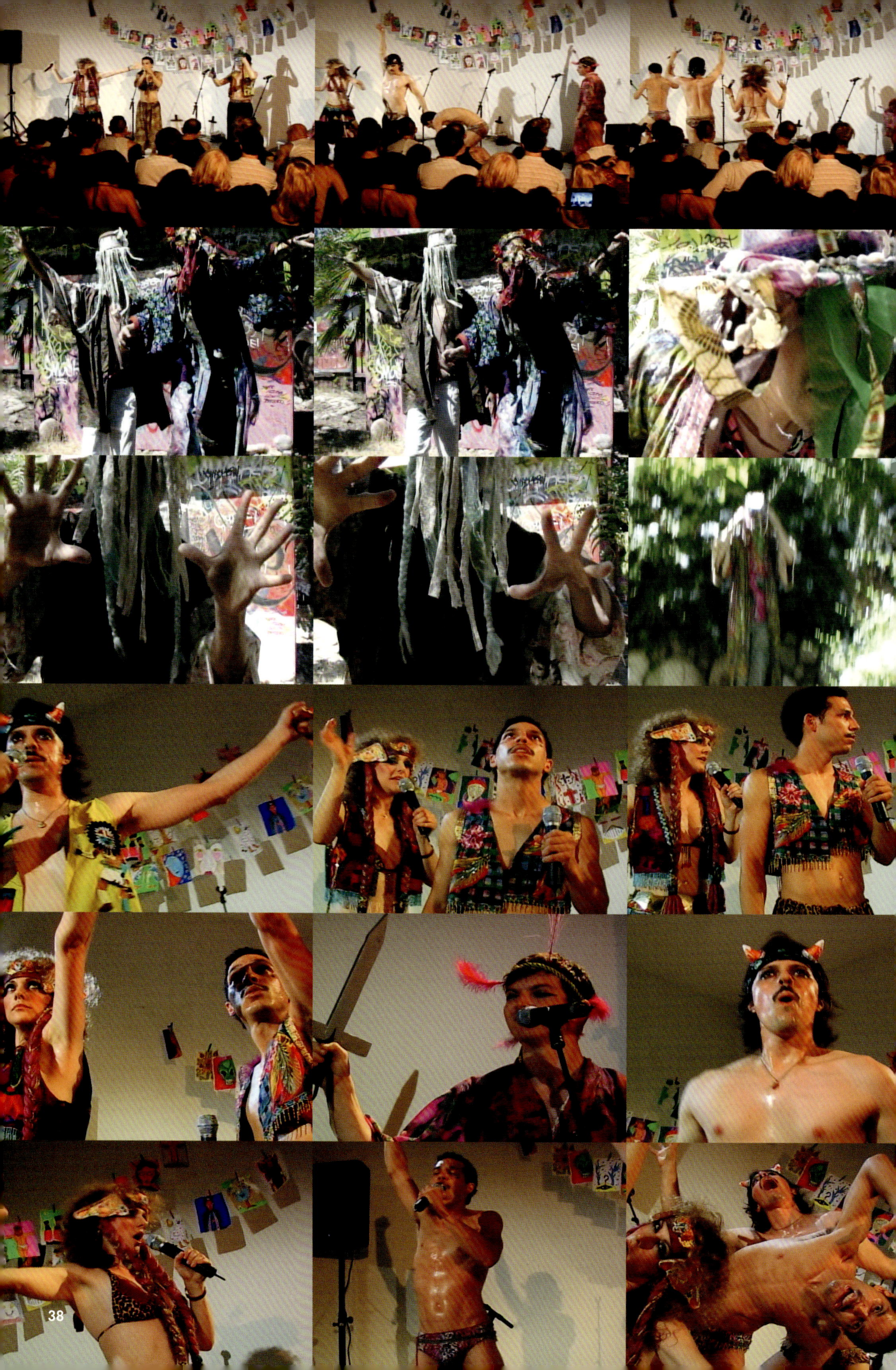

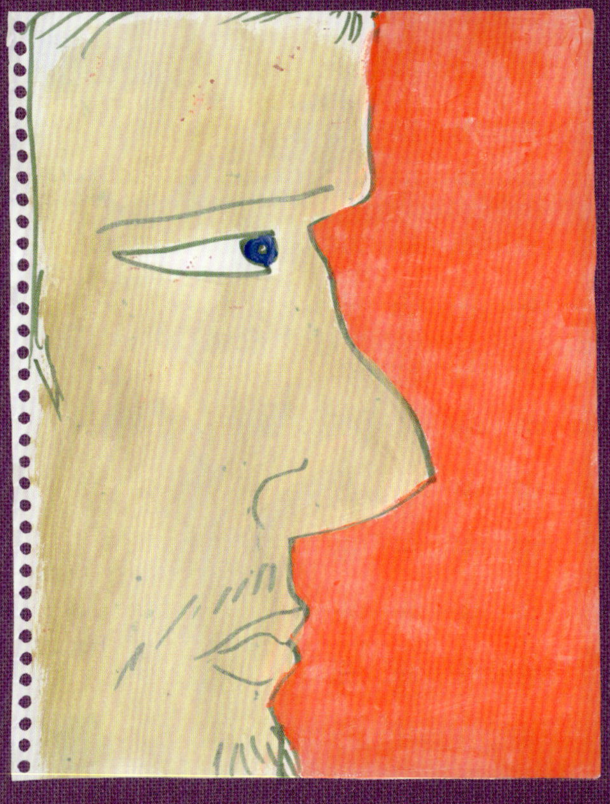
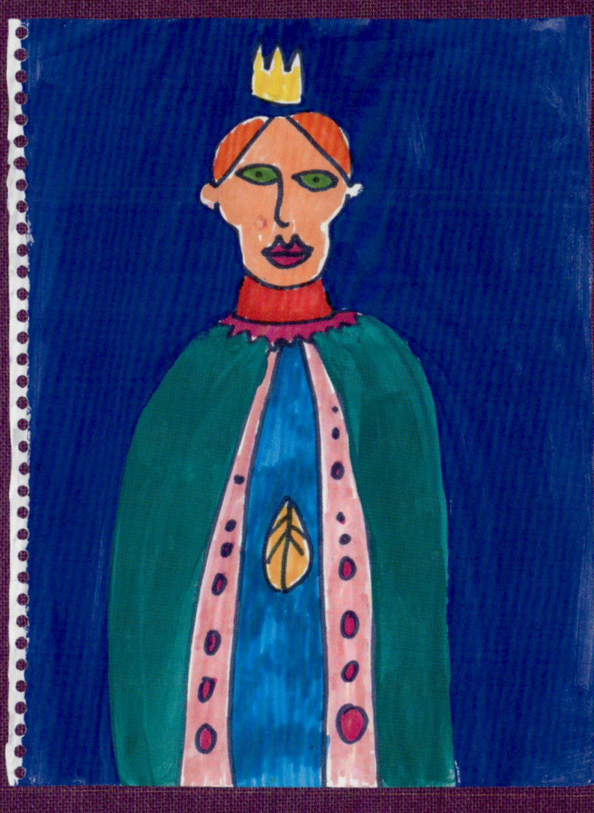
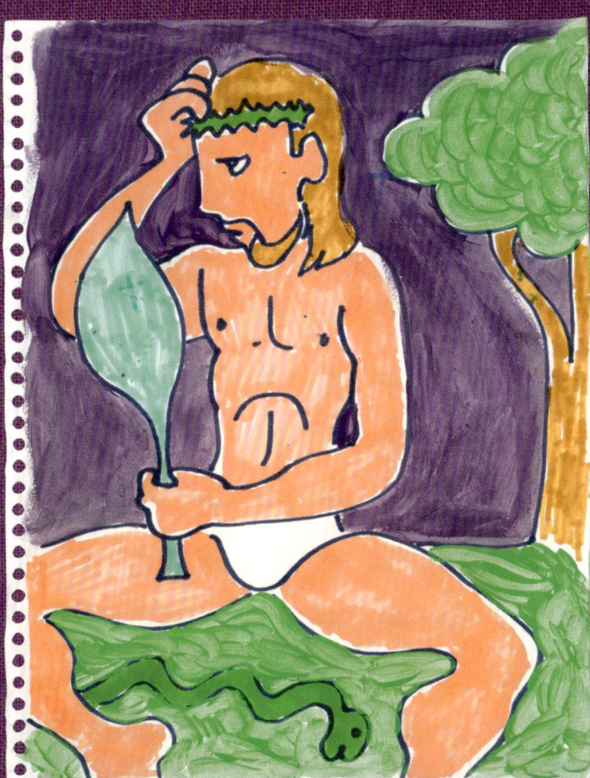
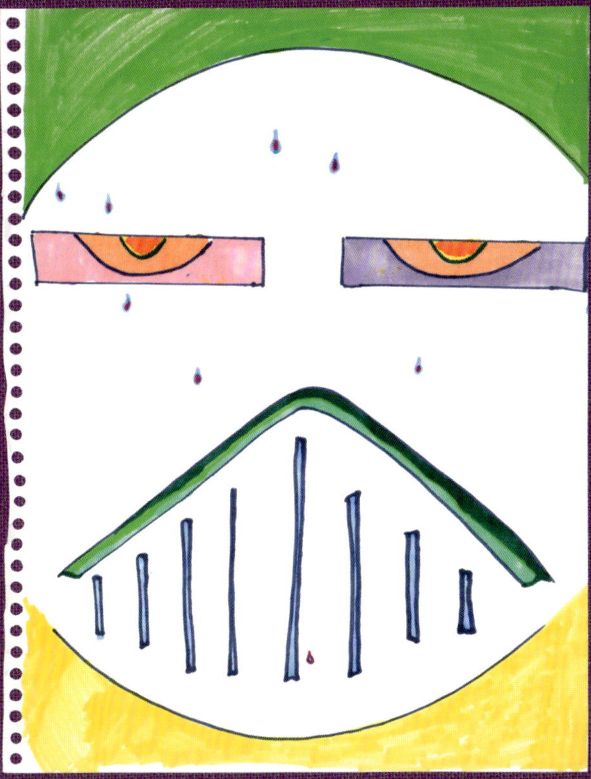

***Medieval Morality*, 2004/2006. Performance photographs and drawings, Peres Projects, Berlin**

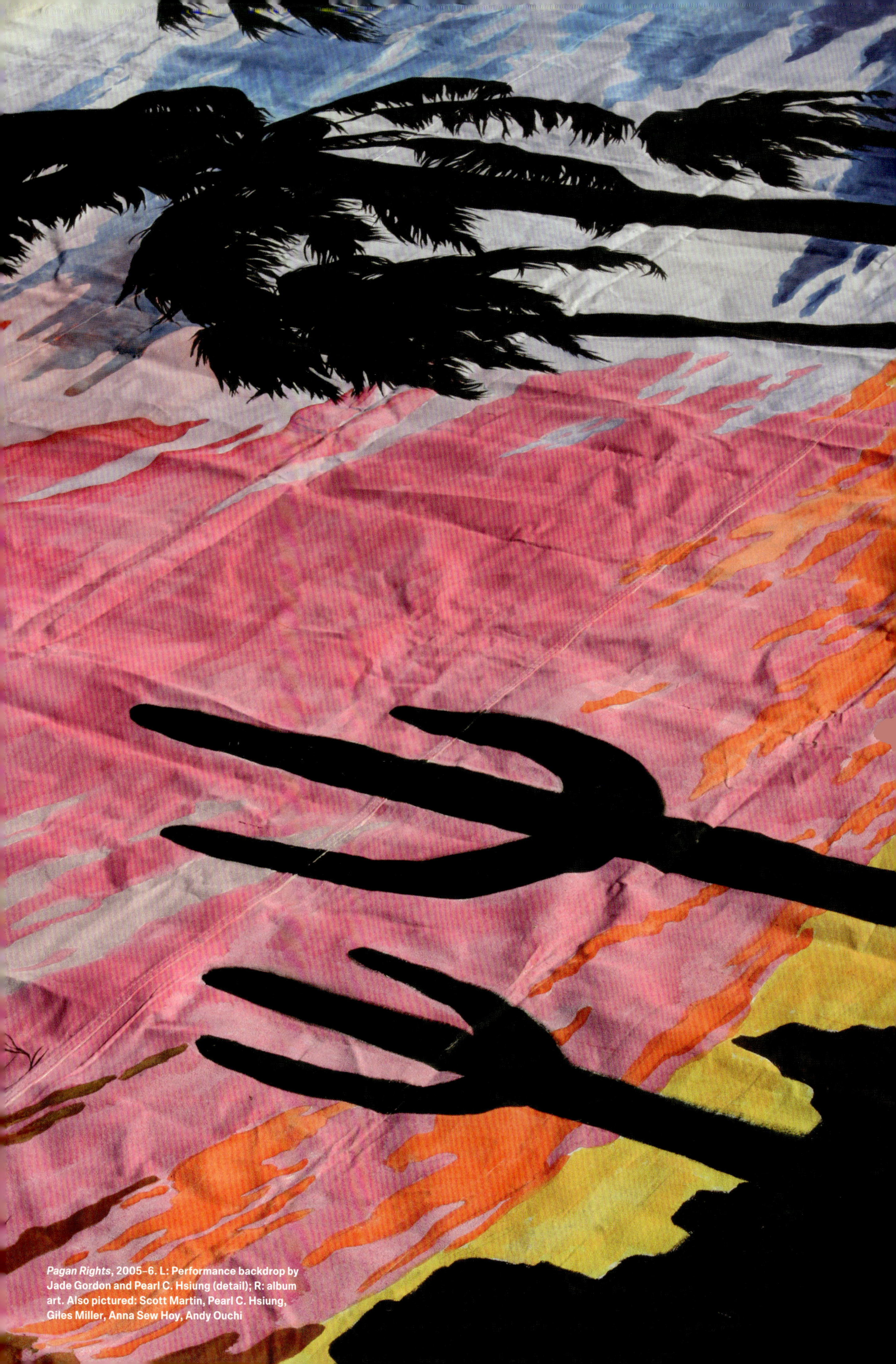

Pagan Rights, 2005–6. L: Performance backdrop by Jade Gordon and Pearl C. Hsiung (detail); R: album art. Also pictured: Scott Martin, Pearl C. Hsiung, Giles Miller, Anna Sew Hoy, Andy Ouchi

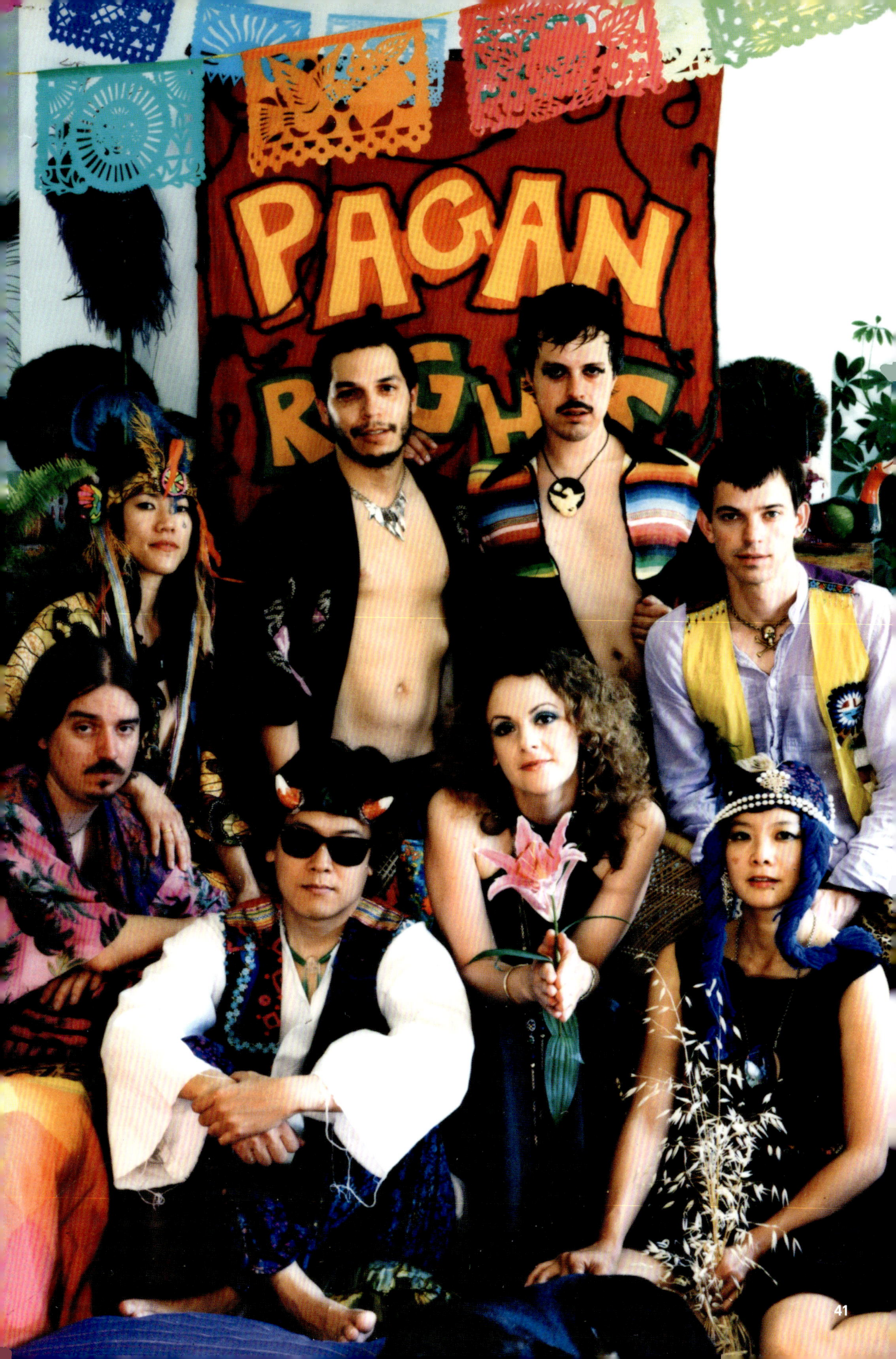
PAGAN

Pagan Rights, 2006. Storyboard drawings and production photographs

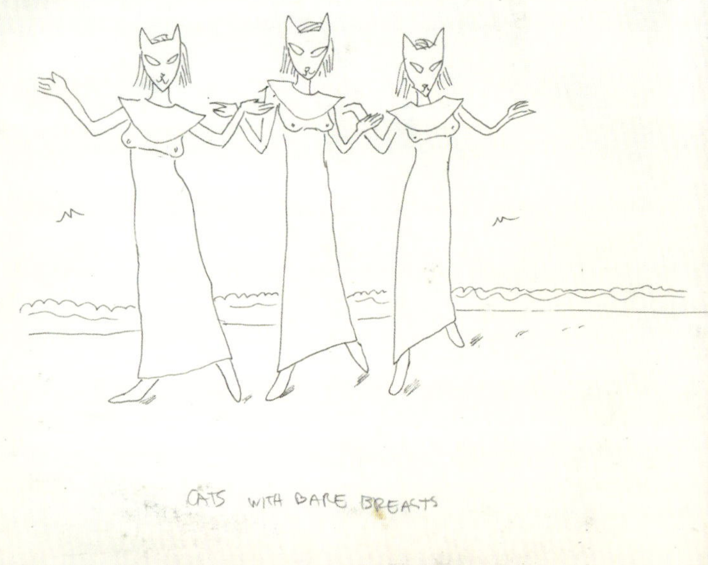

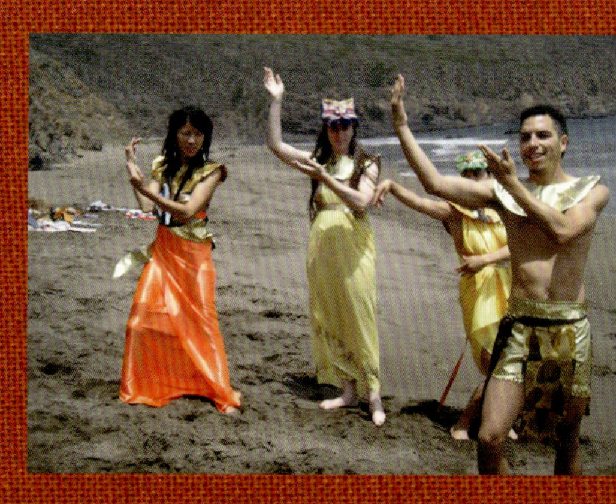

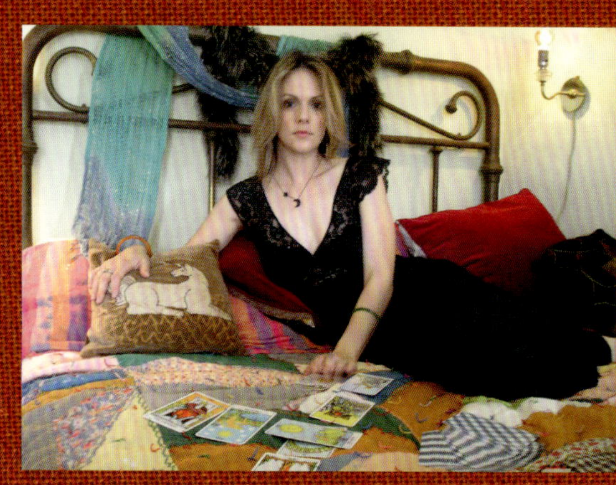

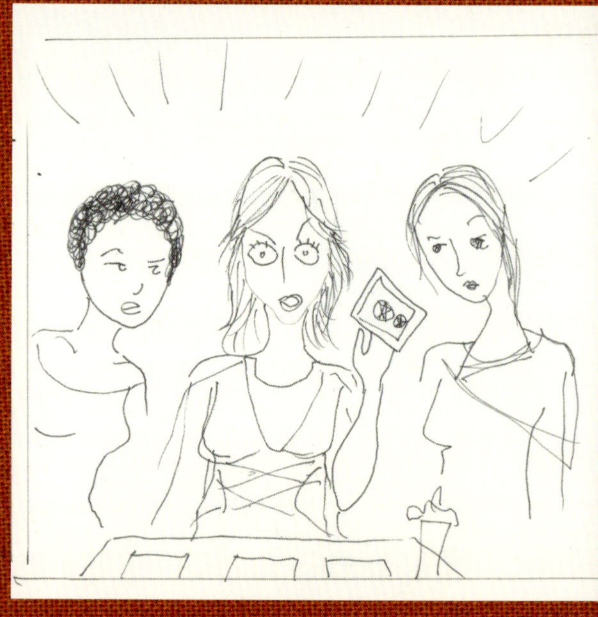

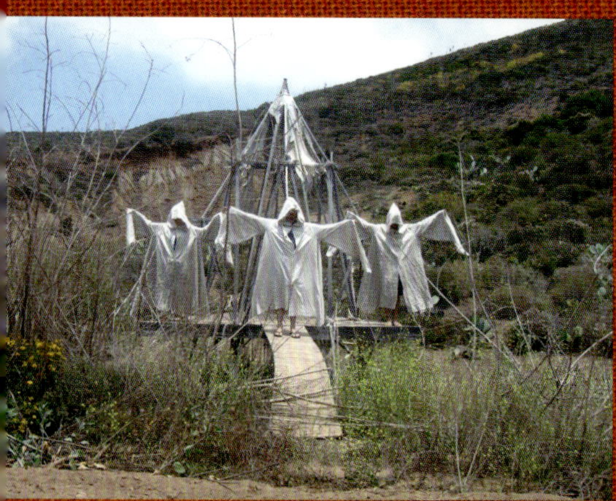

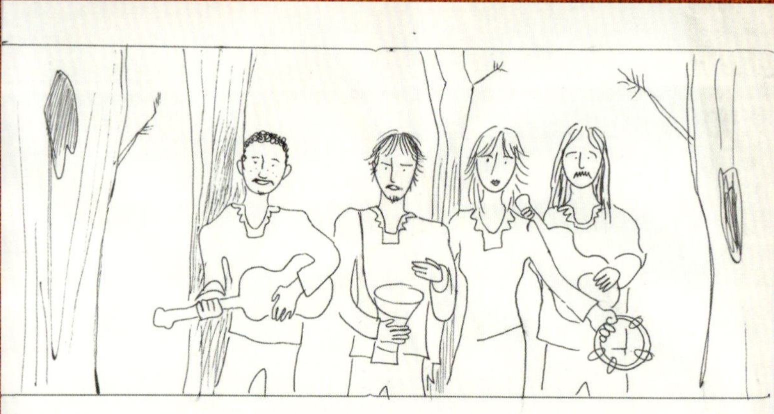

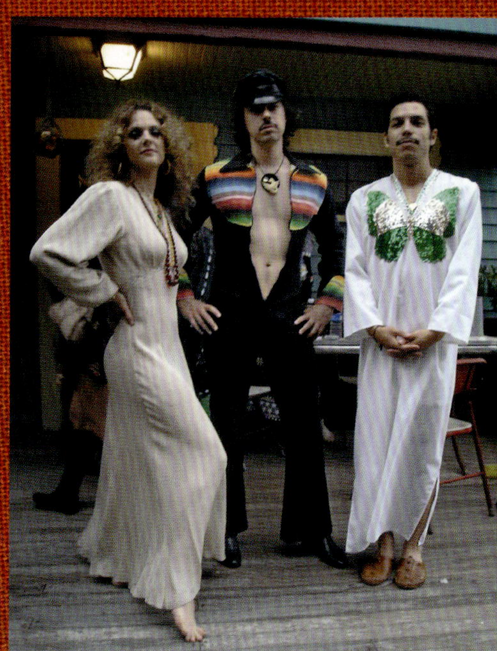

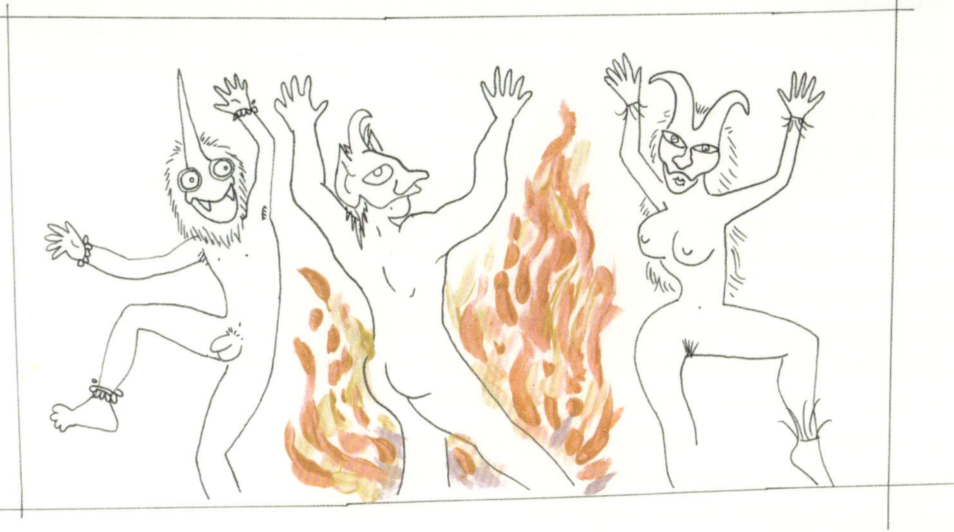
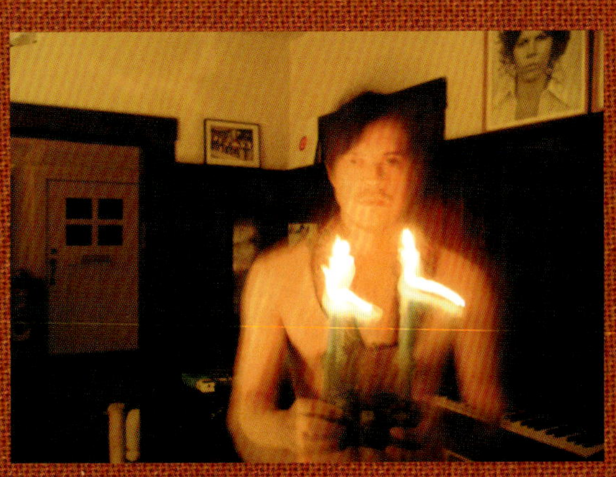
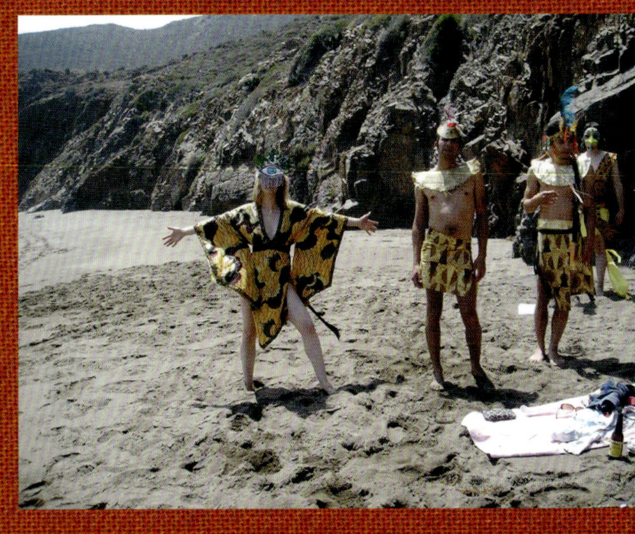
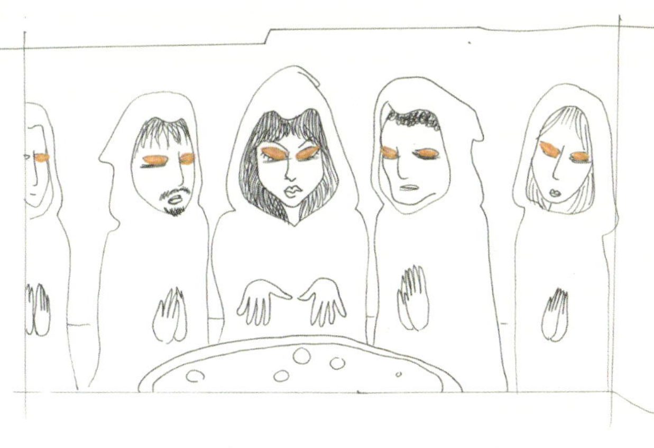
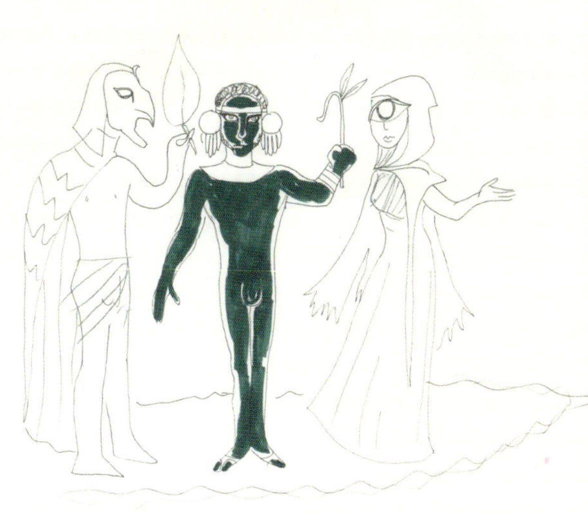
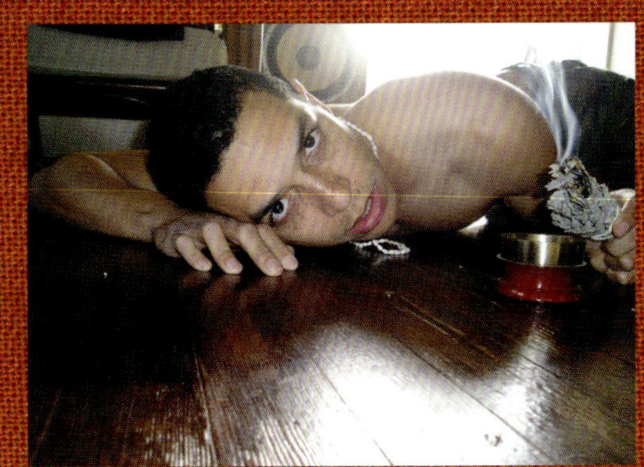

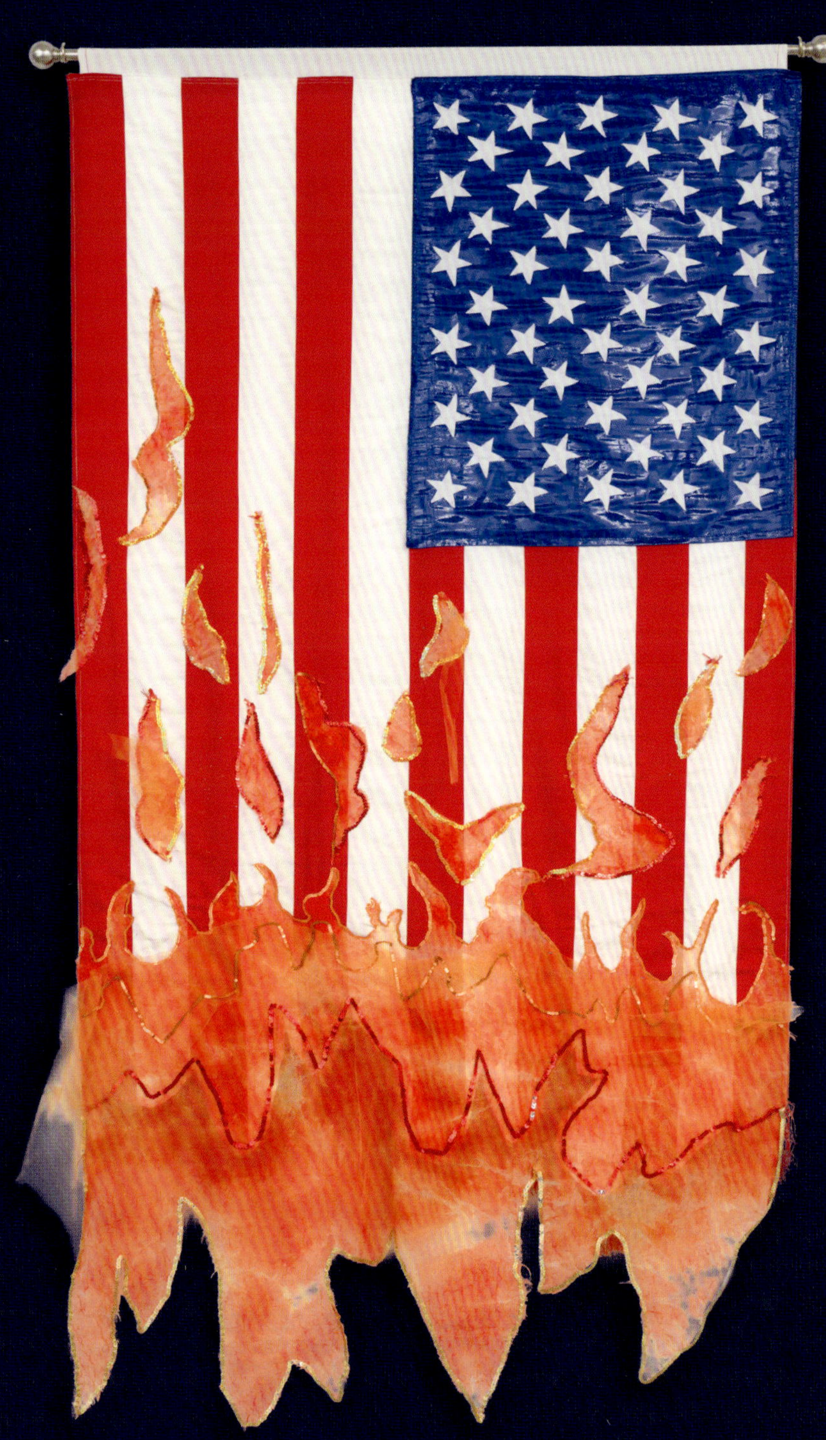

L: *Burning Flag*, 2005/2021, textiles, sequins, and acrylic, 75½ × 41 in. (191.8 × 104.1 cm); R: *Pagan Rights*, 2006. Stills from video, color, sound, 16:18 min.

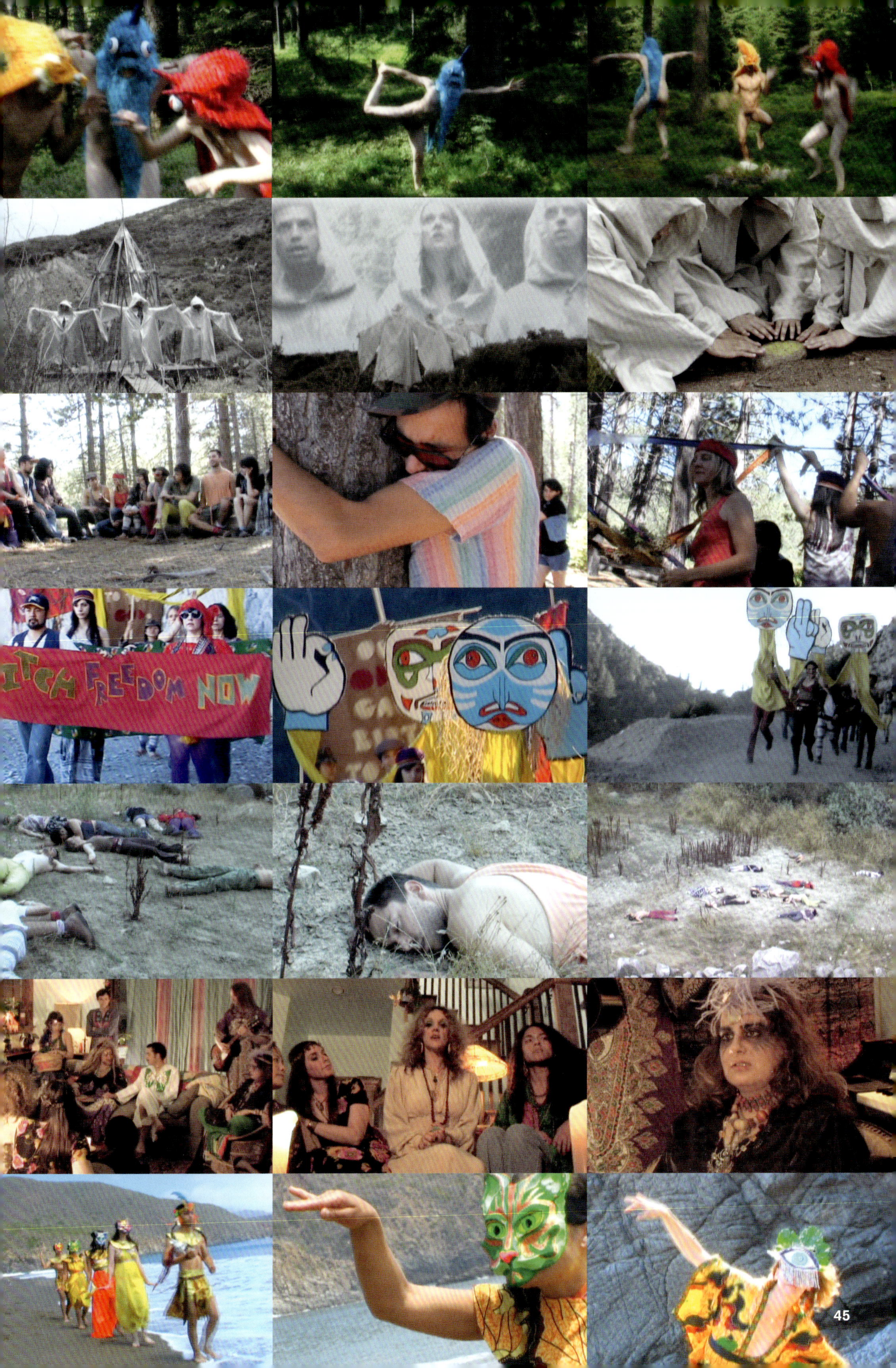
ITCH FREEDOM NOW

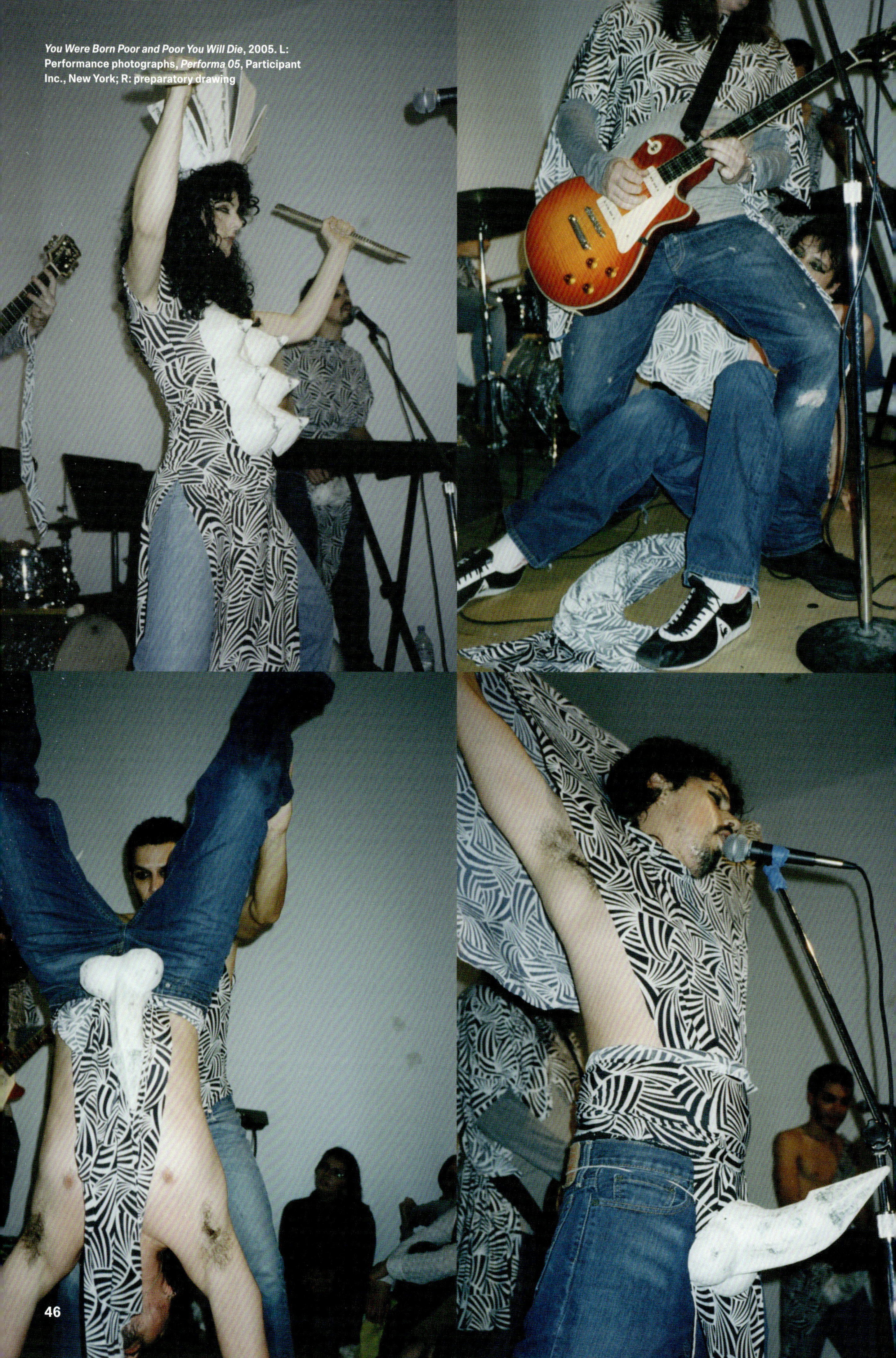

You Were Born Poor and Poor You Will Die, 2005. L: Performance photographs, *Performa 05*, Participant Inc., New York; R: preparatory drawing

YOU WERE BORN MIDDLE CLASS
THAT WON'T LAST
YOU WERE BORN MIDDLE CLASS
& POOR YOU WILL DIE

YOU WERE BORN RICH & RICH YOU WILL DIE
& & POOR YOU WILL DIE

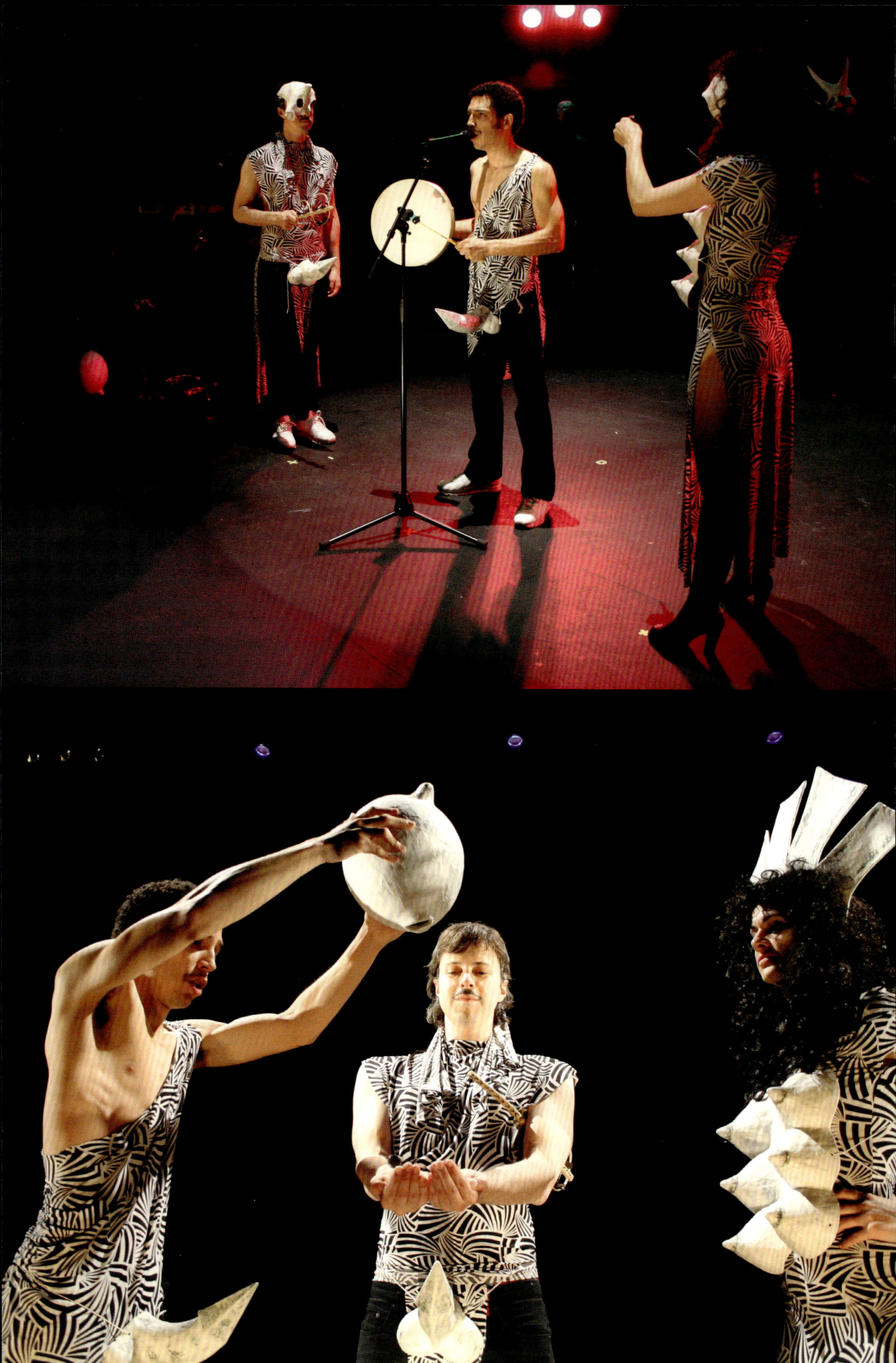

You Were Born Poor and Poor You Will Die, 2006. Performance photographs, Roy and Edna Disney/CalArts Theater (REDCAT), Los Angeles

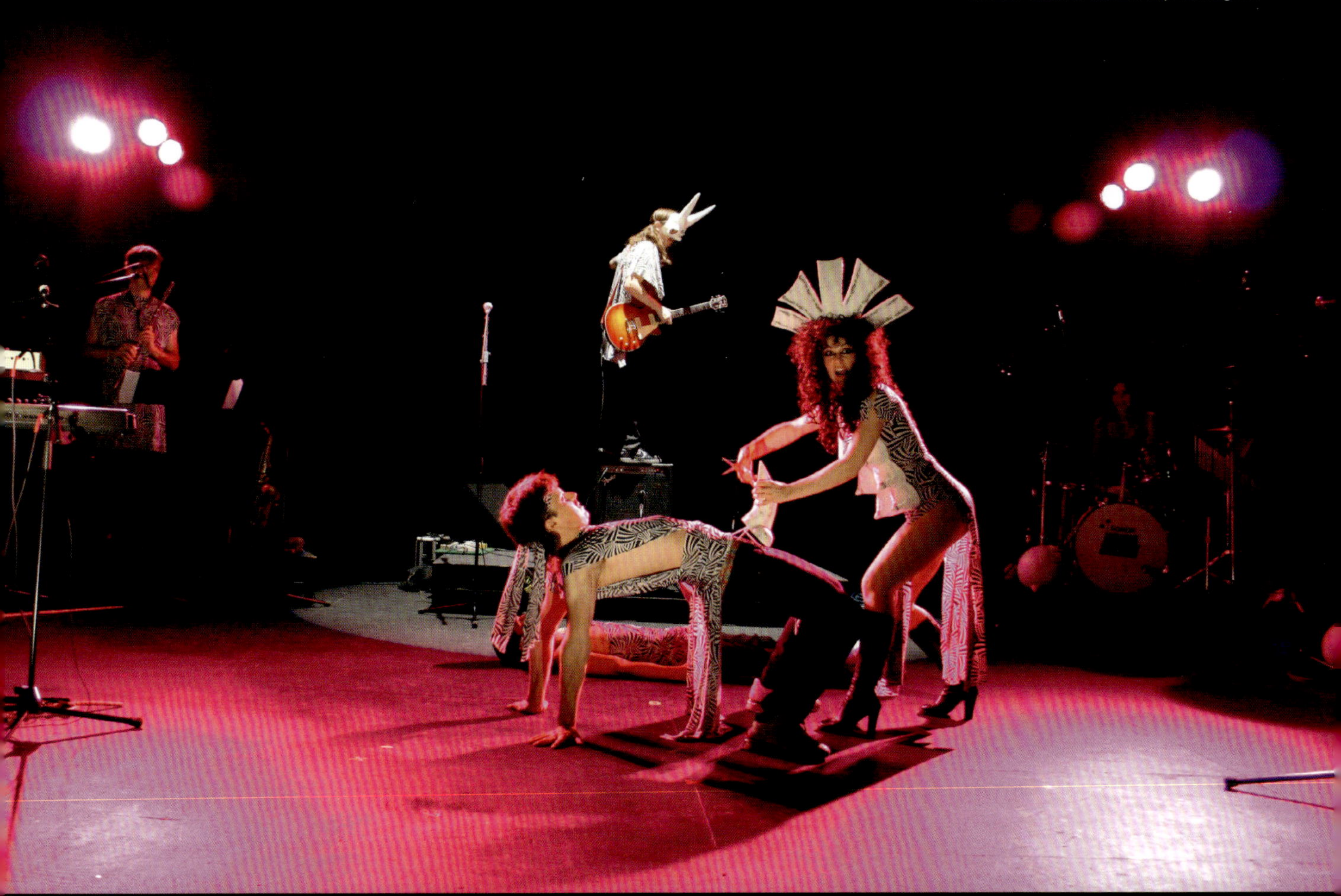

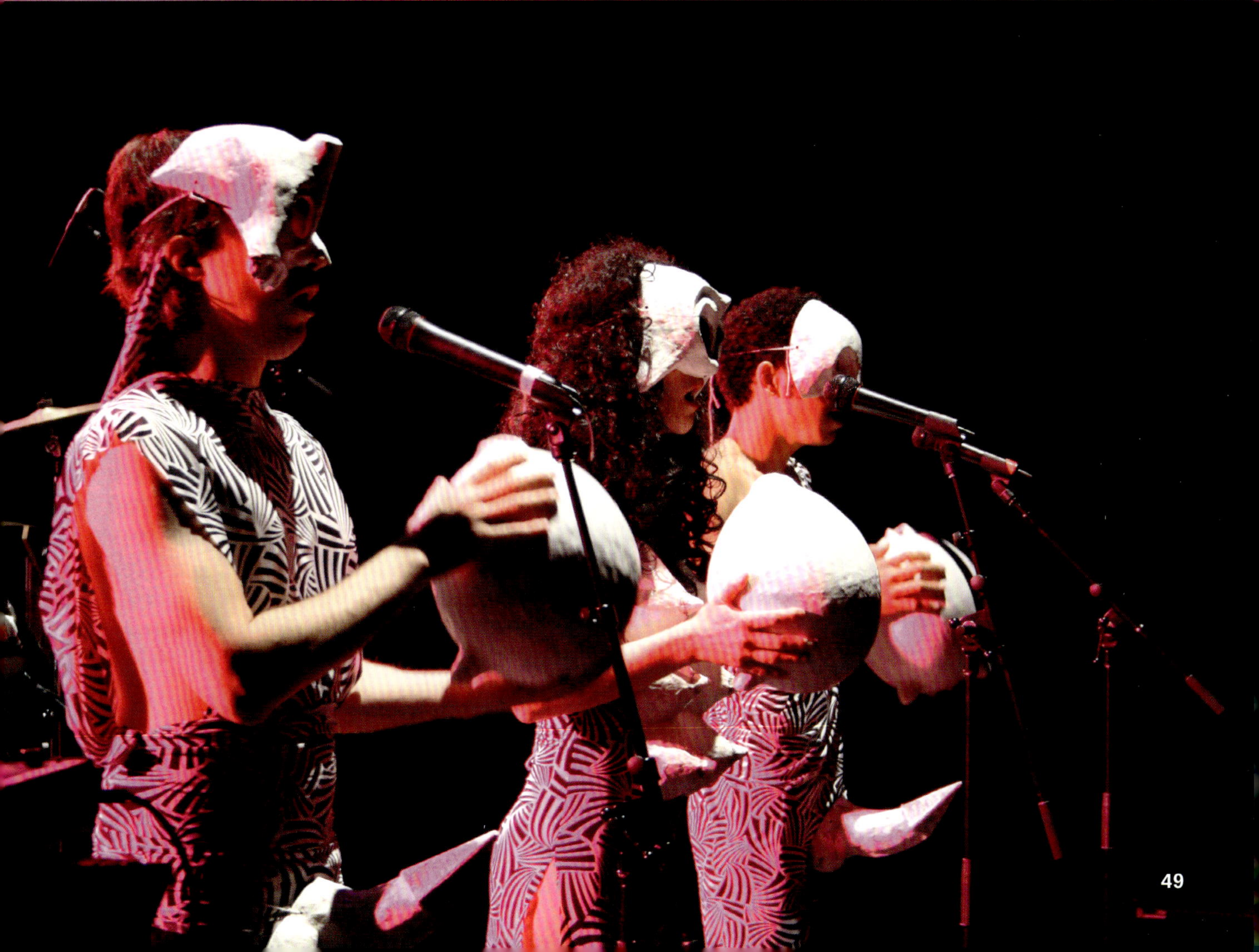

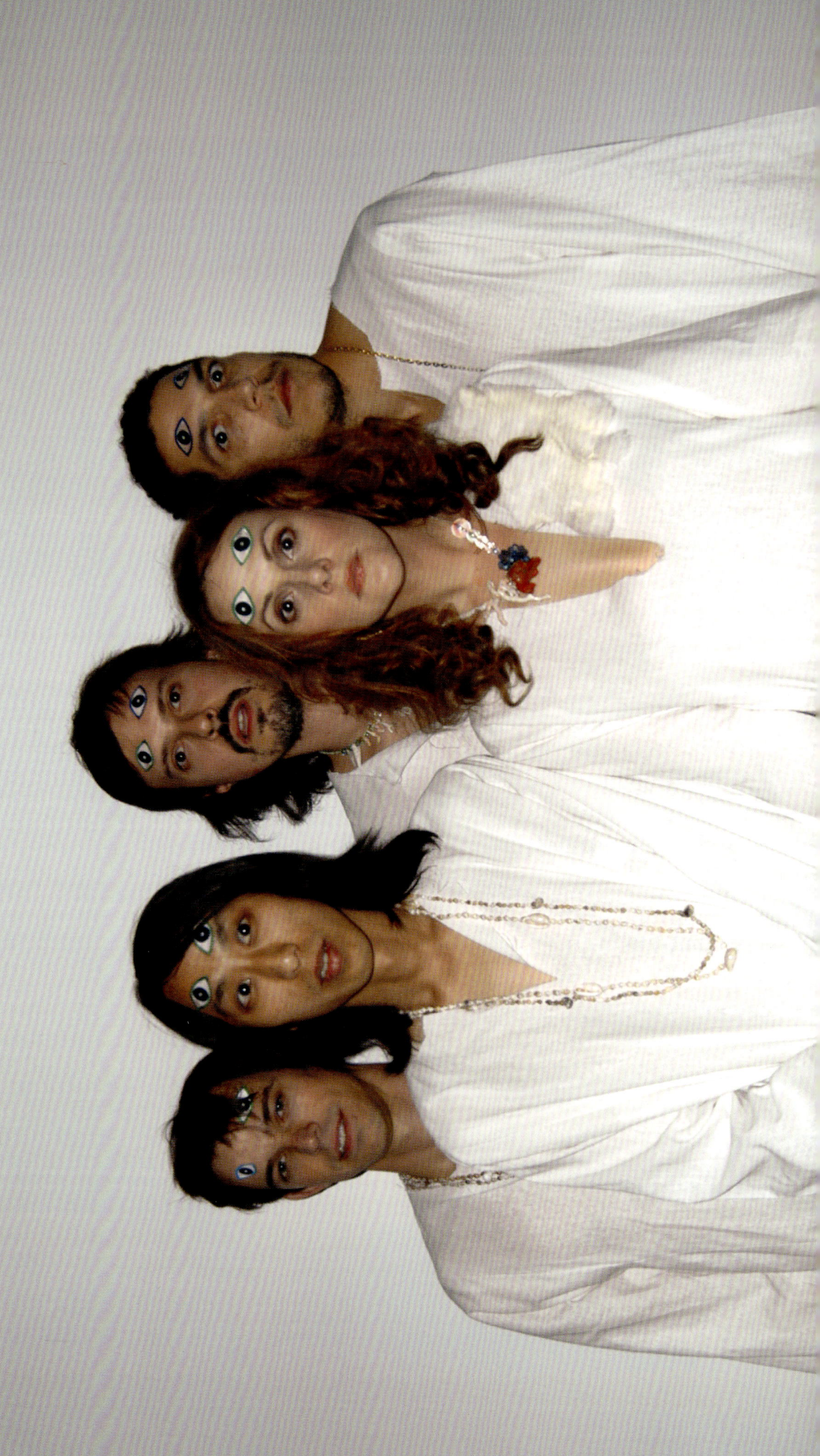

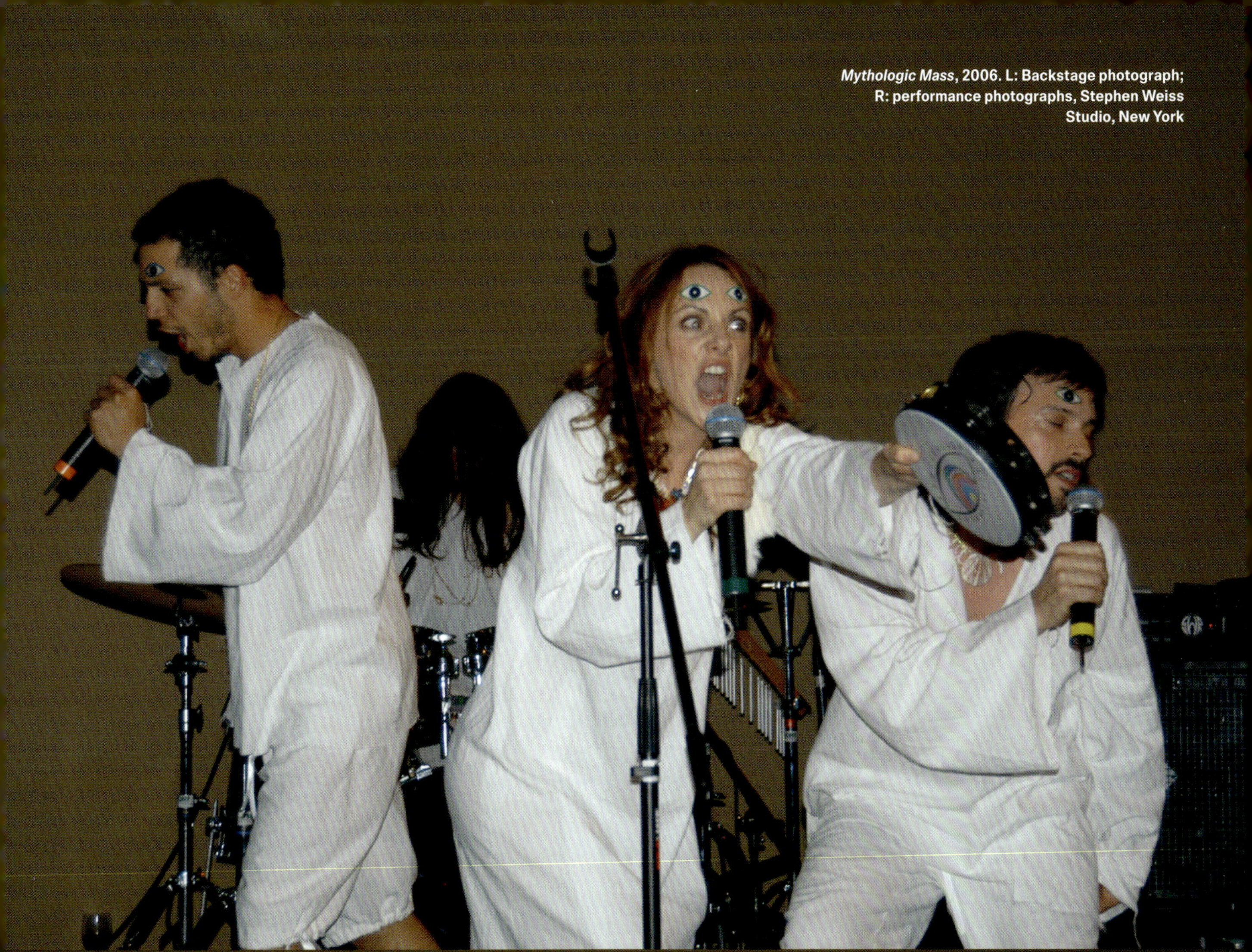

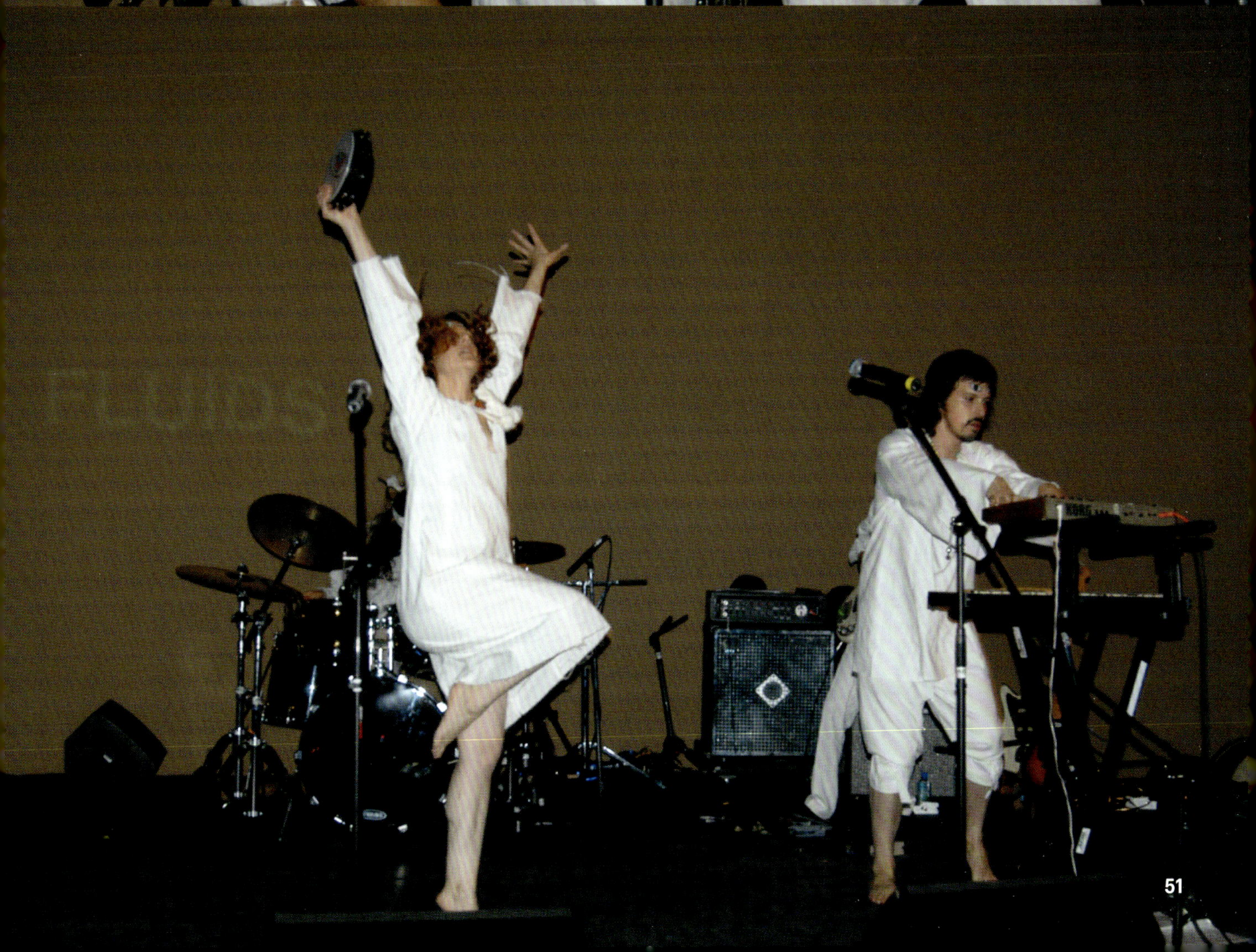

Mythologic Mass, 2006. L: Backstage photograph; R: performance photographs, Stephen Weiss Studio, New York

SITE-SPECIFIC SPECTACLE

Malik Gaines

My Barbarian's work uses performance to obviate, or understand, or criticize peoples' entanglements with each other, just as we three had entangled ourselves. Our earlier preparation playing a music ensemble/theater troupe/art group interested in crossing each of those boundaries led to a series of performances that used the far-flung sites of their enactment to play out specific ways—from the historical and political to the phenomenological and spatial—that "humans" may be "together." This is, of course, a violent and disturbing history, with occasional moments of brilliant collectivity, coordinated production, and love.

When asked to do a performance in the snow outside the Aspen Art Museum, we thought of classical theater forms that can be seasonal and landed on a version of a Noh drama that could convey the story of tourists from a climate-changed future who travel to the past to go skiing. Masked theatricality and formal gesture met the real time and place of the *après-ski* audience, with their local tangle of wealth and environmentalism. For a Canada Day performance at Toronto's Power Plant, we tapped into a Bush-era fantasy about supposedly liberal Canadian policies and became a team of ridiculously nationalistic superheroes, the Gods of Canada, who celebrate public health care, gay marriage, decriminalized marijuana, and other ideas that hadn't yet taken hold in the US in a rock-opera pageant replete with a custom-flag-flying sail-by. This playful approach to site offered a kind of specificity we were seeking, but it also opened up real questions about what it means to show up somewhere on an art budget and tell the locals what you think you know about them.

We arrived in Aspen after a long drive from LA and found that we would be performing outdoors in the middle of what seemed like a dog park. We decided that we would create our own stage and spent the day digging out a trench in the snow. We altered our costumes by cutting up old sweaters purchased at a local thrift shop and fashioned makeshift legwarmers, headbands, and fingerless gloves to keep us warm in our gold unitards. The high altitude made the choreography tough. We (breathlessly) performed in daylight for a confused audience of rich ladies holding Pekingese dogs in mink sweaters. —Jade

Referencing the Canadian superhero team Alpha Flight, this project gave me the chance to cosplay a version of the Quebecois separatist mutant Northstar, the first Marvel Comics character to declare "I am gay!" —Alex

These performances ironized our own relation to the site, uneasily. Later on, when invited to work on a project for a Baltic Triennial in Vilnius, Lithuania, we paired with a talented up-and-coming musical trio there, Liūdni Slibinai, to try to communicate about a history displayed to us in tourist sites like the KGB Museum, where we first met in a preserved prison cell to play theater games. The more time we spent there, the more we discovered that a celebrated national history of partisan resistance to Soviet occupation barely papered over brutal antisemitic violence that had never been culturally processed. A curator in an isolated Jewish history museum clutched documents in her hands, proving a point that was not widely accepted. This all happened at the time of the Lehman Brothers collapse, which crashed the Lithuanian national airline, so we flew through Helsinki to get to this EU art capital from LA. There wasn't enough ironically critical performance art in the world to untangle this historical knot. With all of this in the surround we used the costumes of partisan resistance

We first saw Liūdni Slibinai, or Sad Three-Headed Dragon (Dominykas Vaitiekūnas, Vaidas Kublinskas, and Aistė Lasytė), onstage in a recital at the performing arts school, doing satirical versions of Lithuanian folk songs. It was like looking into a Baltic mirror. When we reached out to them they thought we were their friends playing a joke, pretending to be from LA. —Alex in *Forest Brothers & Sisters* (2009) to ask who can and cannot access this history. Unable to answer that question fully, we focused on the present act of communicating with our collective double. In a live performance, they taught us Lithuanian folk dances, and we taught them dances in the style of Beyoncé, which they presumably already knew.

In this period of My Barbarian's work, there are problems of costuming. We saw in our favorite performance art influences—such as Vaginal Davis, the group Asco, and conceptual feminist Eleanor Antin—alienated staging attitudes, including toward costumes. This distanciation, resembling Brechtian criticality, queer camp zaniness, and disidentificatory technique, allowed for a performance of "positions and attitudes," as we described it in the later masked work *Shakuntala Du Bois* (2012), rather than authentic identities. As a group of three people marked by different races, ethnicities, genders, and sexualities, there were few single costumes we were all authorized to wear. I, as a queer Black person with a white parent, wanted to play both with identificatory fantasies and also with the permission I might have to evade rules of cultural attire. This may play out differently for Jade, a white woman with an English dad, or Alex, with Cuban, Puerto Rican, and Eastern European Jewish grandparents. Pursuing matching garments heightened all of this complexity. We felt this when we all dressed as Dutch sailors in the postcolonial musical *Voyage of the White Widow* (2007), performed in both old Amsterdam and New Amsterdam. Following some gender hijinks and a difficult dance contest during which the audience is symbolically inducted into slavery, the sailor costumes give way to those of mermaids, who oversee the climate apocalypse that will finally destroy this human record.

Andrea Fraser told her students we occupied positions in the field of cultural production. Fassbinder directed his actors to play "attitudes" not characters. My Barbarian was equipped with enough positions to make a field, and, as "slacker Brechtians," an attitude with a bad accent was more doable than a "character." I was also interested in "ethnicity," a paradoxical identity marker suggesting both an authentic cultural origin and its self-conscious performance. So I played loungy Latin lover wannabes (copying Raul Julia's copy in *One from the Heart*) and kitschy mystics (shades of Guillermo Gómez-Peña's rasquache futurism), but with a queer attitude. —Alex

Attempts to signal Indigenous positions through costume have been difficult. In earlier work, like *Pagan Rights* (2006), we were reenacting California countercultures that sometimes appropriated Native materials, with a beaded headband here and there. A friend of ours was in a gay shaman collective, so we wrote a song about that. As we developed more historically situated pieces, it was important to recognize indigeneity as a foundation of modernity. In *Non-Western* (2007–8), our quick-change Western, we played numerous characters in a mythic Pueblo de Los Angeles, all of whom are adrift in coloniality in a time when "California" was moving between sovereign powers. Dedicated to the instability of our own city, we performed this show in brightly colored costumes with rapidly changing accessories in Madrid, Los Angeles, Santa Barbara, San Diego, and Tijuana. In our musical, the most radical thinkers in the pueblo are the Indians, who are oppressed by the nuns and the landowners and finally lead the enslaved people and the animals in a violent revolution. To play Indian (as differentiated from my other characters of cowboy, enslaved woman, coyote, colonial officer, nun, and half of a magical pterodactyl), I would put a fuchsia feather in my hair to match my fuchsia dance pants and vest. Jade would casually wrap a lime green woven shawl around her lime green saloon gal outfit. These were not caricatures, but signals. While dressing up as Indian is now better understood as part of a repertoire of erasure, we needed to represent these characters if we were going to try to depict "The West," but we were also interested in critically engaging that very repertoire with the serious power that circulates in performance.

I feel less confident now about the angular disco routine we did in flashy gold custom Aztec dance costumes at the Espacio Escultórico in Mexico City in 2010. I know why we did it. We were unraveling the utopian modernism embedded in the founding of the museum we were working in, Museo Experimental el Eco, which synthesized European avant-gardism with pre-conquest forms. Exploring the history of the space, we reenacted a lesbian bar with local cabaret stars Las Reinas Chulas, we made video murals featuring museum visitors on a green screen, we held a comic séance with an audience to communicate with architect Matthias Goeritz and also with Trotsky, and we danced in a historic land-art piece in various costumes, from the Bauhaus-esque to the attire of a mariachi band.

Ecos de los Ecos de los Ecos (2010) followed other pieces that were turned in on the museums where they were sited. *The Case of the Stairs* (2008) was an elaborate floor show to accompany the rededication of a stairway at the Los Angeles County Museum of Art (LACMA). *The Fourth Wall* (2009) was a deep dive into LA's Museum of Contemporary Art, following a highly publicized financial disaster. The only flexible budget left was a grant for social practice projects, so the museum used our intervention to fund the opening of a collection show. We did interviews with staff about the crisis and documented the installation of the exhibition, and fused that footage into a series of scenes and dances that happened around the museum. This culminated in a flashy musical mediation on "Transparency" that used live feeds to project performances throughout a particularly opaque museum.

As our work developed in this period, we took up the art context not only for performances but for new video work as well. Previously having made music videos, we began expanding that category into video installations that could crystallize specific ideas from our hyper-narrative performances. *The Golden Age* (2007) stages the slave dance from *Voyage of the White Widow*. We three sailors demonstrate the moves, in girl-group style, for an audience who is required to learn them. "You put your hands in chains, shake that chain, shake that chain." "You can cook and serve, cook and serve." "They took your baby away, your baby away." The catchy refrain repeats the question "Who put the gold in the Golden Age?" This work takes up problems of Black performance and disperses them across non-Black performers, attempting to make the requirements for visibility and compulsory production everyone's. Drawing from the *Non-Western* performance, the two-channel video installation *Hacia una Postura Izquierdista (Toward a Leftist Positionality)* (2007) depicted a radical cell coolly exploring violence against a ruling class. "Masters of materials, corruptors of the earth, they don't need your labor, they don't make anything, they steal and steal, they simply murder and steal." Unlike a lot of the art we were seeing around us, our work was trying to talk explicitly about real things.

We also made two video series based on television, which allowed us to pursue entire genres and their forms of reading in the same way we had played with costume in live performance. *The Night Epi$ode* (2009) came when we had no money but a first solo show planned at New York's Participant Inc. We made a four-channel installation of episodes influenced by Rod Serling's *Night Gallery*, which allowed us to use cheap B-horror clichés to allegorize social problems connected to the economic collapse of the late 2000s and political fights around access to health care. At the opening, we performed as the nightmare curators who host the series, offering a *Death Panel Discussion*. Years later, for *Double Agency* (2015), we used a *Mission: Impossible* style to portray our sense of being spies in the museum. Shot on location in and around LACMA's galleries, offices, and campus, we dramatized the difficult space between subjectivity and objecthood that performance can occupy with chases and escapes, karate fights, coded messages, and poison gasses. The extended narrative involved a caper around masks from the museum's collection. Jade's undercover persona as a curator proposes a naïvely framed show called *Masks of the World*. In her curatorial meeting she makes the pitch "Masks of the World. A touchy subject? Not really." Later, in a musical finale, her nemesis, played by Jibz Cameron (a.k.a. Dynasty Handbag), chants, "I know the reason for this exhibition: to unleash neoliberal propaganda on the world!" The masks in question were replicas, or forgeries, we had made of masks from the museum's encyclopedic permanent collection. In the final episode they are taken off the wall by ninjas and carried away. Having performed in museums for a decade, using public bathrooms and conference rooms as dressing rooms, being asked not to need drinking water in gallery spaces, spending lots of time talking with security staff about our work, and being treated as the help at more than one special event, it felt poignant to me when we, undercover as the LA County Board of Supervisors, harmonized the question (paraphrasing comments I'd heard philosopher Judith Butler give at the Museum of Modern Art, New York): "Are the objects really so dead? Are the people really so alive? No one knows."

Television is the ideal form for our work, but we have only ever appeared on morning shows on local TV stations in Aspen and San Diego, and in an in-flight video on Air Canada. —Alex

We were informed by LACMA that handling the authentic masks would be impossible, but I was allowed to go into the museum's storage facility to choose and photograph original masks from East Asia, West Africa, Central and South America, and the Mediterranean. I made replicas of these masks using materials such as Aqua-Resin, papier-mâché, brass foil, and water-based clay. —Jade

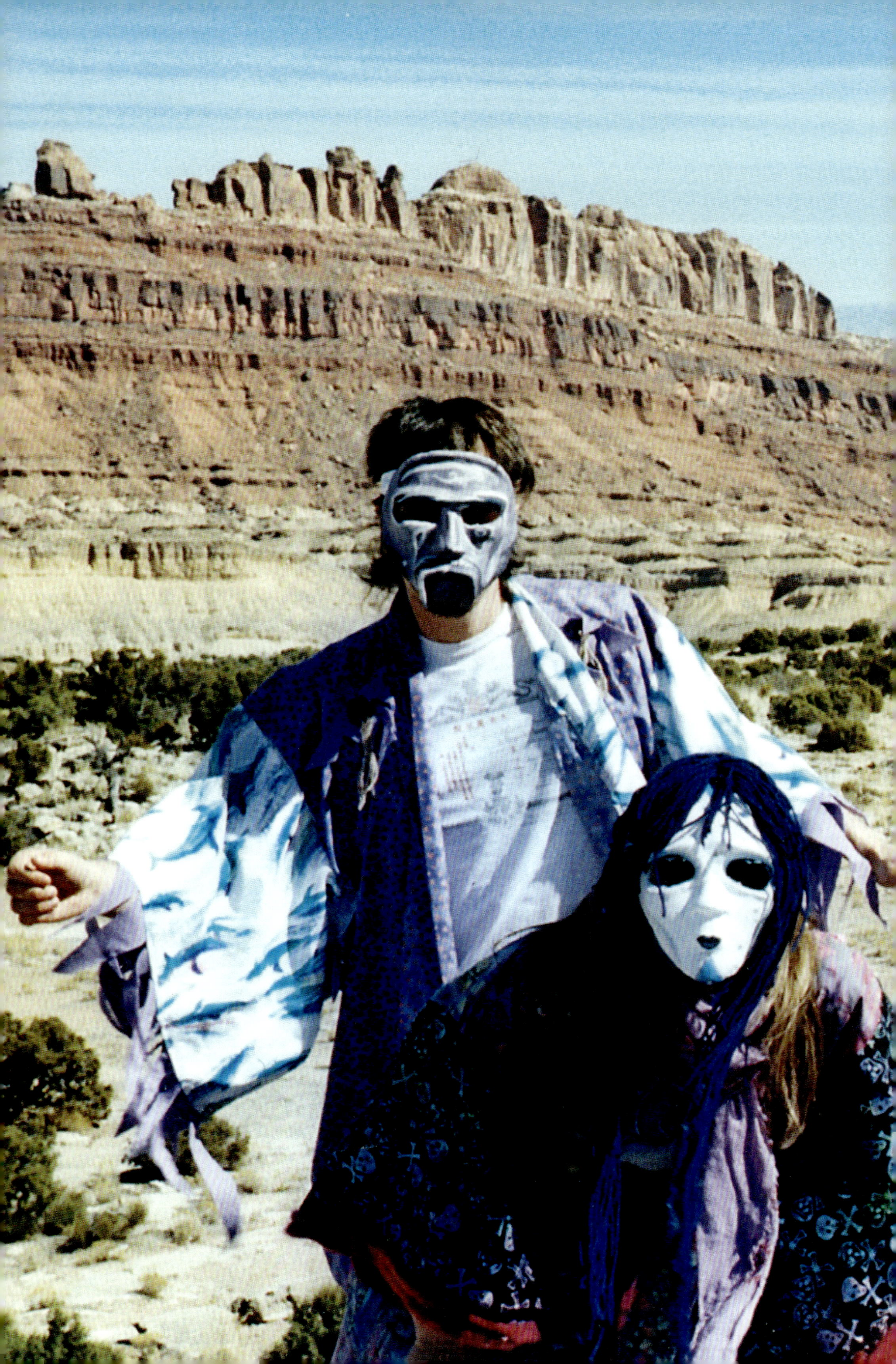

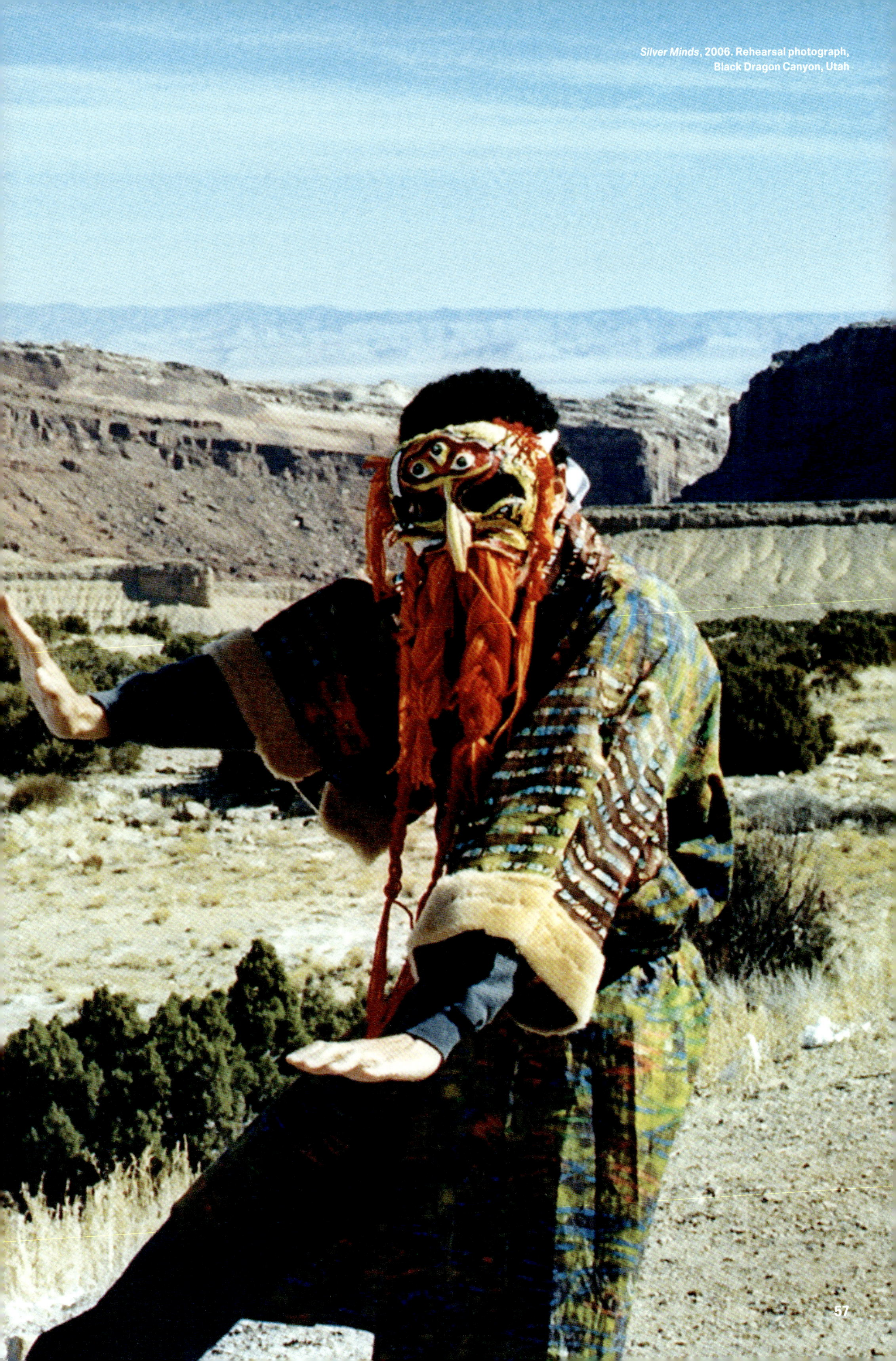

Silver Minds, 2006. Rehearsal photograph, Black Dragon Canyon, Utah

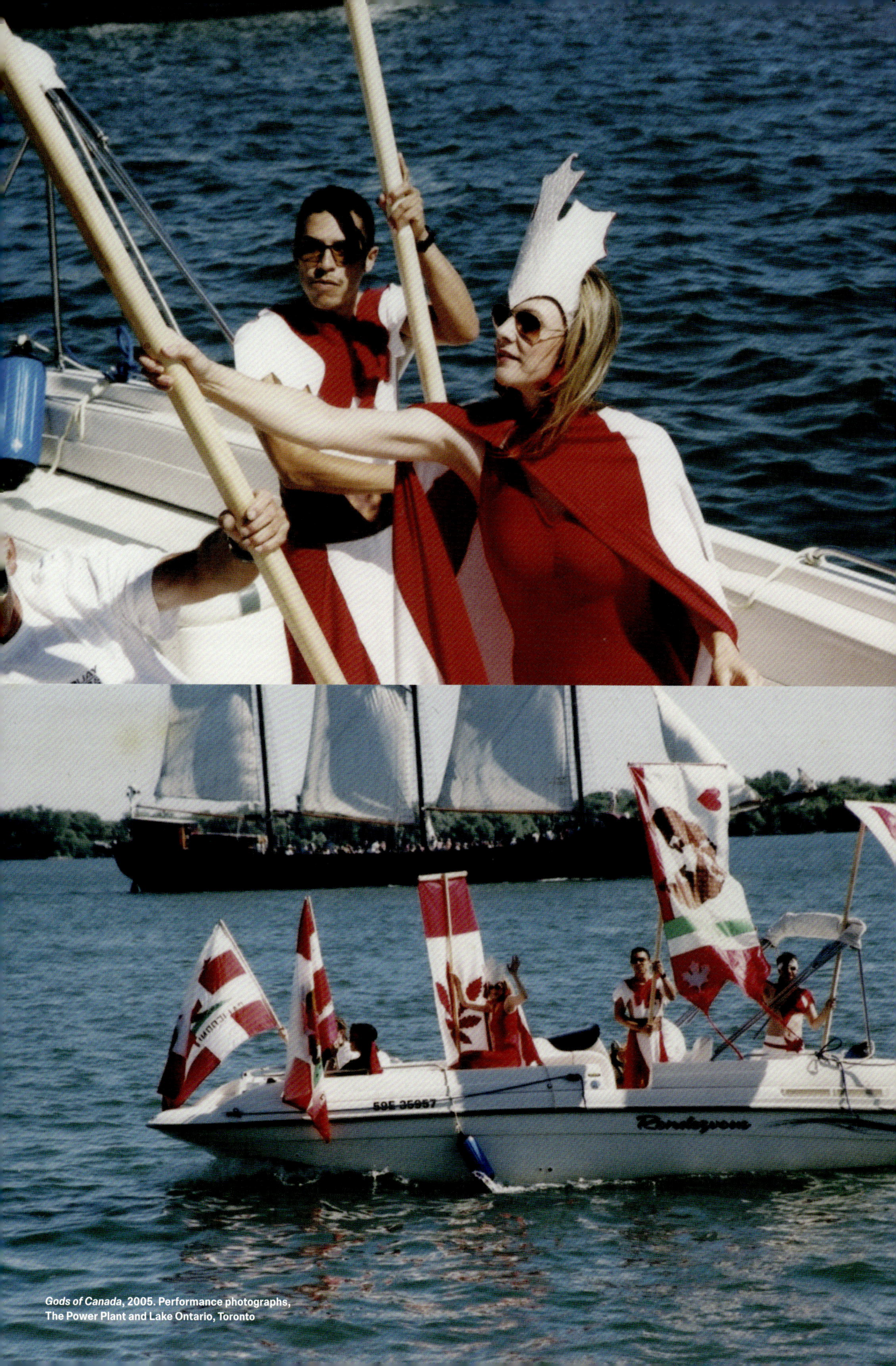

Gods of Canada, 2005. Performance photographs,
The Power Plant and Lake Ontario, Toronto

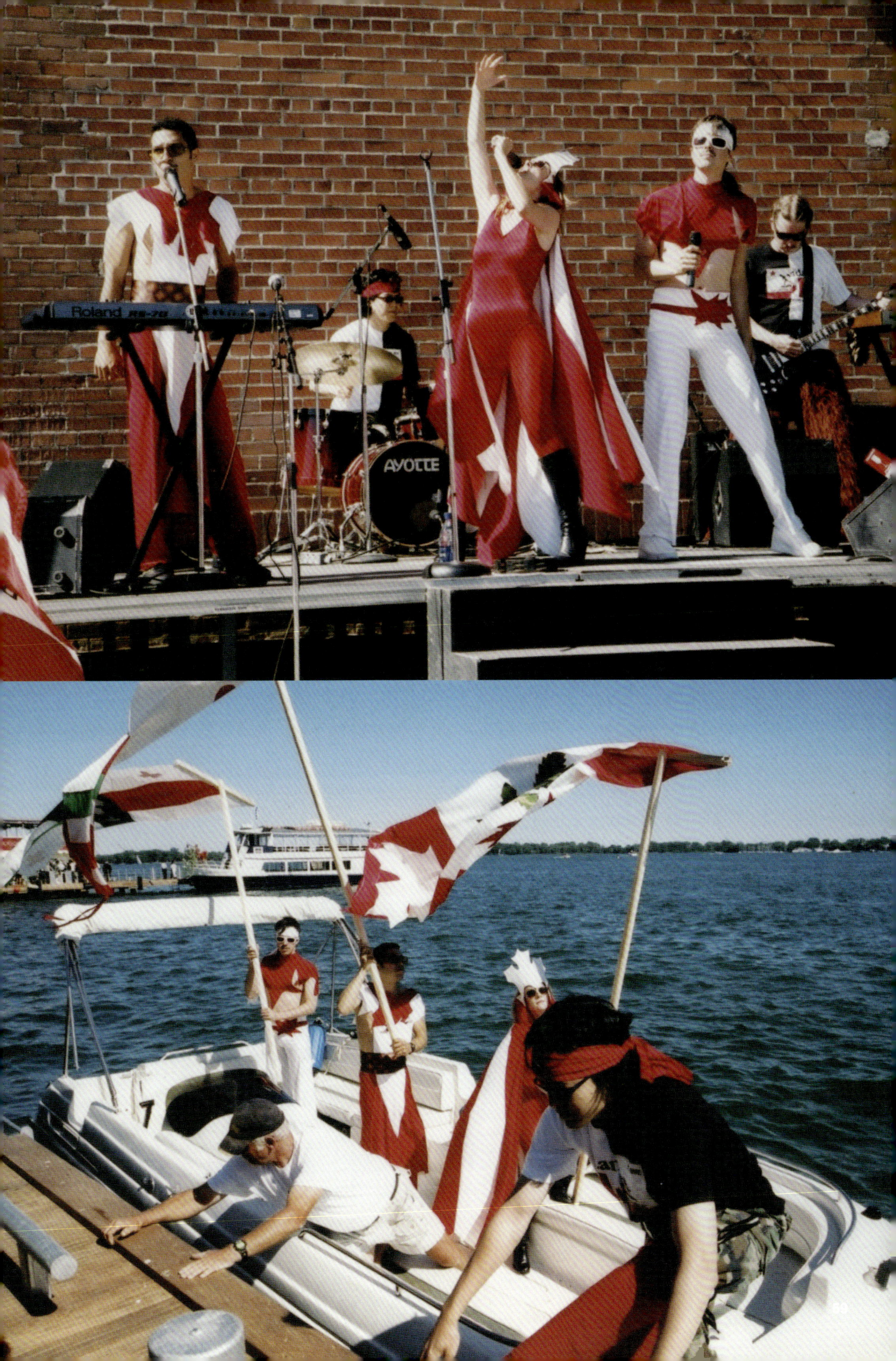
Roland
AYOTTE

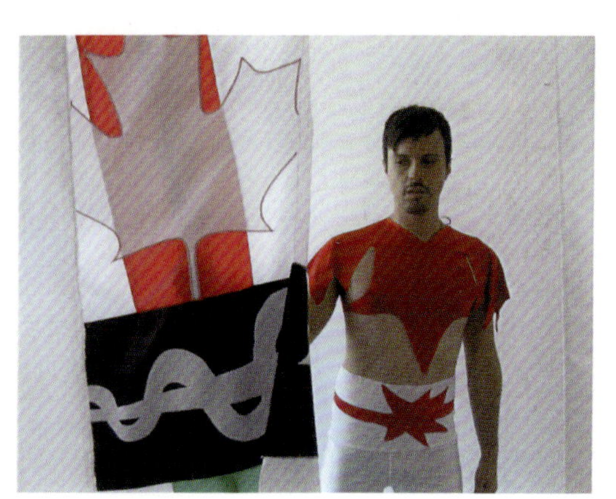

White Coal

True Identity: Jacques Pouvoir
Occupation: Olympic Hockey Star
Origin: Quebec City, Quebec

History: Jacques Pouvoir and his twin sister Jacqueline, a.k.a. Borealis (not pictured), were born to a rich industrilaist family in Quebec. The twin babies glowed with an aura of clean burning bio-electricity. Sent by their parents to Lawrence Livermoor Labs in California, the two children were expirmented on. Jacques and Jacqueline eventually escaped to San Francisco, where they lived as petty thieves who used their super powers for ill until they were discovered by Dr.Patient and Professor Elora Gorge, who convinced them to return to their native land and hone their skills for the benefit of Canada. Keen to bring glory to Quebec, and prove himself to his conservative family, Jacques became a gold medal winning hockey player at the Winter Olympics. As White Coal, he is a controversial super-hero known for making intemperate comments about political issues, such as support for French-Canadian secession, drug use and same-sex separatism.

Powers: White Coal has complete control over the bio-electric currents of his own body: able to perform super-human feats with his augmented physical prowess and super speed; he is an excellent athlete and dancer. Able to emit a blast of nervous energy into his opponents he can cause seizures in others, and with the aide of currents which surround the earth, he can fly.

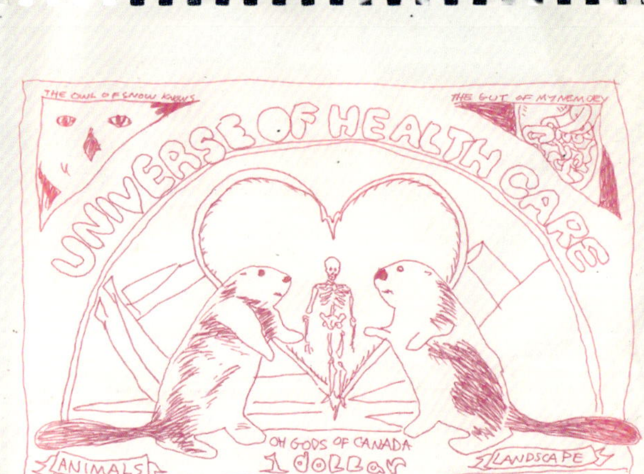

OOOO- A-A-AH A-A-AH, OOOO- A-A-AH A-A-AH
OOOO- A-A-AH A-A-AH, OOOO- A-A-AH A-A-AH
OOOO THE GODS OF CANADA!

DOI DOI DOI DOI
DOI DOI DOI
FORTY-THOUSAND YEARS AGO
GLACIER RIPPED THE LAND WITH WHITE CLAWS
AN ICE CORRIDOR
A NORTHERN DOOR
DAWN WITHOUT A SUN
PRIMORDIAL FORCES
BATTLES RUMBLE
SILENT MEDITATIONS

SEDNA! GUELPH! TUNDRA! FLINT! ELORA! TUNDRA!
SEDNA! GUELPH! TUNDRA! FLINT! ELORA! TUNDRA!

GODS OF CANADA
GODS OF CANADA

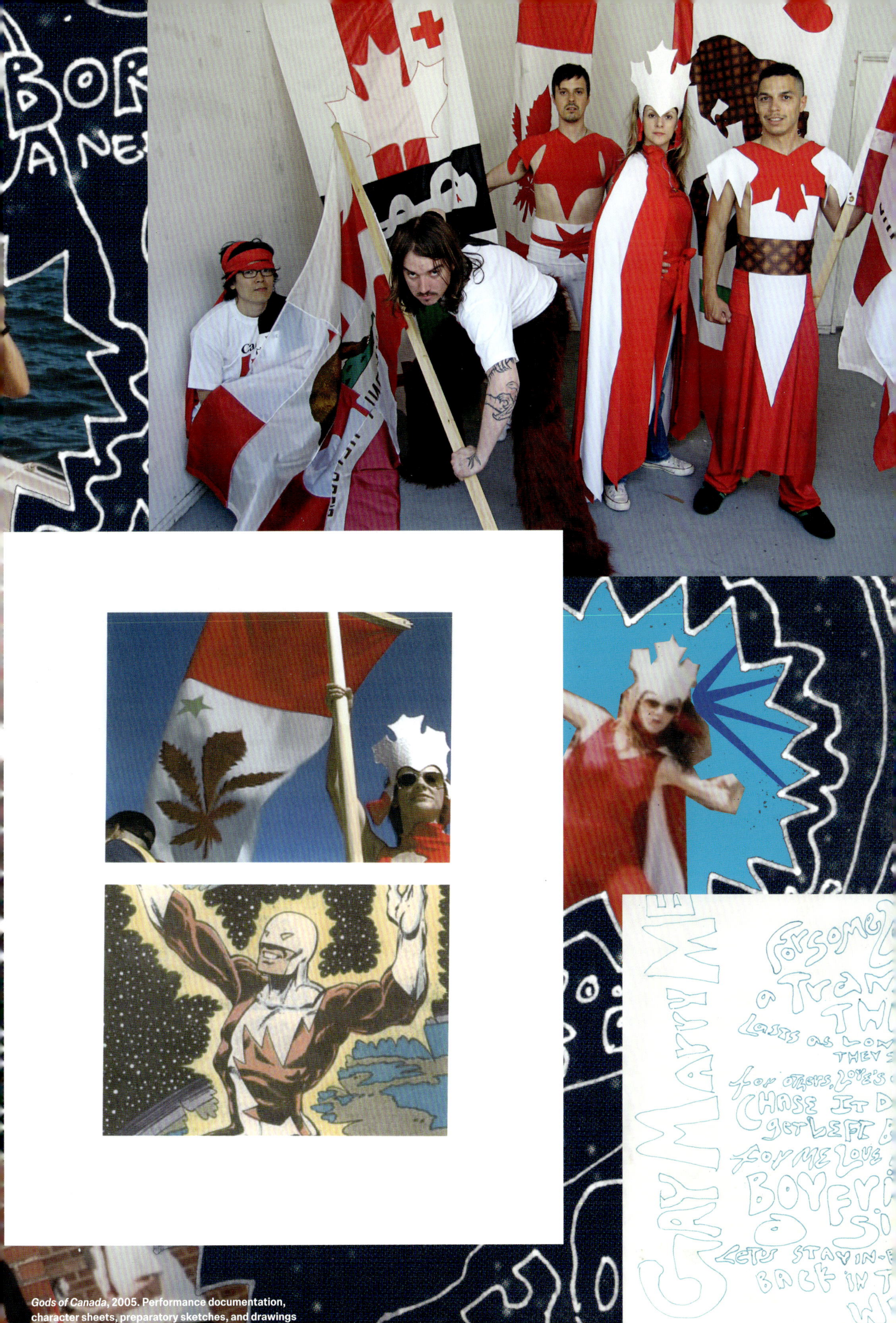

Gods of Canada, 2005. Performance documentation, character sheets, preparatory sketches, and drawings

INTERNATIONAL PERFORMANCE ARTISTS
HIGH-FLYING
TIME AND SPACE
DO WE MEET CRITERIA?

RECALL THE 70'S
AND YOU'RE LOOKING AT THE
NOW NOW NOW!

INTERNATIONAL PERFORMANCE ARTISTS
HIGH-FLYING
TIME AND SPACE
DO WE MEET CRITERIA?

MAKE ART THAT'S GUTSY
AND DISSOLVE THE OBJECT
LIVE LIVE LIVE!

WE COME FROM
CALIFORNIA
WHERE THE RICH ARE
LEFTISTS
WHY SHOULD YOU GIVE US
5,000 EURO
5,000 EURO

INTERNATIONAL PERFORMANCE ARTISTS
HIGH-FLYING
TIME AND SPACE
DO WE MEET CRITERIA?

DOES IT SHOW EVIDENCE OF
A RELEVANT CRITIQUE OF THE
MODE MODE MODE!

WE COME FROM
AMERICA
THEY WONT GIVE US
MONEY
WE'LL NEED, TO BE EFFECTIVE:
5,000 EURO
5,000 EURO
5,000 EURO
5,000 EURO
5,000 EURO
5,000 EURO

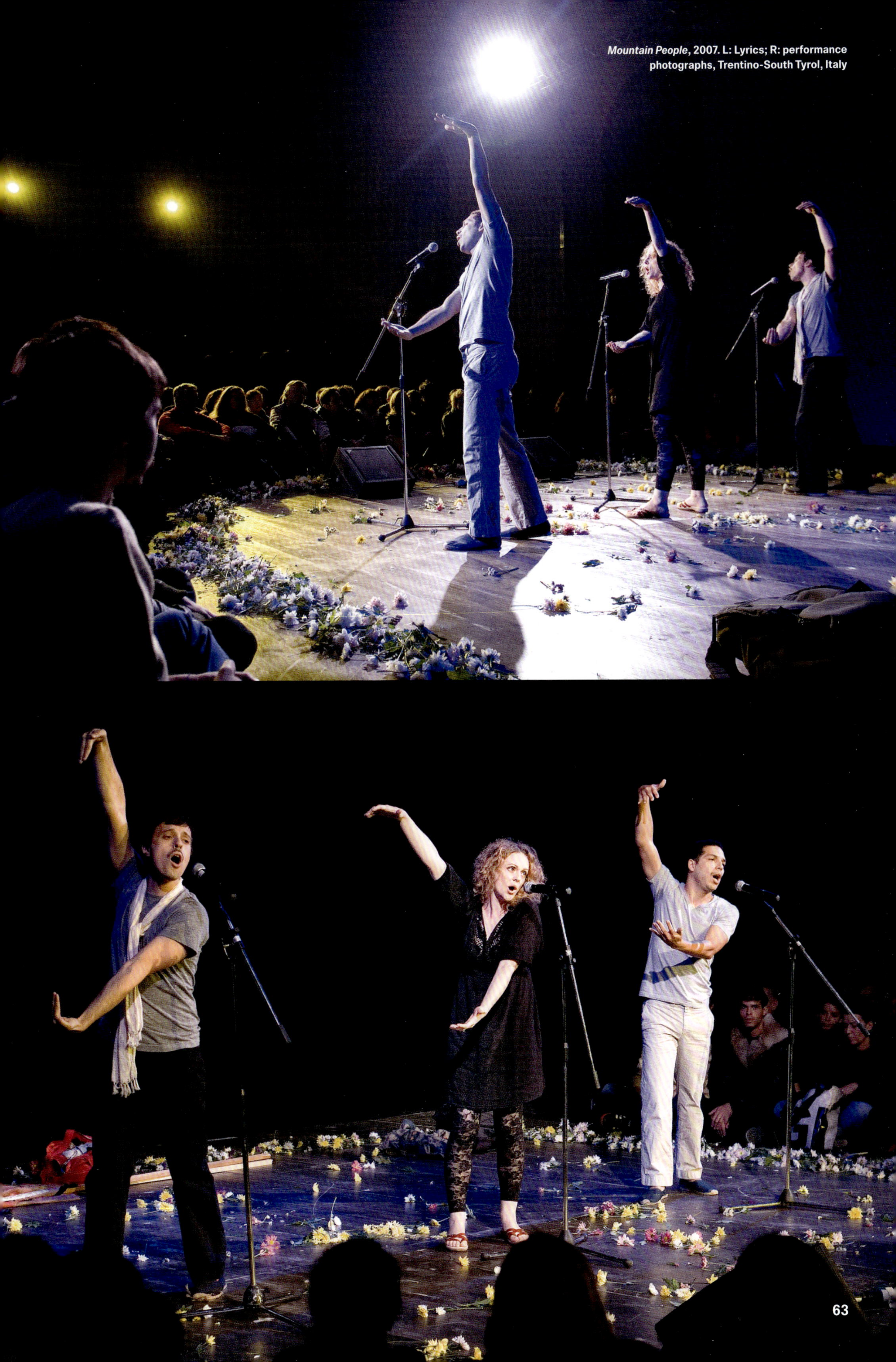

Mountain People, 2007. L: Lyrics; R: performance photographs, Trentino-South Tyrol, Italy

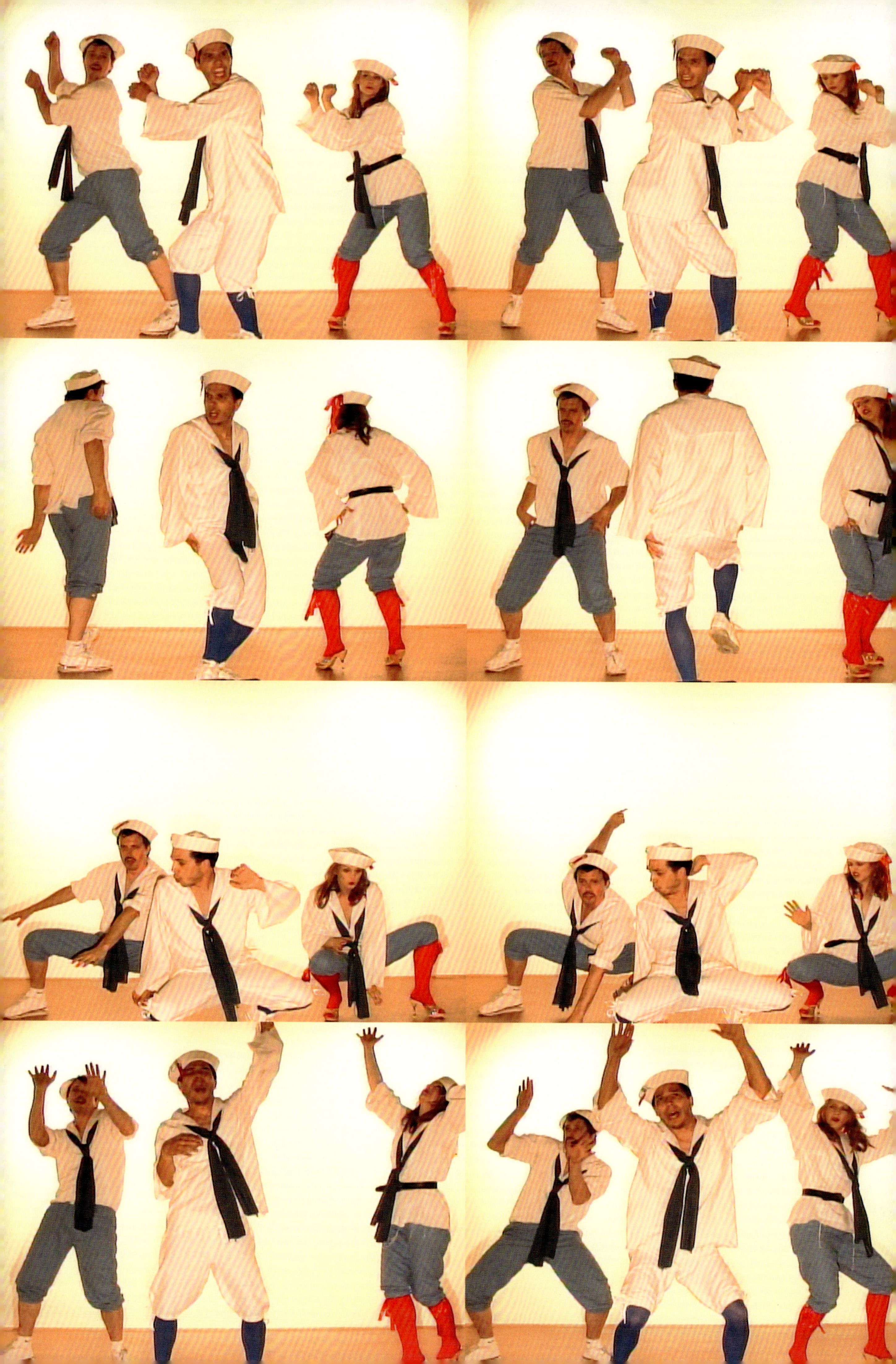

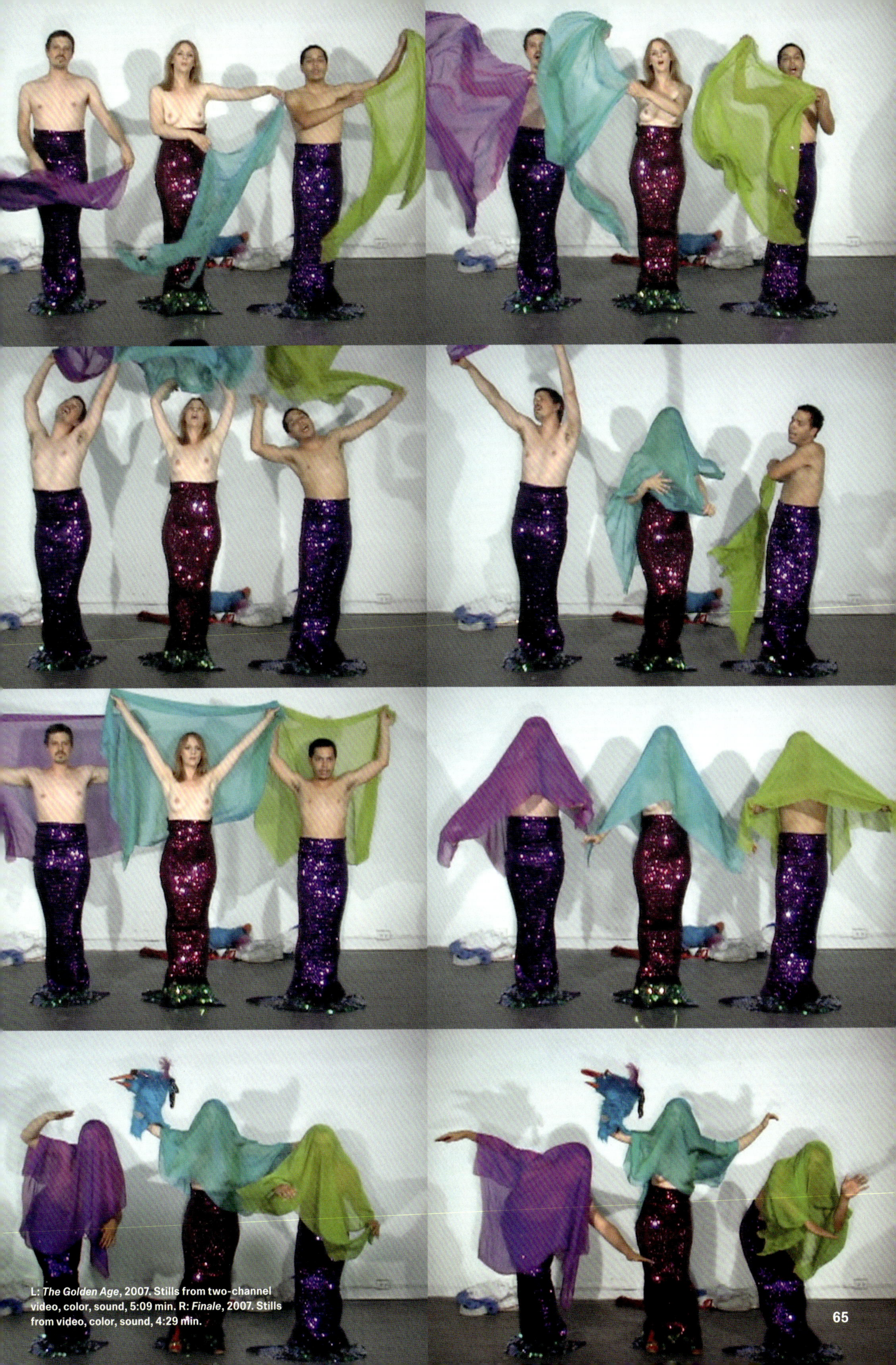

L: *The Golden Age*, 2007. Stills from two-channel video, color, sound, 5:09 min. R: *Finale*, 2007. Stills from video, color, sound, 4:29 min.

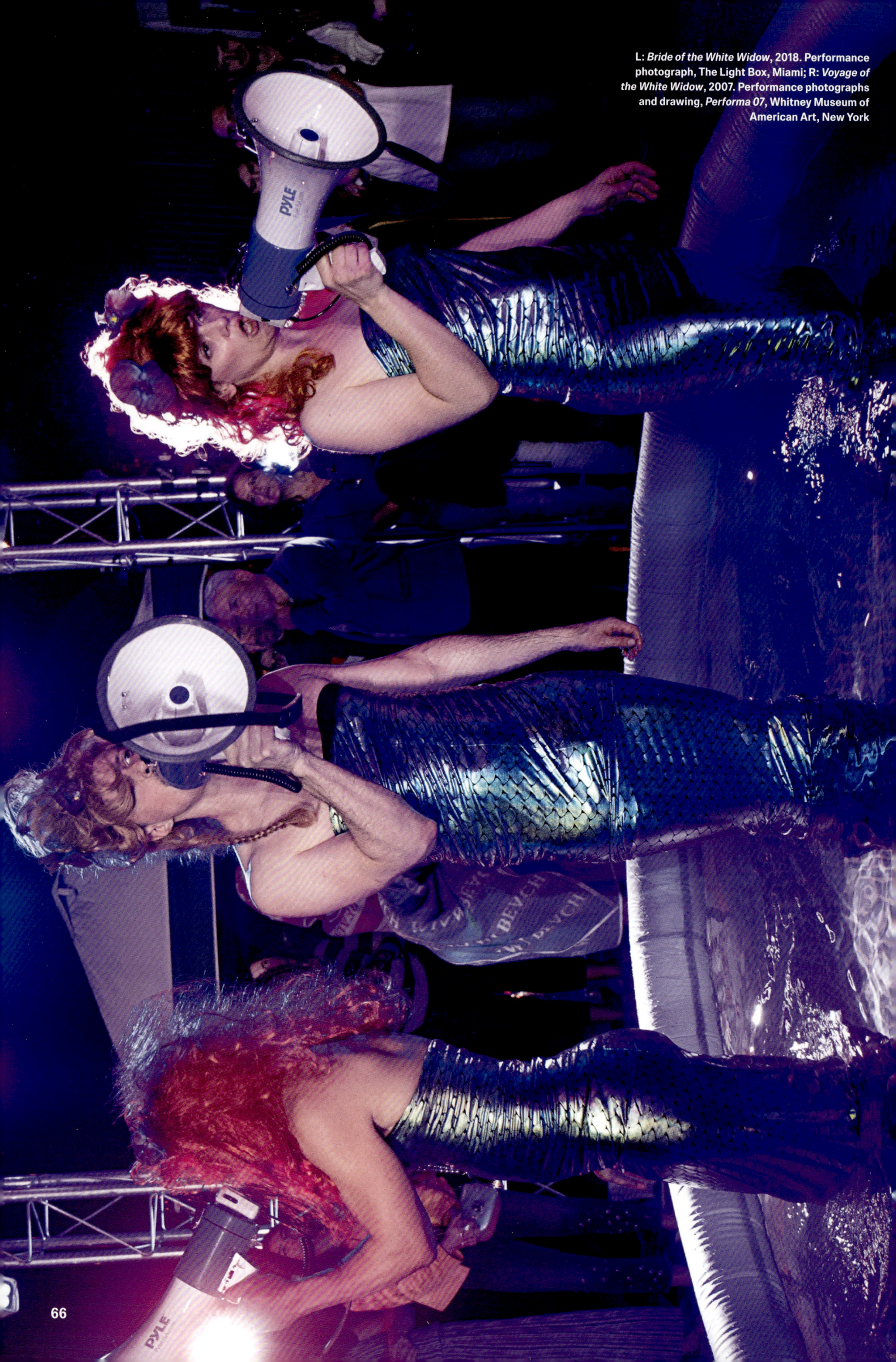

L: *Bride of the White Widow*, 2018. Performance photograph, The Light Box, Miami; R: *Voyage of the White Widow*, 2007. Performance photographs and drawing, *Performa 07*, Whitney Museum of American Art, New York

MUNDO NOVO

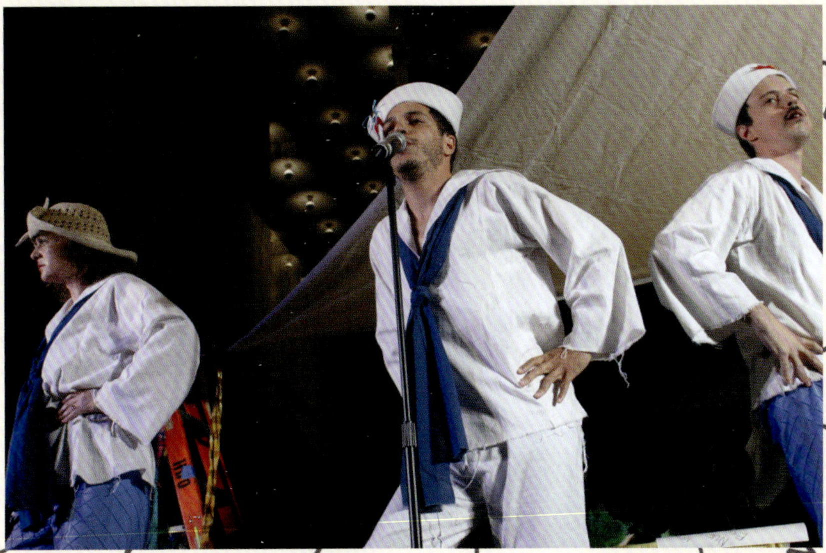

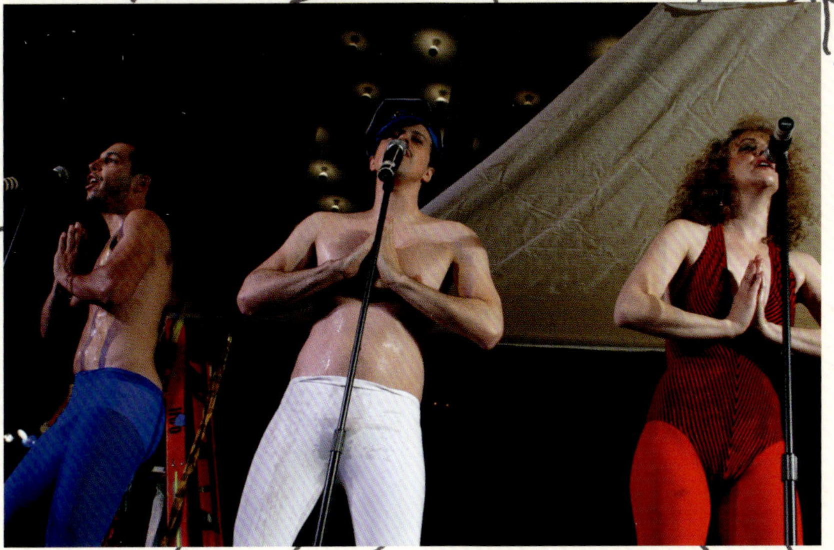

AMSTERDAM

RUSSLAND

CHINA

JAPON

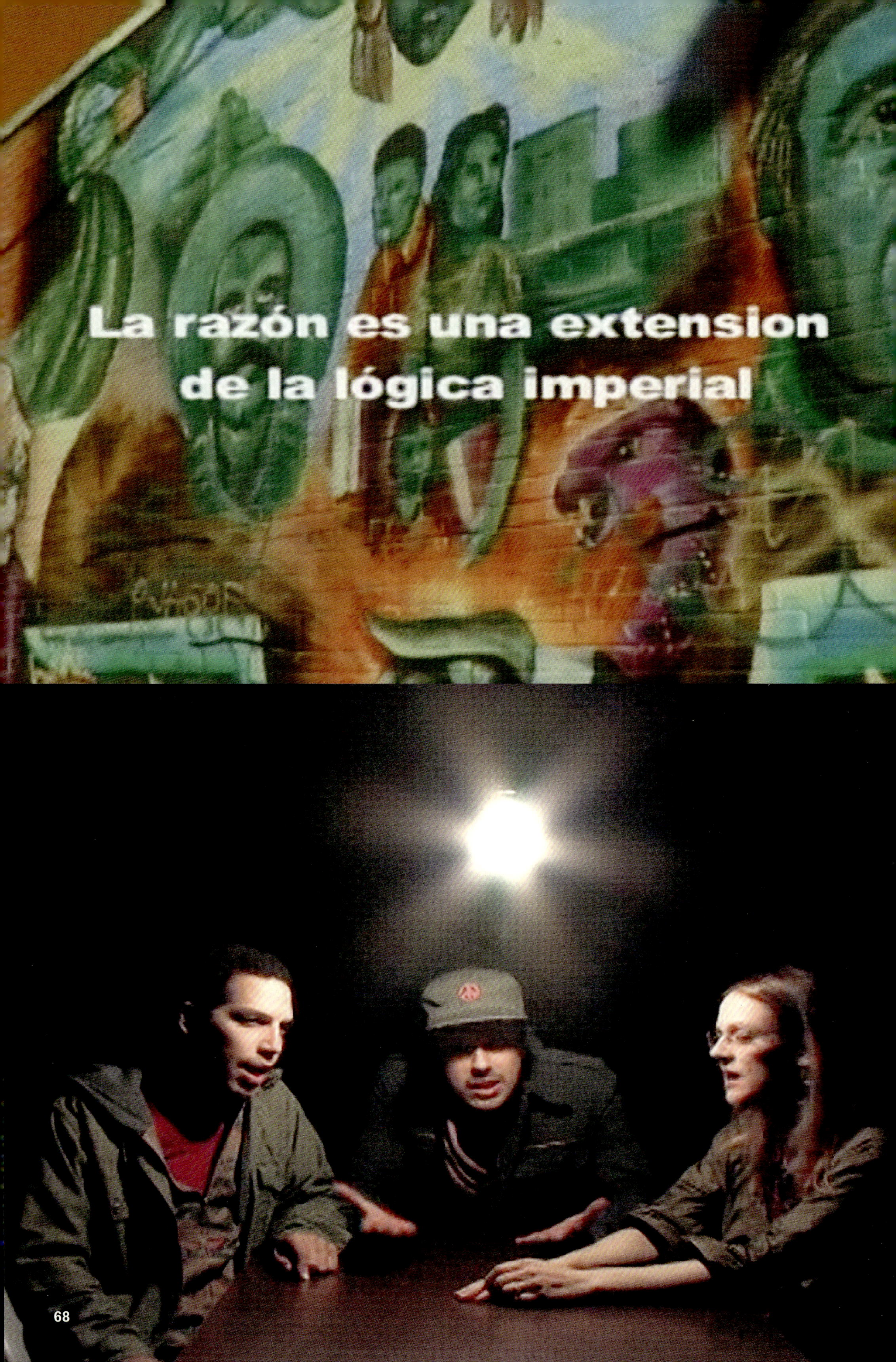
La razón es una extension
de la lógica imperial

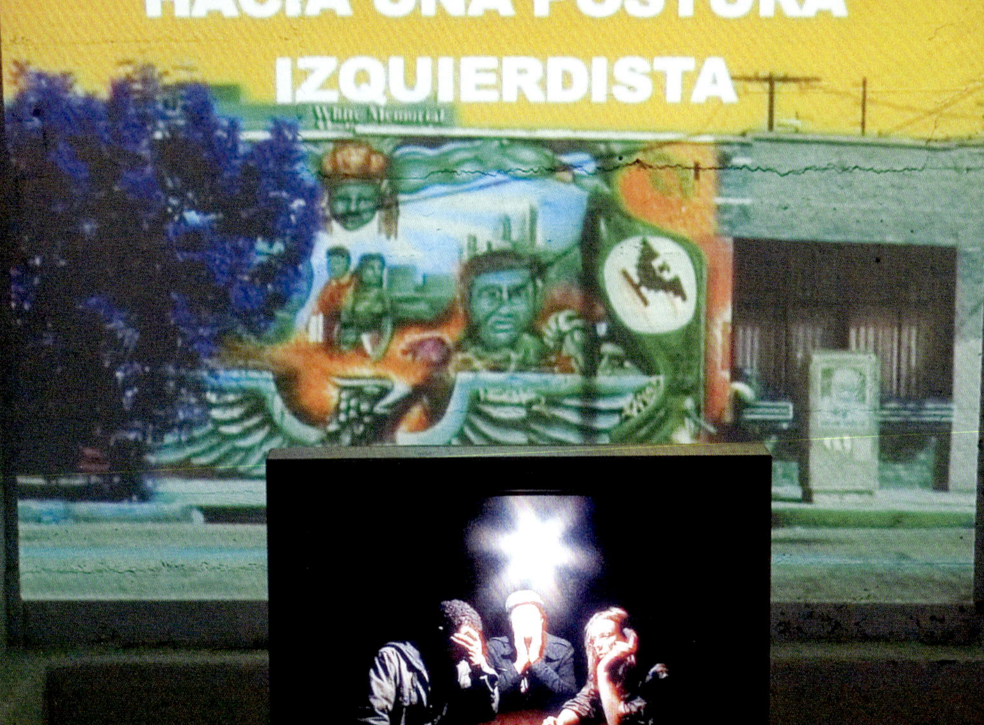
HACIA UNA POSTURA
IZQUIERDISTA

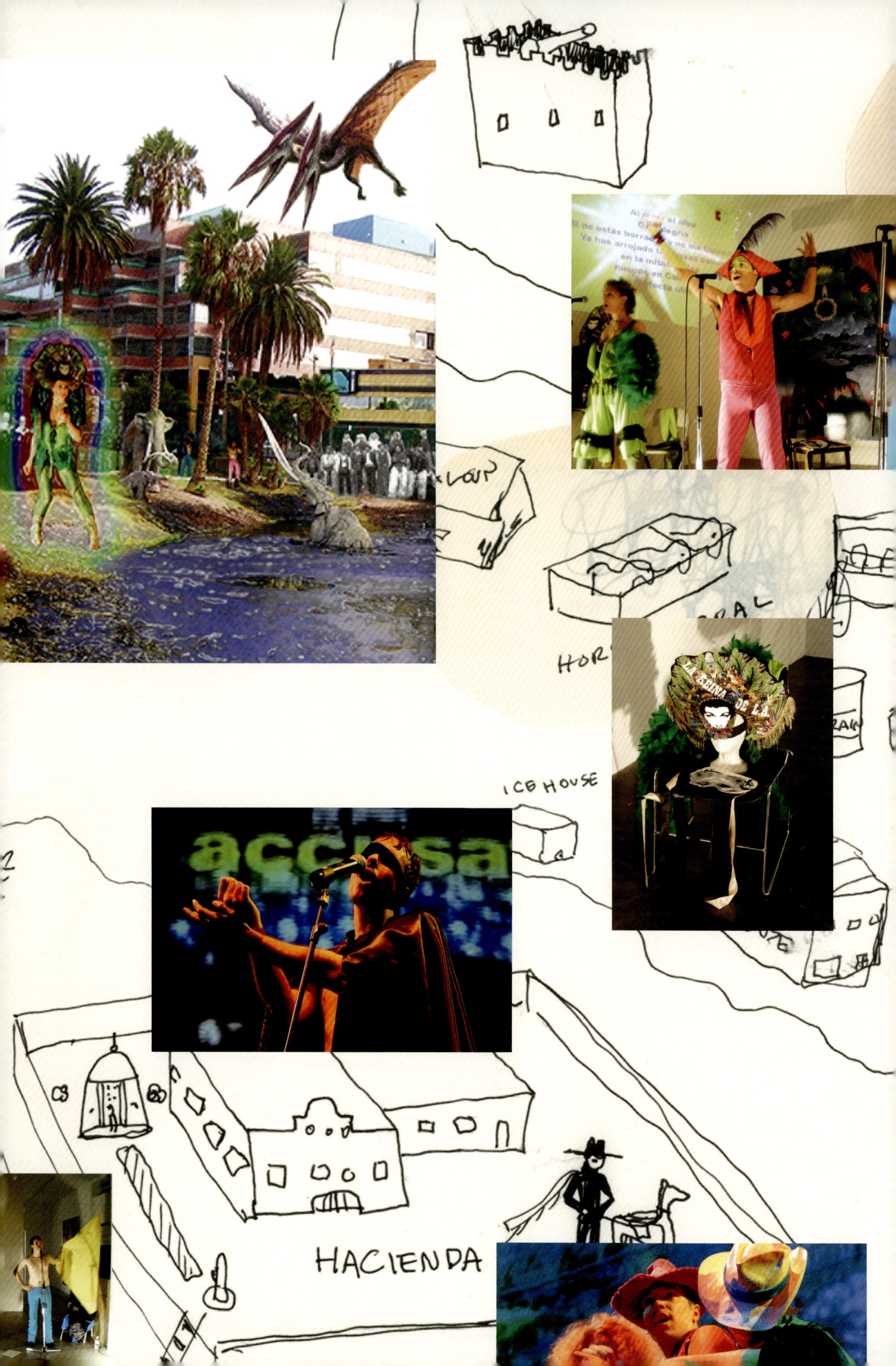
ICE HOUSE
HACIENDA
accusa

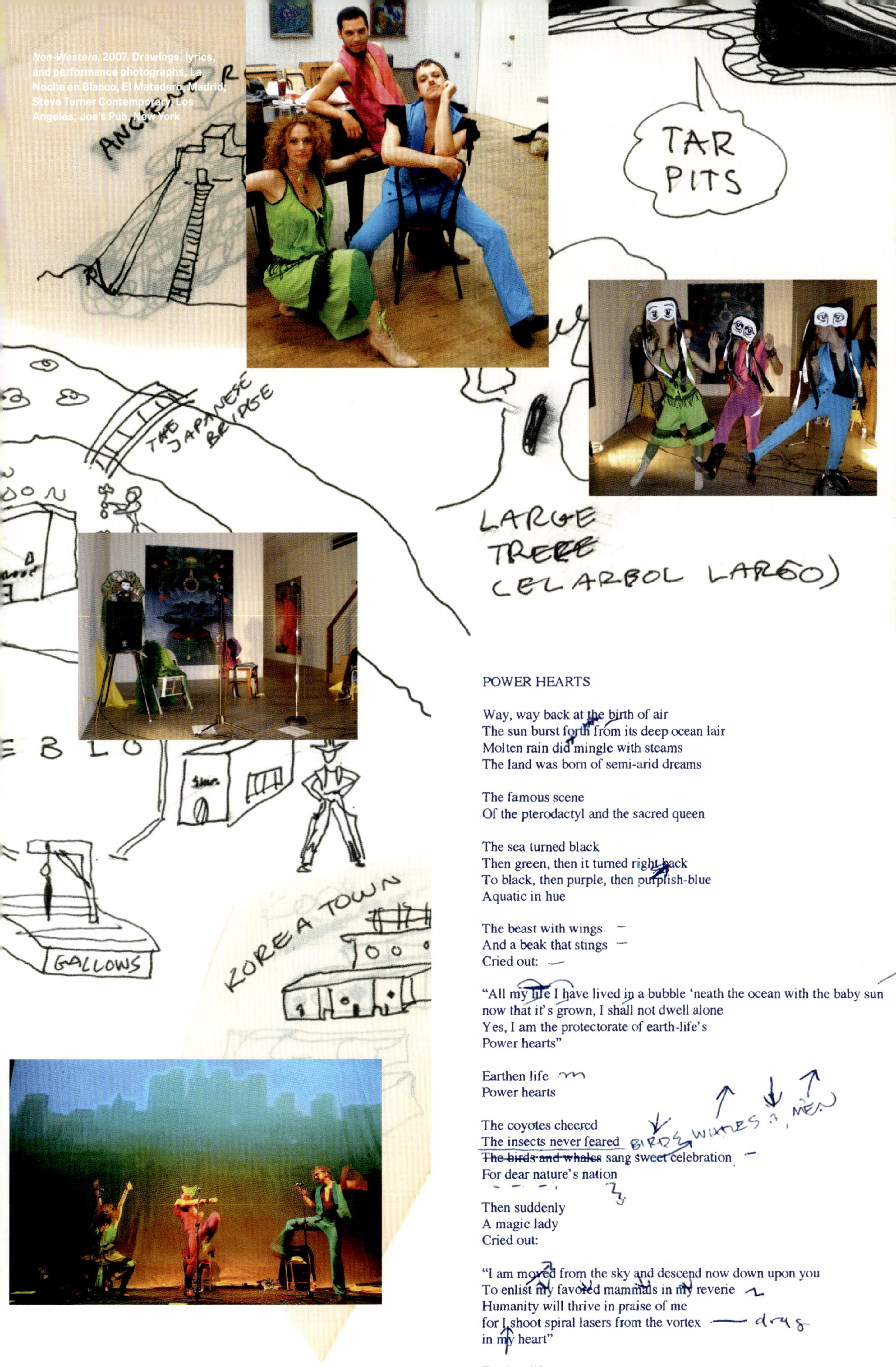

POWER HEARTS

Way, way back at the birth of air
The sun burst forth from its deep ocean lair
Molten rain did mingle with steams
The land was born of semi-arid dreams

The famous scene
Of the pterodactyl and the sacred queen

The sea turned black
Then green, then it turned right back
To black, then purple, then purplish-blue
Aquatic in hue

The beast with wings
And a beak that stings
Cried out:

"All my life I have lived in a bubble 'neath the ocean with the baby sun
now that it's grown, I shall not dwell alone
Yes, I am the protectorate of earth-life's
Power hearts"

Earthen life
Power hearts

The coyotes cheered
The insects never feared
~~The birds and whales~~ sang sweet celebration
For dear nature's nation

Then suddenly
A magic lady
Cried out:

"I am moved from the sky and descend now down upon you
To enlist my favored mammals in my reverie
Humanity will thrive in praise of me
for I shoot spiral lasers from the vortex
in my heart"

Non-Western, 2007. Drawings, lyrics, and performance photographs, La Noche en Blanco, El Matadero, Madrid; Steve Turner Contemporary, Los Angeles; Joe's Pub, New York

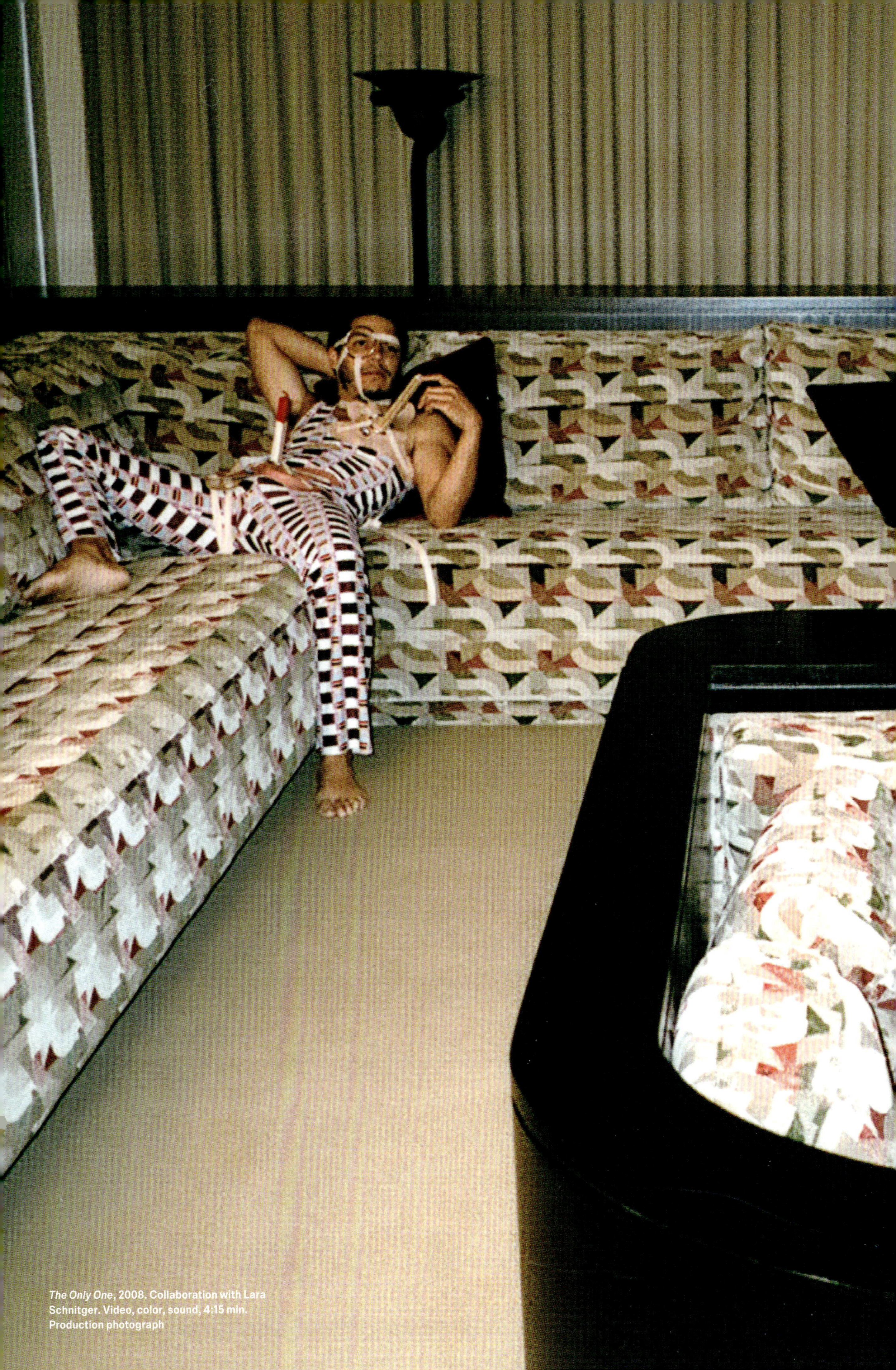

The Only One, 2008. Collaboration with Lara Schnitger. Video, color, sound, 4:15 min. Production photograph

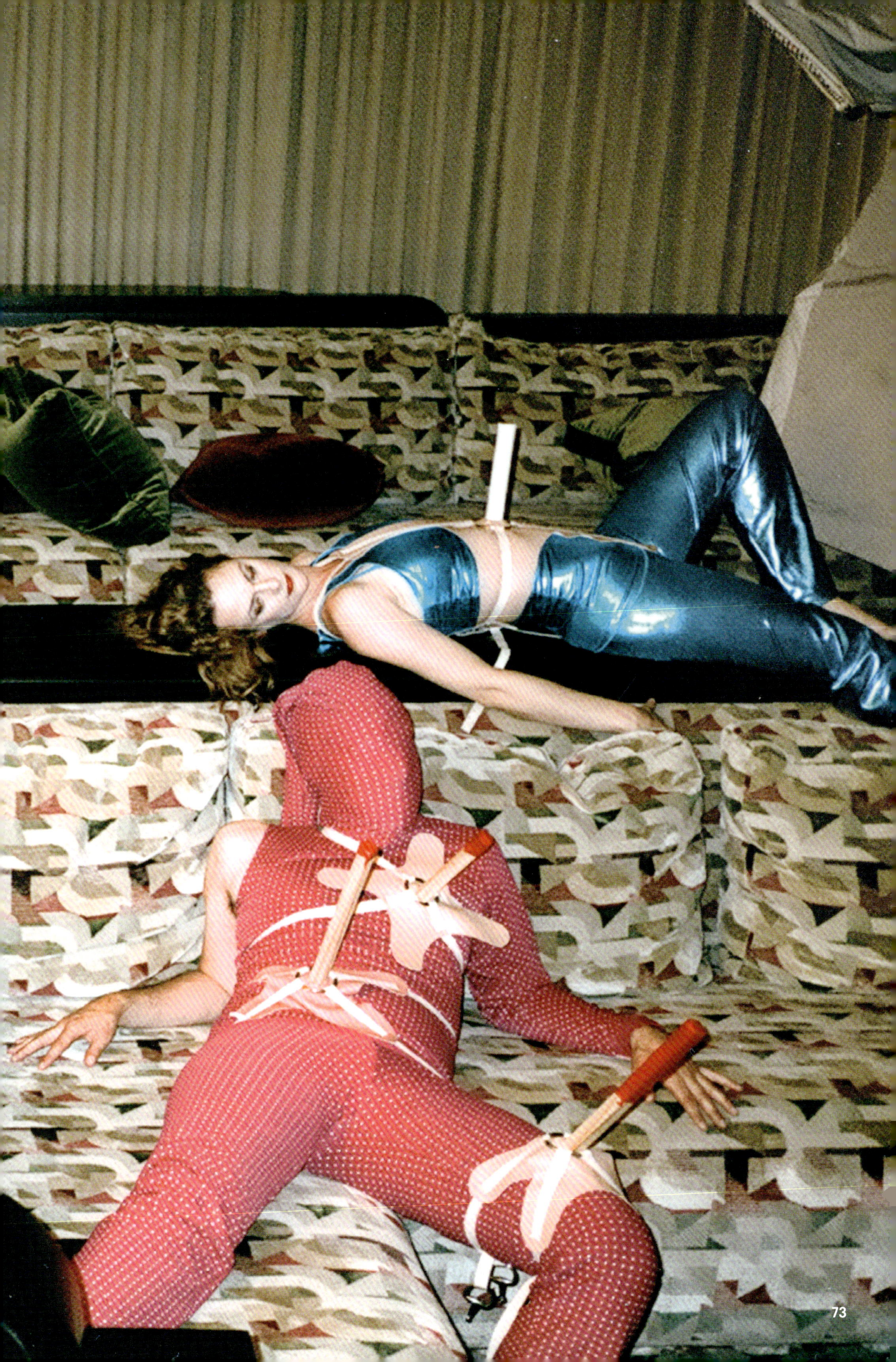

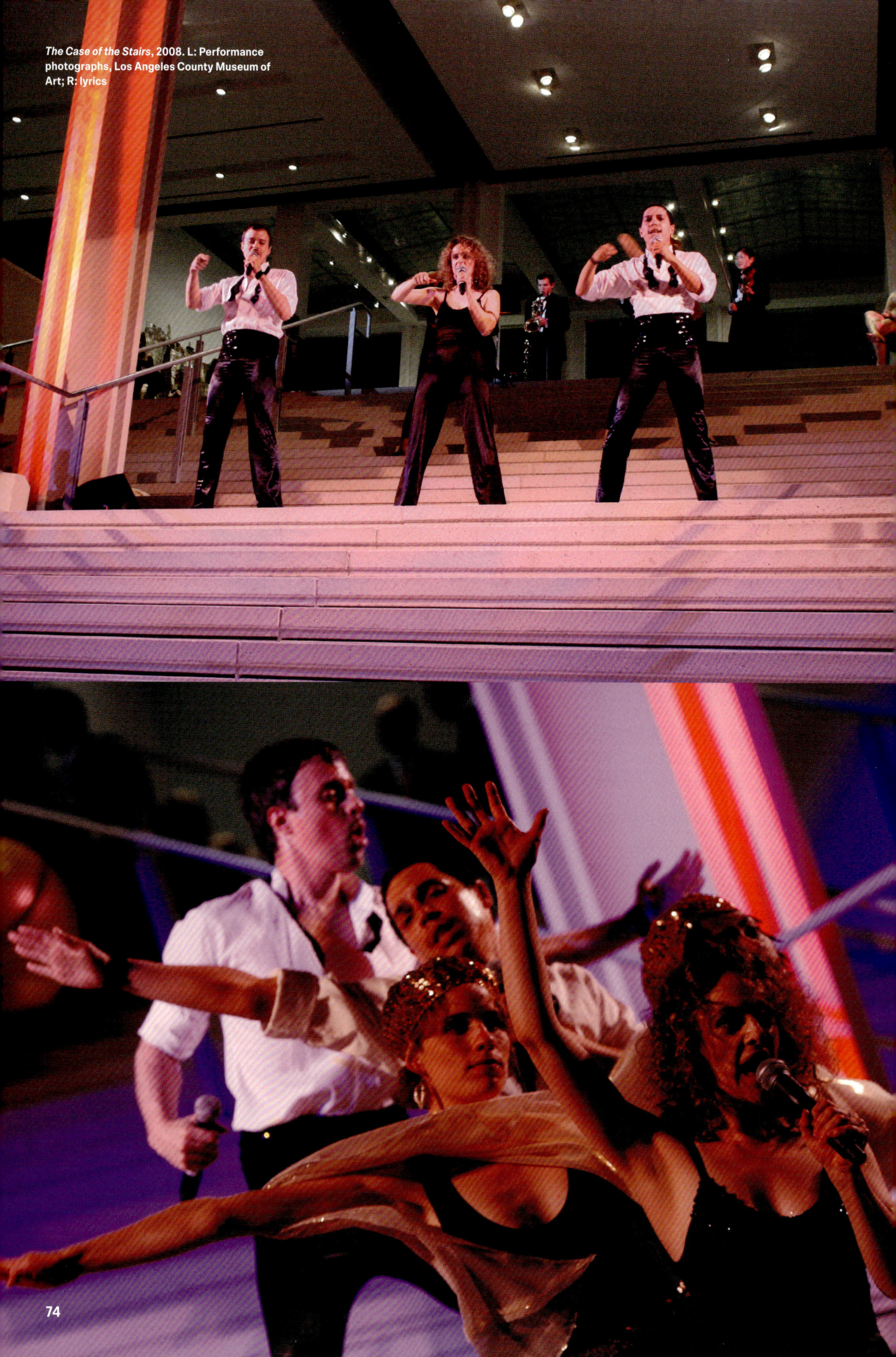

The Case of the Stairs, 2008. L: Performance photographs, Los Angeles County Museum of Art; R: lyrics

Painter: I must paint the lady of the house. X 5 THE PORTRAIT OF A LADY ~~[illegible]~~ SHADY IT SHAN'T ~~SHALL~~ BE

Painter paints the lady. ~~SERENITY/ NOBILITY~~

~~The Painting is revealed, it's the maid!~~ WHEN THE PAINTING WAS LATER REVEALED, IT WAS A PORTRAIT OF THE MAID

Lord of the House: Brazen Modernity!

ALL: BRAZEN MODERNITY!

ALL: BRAZEN MODERNITY!

THE ARTIST PAINTS THE LADY OF THE HOUSE

THE PORTRAIT OF SOME LADY

J3A: THE PORTRAIT OF SOME LADY

SCENE 3: Untouched

THE SHOOTOUT

JMA, HL pull out guns and point them at each other.

J: Don't make me do this!

M: I don't wanna hurt nobody!

A: I don't wanna hurt nobody niether!

H: Don't make me do this!

L: Put down the gun!

J: Put down the gun!

M: I'm gonna put down the gun…

A: I'm putting down the gun…

H: Don't make me do this!

L: Put down the gun!

All shoot each other. Everyone acts dead.

SCENE 4: The Apartment

A: The Stairs go up up up
Footsteps tip tap tip tap upon the pavement
Lonely lonely, smoking a lot, of pot

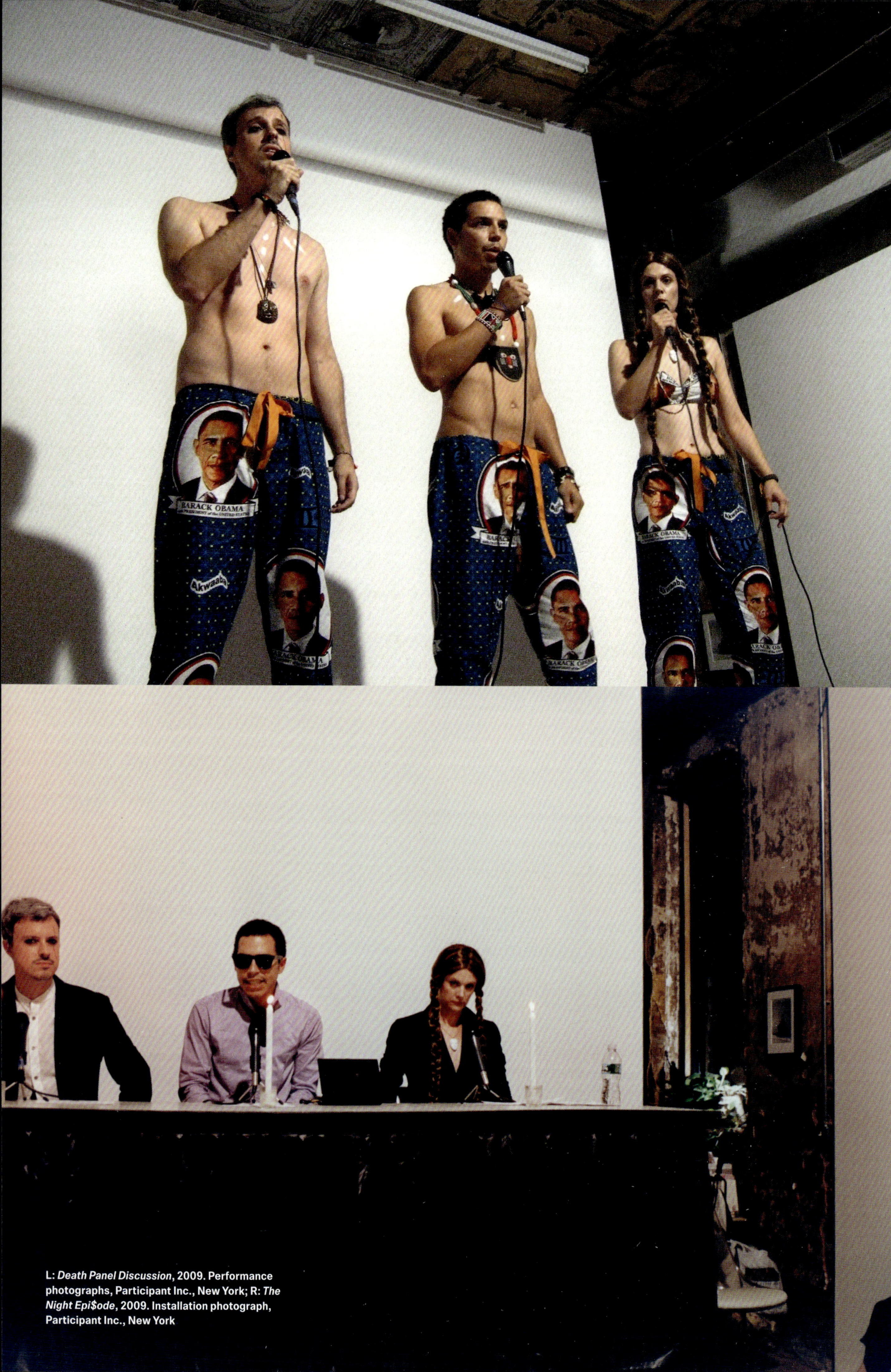

L: ***Death Panel Discussion*, 2009. Performance photographs, Participant Inc., New York; R: *The Night Epi$ode*, 2009. Installation photograph, Participant Inc., New York**

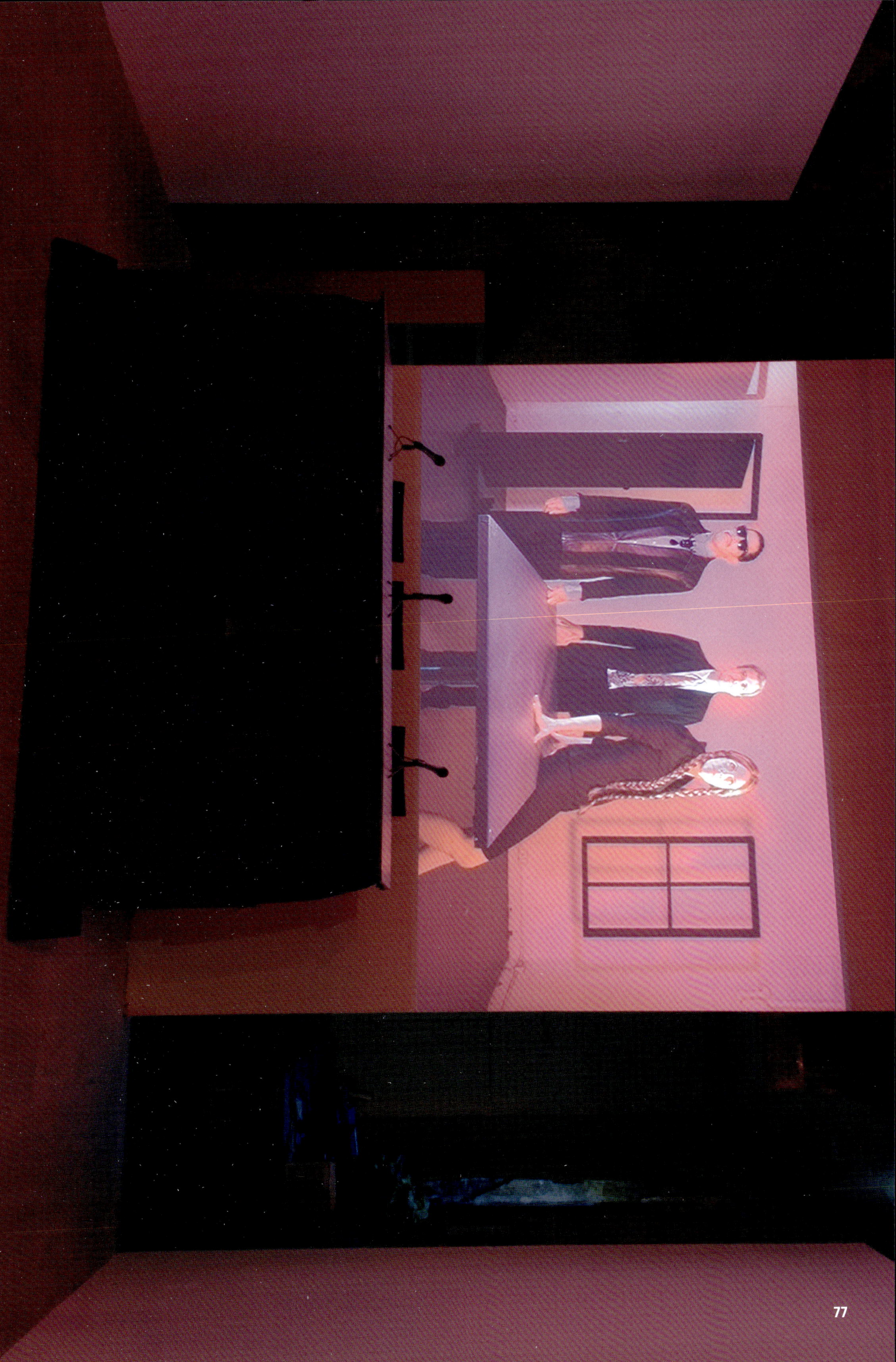

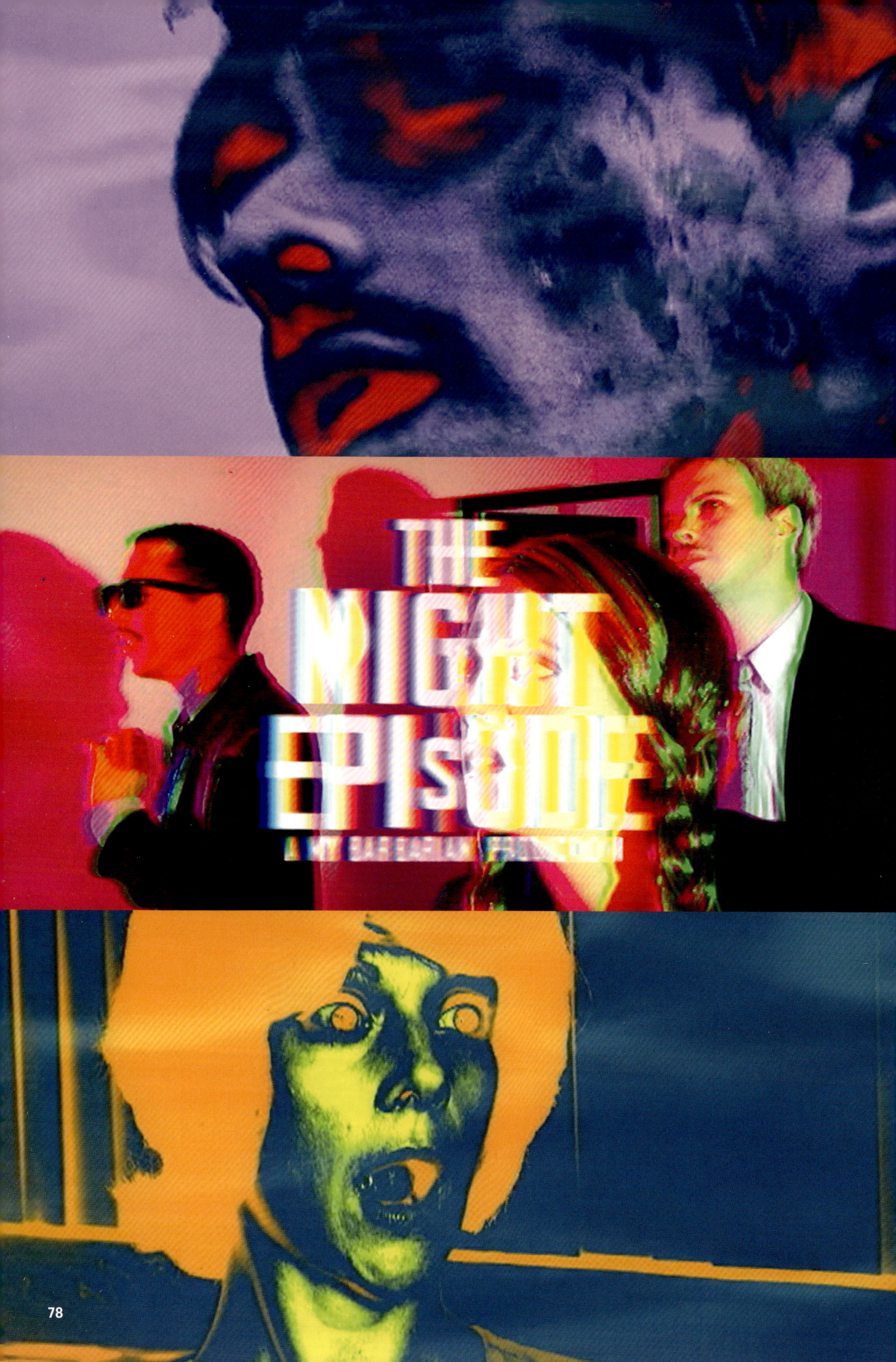
THE
NIGHT
EPISODE

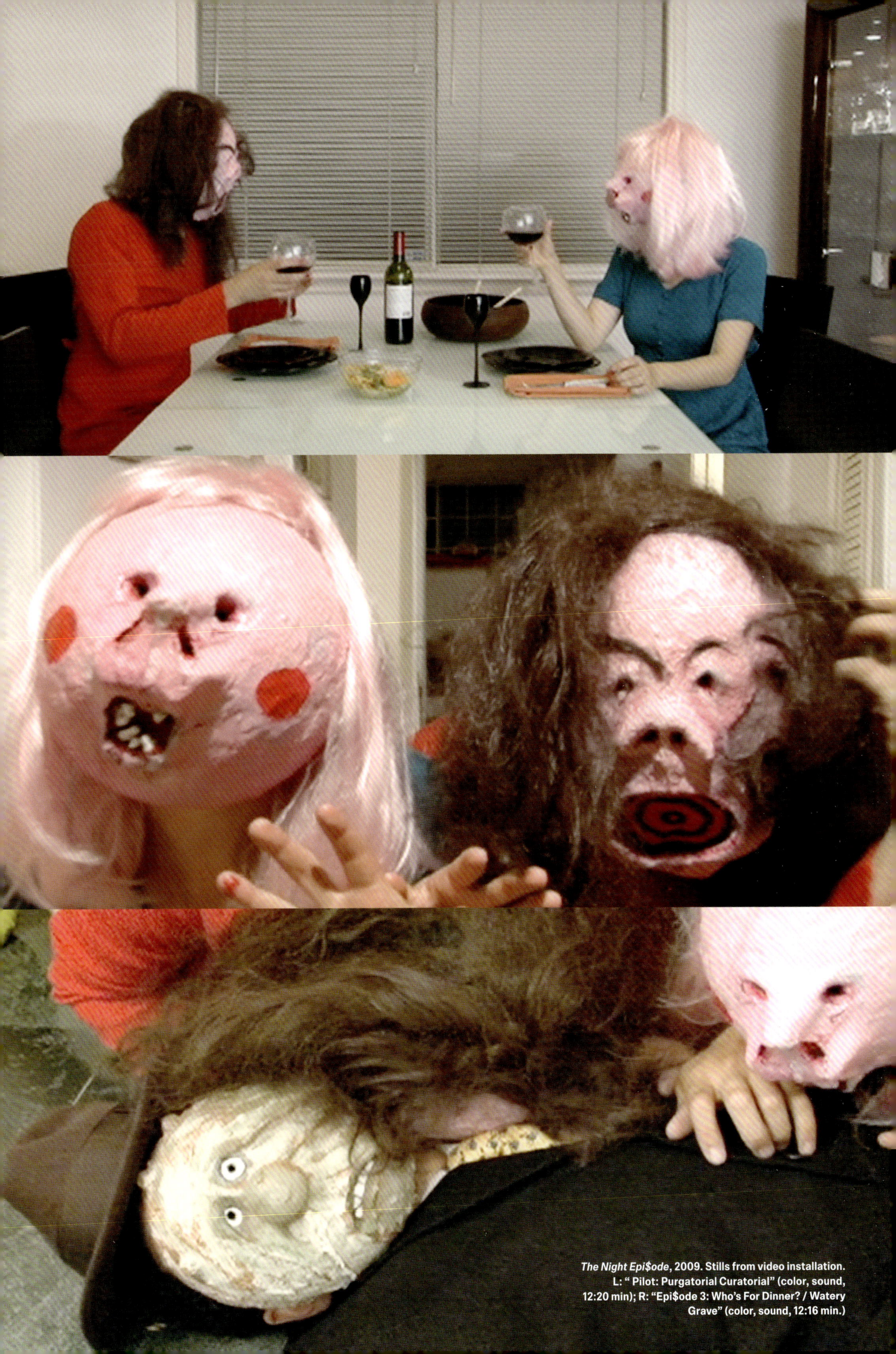

The Night Epi$ode, 2009. Stills from video installation. L: " Pilot: Purgatorial Curatorial" (color, sound, 12:20 min); R: "Epi$ode 3: Who's For Dinner? / Watery Grave" (color, sound, 12:16 min.)

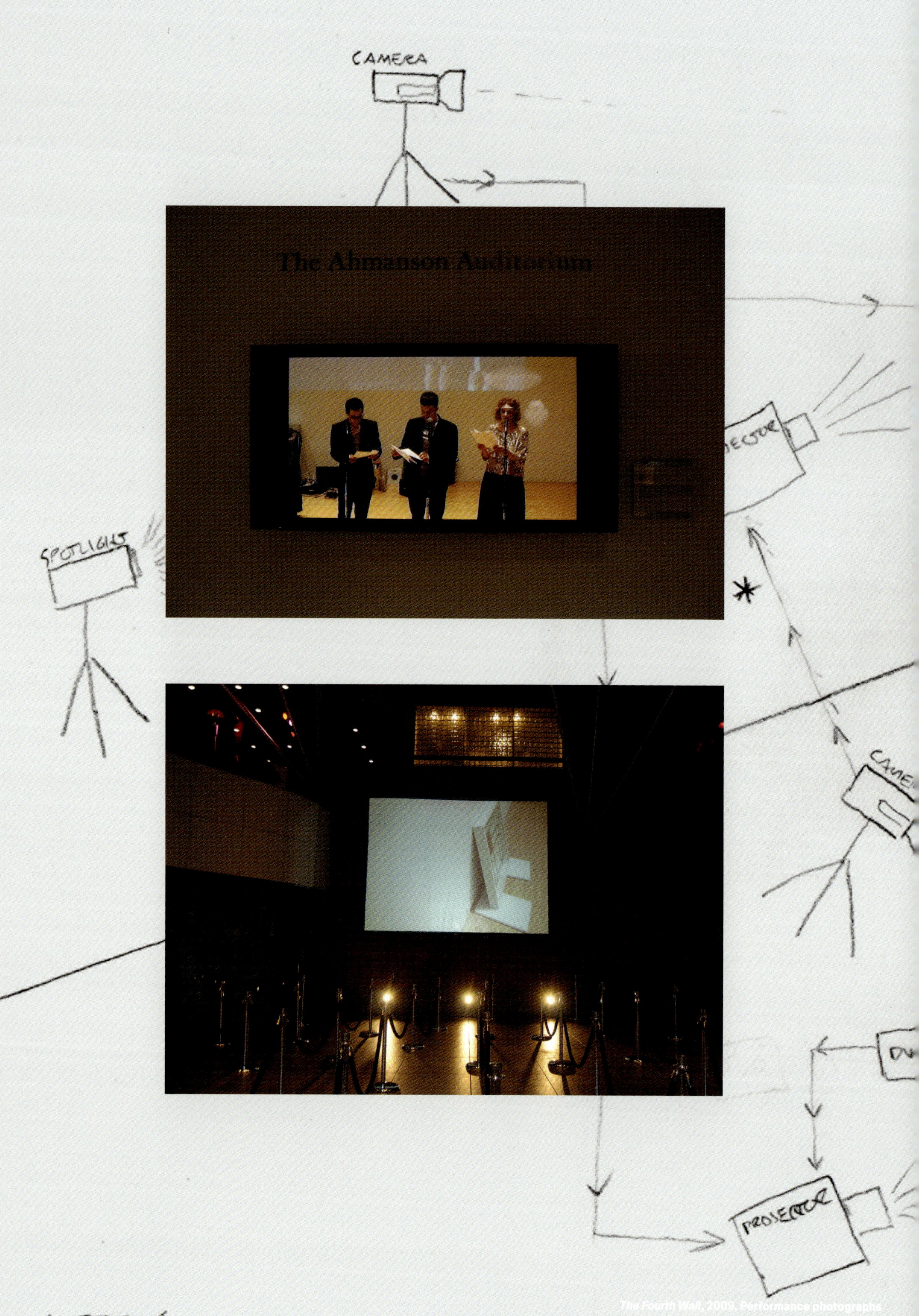

The Fourth Wall, 2009. Performance photographs and drawings, Museum of Contemporary Art, Los Angeles

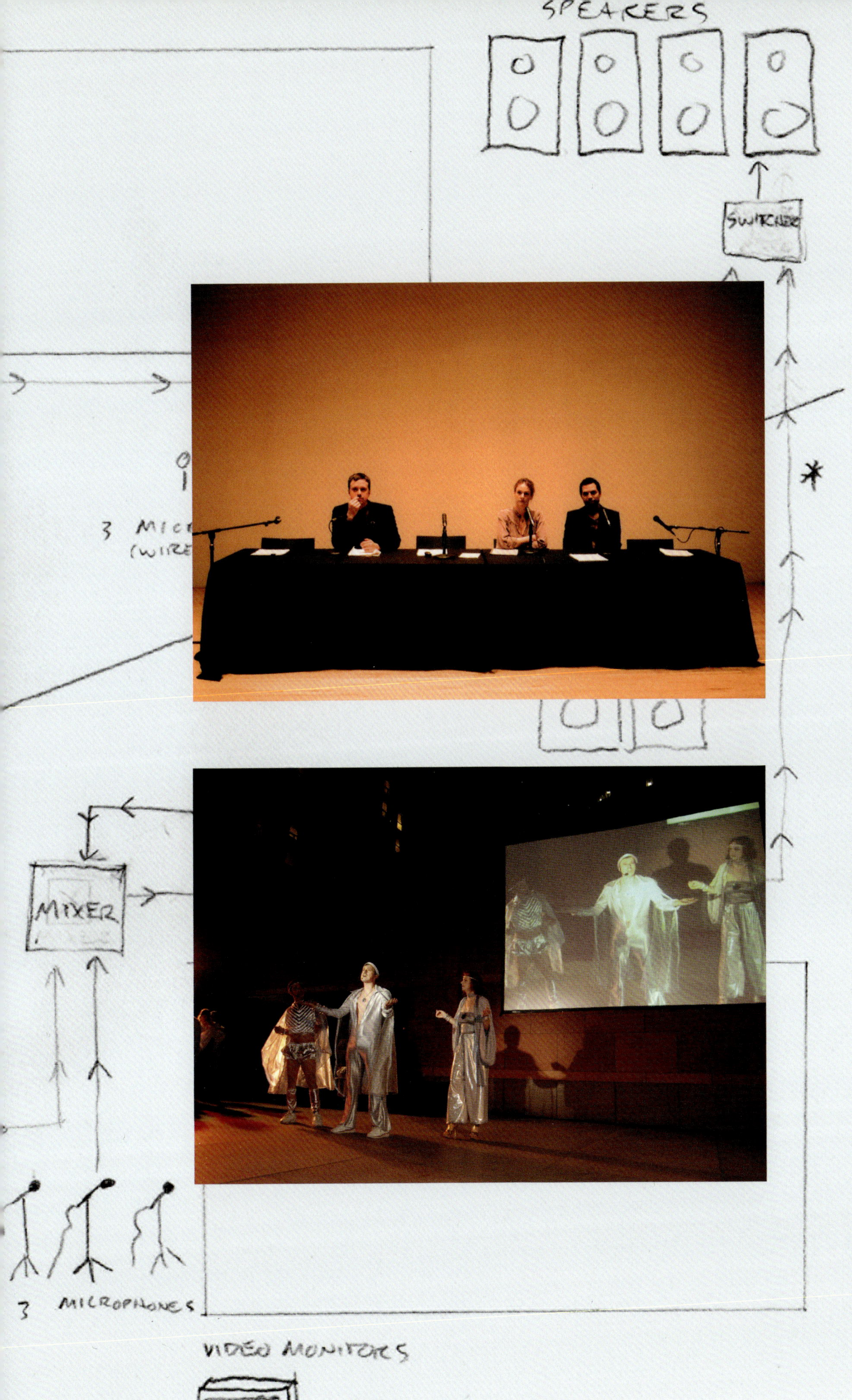
SPEAKERS
SWITCHER
3 MIC
(WIRE
MIXER
3 MICROPHONES
VIDEO MONITORS
?
x 4

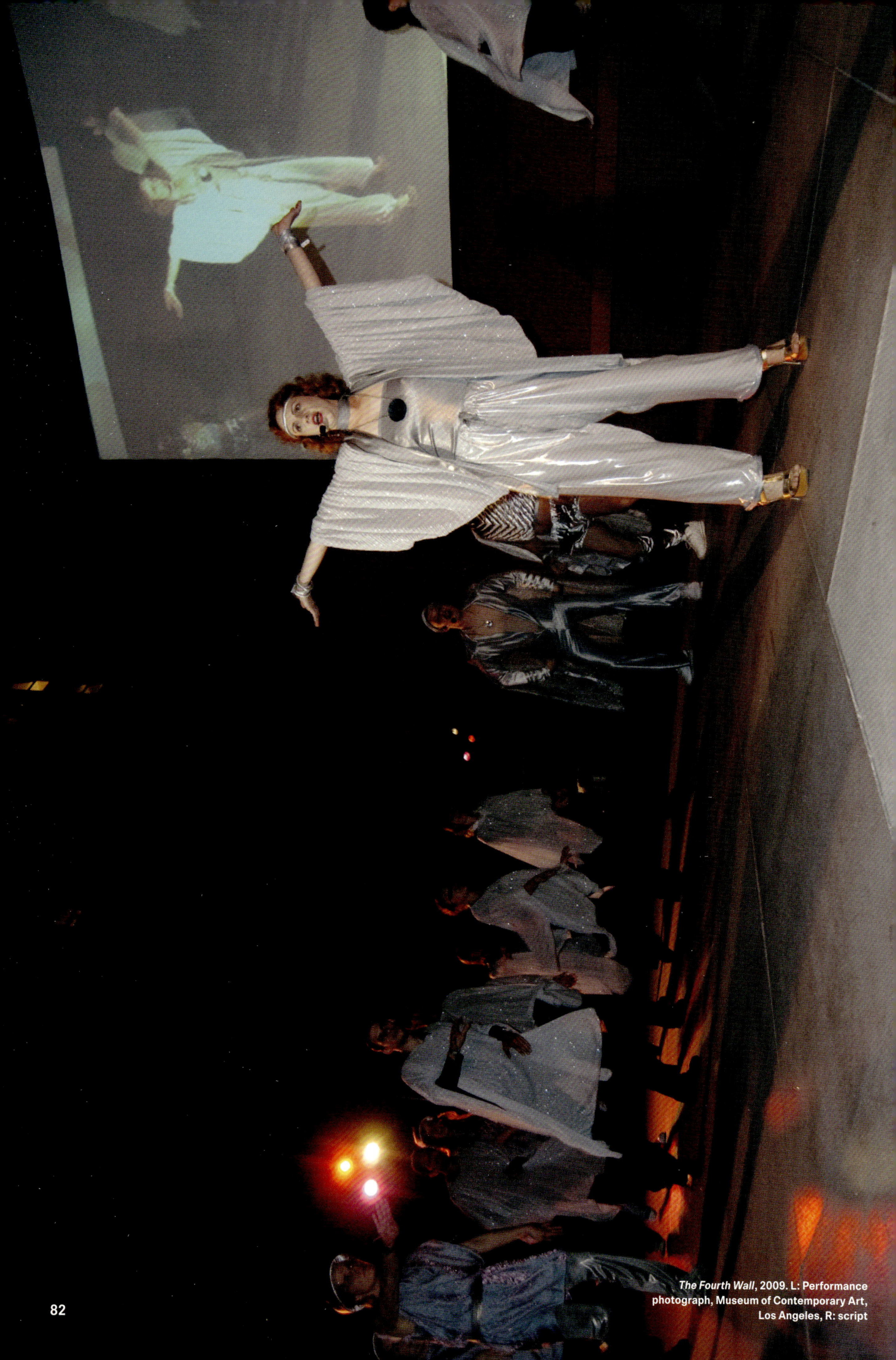

The Fourth Wall, 2009. L: Performance photograph, Museum of Contemporary Art, Los Angeles, R: script

J: What was your first museum experience?
Oo oo oo oo oo oo oo oo oo (J/M/A)
M: When did you decide that you would pursue working in one?
Oo oo oo oo oo oo oo oo oo
A: When did you start at MOCA?
Oo oo oo oo oo oo oo oo oo
J: What show was up?
Oo oo oo oo oo oo oo oo oo
M: What is the best show MOCA ever did?
Oo oo oo oo oo oo oo oo oo
A: What was the worst? Why?
Oo oo oo oo oo oo oo oo oo
J: Where in the museum building do you feel most comfortable? Where do you feel least comfortable?
Oo oo oo oo oo oo oo oo oo
M: What do you like and/or dislike about the architecture?
Oo oo oo oo oo oo oo oo oo
A: What is the museum's responsibility to the public?
Oo oo oo oo oo oo oo oo oo
J: What is its responsibility to private donors?
Oo oo oo oo oo oo oo oo oo
M: What is its responsibility to living artists?
Oo oo oo oo oo oo oo oo oo
A: Do you feel secure in your job?
Oo oo oo oo oo oo oo oo oo
J: Can you describe the feeling within the institution during the period of crisis?
Oo oo oo oo oo oo oo oo oo
M: What were some of the misperceptions, or points missed (among the public, the press, donors and supporters, and artists) when MOCA's financial problems went public?
Oo oo oo oo oo oo oo oo oo
A: What would be so bad about selling off the collection?
Oo oo oo oo oo oo oo oo oo
J: Are you now, or have you ever been, an artist?
Oo oo oo oo oo oo oo oo oo
M: Do you collect art?
Oo oo oo oo oo oo oo oo oo
A: What is a piece from the MOCA collection that has special meaning for you? Is it in the collection show?
Oo oo oo oo oo oo oo oo oo
J: What does this collection say about art history?
Oo oo oo oo oo oo oo oo oo
M: Is there a piece missing from the collection show that you would like to have included?

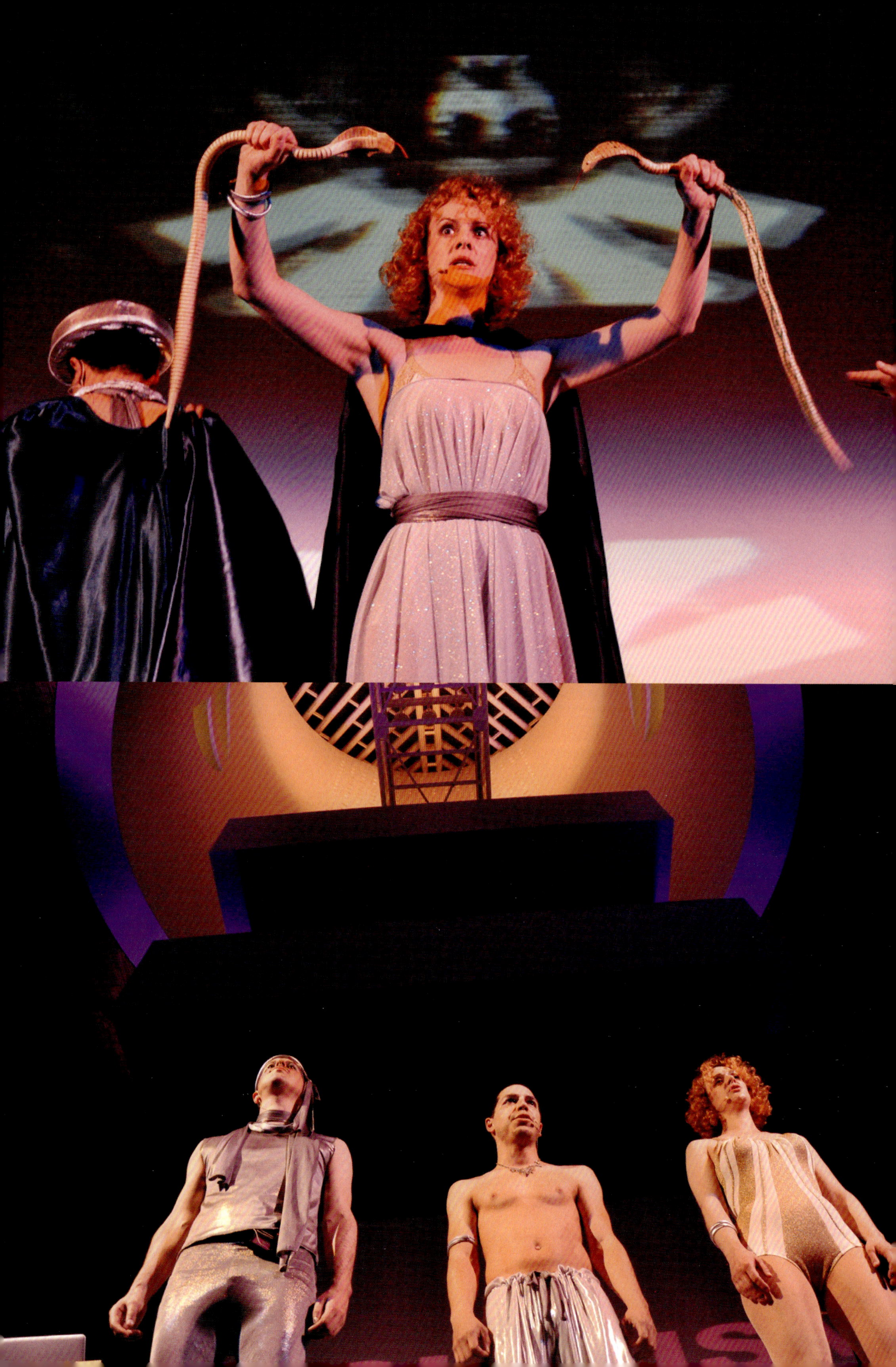

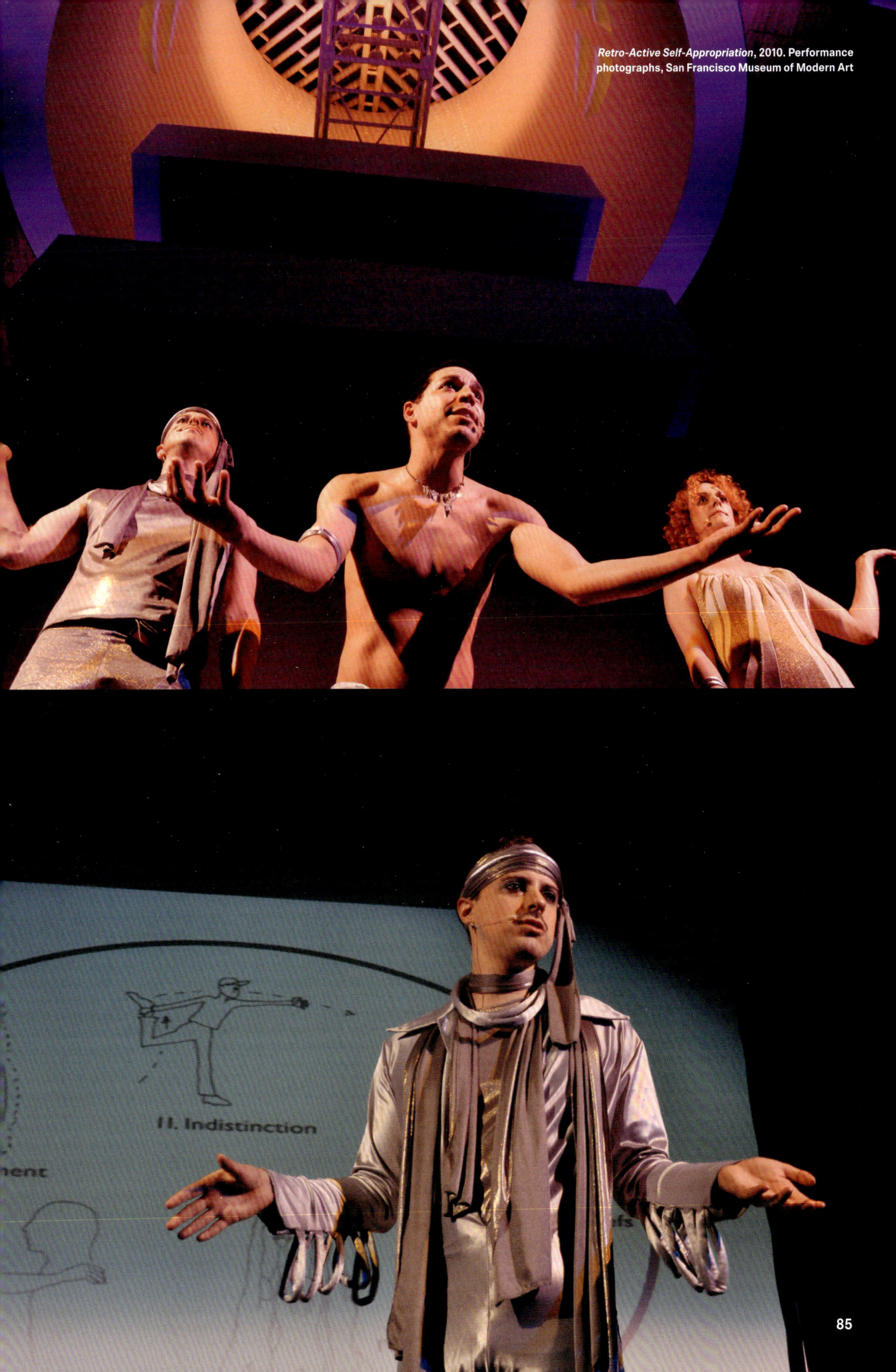

Retro-Active Self-Appropriation, 2010. Performance photographs, San Francisco Museum of Modern Art

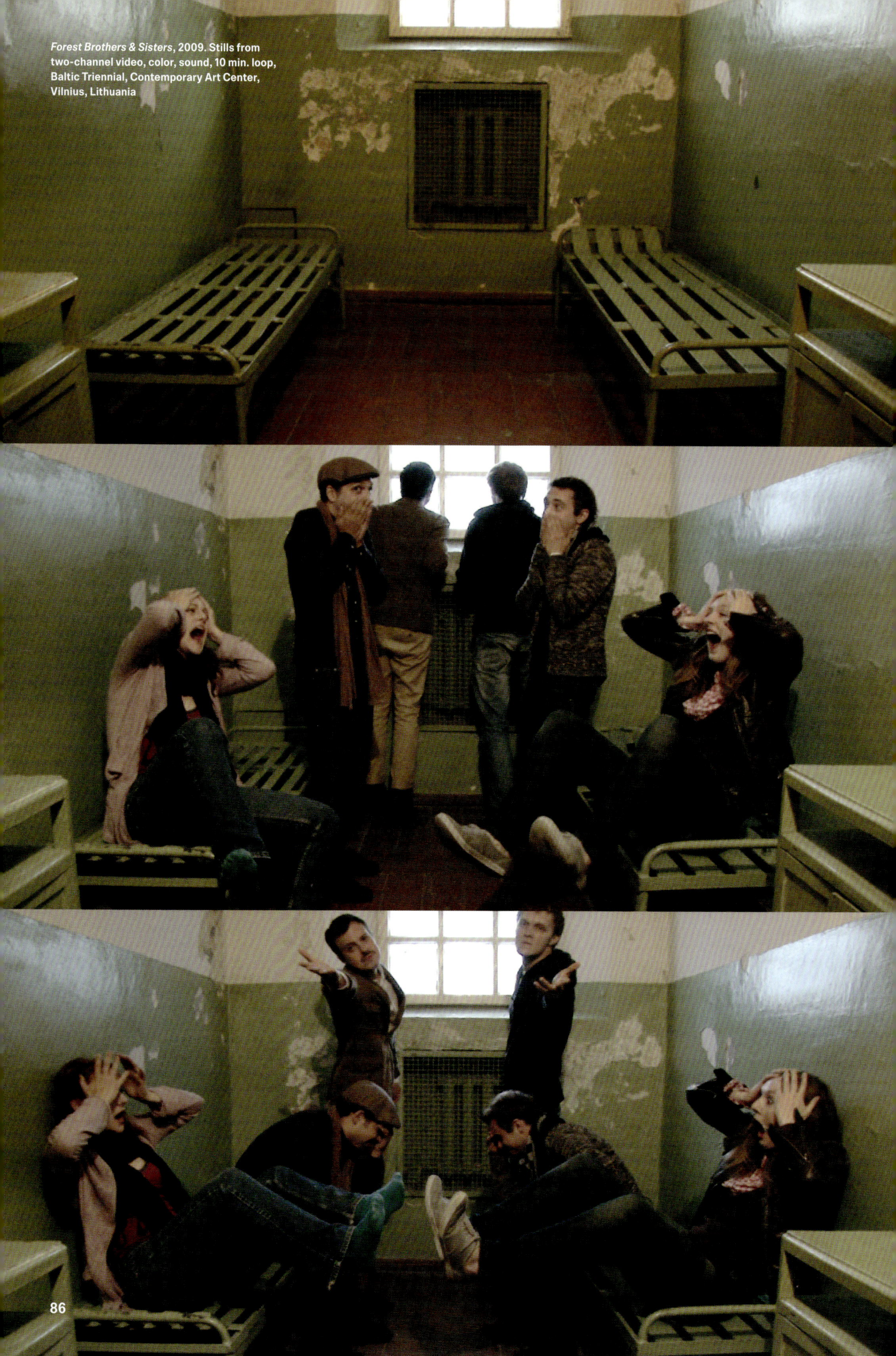

Forest Brothers & Sisters, 2009. Stills from two-channel video, color, sound, 10 min. loop, Baltic Triennial, Contemporary Art Center, Vilnius, Lithuania

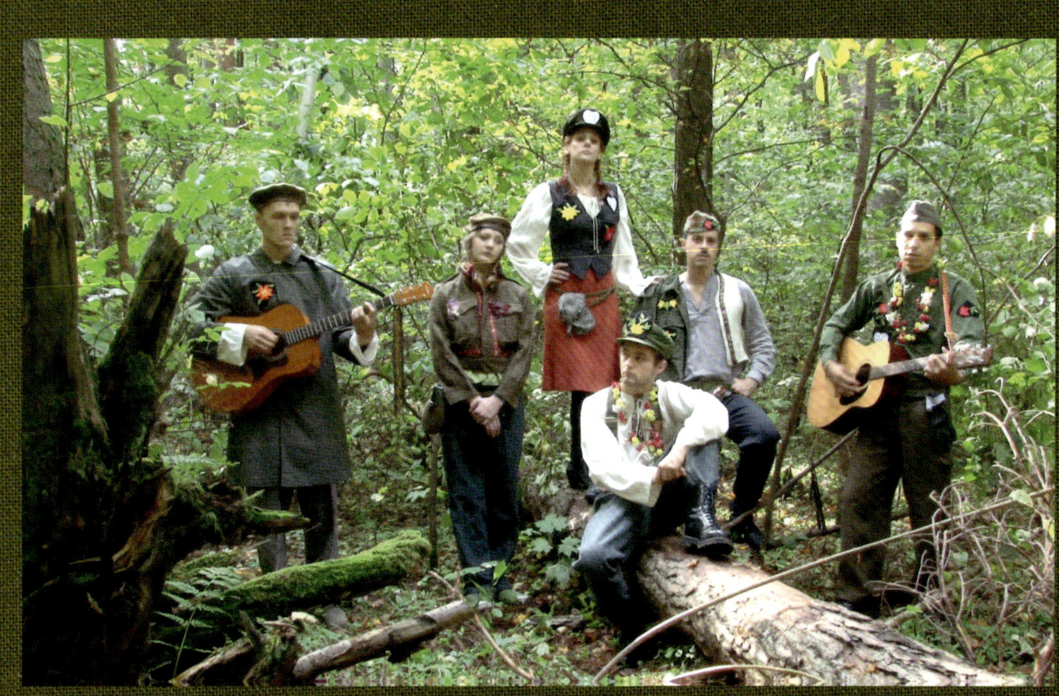

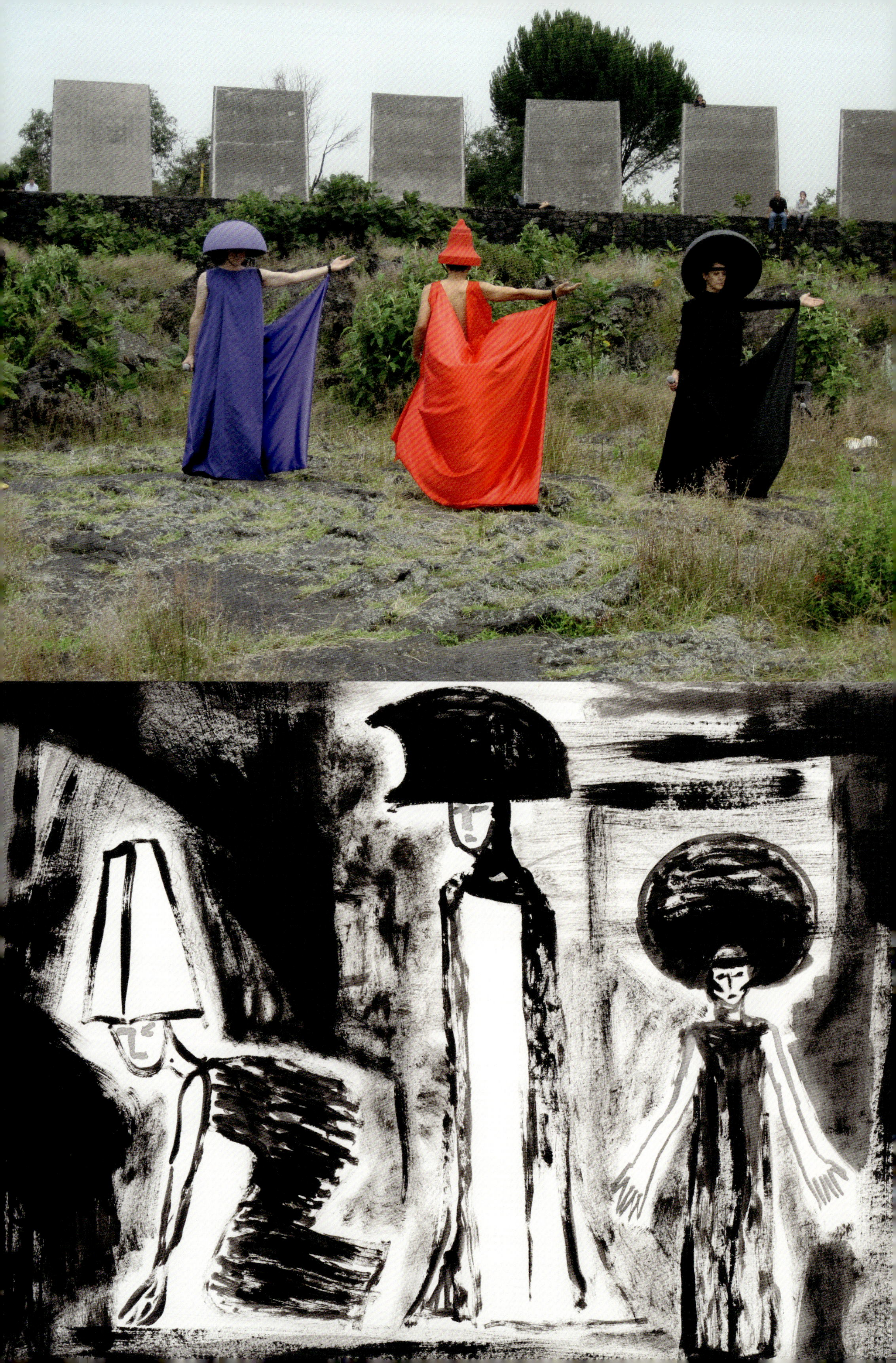

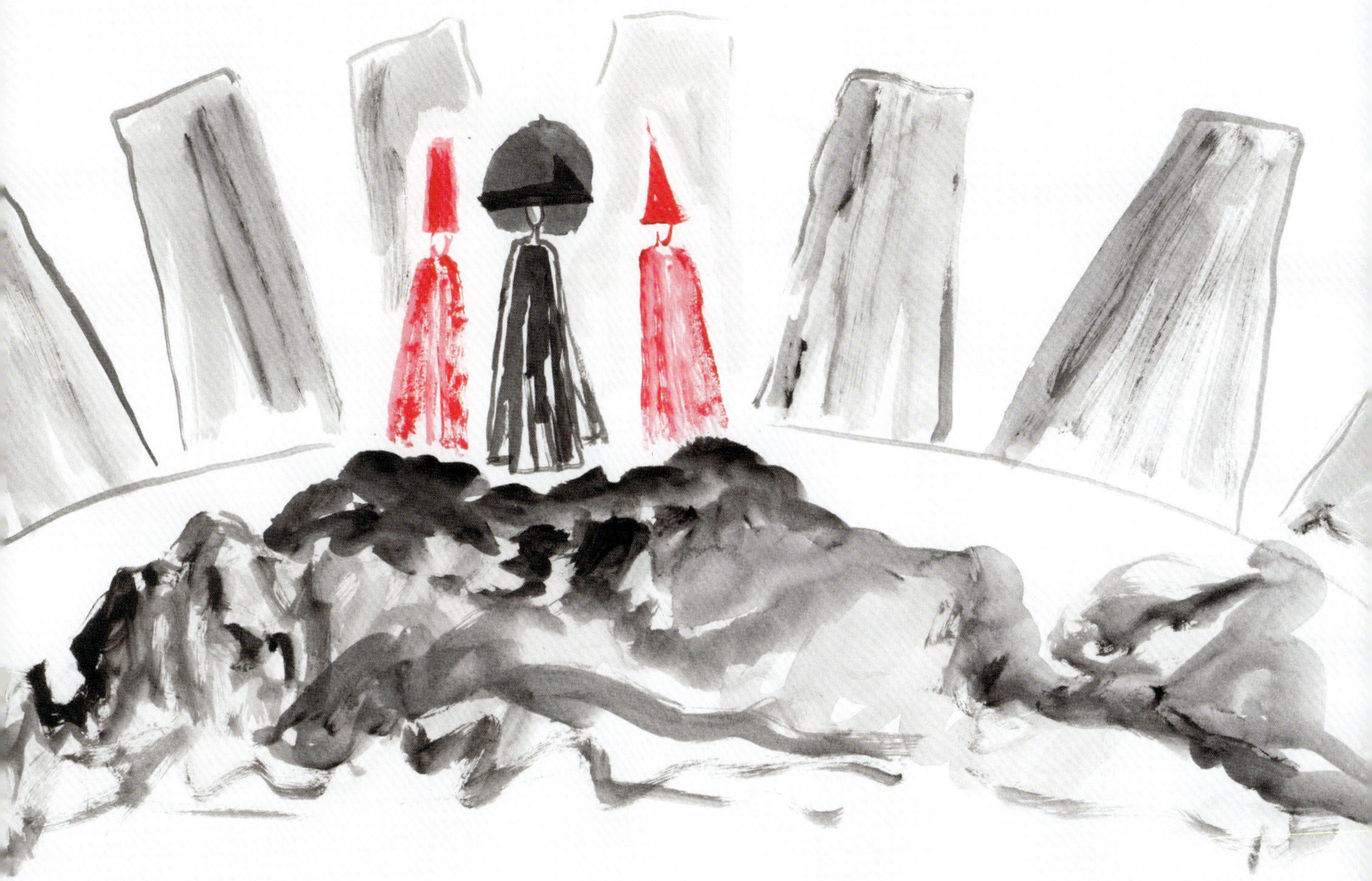

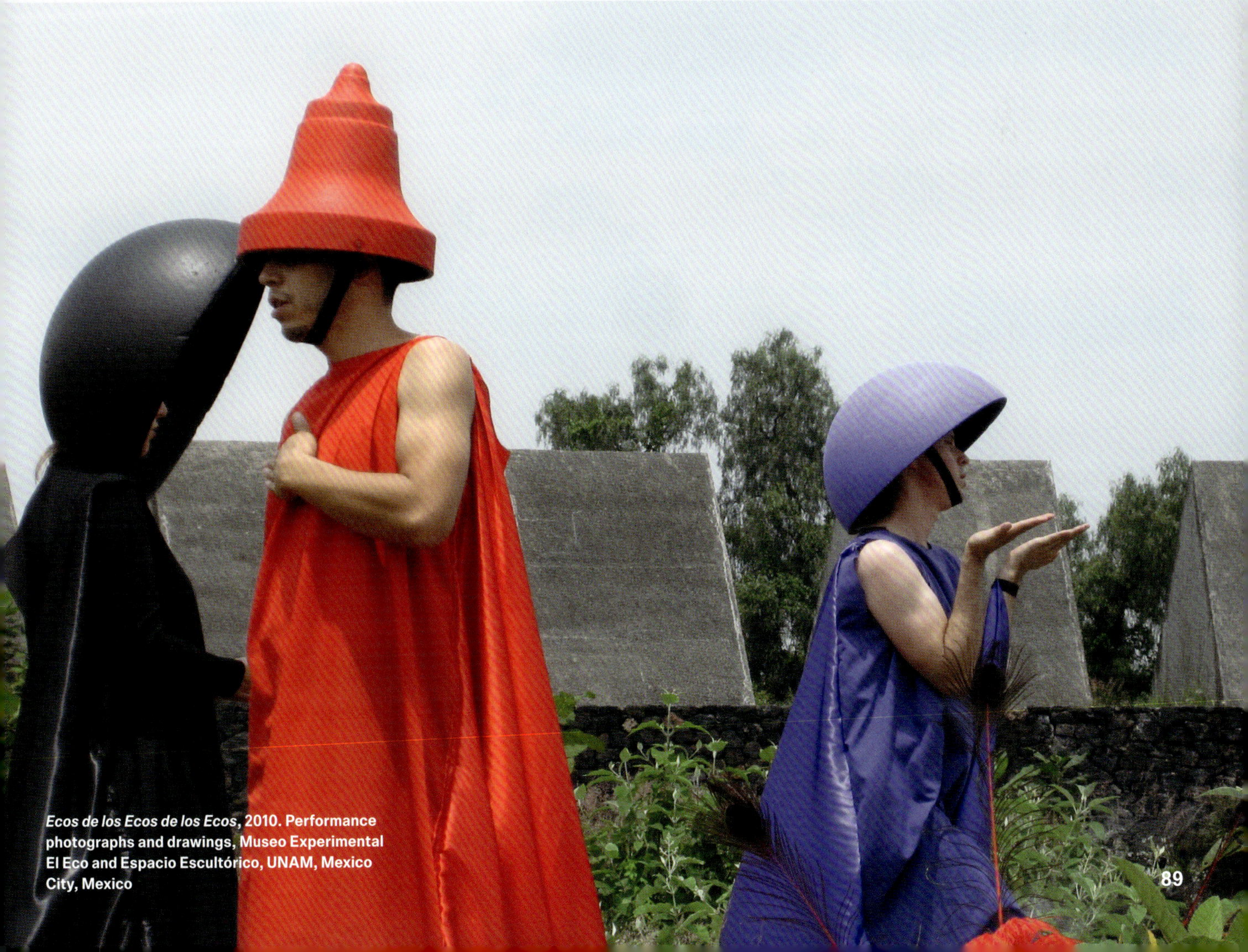

Ecos de los Ecos de los Ecos, 2010. Performance photographs and drawings, Museo Experimental El Eco and Espacio Escultórico, UNAM, Mexico City, Mexico

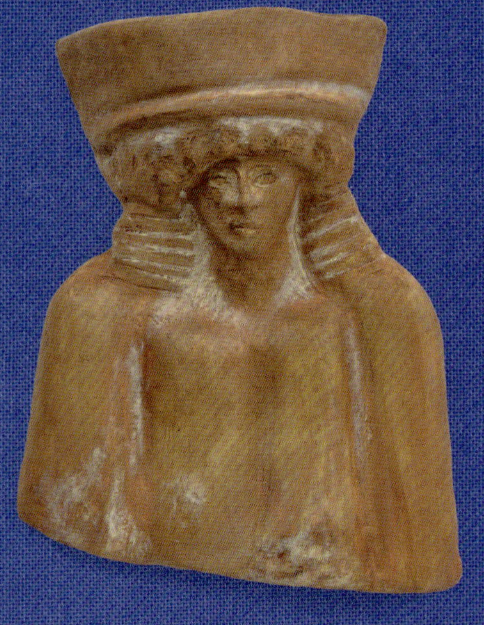

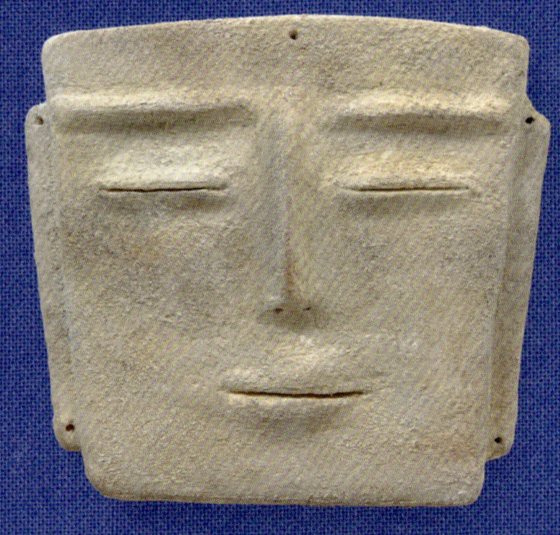

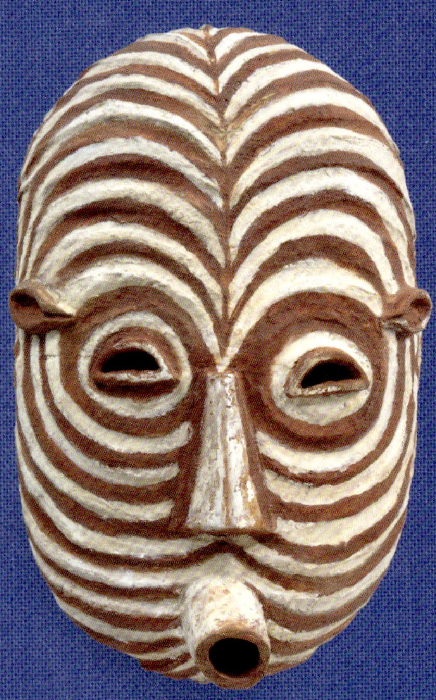

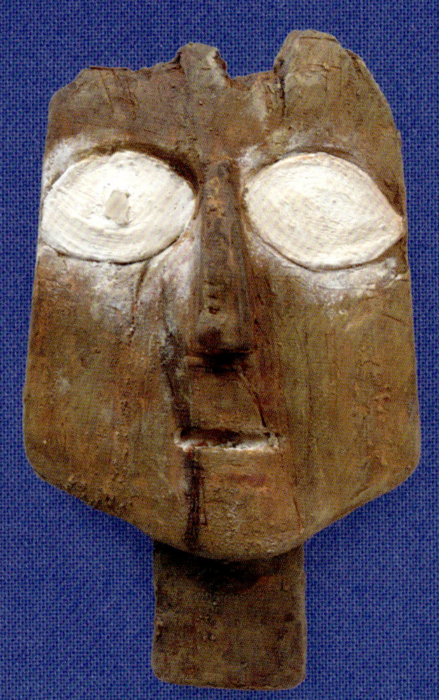

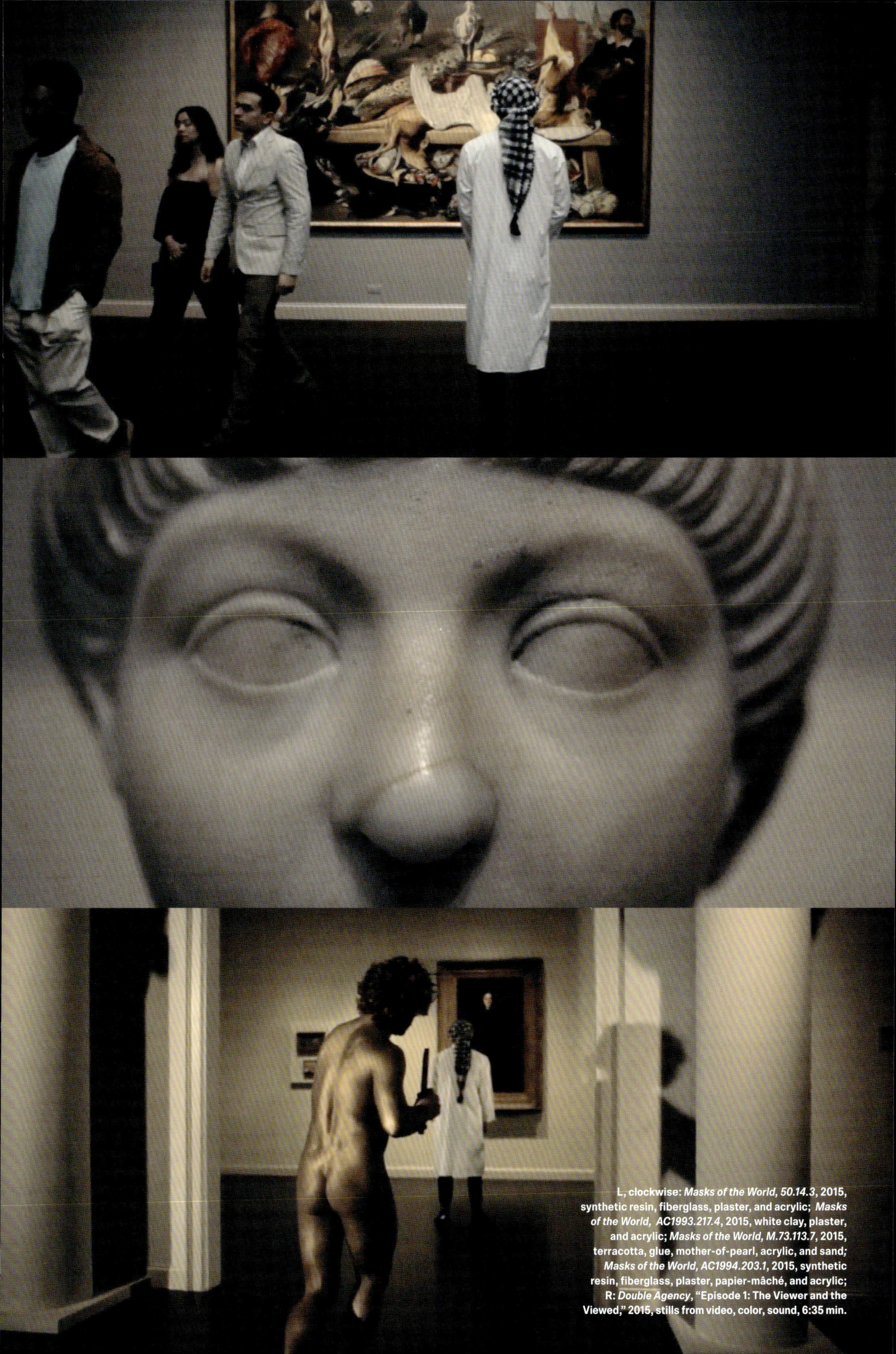

L, clockwise: *Masks of the World, 50.14.3*, 2015, synthetic resin, fiberglass, plaster, and acrylic; *Masks of the World, AC1993.217.4*, 2015, white clay, plaster, and acrylic; *Masks of the World, M.73.113.7*, 2015, terracotta, glue, mother-of-pearl, acrylic, and sand; *Masks of the World, AC1994.203.1*, 2015, synthetic resin, fiberglass, plaster, papier-mâché, and acrylic; R: *Double Agency*, "Episode 1: The Viewer and the Viewed," 2015, stills from video, color, sound, 6:35 min.

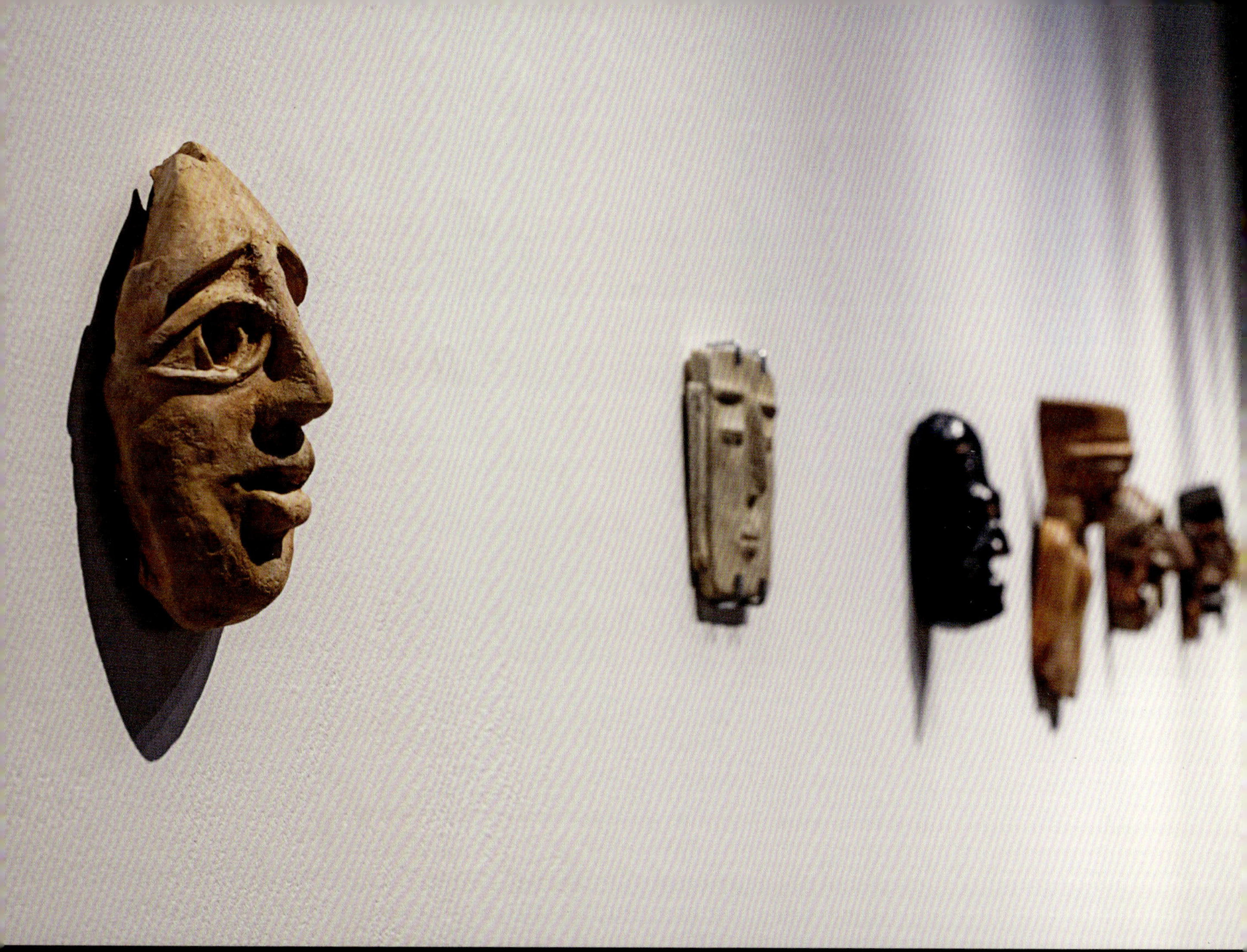

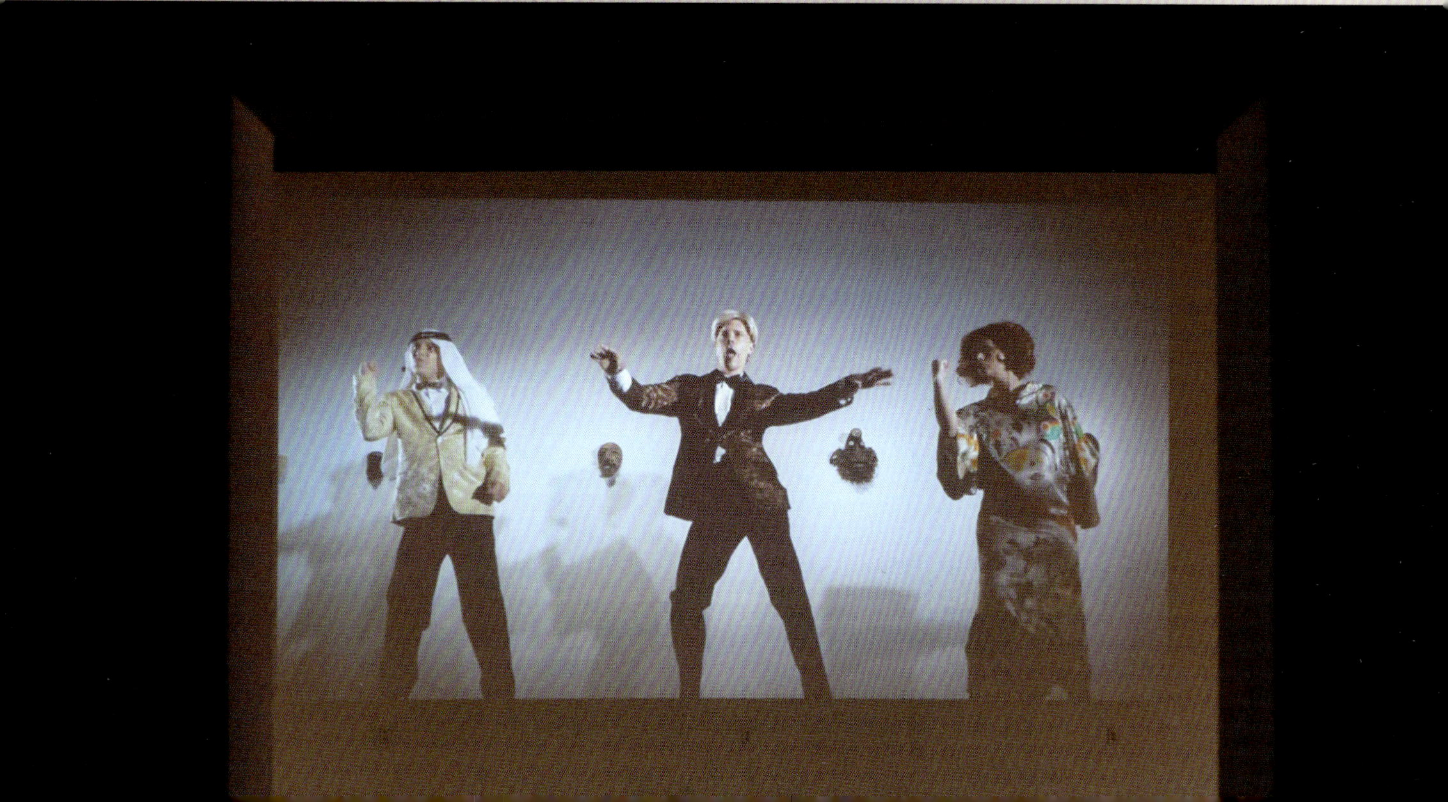

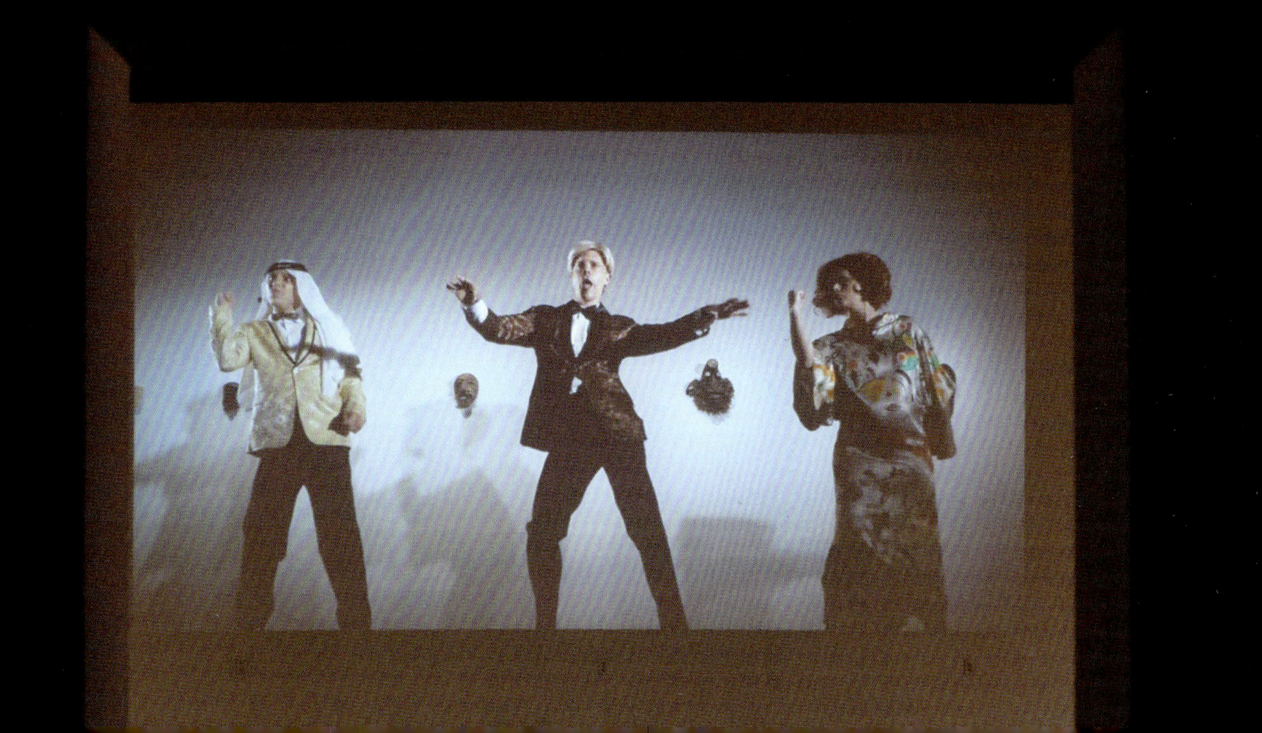

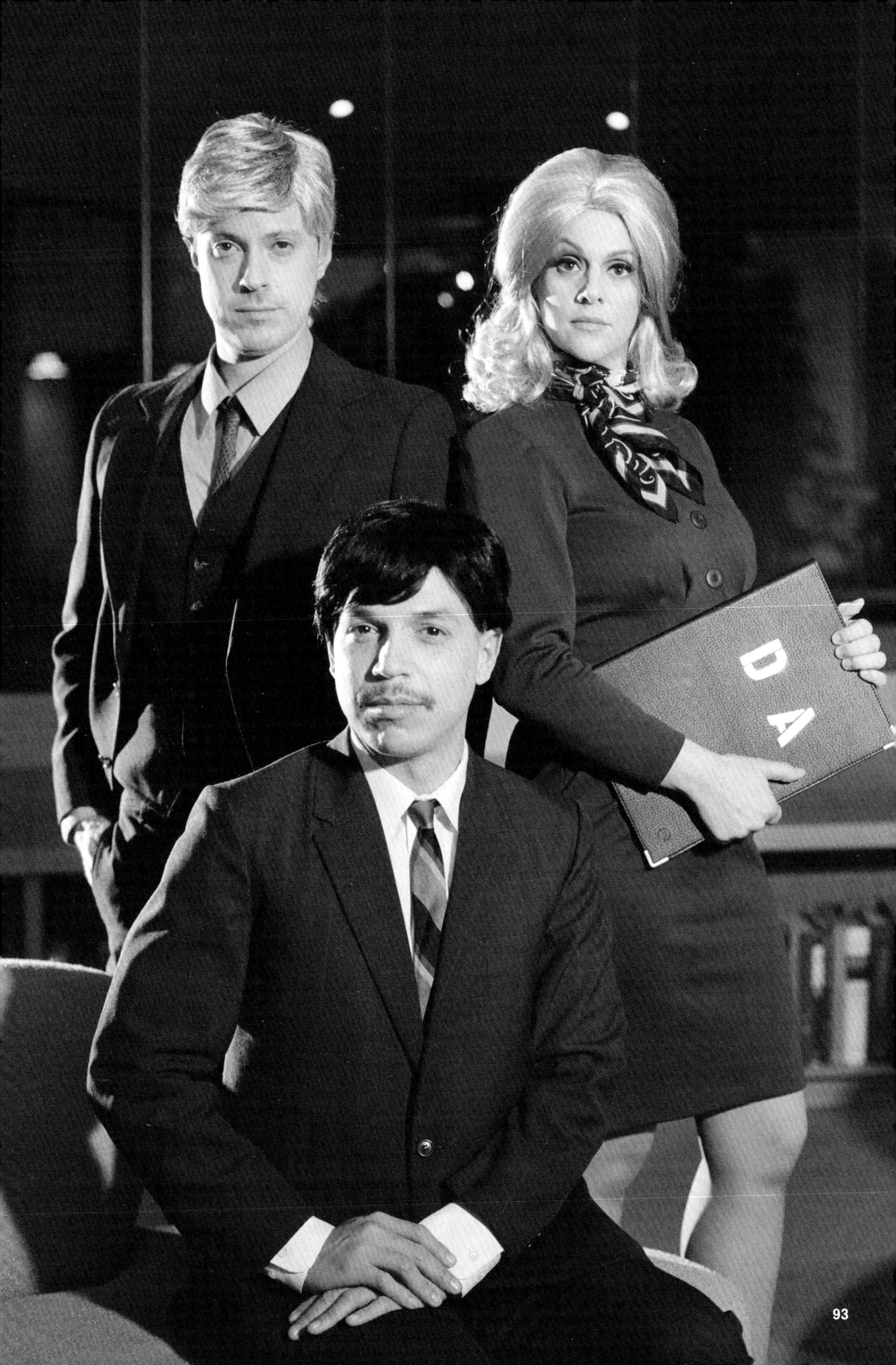
DA

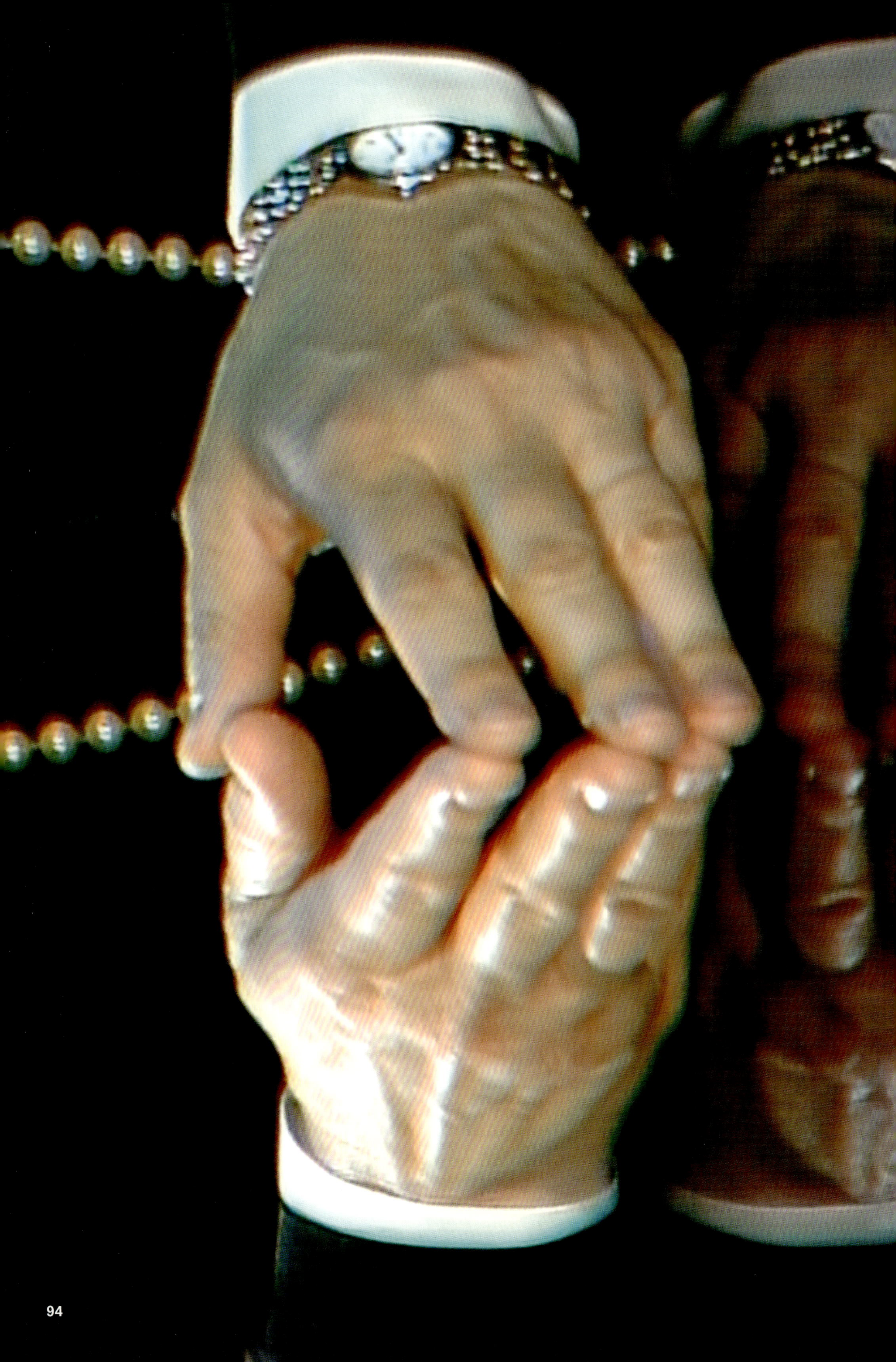

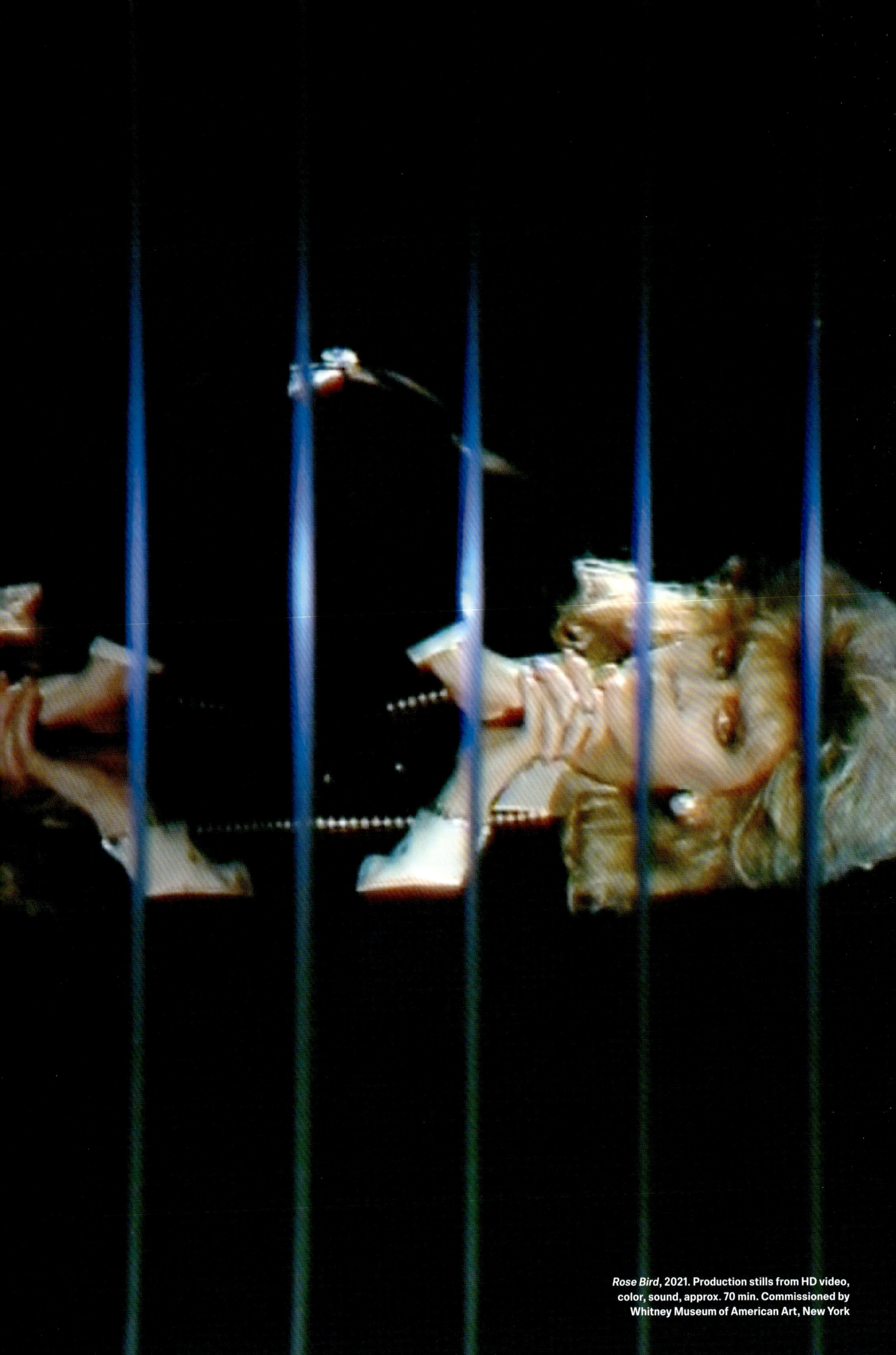

Rose Bird, 2021. Production stills from HD video, color, sound, approx. 70 min. Commissioned by Whitney Museum of American Art, New York

POST-POLITICAL THEATER

Jade Gordon

My Barbarian's work up to the late 2000s was influenced by queer camp humor, Brechtian alienation, Artaud's ritual theater, 1960s radical theater collectives like the Living Theater and Rainer Werner Fassbinder's antitheater, and Augusto Boal's Theater of the Oppressed (TO). The *Post-Living Ante-Action Theater* (PoLAAT, 2008–16) was a response to questions about performance and politics, a way to codify our strategies and teach them to others.

The five principles of the PoLAAT are 1) Estrangement, 2) Indistinction, 3) Suspension of Beliefs, 4) Mandate to Participate, and 5) Inspirational Critique. The project was originally somewhat parodic, but as the workshops developed it became clear to us that we actually use these strategies in performance and that they can be useful for others. The PoLAAT was a pedagogical response to our own educations; we were all in school and transitioning into teaching professionally while we worked on this commission from the New Museum, New York, in dialogue with the museum's education and public programs curator Eungie Joo. Eventually we made a handbook, complete with diagrams, worksheets, and sheet music. —Alex

After its development at the New Museum, New York, in 2008, the PoLAAT traveled to multiple international sites. In each location it brought together groups of local participants for a workshop and public recital. The PoLAAT began during the 2008 Democratic primary and returned to the New Museum during the run-up to the election in 2016. For the final PoLAAT workshops we reunited with a group of former participants from previous iterations of the project.

The year after the PoLAAT began I went back to school for a master's degree in applied theater at the University of Southern California. My program was based in community activism and Freirean pedagogy. I was training to become a practitioner of Boal's techniques. A TO practitioner approaches collaboration without a preconceived plan or desired outcome. Instead, Boal's "joker," or facilitator, holds a neutral position, allowing the communities' needs and desires to be foregrounded. The joker is a wild card, stirring things up but ultimately acting in service to others.

The tension I felt between using political theater as a tool to make art and using it as a tool for social change was painful. I'd spent ten years onstage making a spectacle of myself, so the part of neutral facilitator wasn't easy to play. I had questions: Is social practice exploitative? Can I still have a starring role? Do we need an invitation from the communities we're working with? Is it weird that the invitations we did get were from art institutions who profited from the creative capital we generated through "community engagement"? Ultimately, I had to be okay with the fact that My Barbarian was not an activist theater troupe but rather an art collective that invited audiences to critically question with us.

In institutions, this followed a wave of high-end artists who had introduced social processes as art objects, so now we could reenact leftist theater as a budget line. I thought of that reenactment as a subsidized rehearsal for acting outside of the institution; a kind of philosophical labor.—Malik

Around the time I was finishing my MA program in 2010, and in response to the stripped-down visual aesthetics of community-based theater I'd been studying, I traveled to a clown school in Northern California for an intensive two-week mask workshop. I came back to LA with a papier-mâché mask-making technique. Most of the students in the workshop were clowns in training. After a morning session of mask-making we'd move into a mirrored dance studio to test out our creations through improv. We were told to "crown the mask," adding a matted wig or questionable hat. Then we'd figure out a look from a bin full of thrift store clothes. In clown school, a baggy blazer equals "funny" and hat acting is always a thing. Through a series of physical theater jams we'd find out whether or not a mask "prints" in performance, making the viewer forget there is a human face underneath. If your mask didn't "print," you'd go back into the art studio.

I made a set of contemporary commedia masks using the new techniques for *Broke People's Baroque Peoples' Theater* (2009–). Borrowing more from the Cockettes than Grotowski, it was a trashy poor theater. Like Bread and Puppet Theater, we used cheap materials. As Boal wrote in his 2004 essay "Aesthetics of the Oppressed": "Every group should produce a collective creation under the title THE HUMAN BEING IN GARBAGE, using cleaned garbage from their communities or workplaces." The project comprised multiple full-length videos; props, masks, and wigs; and a puppet theater modeled on a miniature Italian baroque theater we had seen at a museum in Vilnius, Lithuania. *Broke People's Baroque Peoples' Theater* was a multi-year project first performed at the Kitchen in New York, with a solo exhibition at Human Resources, Los Angeles (in 2011 and 2012, respectively).

Further exploring this notion of post-political mask work, My Barbarian adapted Fassbinder's *Blood on the Cat's Neck*, commissioned by the Goethe-Institut New York and presented in an installation in their East Village gallery space in December 2014. The piece included a set, video projections, and a series of dolls and masks based on members of Fassbinder's antitheater troupe. The characters were cynical, abusive, and anxious, with names describing their social positions, such as Butcher, Cop, Girl, Teacher, Model, Mistress, etc. They represented negative attitudes, all of them dissatisfied yet resigned to inaction.

"Post" as in so extra, but also over it, but also something after, like an after-hours. —Malik

The politics of motherhood informed our next two projects. There isn't a lot of guidance on how to navigate and maintain a collaborative performance art practice as a mother. My ability to participate in every My Barbarian performance changed when I had children. I had to sit out several projects, and it was difficult to see the work move forward without me. It tapped into anxieties I already had about being an artist and a mother, but ultimately it was good for the collective. We were able to expand the circle to include other performers and musicians. One of the reasons My Barbarian has been able to maintain our collaborative practice for over twenty years has been this kind of flexibility; our ability to move in and out of the three of us to a larger group and back to the core. We refer to MB as a machine powered by its own momentum, but it's actually more like an organism opening up, breathing, exhaling, and cycling through the process again.

The work from this period was very invested in performances of care and "the mother" as social position, not biologically determined category. Another performance from this period, *Counterpublicity* (2014), reenacted the activism of Pedro Zamora, who used MTV's *The Real World* to educate its audience about AIDS, sexuality, and identity. The piece was based on writings by José Esteban Muñoz, and was adapted into a video for Visual AIDS' Day Without Art screening series. —Alex

Hystera Theater began at Art Basel Miami Beach in 2008. The title was taken from the French philosopher Luce Irigaray's feminist rereading of Plato's *Allegory of the Cave*, which draws parallels between the cave and the womb. The 2009 version of the work was a performance and installation inside a shipping container lined with ten large, handsewn, dyed-red linen banners. Stitched onto the banners were prophetic messages from our project *You Were Born Poor and Poor You Will Die* (2005) and slogans such as "I Heart Mimesis" and "A Herstory of Menstrualcy." In 2019 we returned to the project and made a full-length vinyl album. This soundtrack accompanied a new twenty-two-minute 16mm film that was a collage of staged ritualistic performances edited together with found footage from 1980s laserdiscs. Included in the footage were clips of death and destruction from a documentary on Pompeii and versions of hysterical maternal grief appropriated from classic Hollywood tearjerkers.

In late 2018, my three-year-old son died of cancer. Collecting, re-watching, and editing together the bits of found footage for our 2019 *Hystera* video helped me process my grief. I was able to better understand my own experience by playing with misunderstandings and misrepresentations. Cathartic explosions of tears often took place in the final scenes of these melodramatic old movies, cut with shots of relieved-looking families walking from gravesites arm in arm as the credits rolled. In this Aristotelian model, the film audiences purge their fears and return home comforted by their normal lives. Real-life grief lingers; there's no sudden release or pat ending.

I had given birth to my eldest son just five months before we first performed *The Mother and Other Plays* at Vielmetter Los Angeles in 2013. Our adaptation of *The Mother* by Bertolt Brecht was also presented the following year at the 2014 Whitney Biennial. The play is based on Maxim Gorky's novel about a factory worker's widowed mother, Pelagea Vlassova, who is enmeshed in an underground Bolshevik cartel and ends up a leader in the cause. She's trying to take care of her kid, who's been put in prison. She's poor and she's worried; her actions don't feel like choices. Brecht's original play suggests that a good mother is a mother who has struggled.

"The Imaginary," as Mary Kelly called it. —Malik

Accompanying the live performance and installation was a thirty-minute video, *Universal Declaration of Infantile Anxiety Situations Reflected in the Creative Impulse* (2013). The title references texts by Melanie Klein and Eleanor Roosevelt and includes guest performances by artists Mary Kelly and Eleanor Antin as well as each of our own mothers, Barbara Gaines, Victoria Gordon, and Irene Segade. It's been especially poignant looking at the video recently, as we've all watched our mothers get older and sicker. My mother is mentally ill and has been hospitalized dozens of times over the past thirty years. She was living with me, my husband, and our new baby the year we shot the video, sleeping downstairs on a twin bed, smoking all the time. I would try to make her go outside, but she's an old hippie and would say, "Man, don't boss me around." I'd come into the kitchen in the morning and everything would be a wreck. It reminded me of the

My mother, who chaired the San Diego chapter of the Gay and Lesbian Student Education Network, gave a talk about the bullying of gender nonconforming behavior. —Alex story of the shoemaker and the elves who come in while everyone is asleep and fix everything up and make life easier. In my fractured fairy tale, my mom was the elf sneaking around at midnight to spread peanut butter all over the place.

We came up with a plan to shoot her in a series of black-and-white photographs, an homage to Chris Marker's 1962 film *La Jetée*. Photographer Farrah Karapetian came over with her camera and took some stills around our house—my mom smoking cigarettes, staring at the baby in his crib, wandering around our neighborhood. I performed a voice-over accompanying the photographs excerpted from a journal my mother kept in the mid-seventies when she was in graduate school and I was a toddler. She wrote things like "Jade is driving me crazy" and "I don't know how I can do this; Jade is so difficult." She was a single mom trying to be super groovy, but in reality it was about survival. I remember finding and reading the journal when I was a kid and being horrified, especially by the part where she wrote that she was questioning "whether I love my child or not." But as a mother struggling with my own young children, living through grief and COVID, I can empathize with her more now than ever.

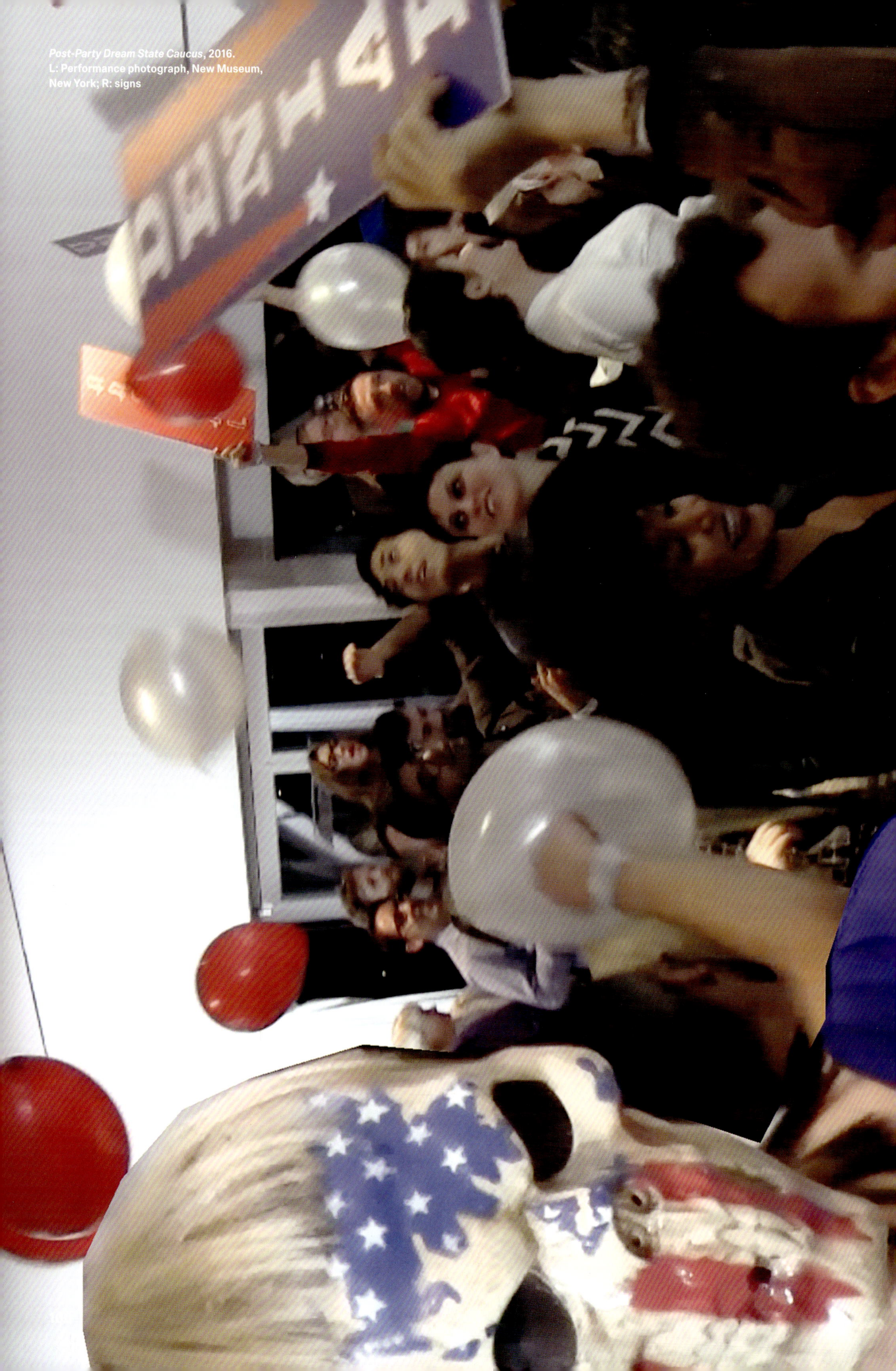

Post-Party Dream State Caucus, 2016.
L: Performance photograph, New Museum, New York; R: signs

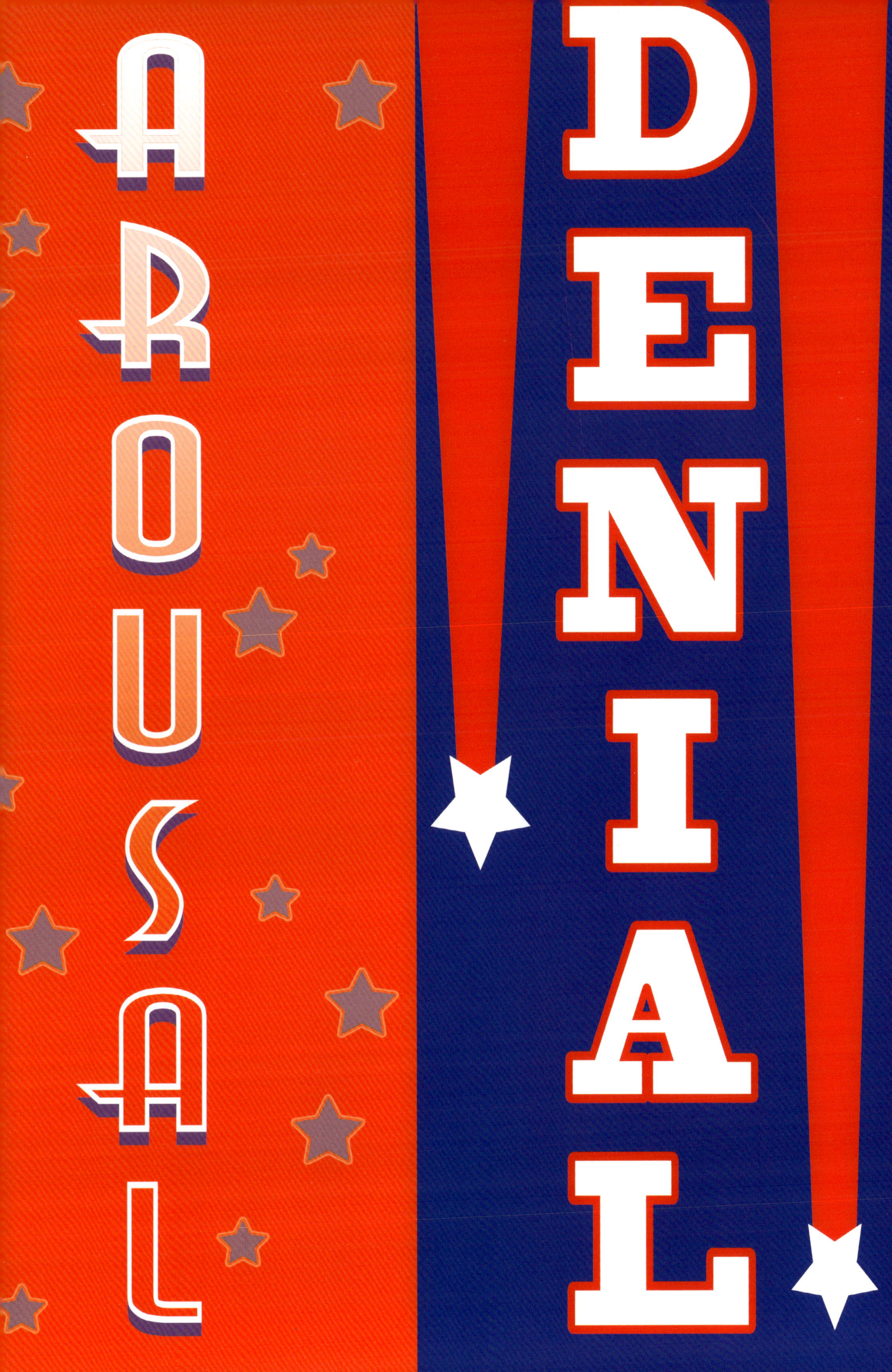
AROUSAL
DENIAL

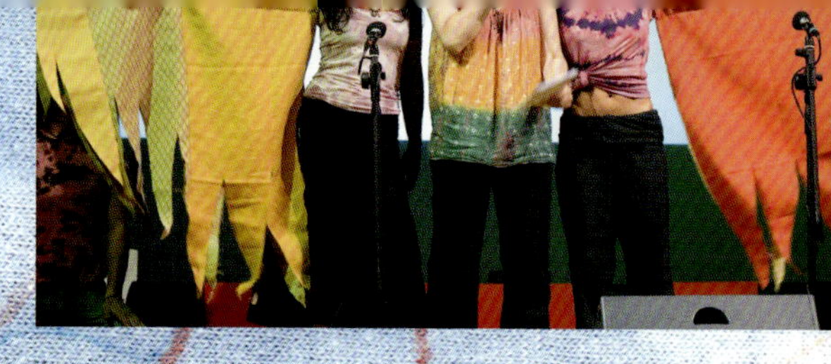
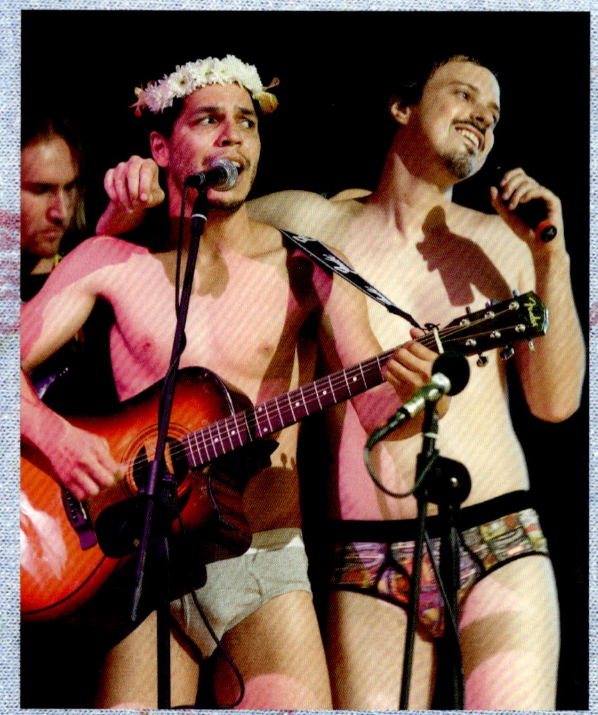
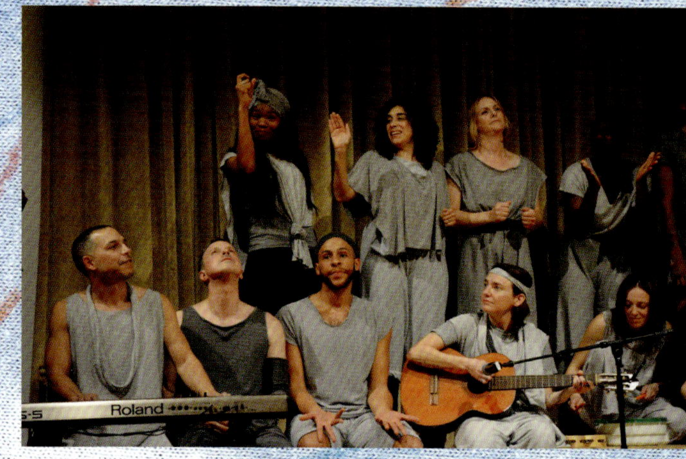
Roland
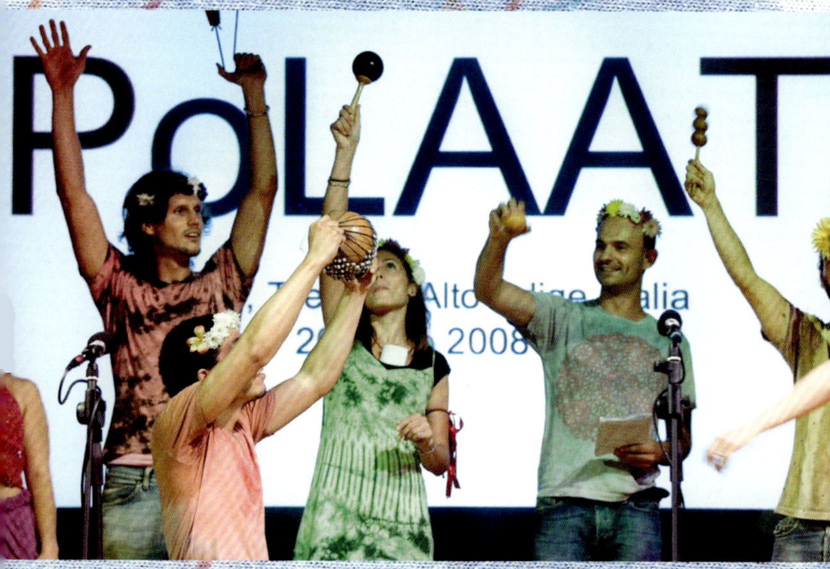
PoLAAT
2008
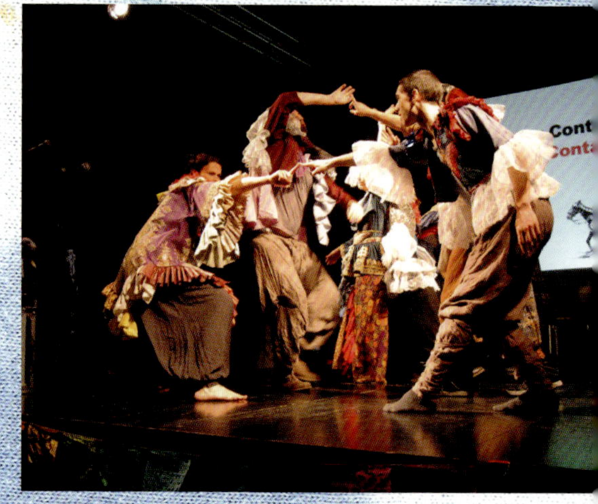
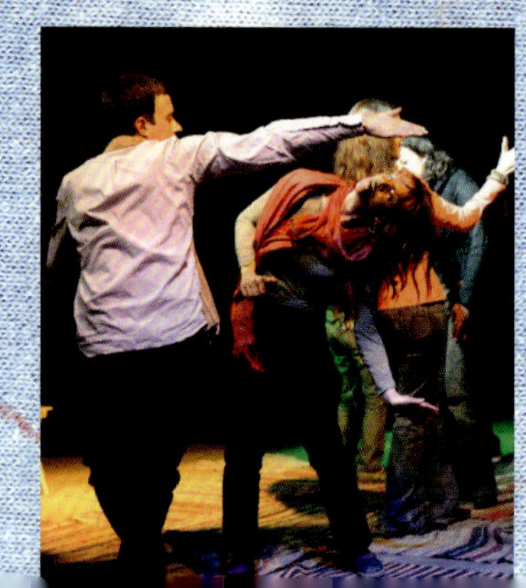
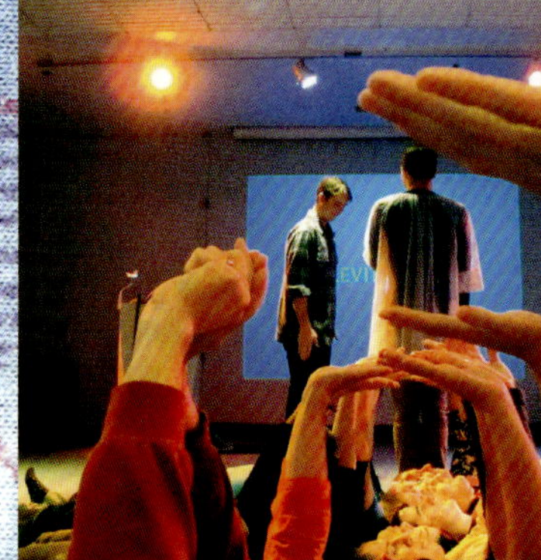

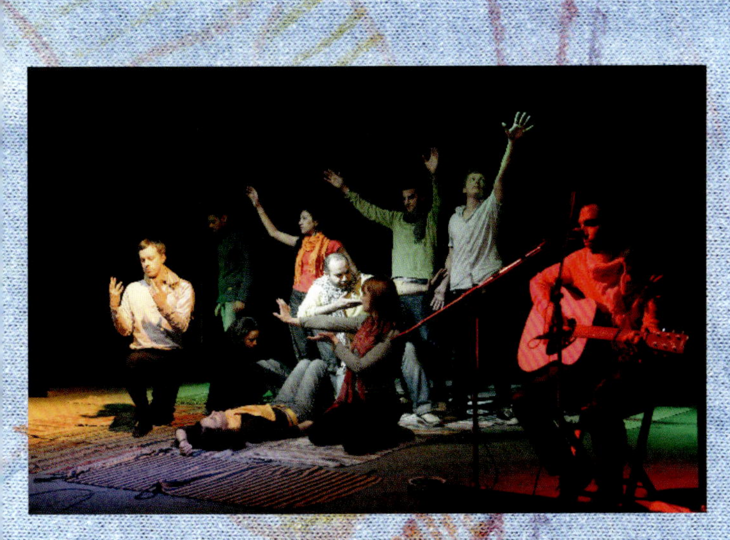

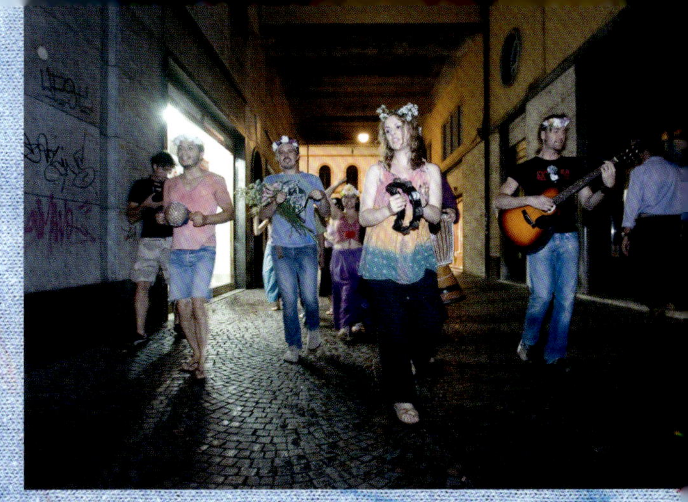

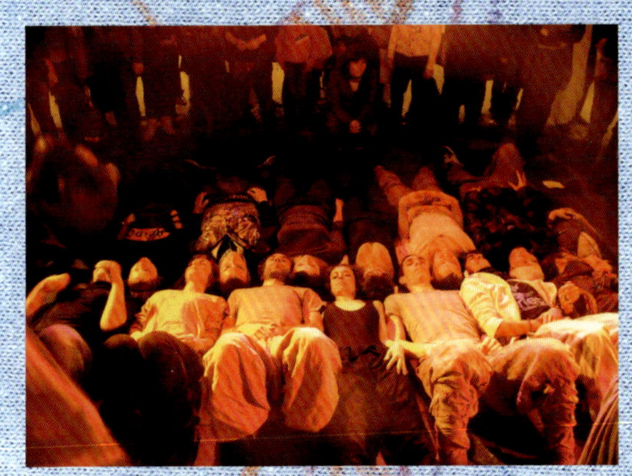

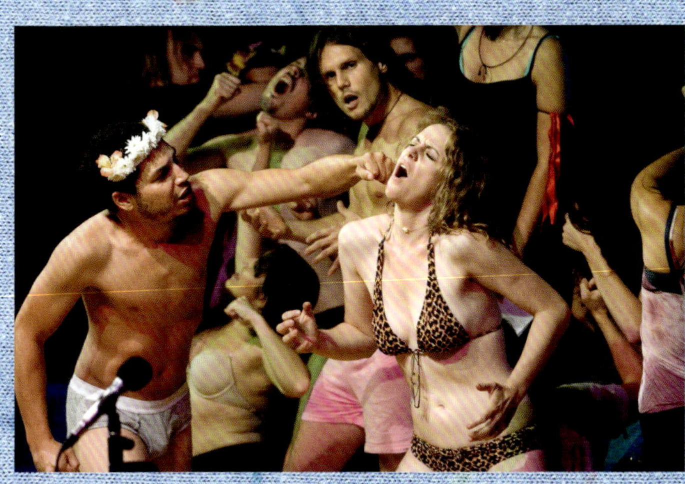

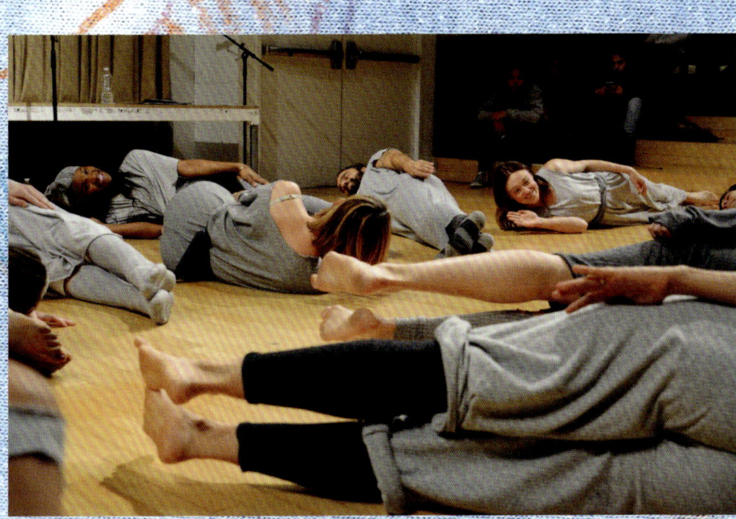

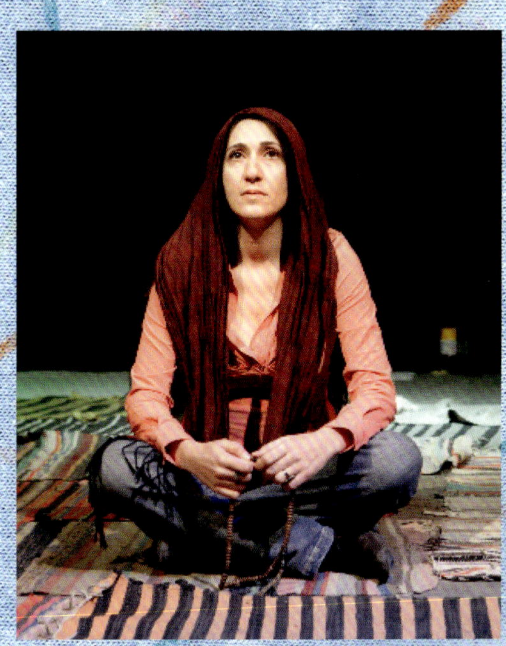

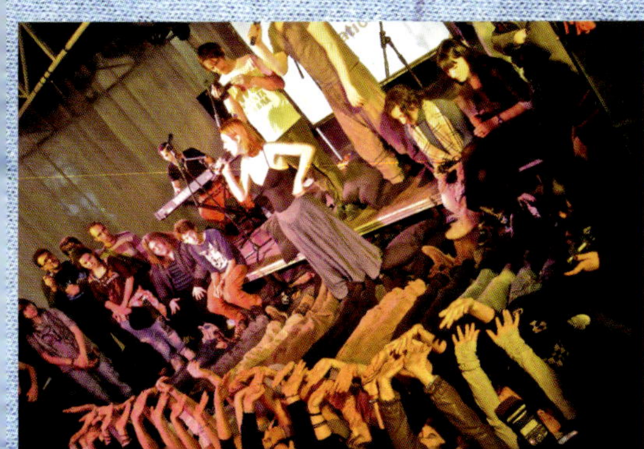

Post-Living Ante-Action Theater (PoLAAT), 2008–16. Performance photographs, El Matadero and ARCO, Madrid; Townhouse Gallery/Rawabet Theater, Cairo; Galleria Civica, Trento, Italy; New Museum, New York; Institute of Contemporary Art, Philadelphia

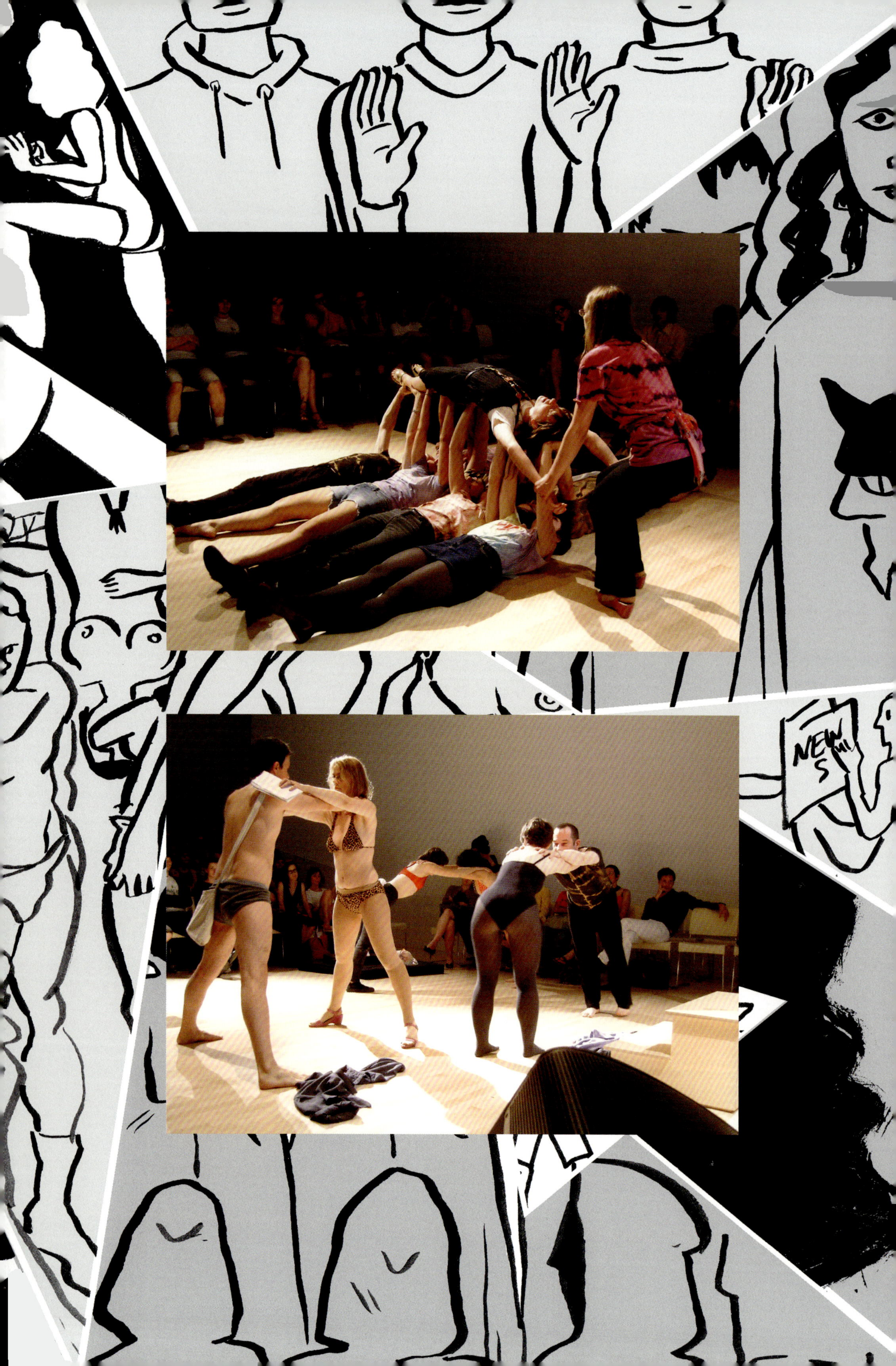
NEWS

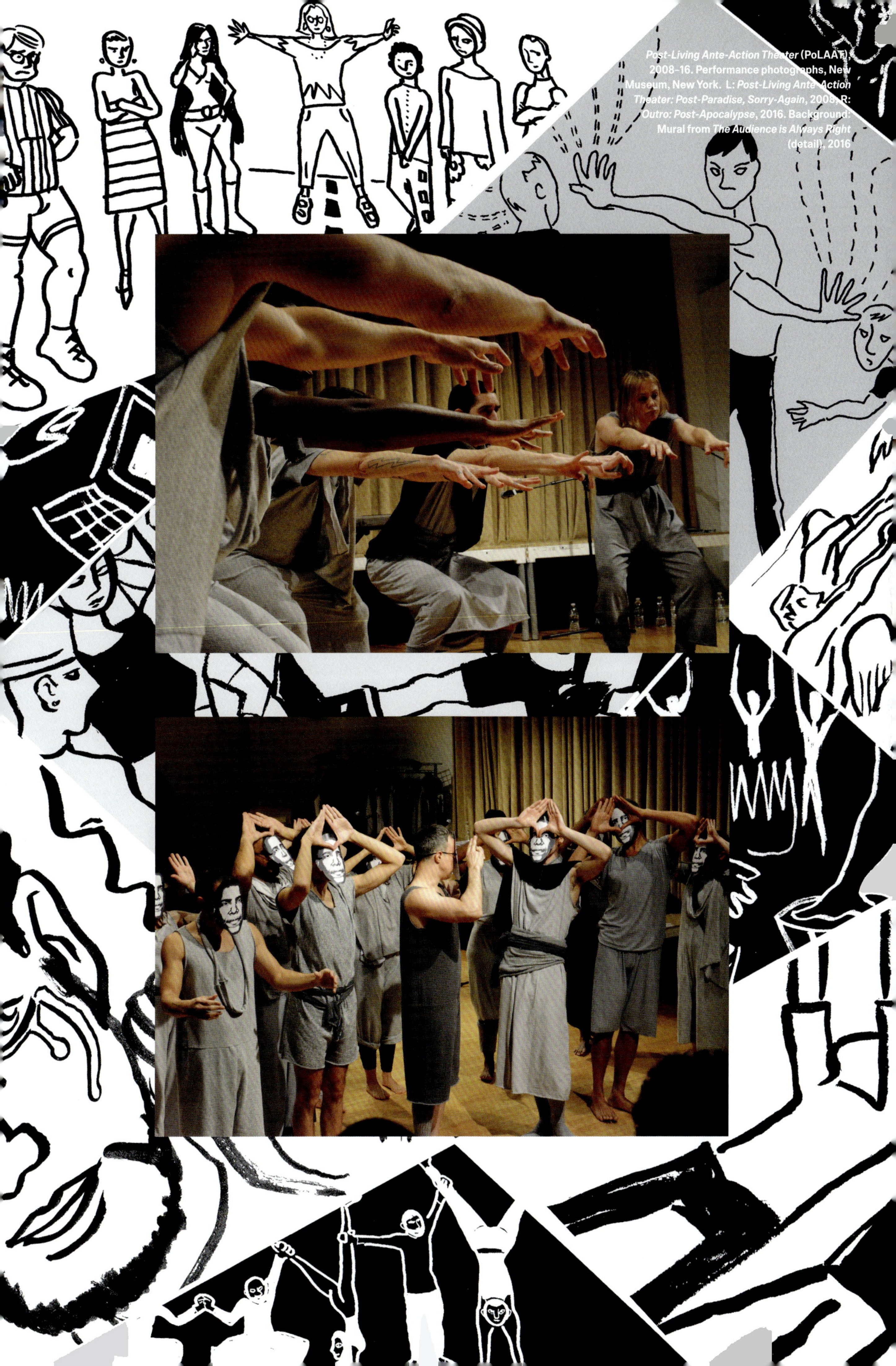

Post-Living Ante-Action Theater (PoLAAT), 2008–16. Performance photographs, New Museum, New York. L: *Post-Living Ante-Action Theater: Post-Paradise, Sorry-Again*, 2008; R: *Outro: Post-Apocalypse*, 2016. Background: Mural from *The Audience is Always Right* (detail), 2016

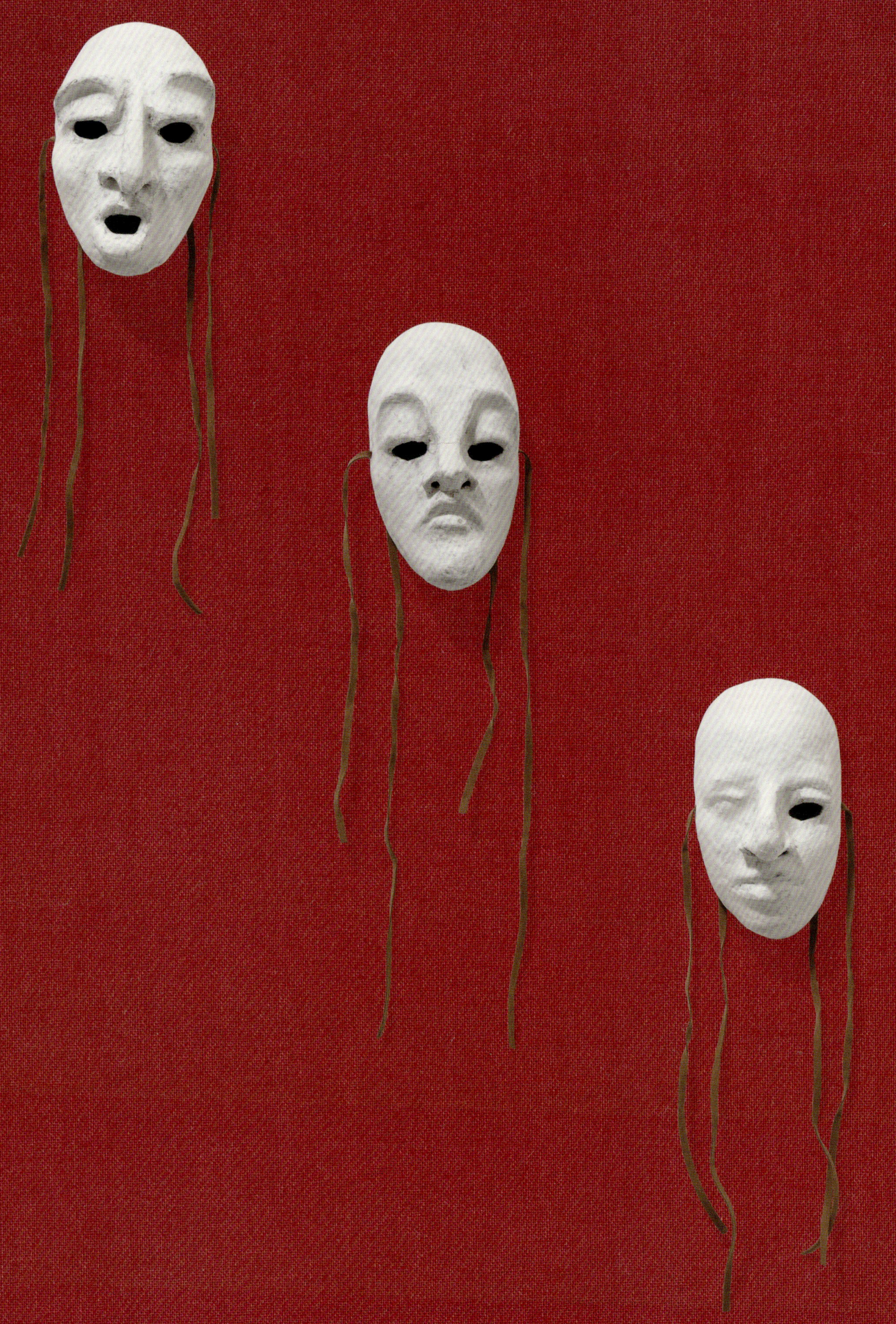

Broke People's Baroque Peoples' Theater, 2011–15. L: *Fire Devil*, *Lady Murasaki MacBeth*, and *Old Fairy* masks, all 2012, papier-mâché, plaster, and leather, various dimensions; R: score

I, Object

Alexandro Segade

Malik Gaines

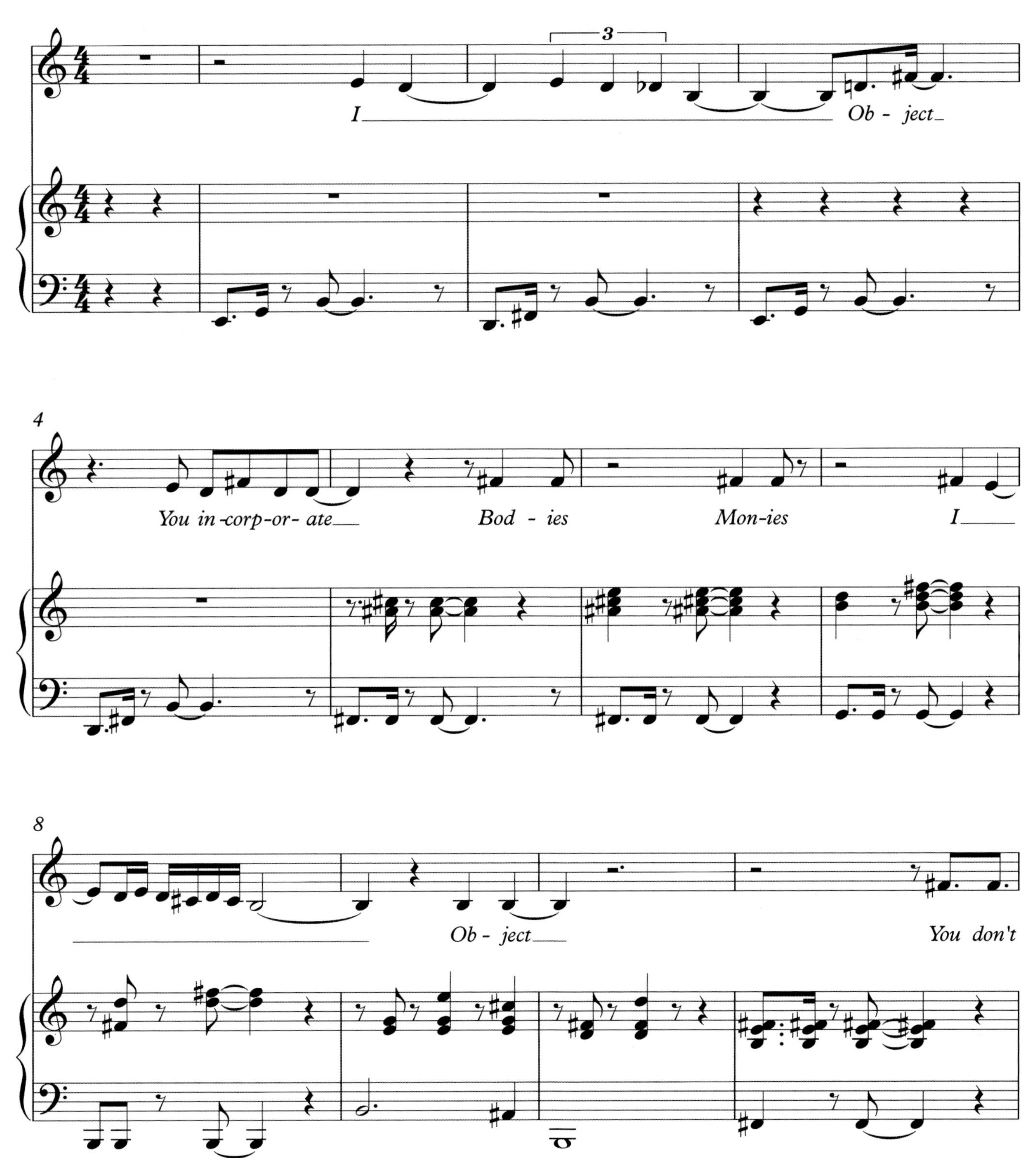

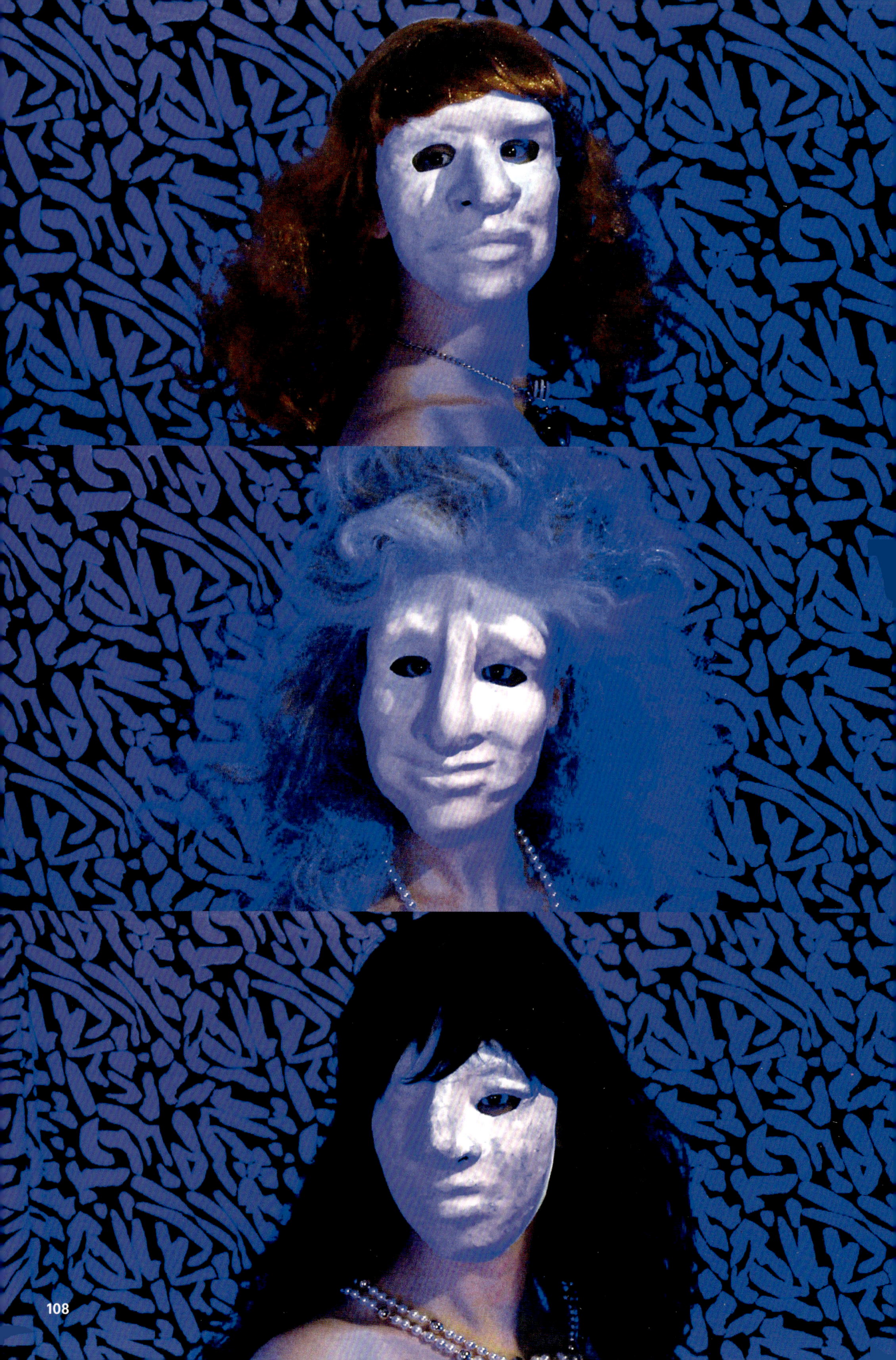

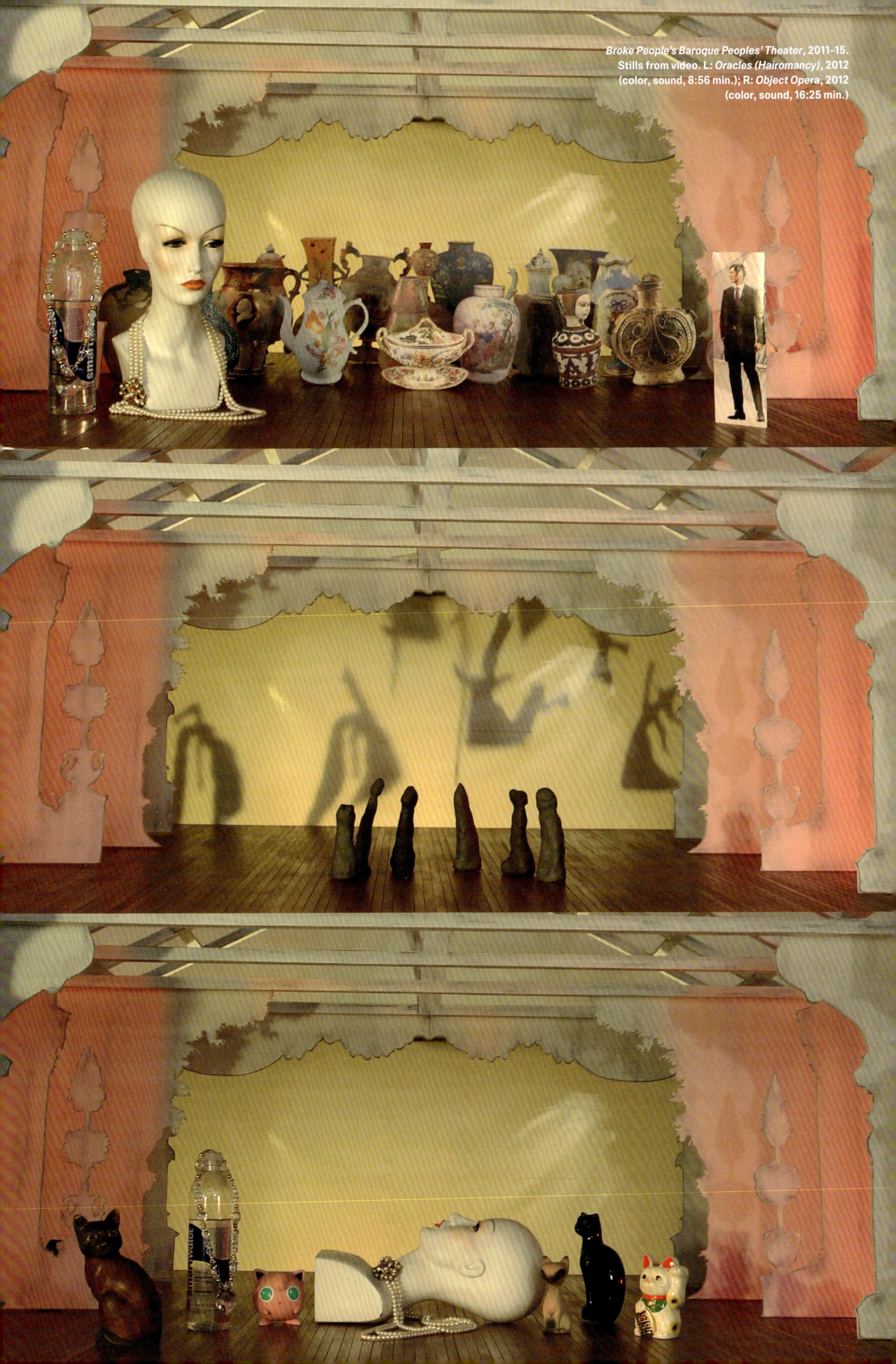

Broke People's Baroque Peoples' Theater, 2011–15. Stills from video. L: *Oracles (Hairomancy)*, 2012 (color, sound, 8:56 min.); R: *Object Opera*, 2012 (color, sound, 16:25 min.)

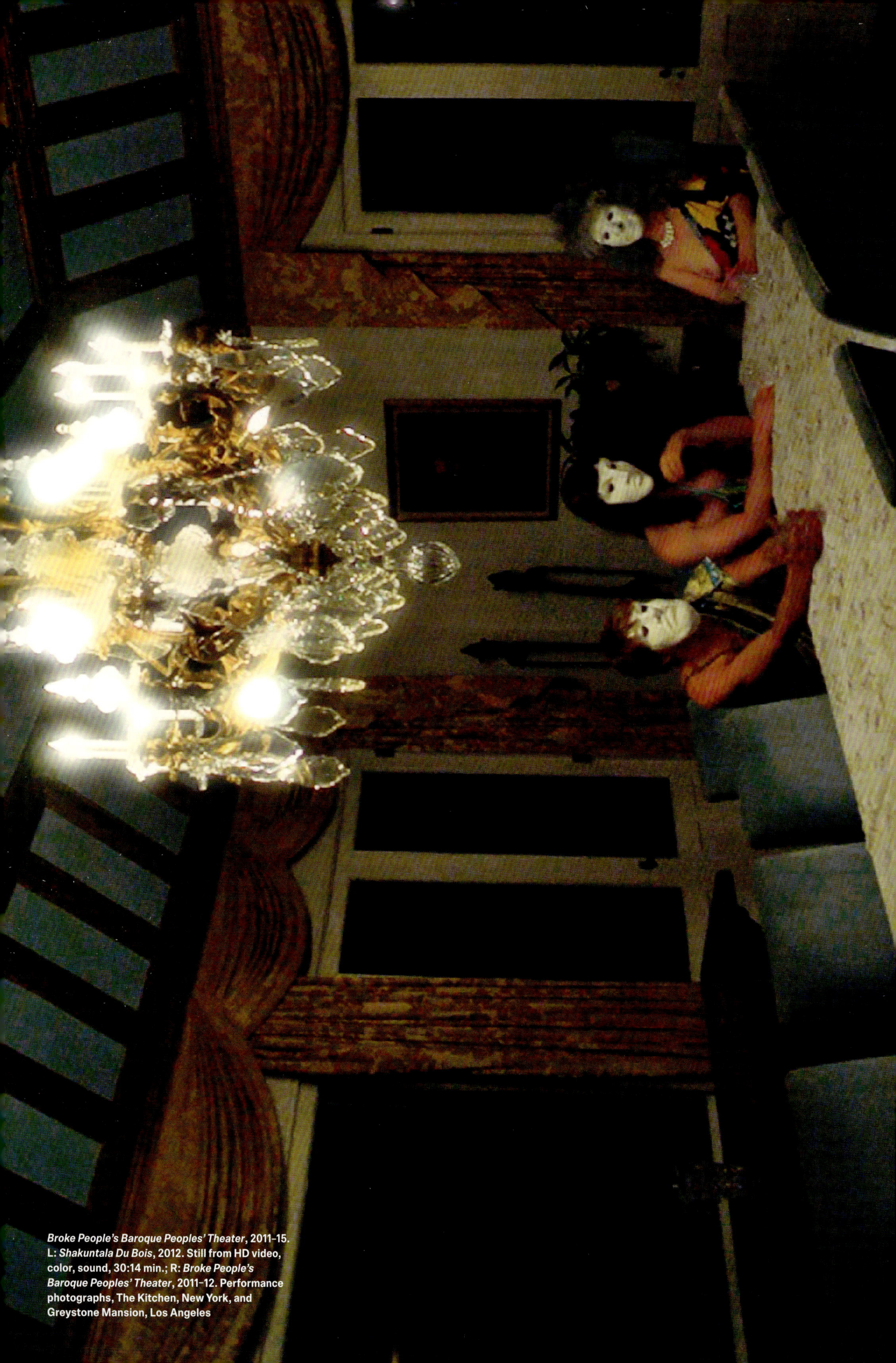

Broke People's Baroque Peoples' Theater, 2011–15. L: *Shakuntala Du Bois*, 2012. Still from HD video, color, sound, 30:14 min.; R: *Broke People's Baroque Peoples' Theater*, 2011–12. Performance photographs, The Kitchen, New York, and Greystone Mansion, Los Angeles

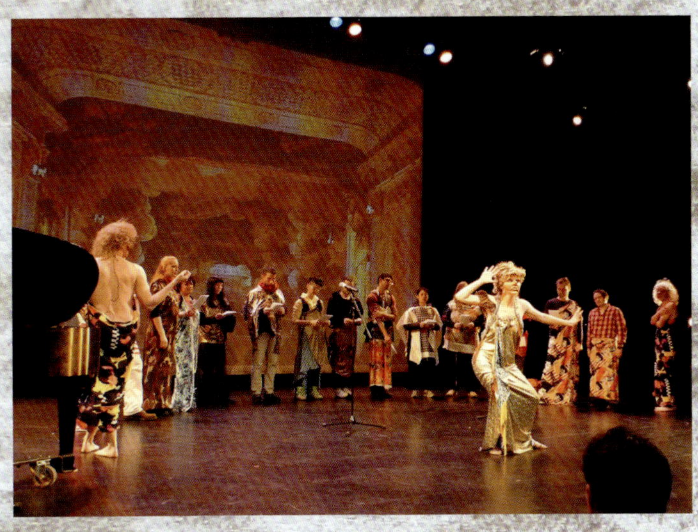

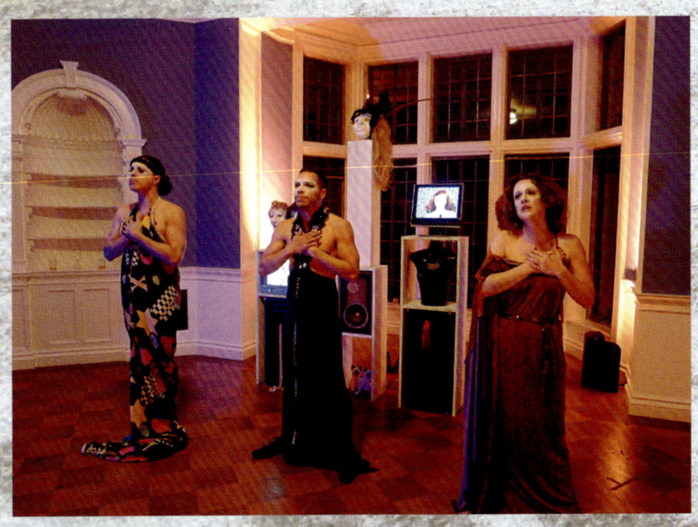

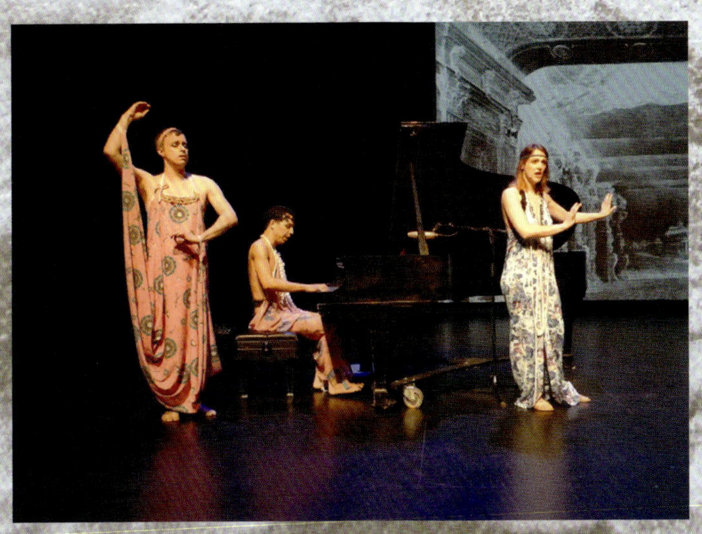

M: You're obsessed with identity.

A: That's why you can't make a living.

J: Be more creative this time.

M: Who has time to be creative?

A: Ouch.

J: I didn't mean to hurt you.

M: No, I hurt my knee. Turn around in circles.

A: What other people think of me is none of my business.

J: I'm bad for business! Relax your body.

PART THREE: Hours of the Day

M: We'd like to invite you to place your body somewhere on the stage or in the aisles. Whichever feels more right. Trust your instincts.

A: You might want to bring your valuables with you, not everyone here is trustworthy.

J: Quickly now, we don't have much time. Go to some part of the room you find yourself inexplicably attracted to.

REPEAT X3

M: Give yourself a little space if you can. Imagine a typical workday. Whatever that means to you. Think about what you do with your body during that day. The positions you take, the objects you manipulate, the things that go in and out of your body, the people you interact with. For each hour of the day, demonstrate your technique of the body.

A: If you are sleeping, sleep.

J: If you are scrubbing, scrub.

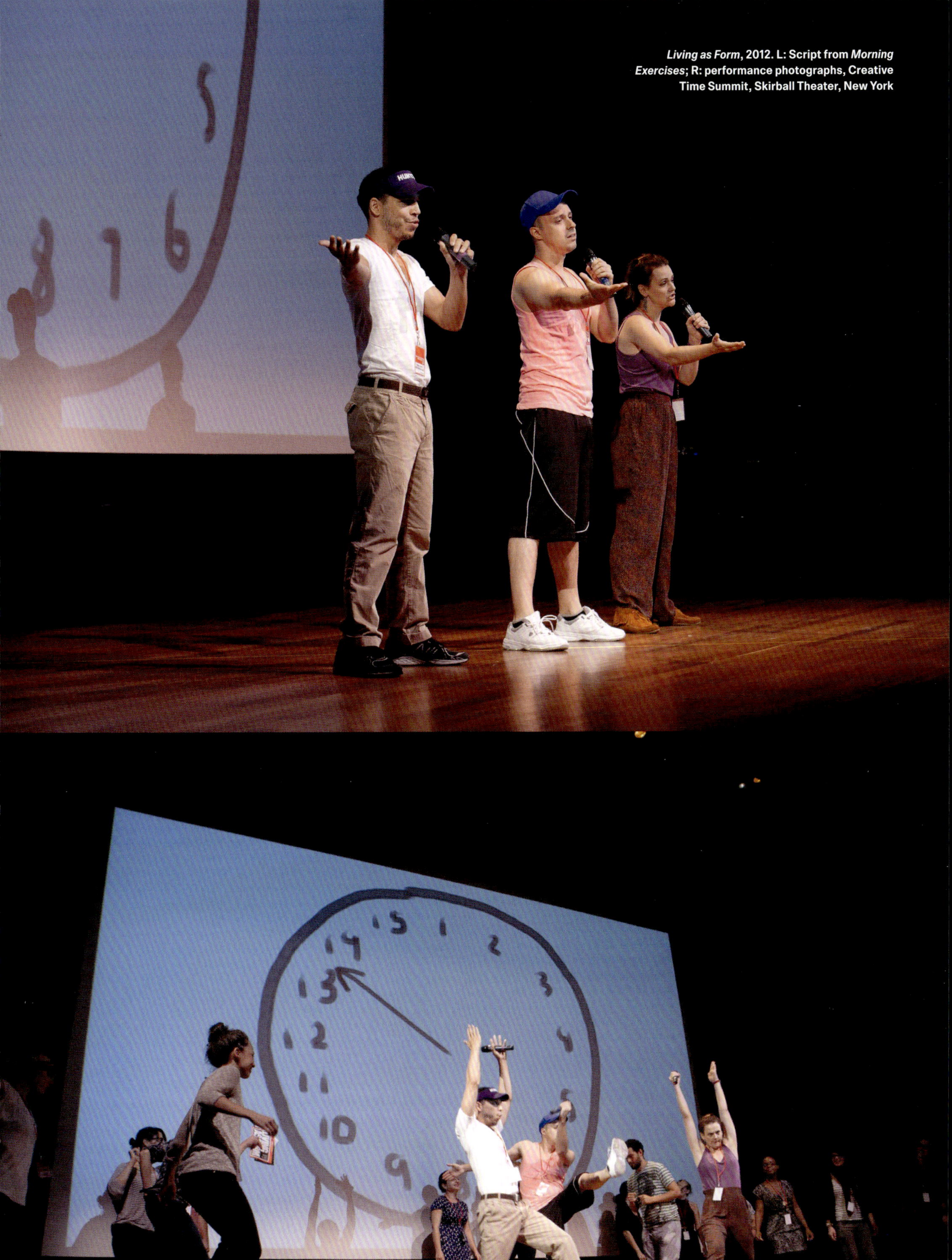
Living as Form, 2012. L: Script from *Morning Exercises*; R: performance photographs, Creative Time Summit, Skirball Theater, New York

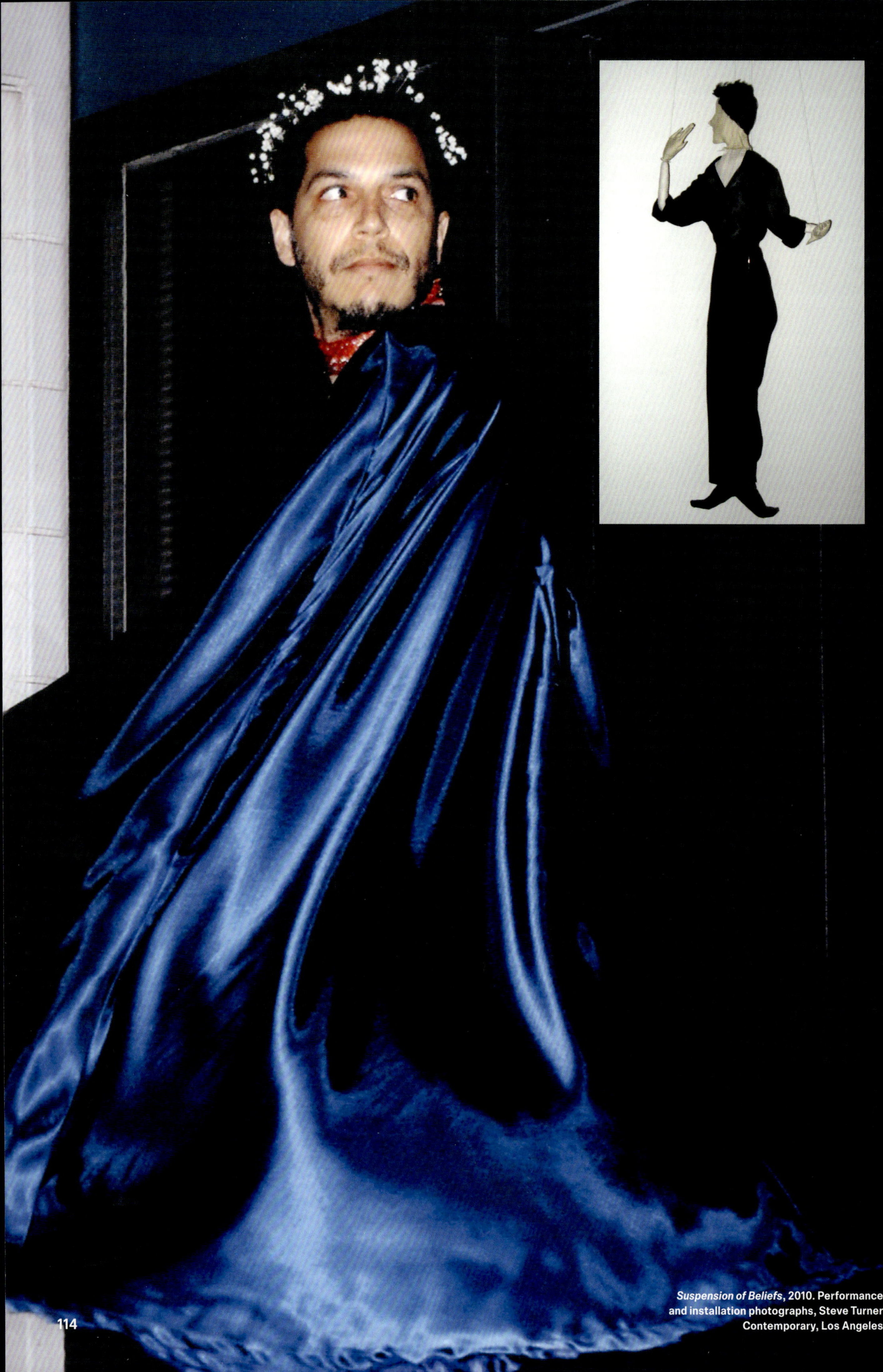

Suspension of Beliefs, 2010. Performance and installation photographs, Steve Turner Contemporary, Los Angeles

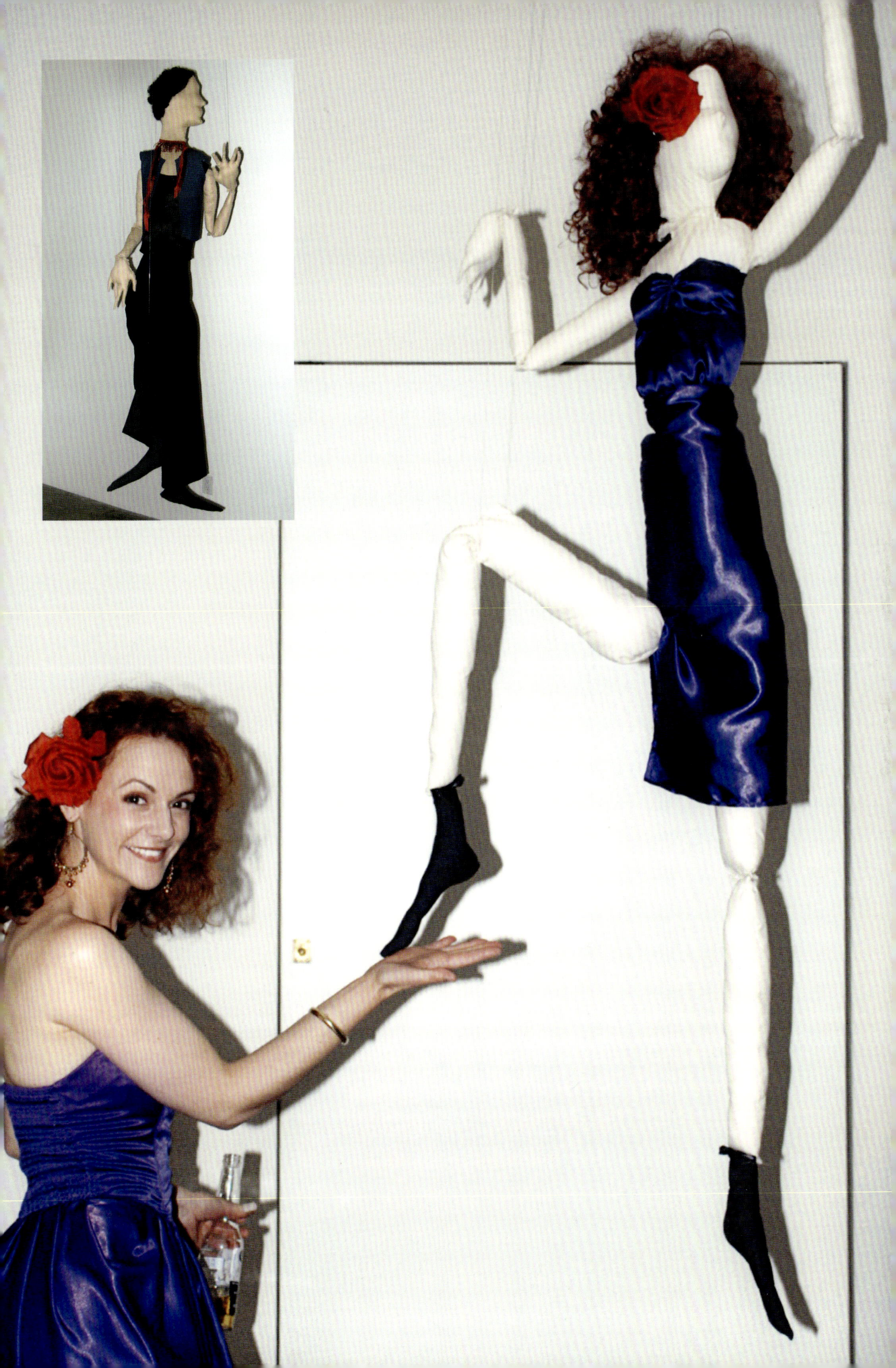

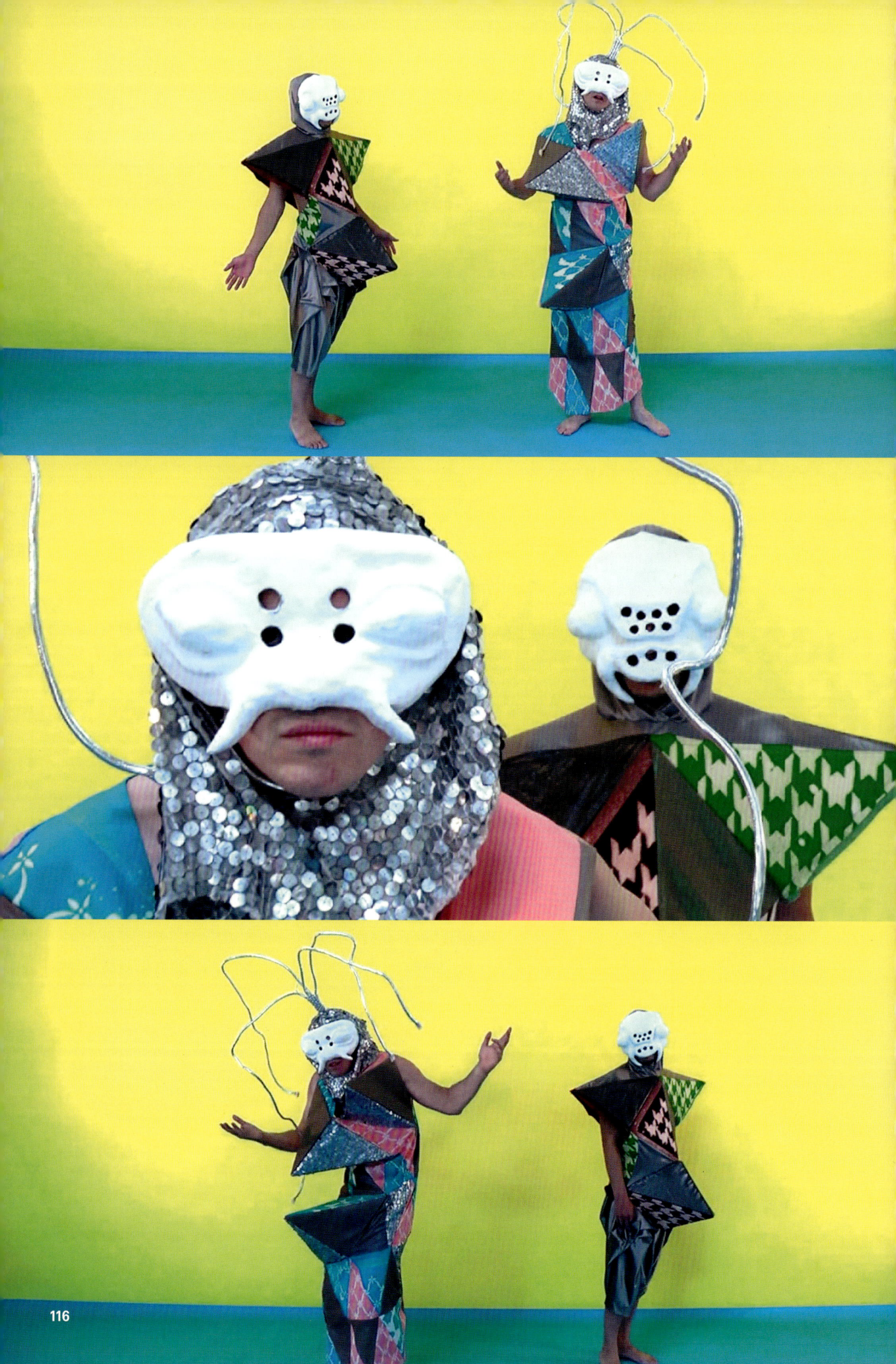

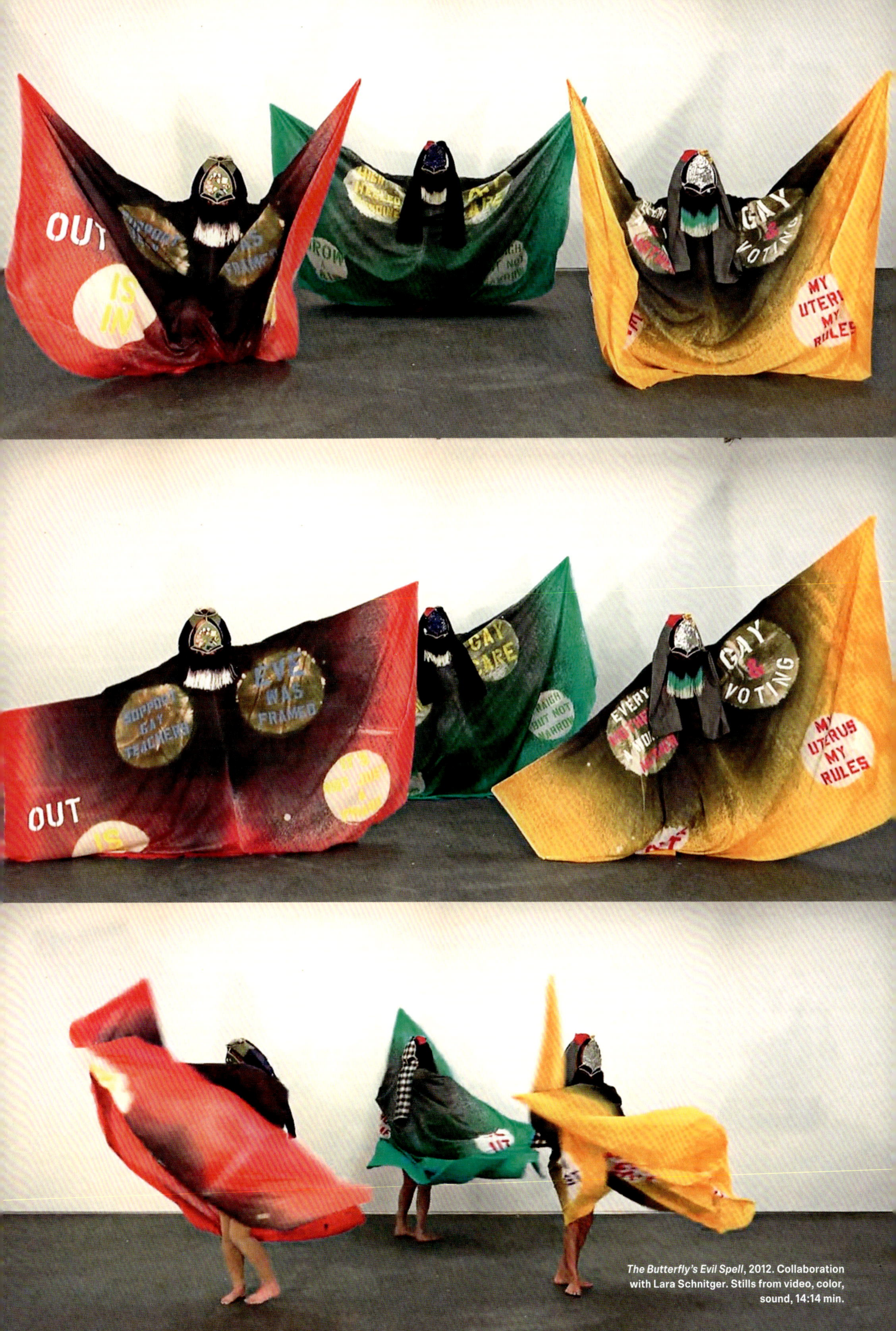

The Butterfly's Evil Spell, 2012. Collaboration with Lara Schnitger. Stills from video, color, sound, 14:14 min.

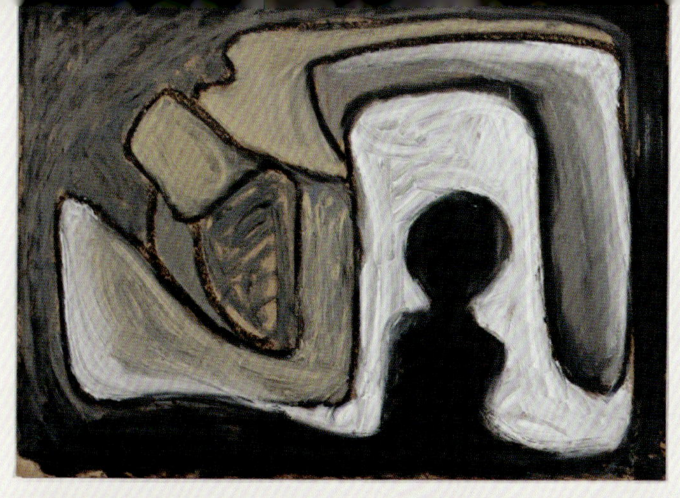

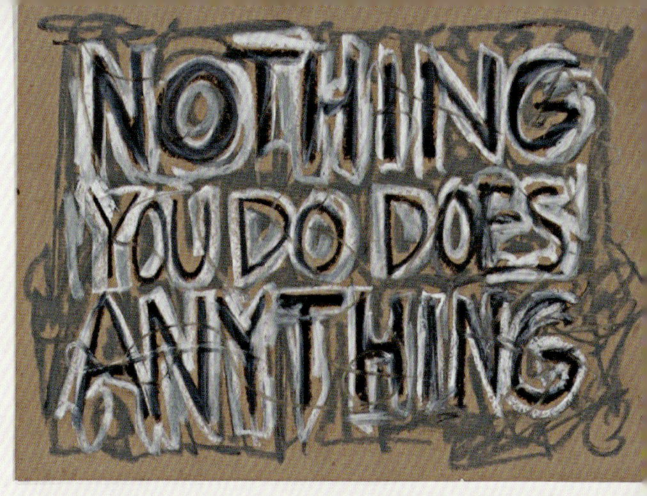

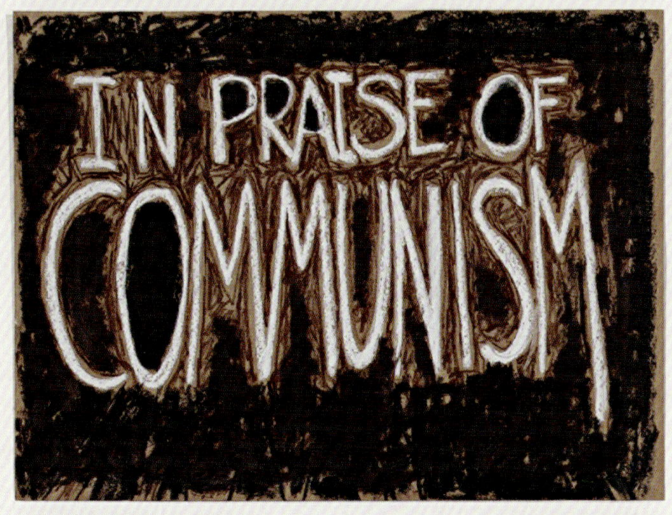

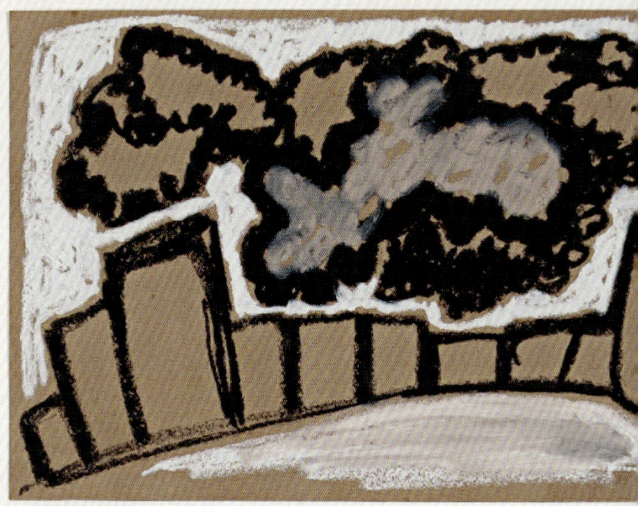

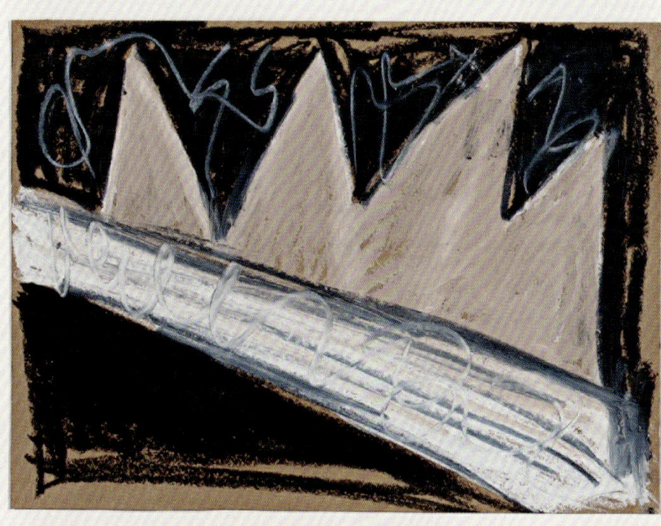

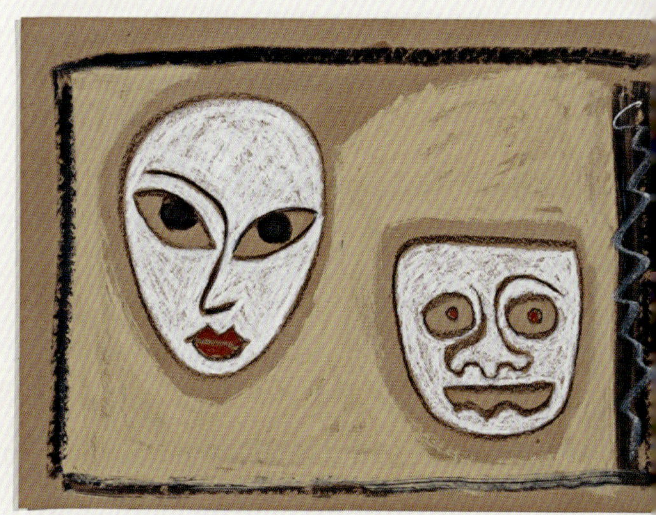

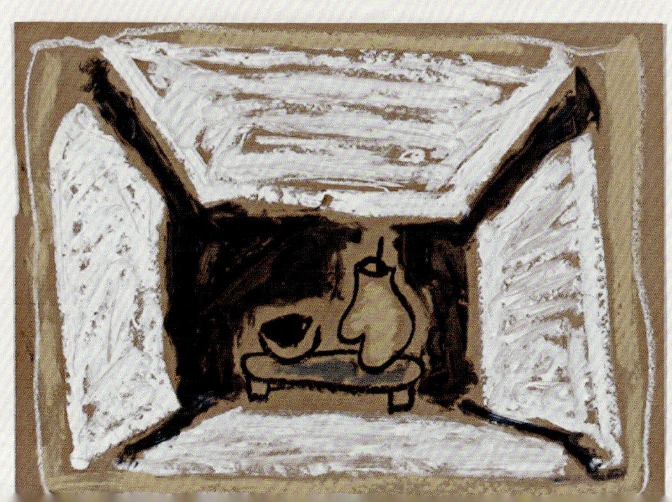

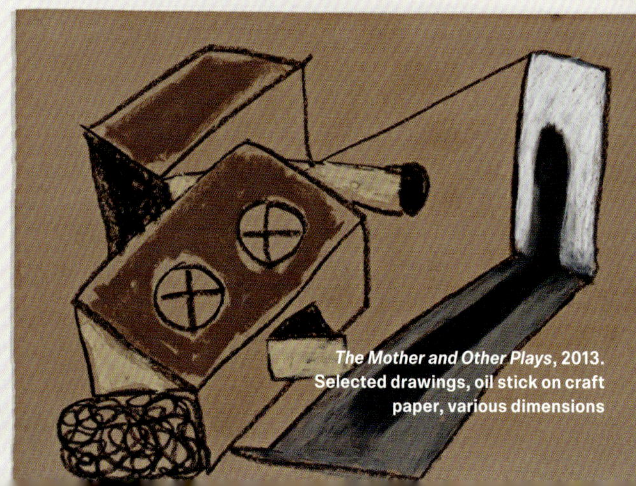

***The Mother and Other Plays*, 2013. Selected drawings, oil stick on craft paper, various dimensions**

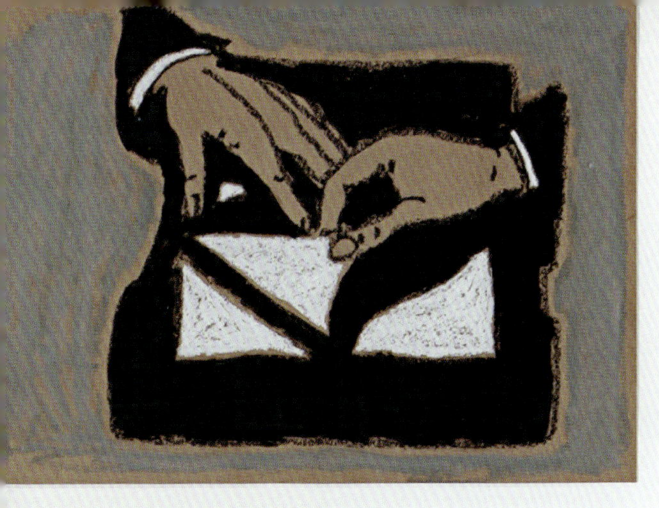

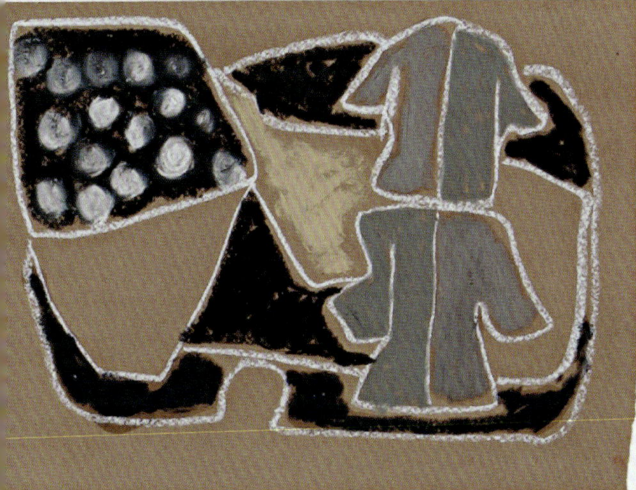
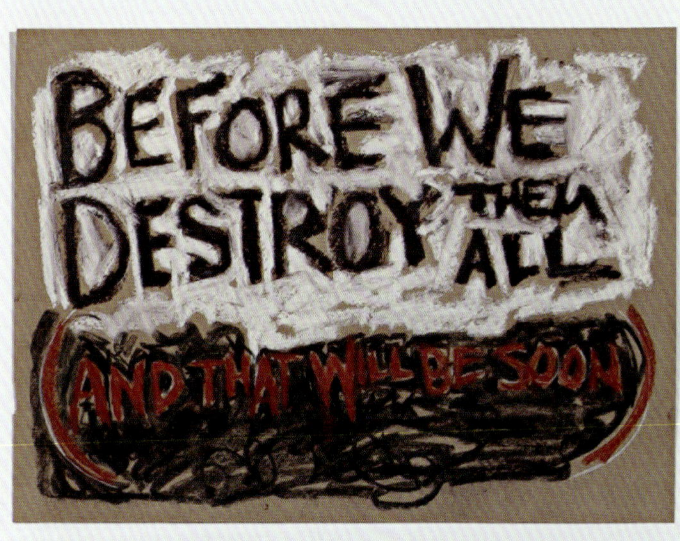
BEFORE WE DESTROY THEM ALL
(AND THAT WILL BE SOON)
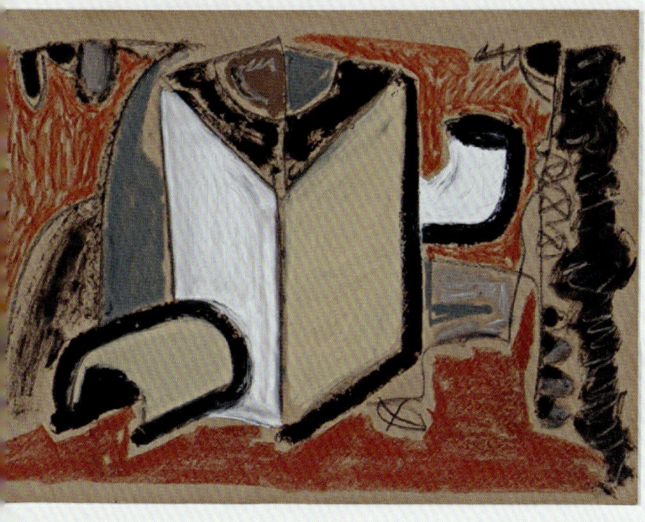
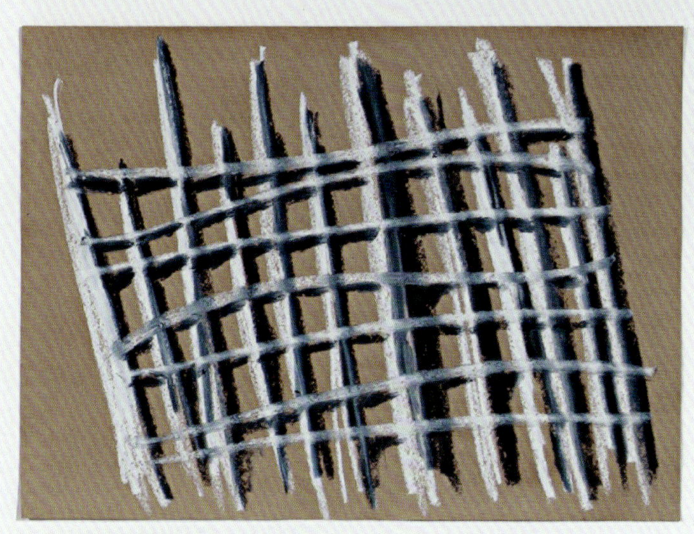
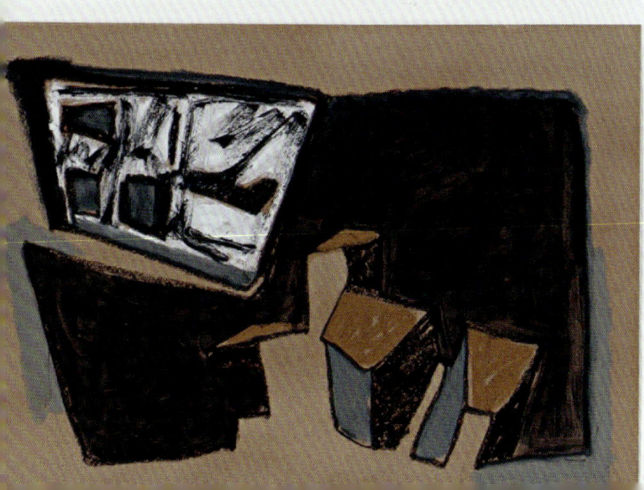
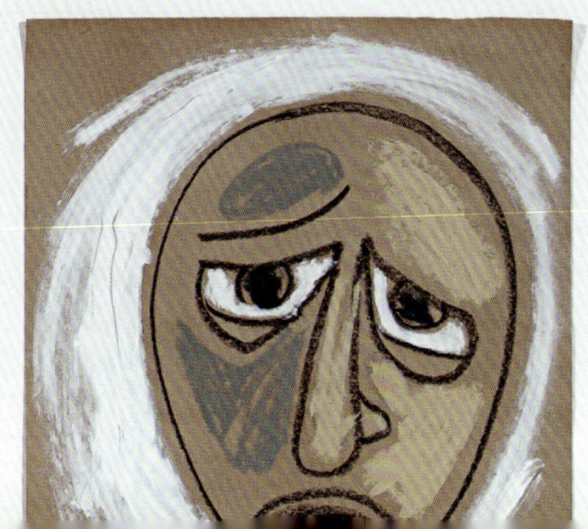

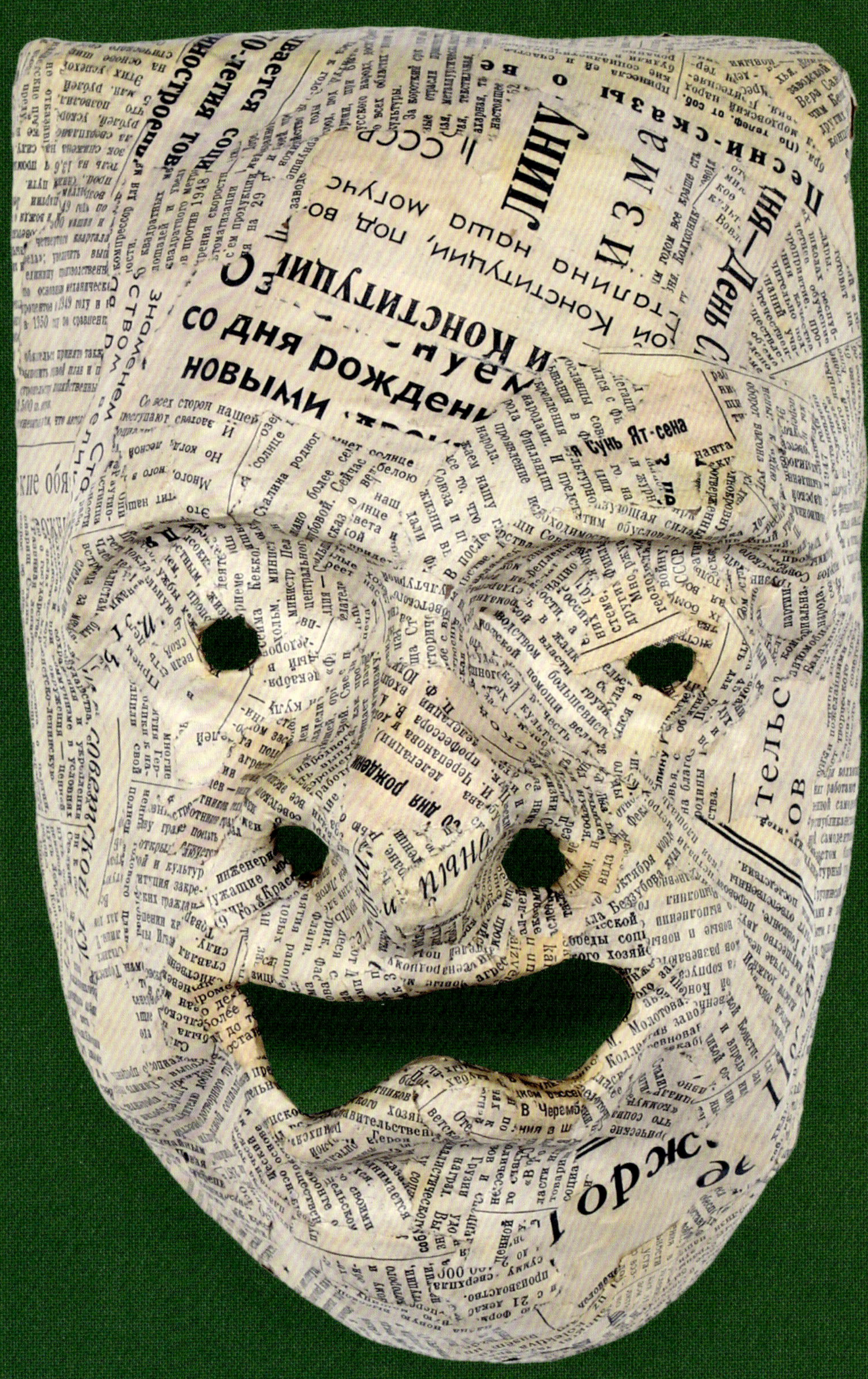
со дня рожден
новыми
Сунь Ят-сена

L: *Peasant*, 2013, papier-mâché, 11 × 6¾ × 5 in. (27.9 × 17.2 × 12.7 cm); R: *The Mother and Other Plays*, 2014. Performance photographs, Whitney Museum of American Art, New York

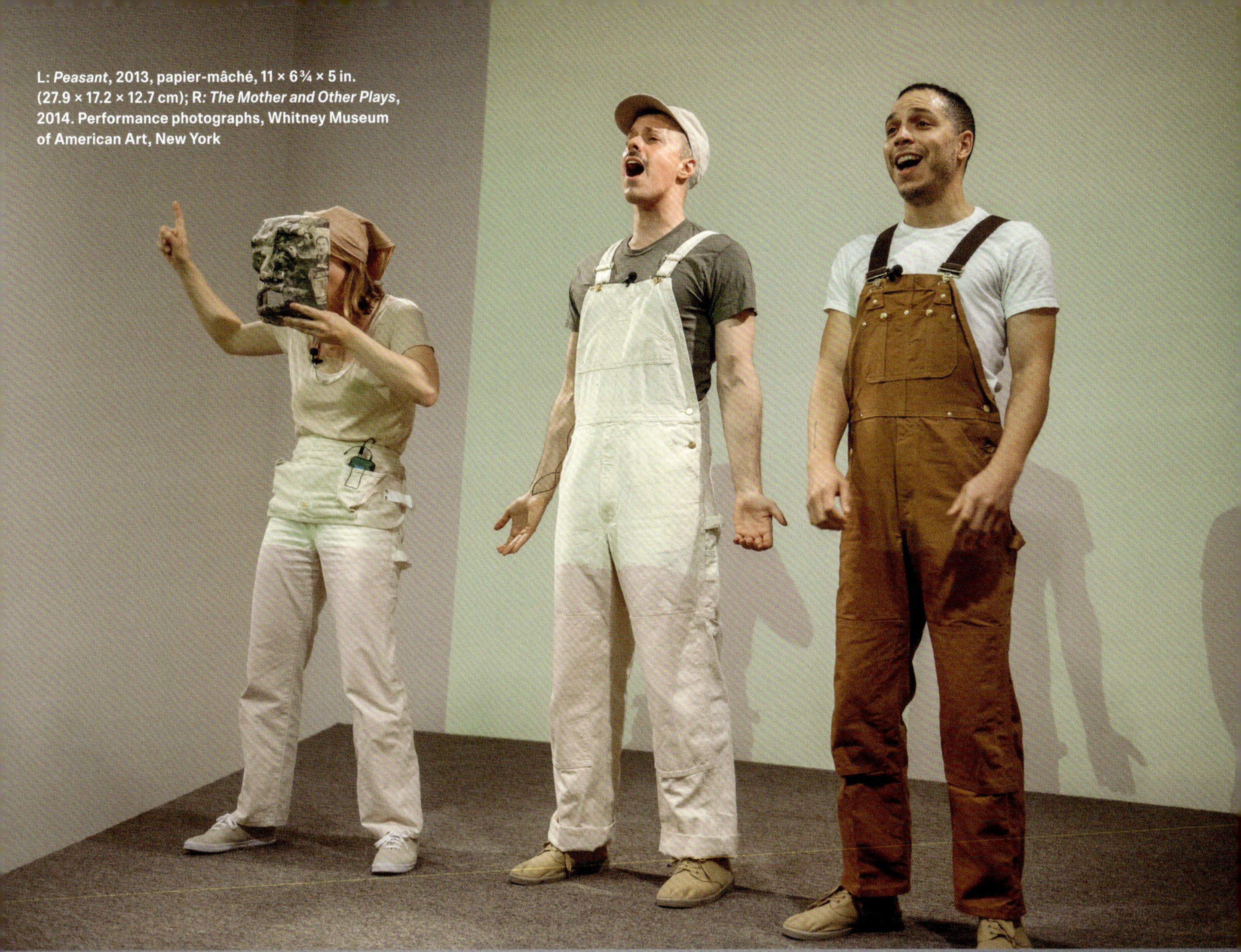

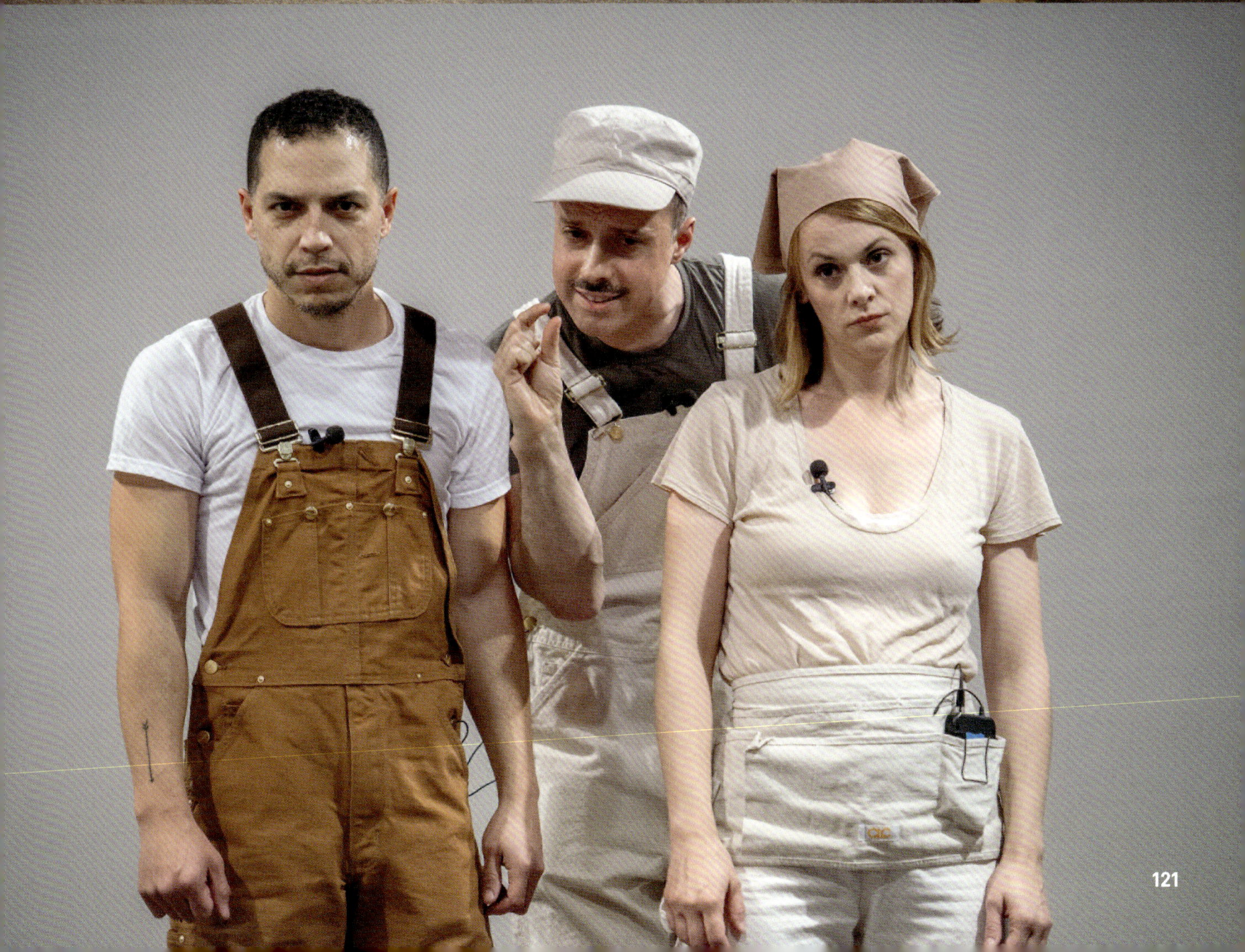

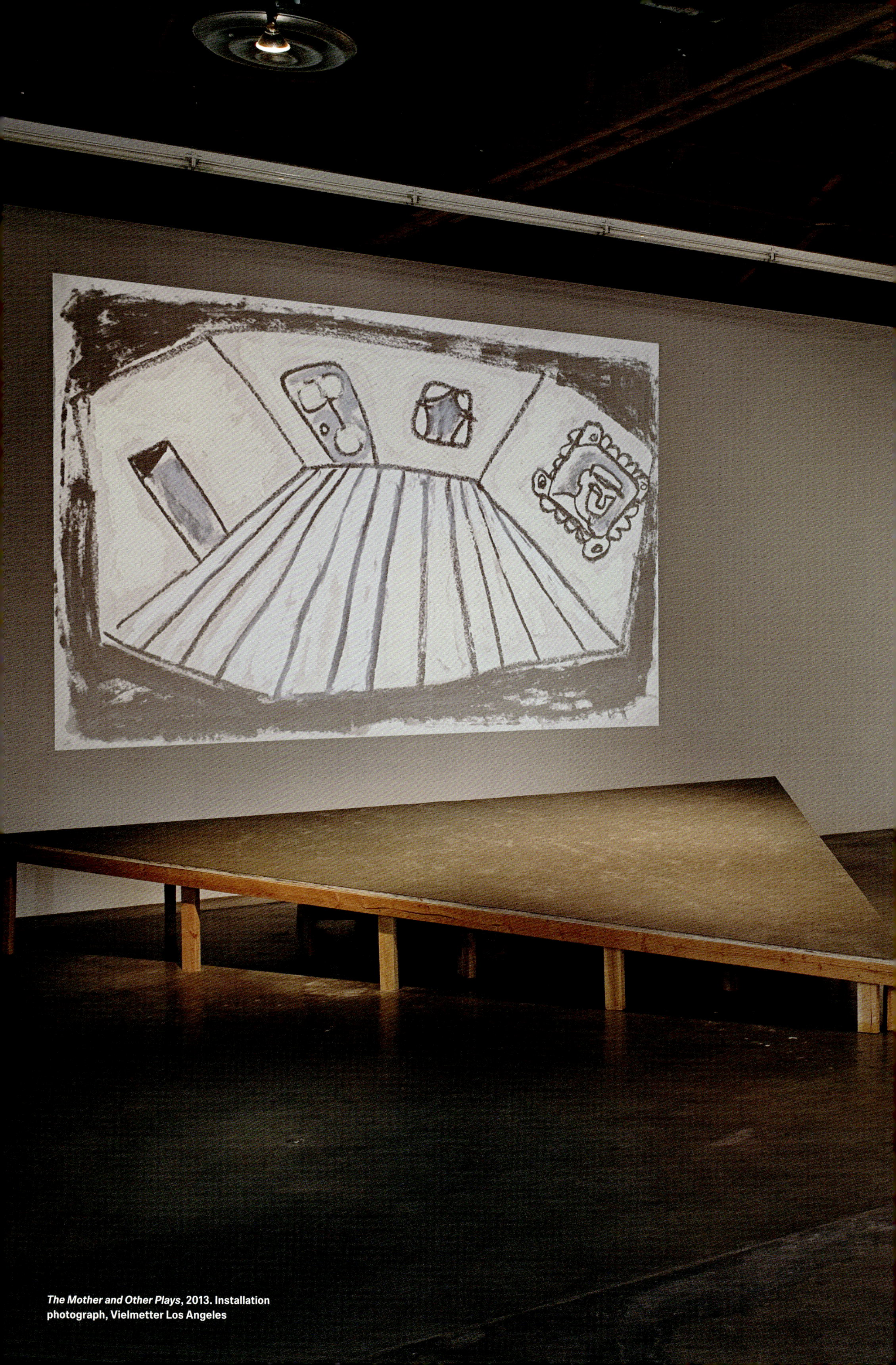

The Mother and Other Plays, 2013. Installation photograph, Vielmetter Los Angeles

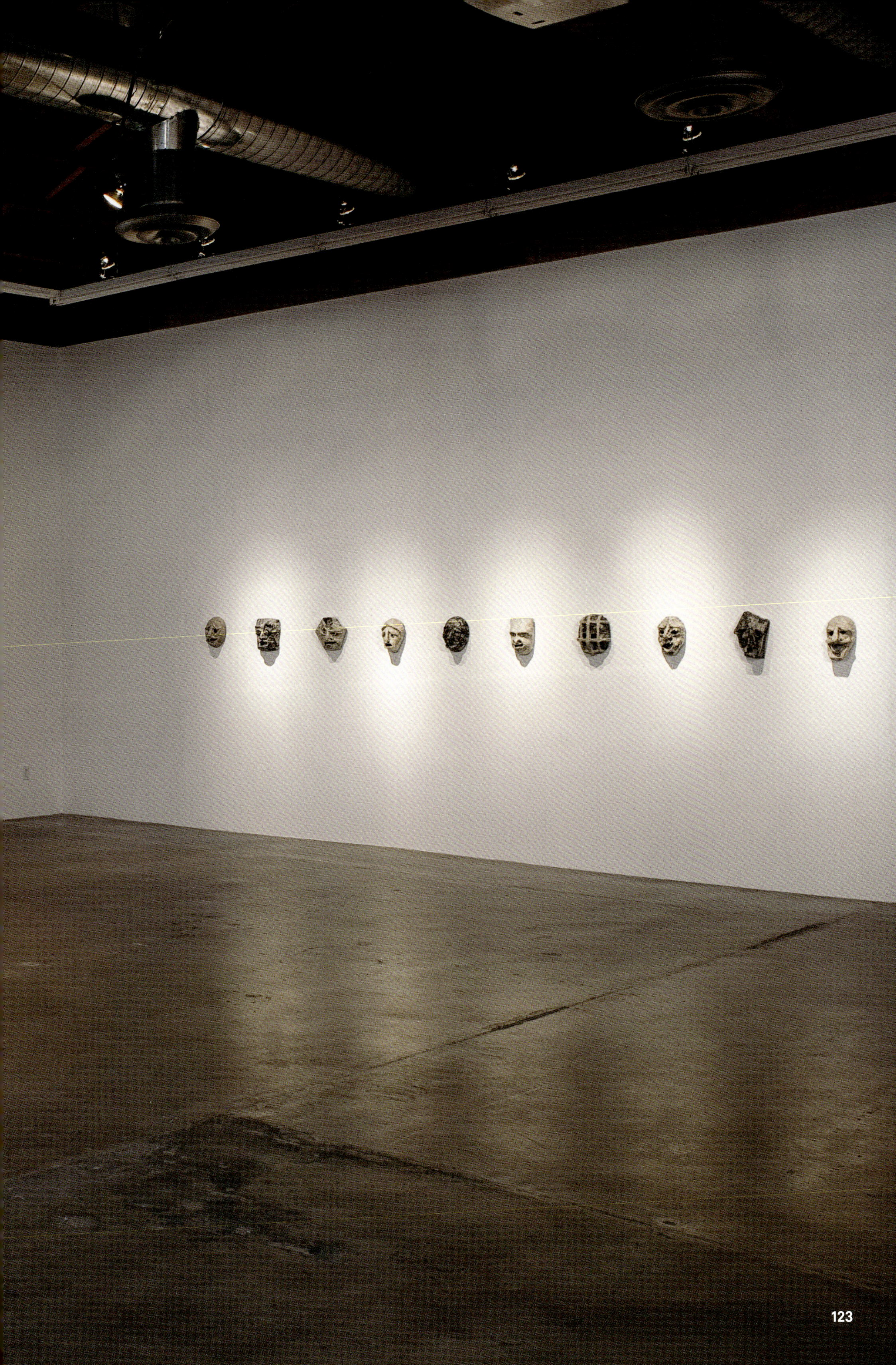

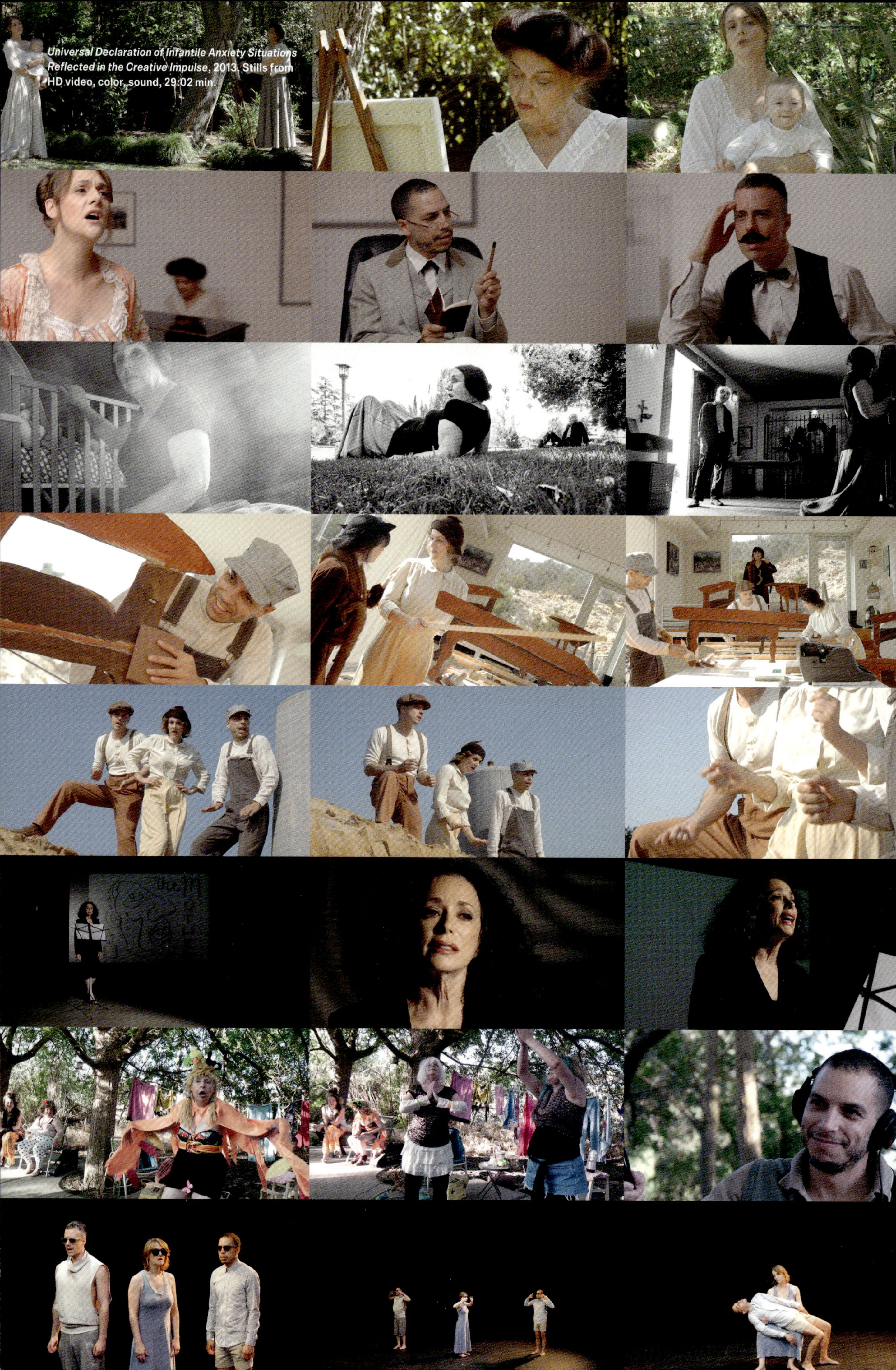

Universal Declaration of Infantile Anxiety Situations Reflected in the Creative Impulse, 2013. Stills from HD video, color, sound, 29:02 min.

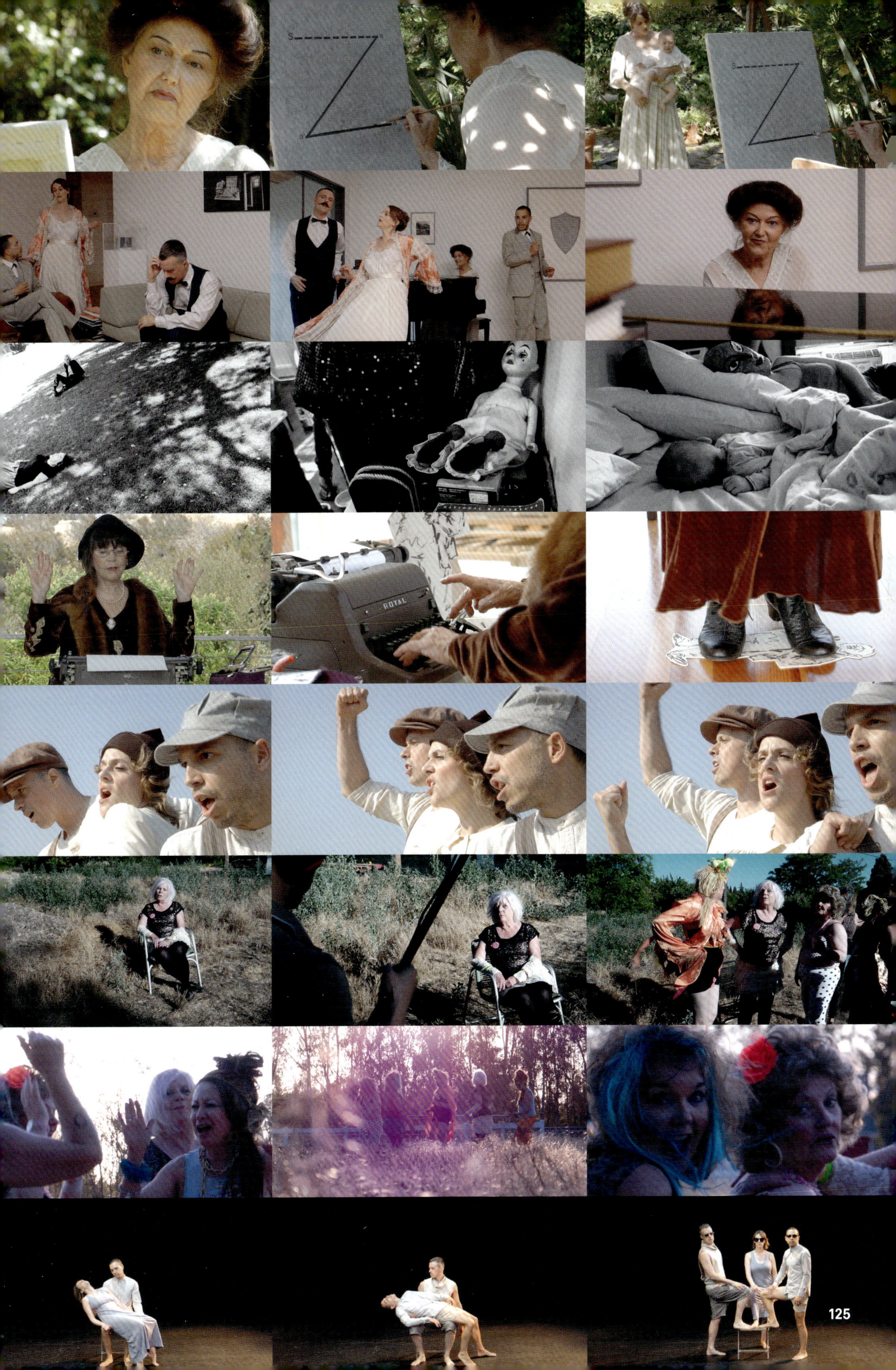

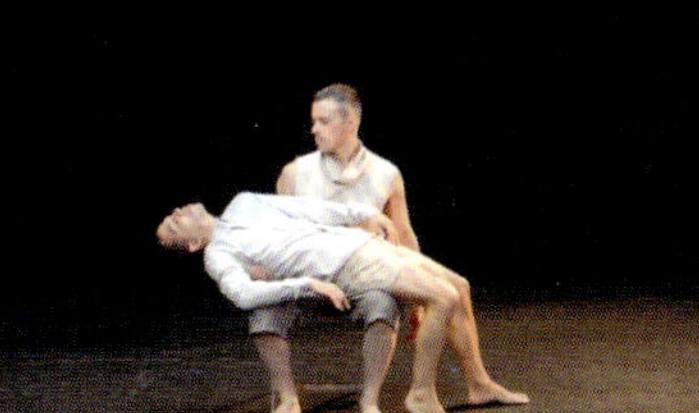
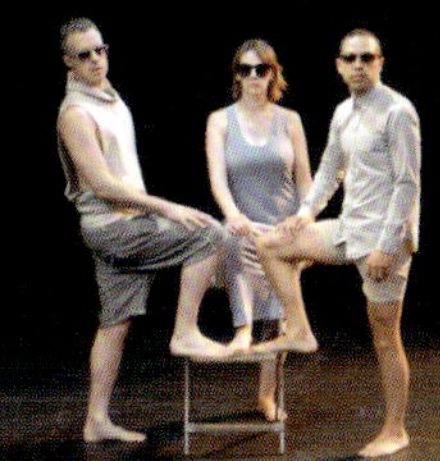

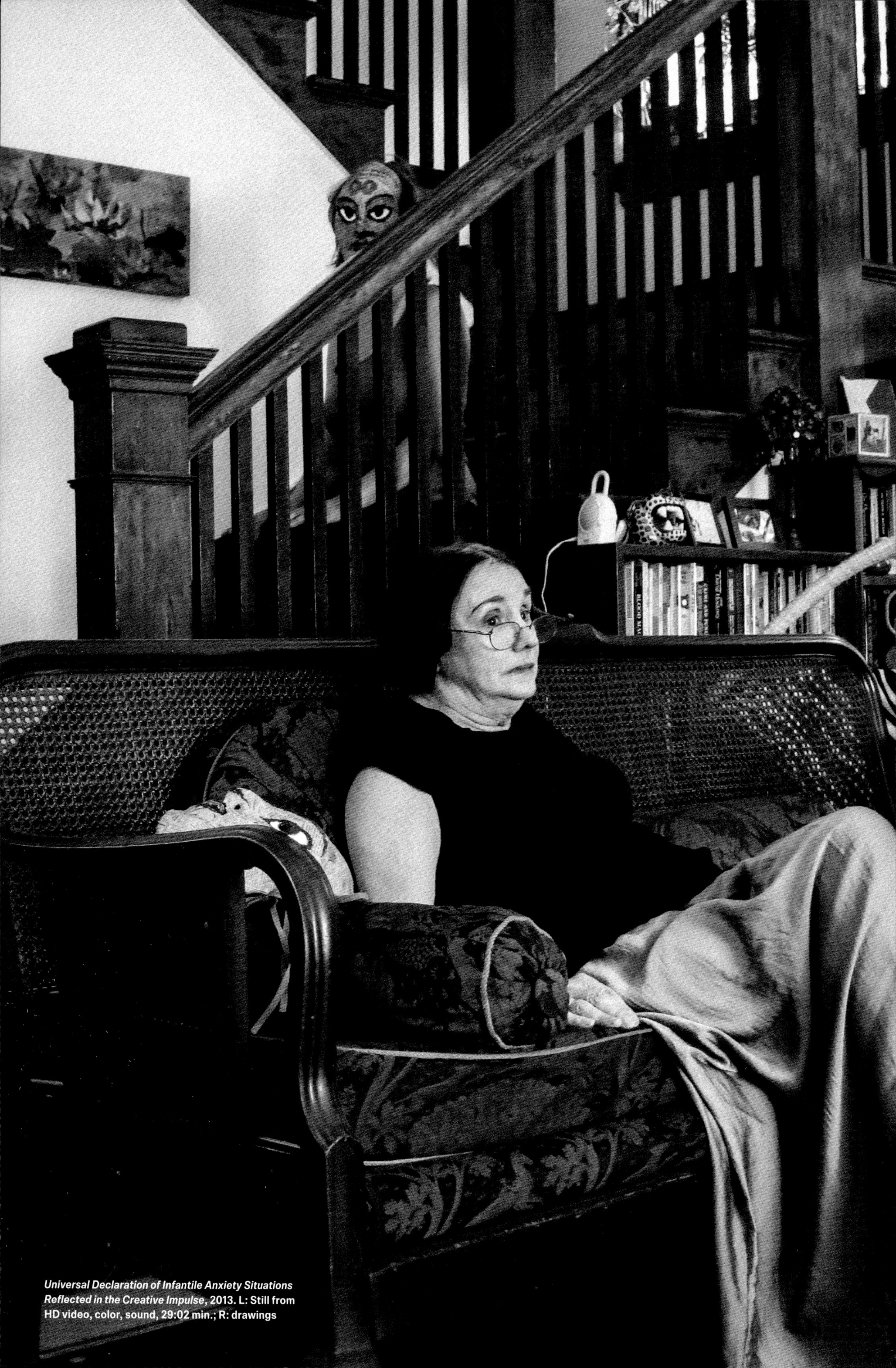

Universal Declaration of Infantile Anxiety Situations Reflected in the Creative Impulse, 2013. L: Still from HD video, color, sound, 29:02 min.; R: drawings

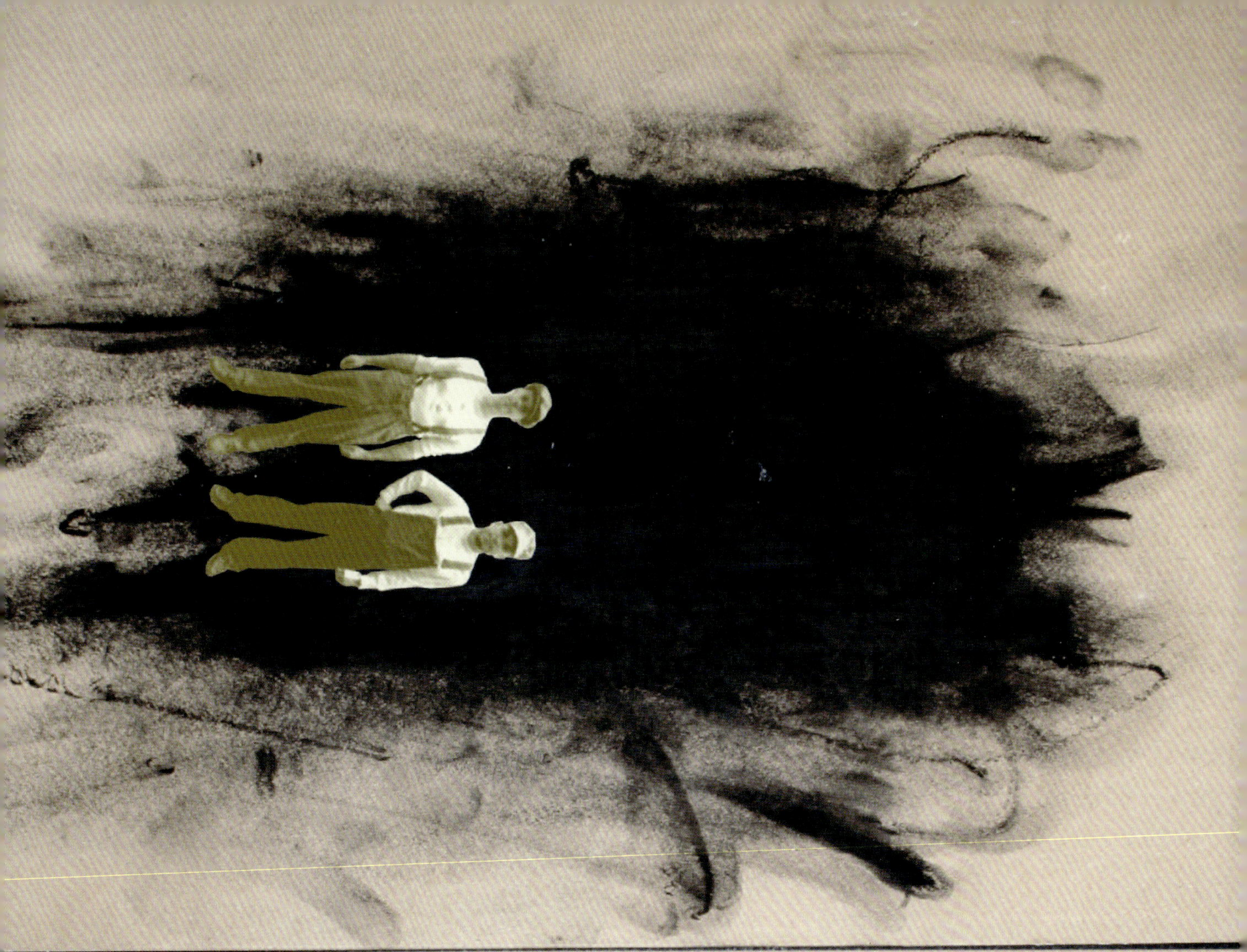

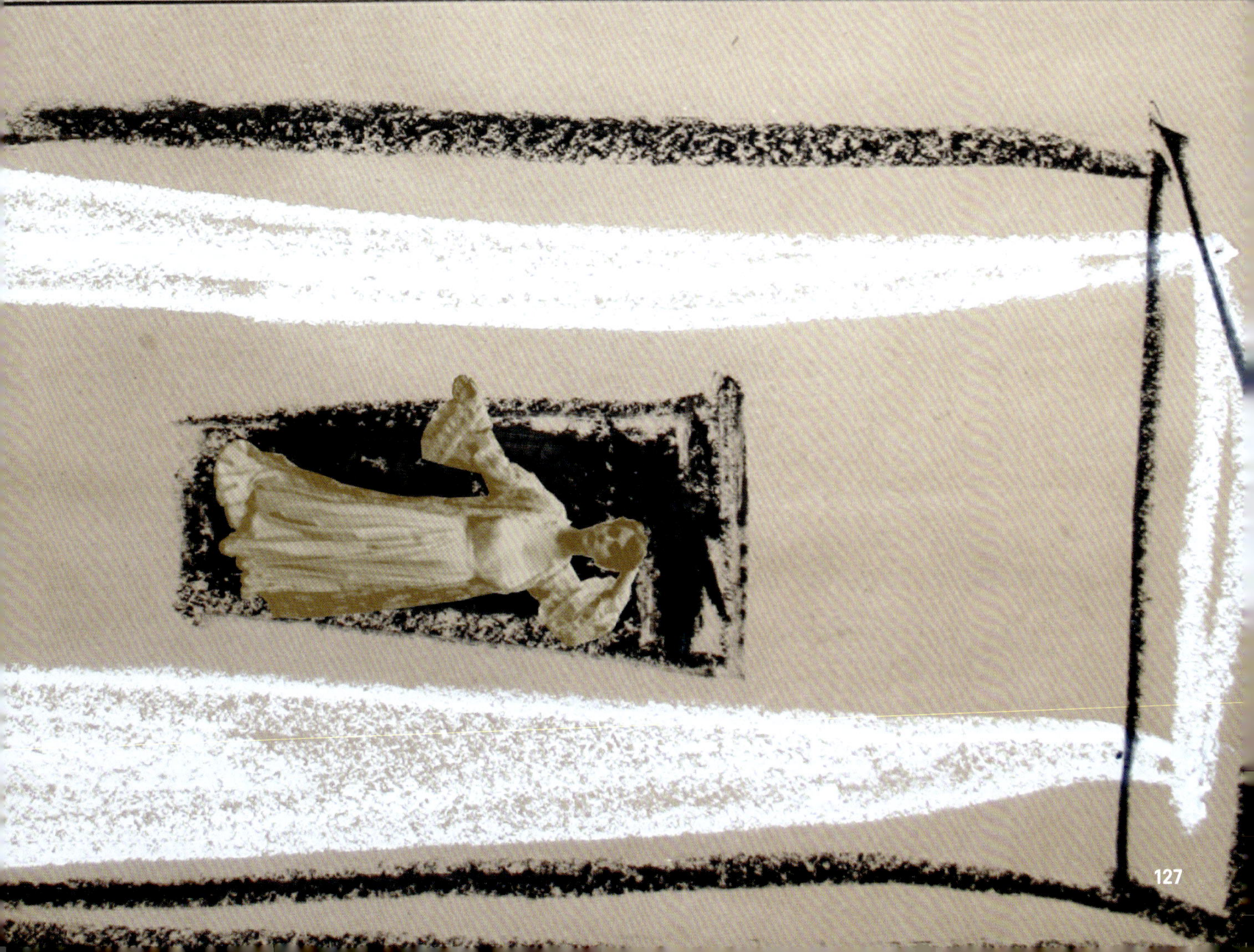

Counterpublicity, 2014. Stills from HD video, color, sound, 11:34 min.

PEDRO
I knew that you were
Republican
I knew you were
Catholic

RACHEL
were you afraid
I'd be
confrontational
with you?

PEDRO
every day I wake up and say
I am going to educate
my community about
my disease

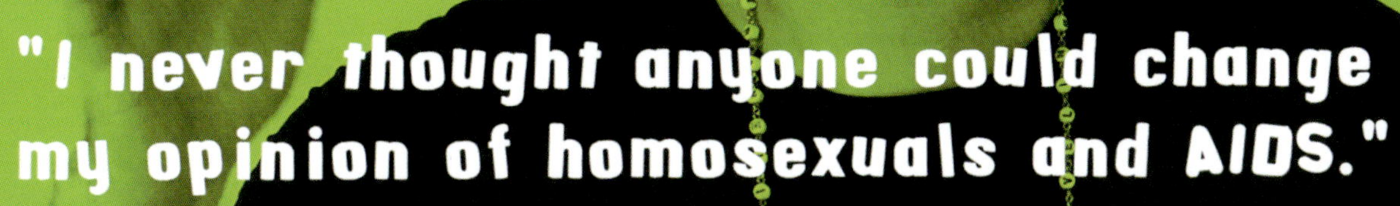

"Because of you I saw the human side of
something that once seemed so unreal to me."

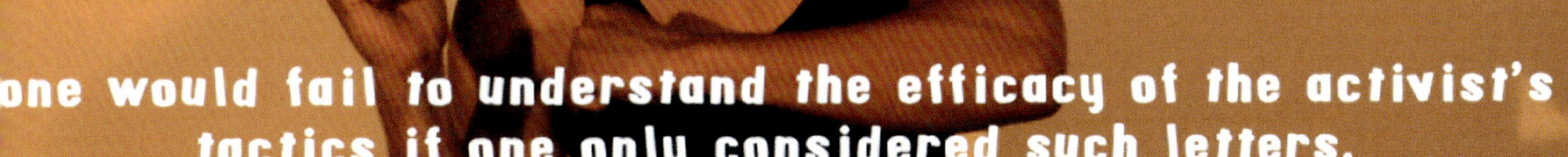

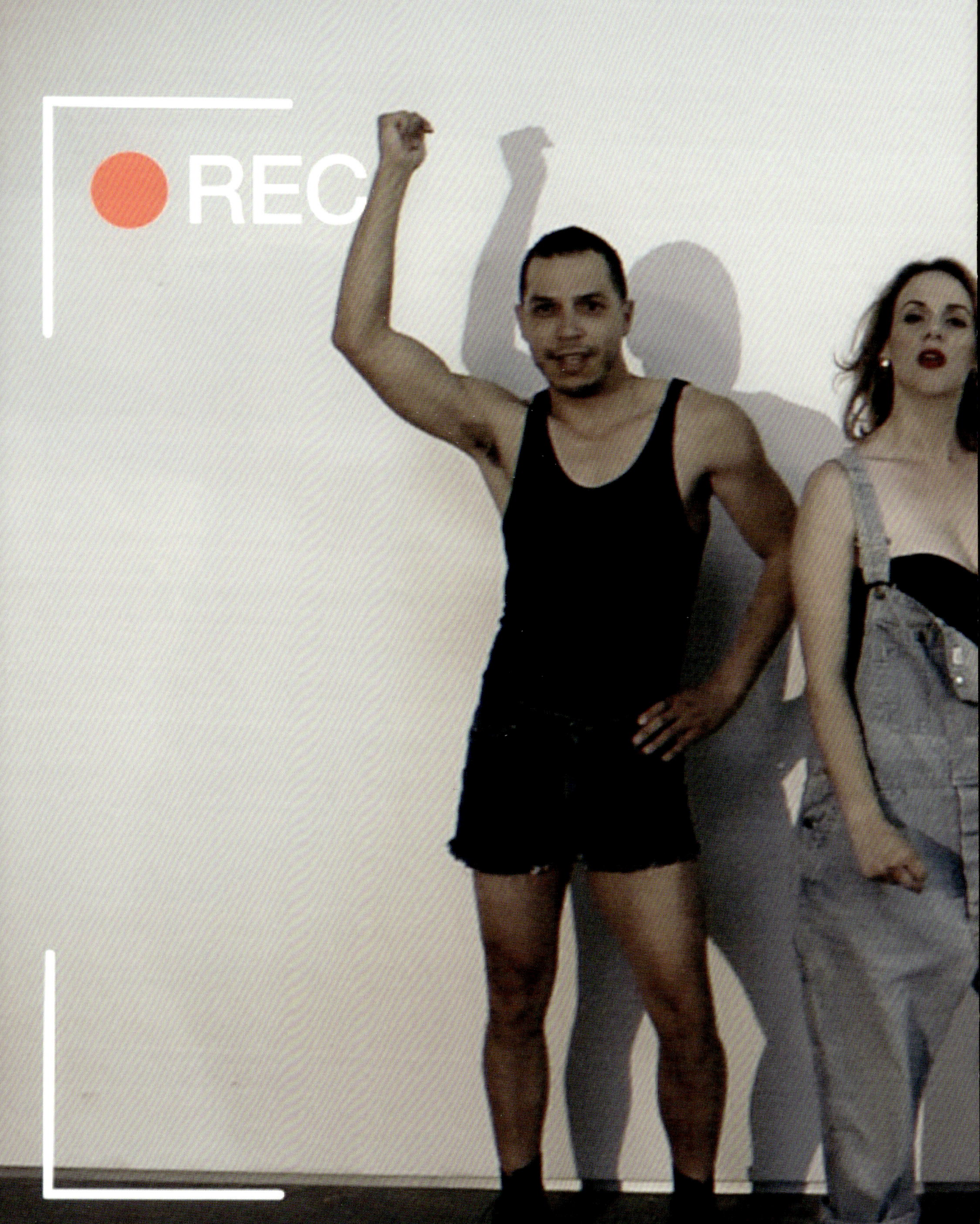
REC

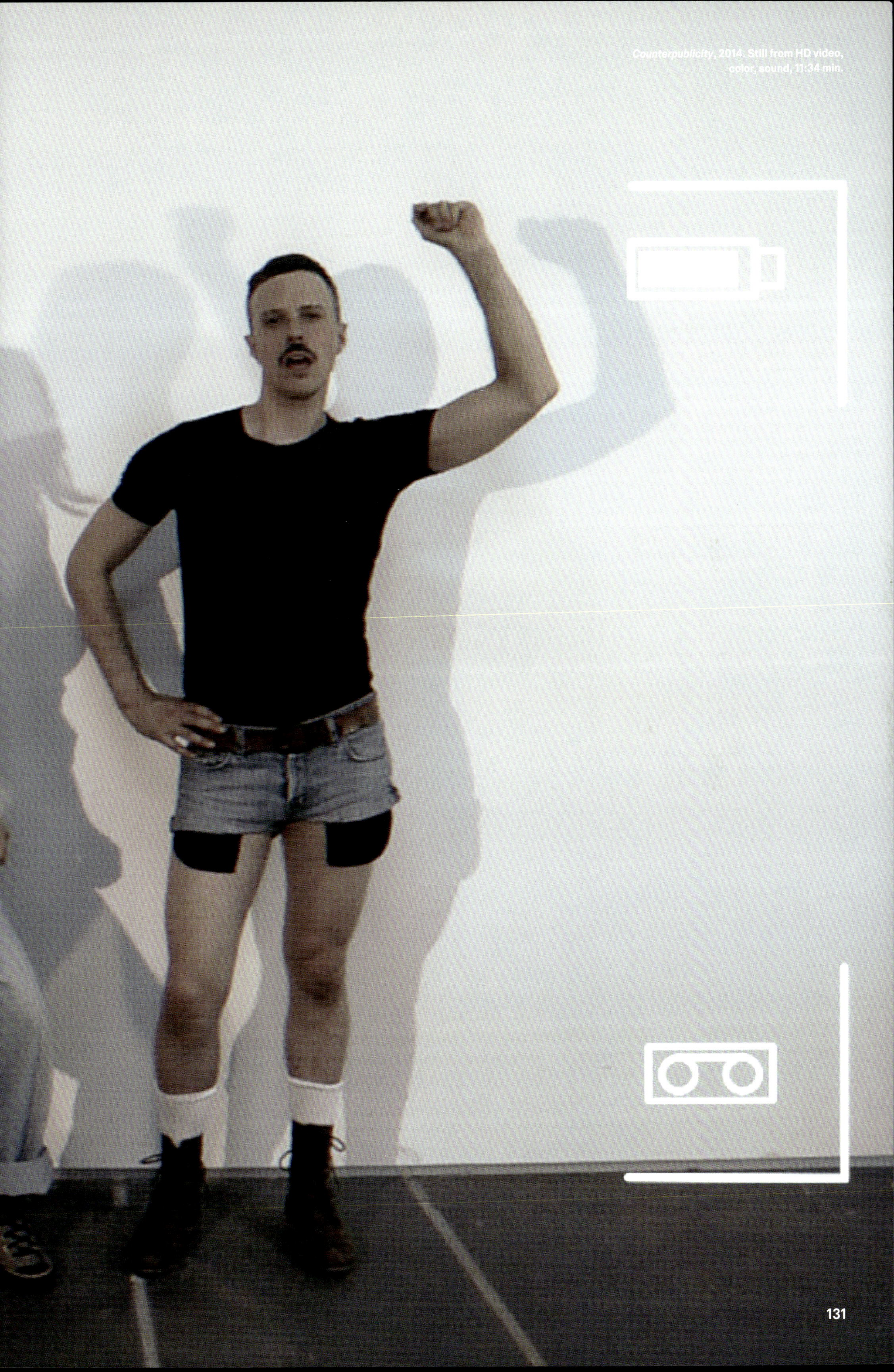

Counterpublicity, 2014. Still from HD video, color, sound, 11:34 min.

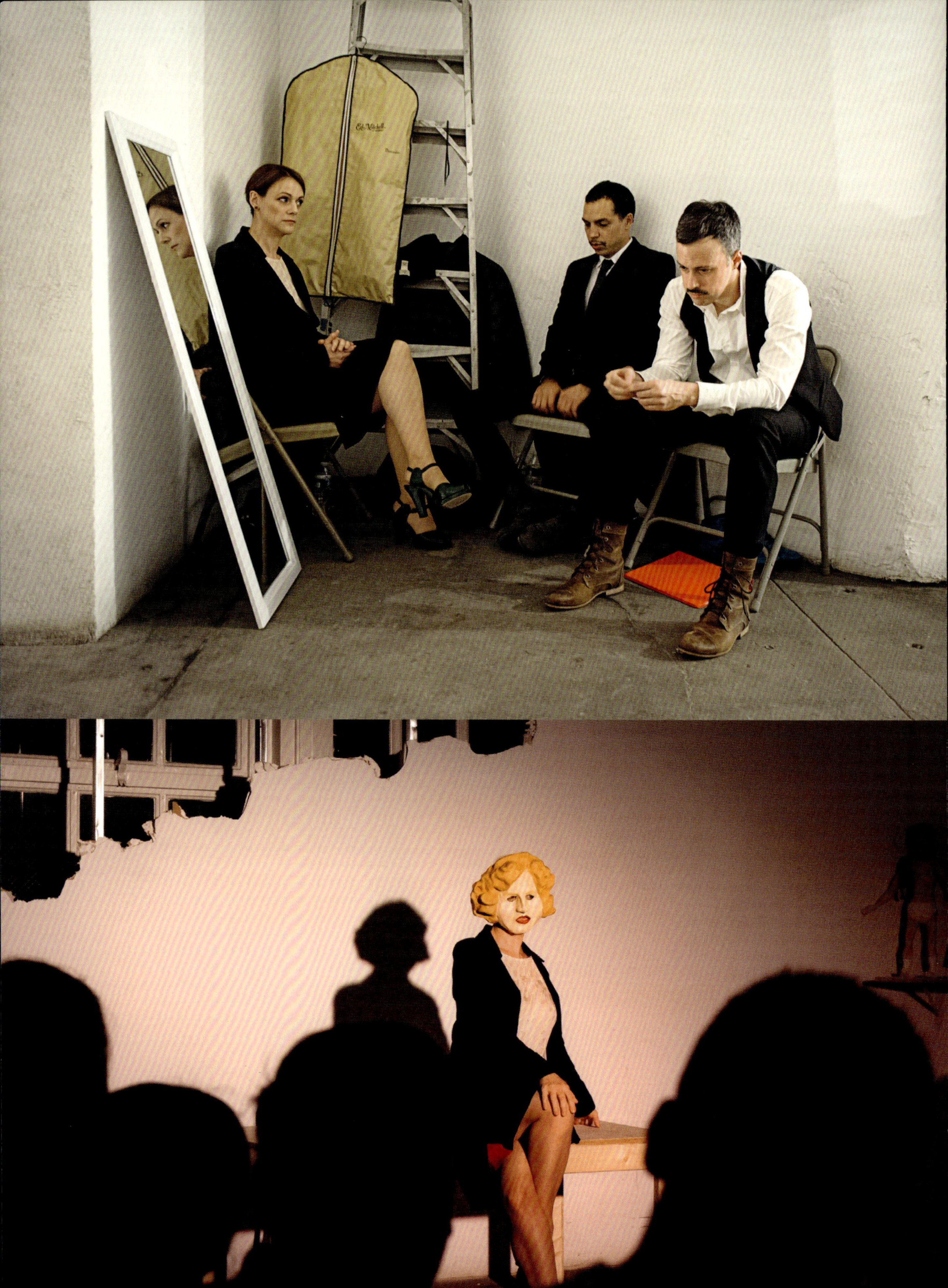

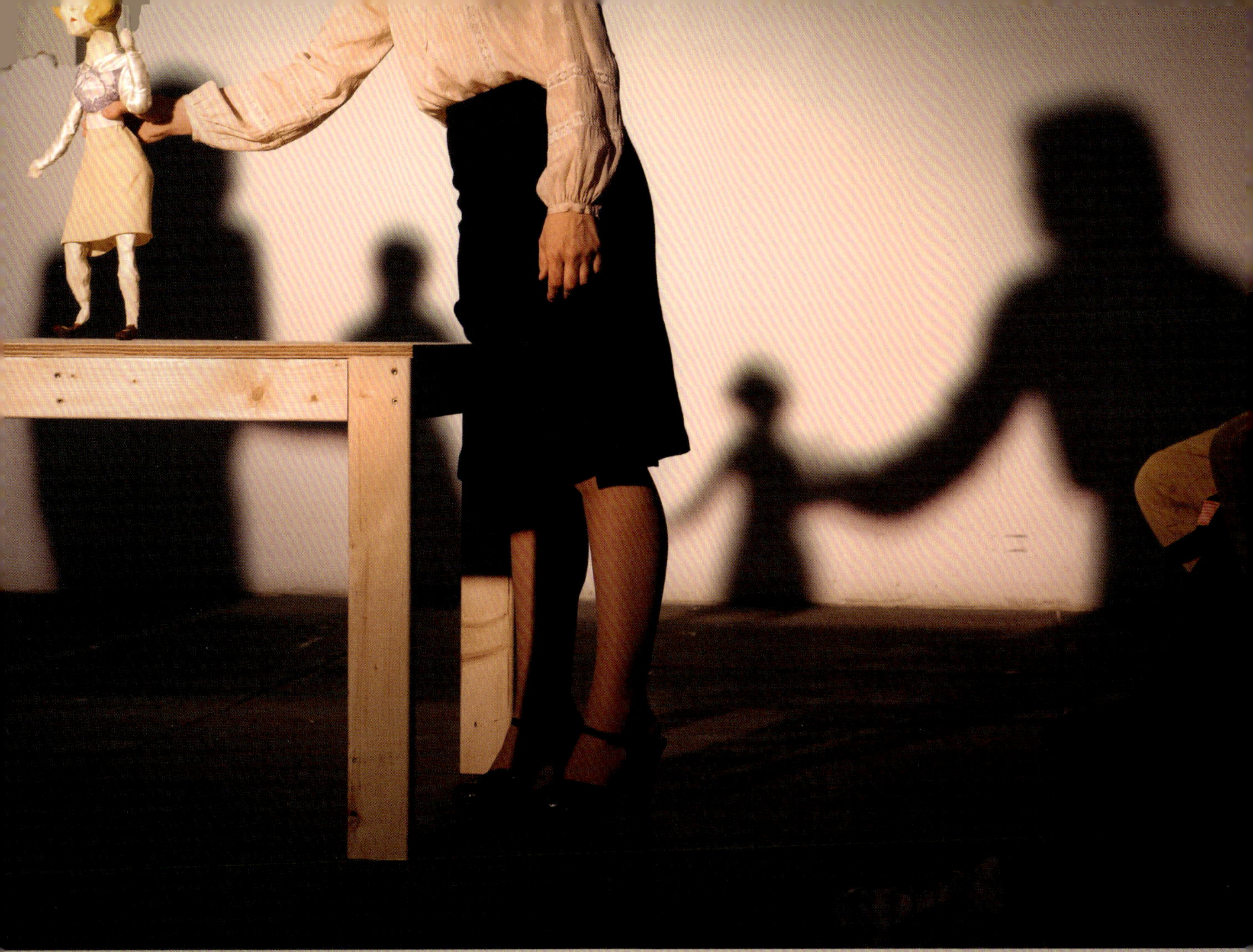

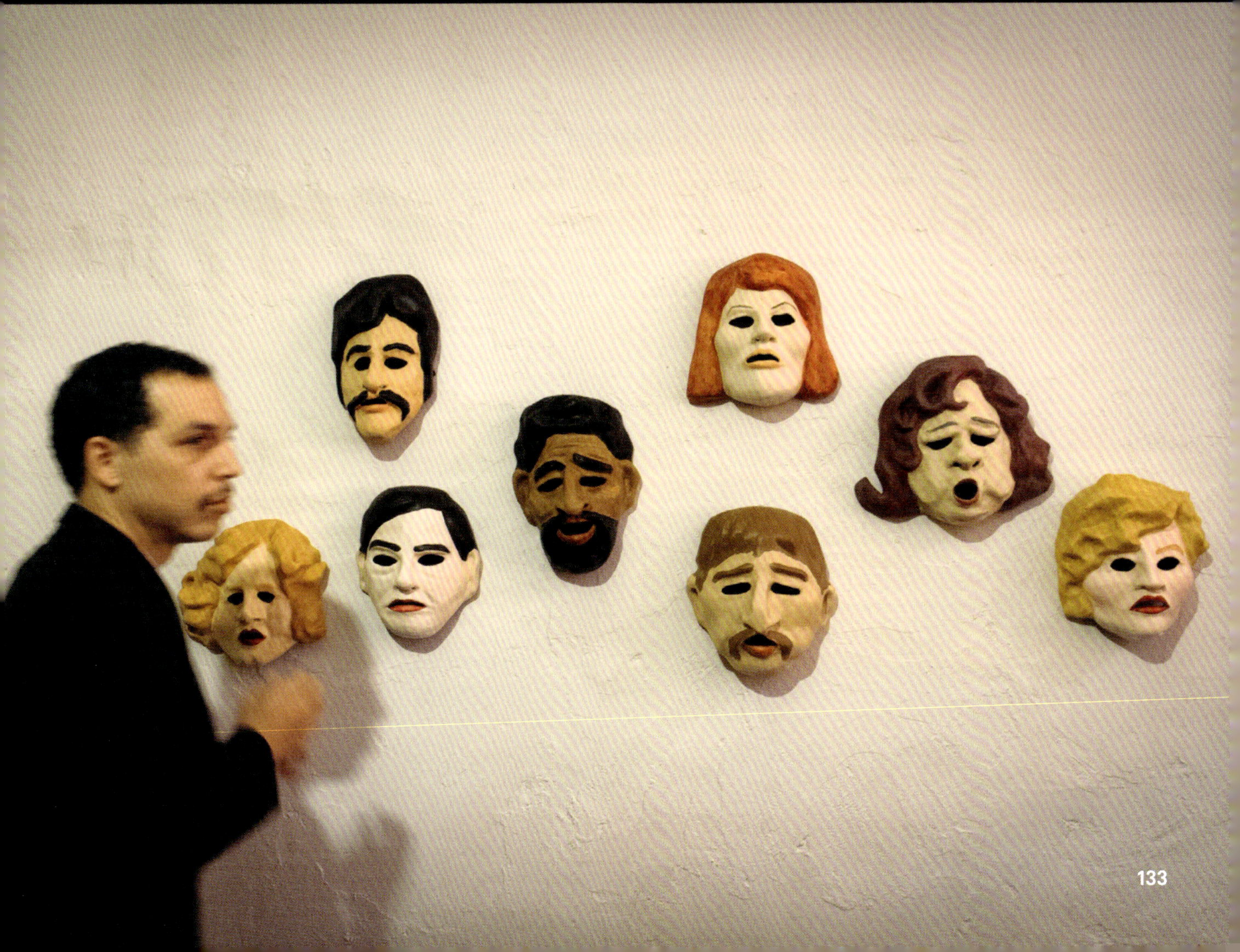

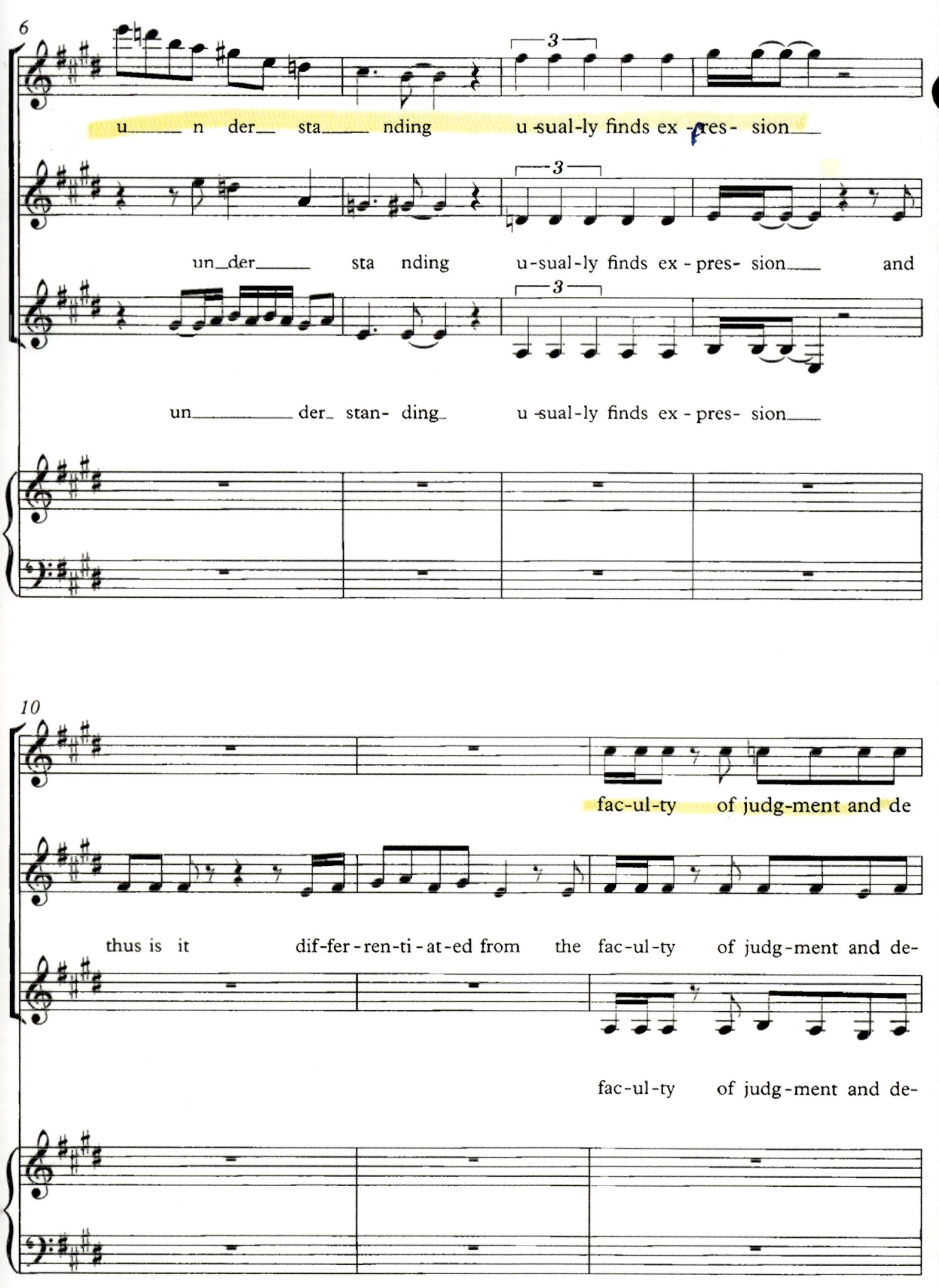
6
u n der sta nding u-sual-ly finds ex-pres- sion
un der sta nding u-sual-ly finds ex-pres- sion and
un der- stan- ding u-sual-ly finds ex-pres- sion
10
fac-ul-ty of judg-ment and de
thus is it dif-fer-ren-ti-at-ed from the fac-ul-ty of judg-ment and de-
fac-ul-ty of judg-ment and de-

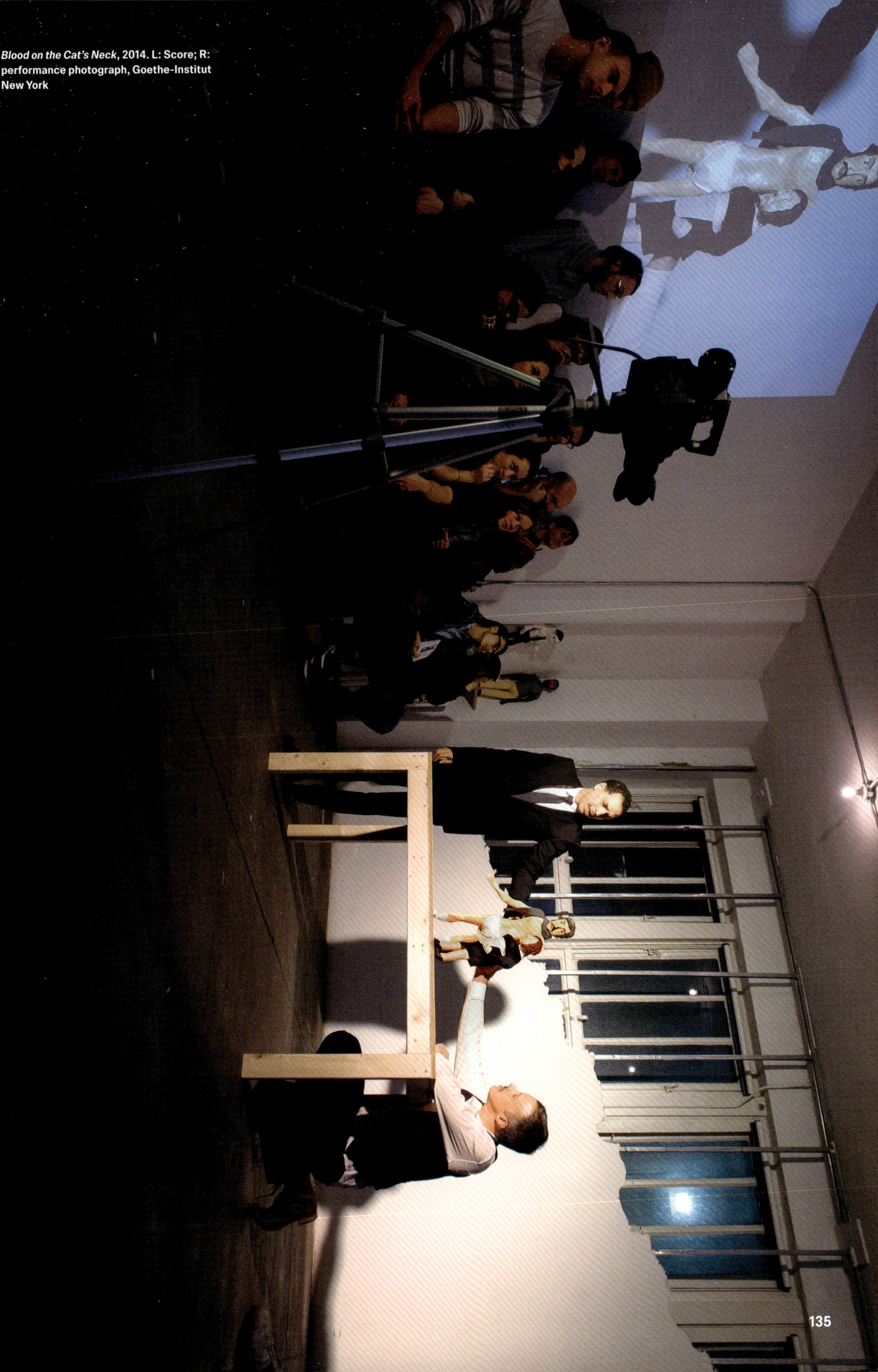

Blood on the Cat's Neck, 2014. L: Score; R: performance photograph, Goethe-Institut New York

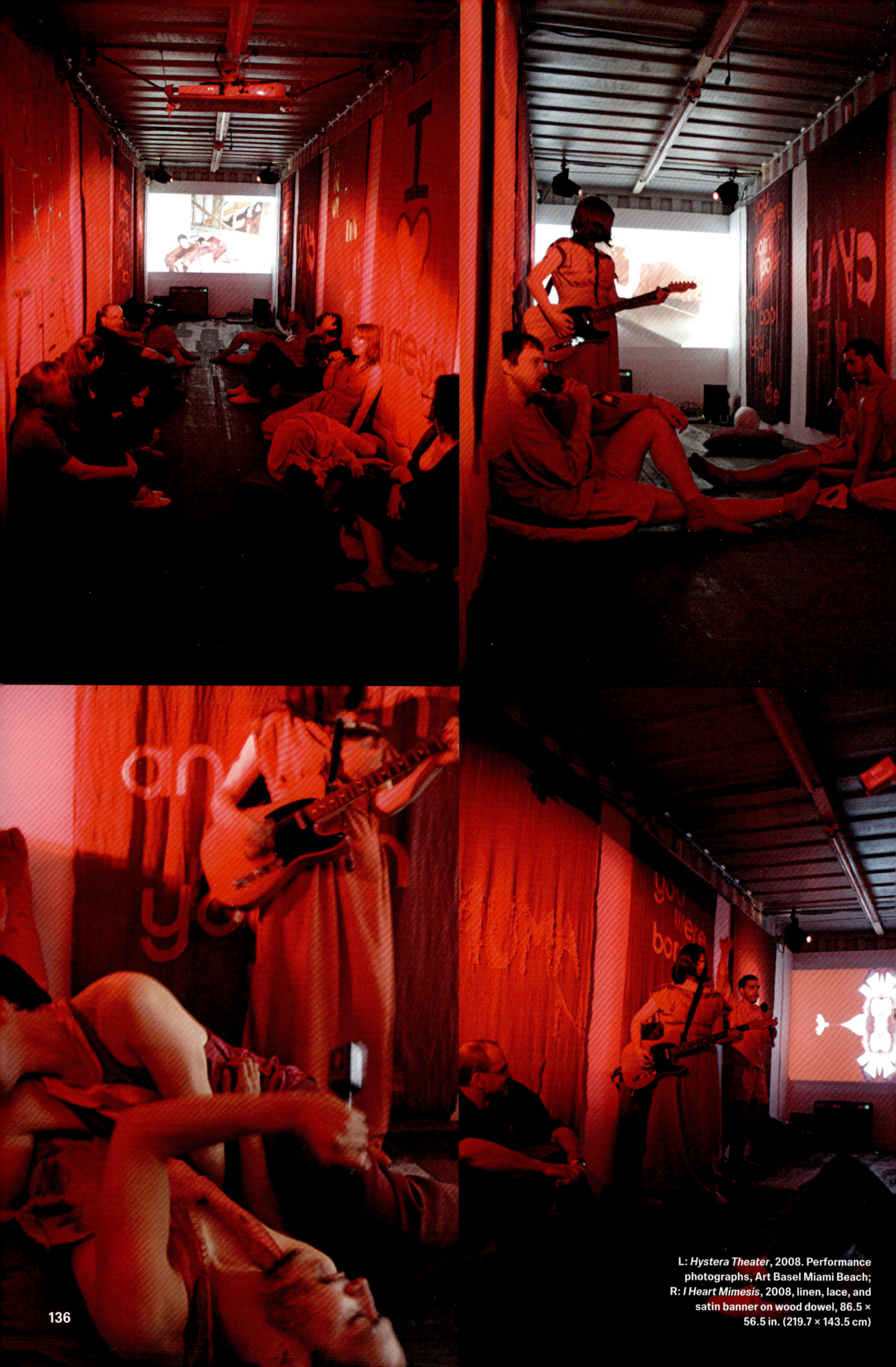

L: *Hystera Theater*, 2008. Performance photographs, Art Basel Miami Beach; R: *I Heart Mimesis*, 2008, linen, lace, and satin banner on wood dowel, 86.5 × 56.5 in. (219.7 × 143.5 cm)

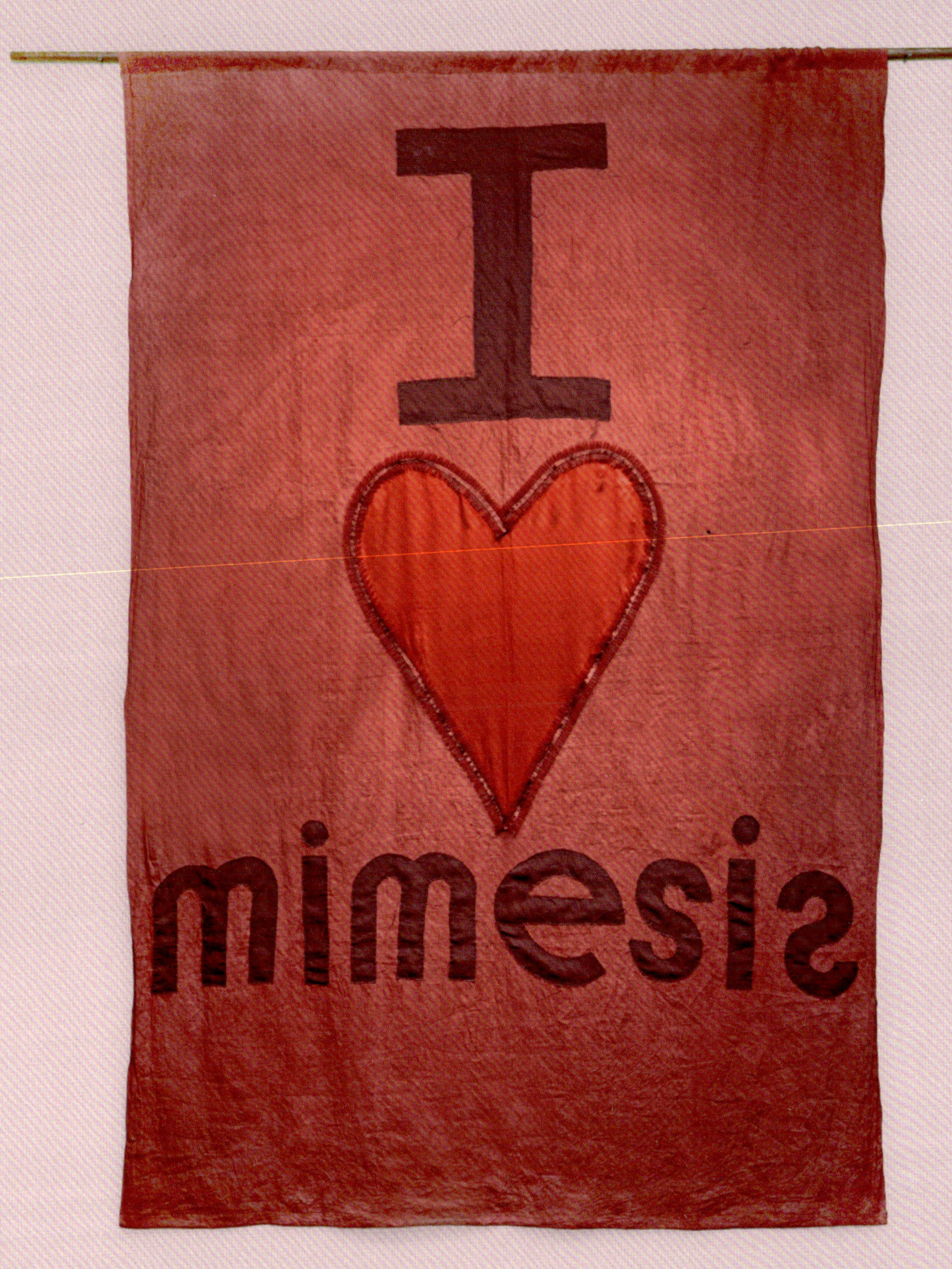
I
mimesis

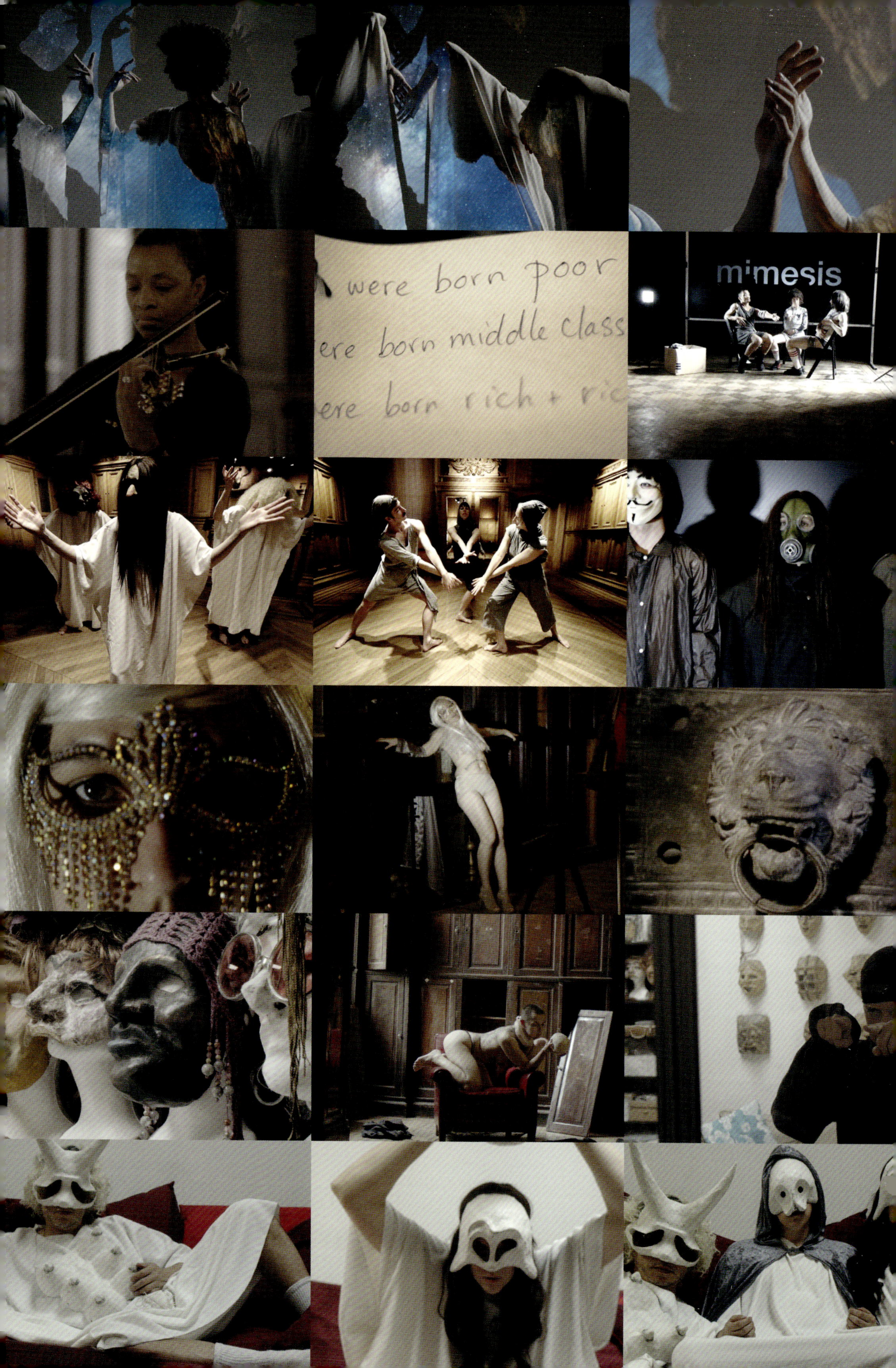
were born poor
ere born middle class
ere born rich + ric
mimesis

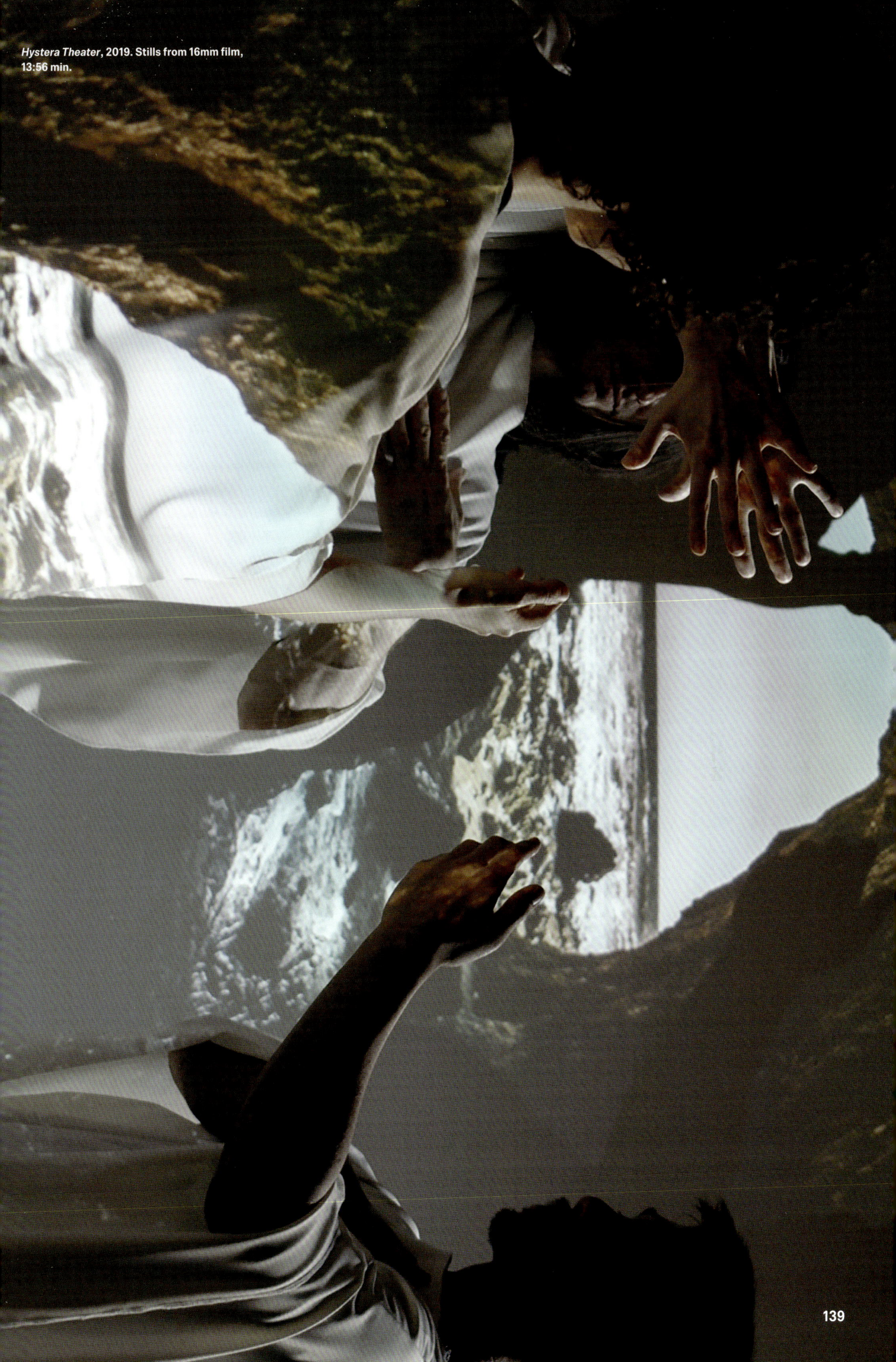

Hystera Theater, 2019. Stills from 16mm film, 13:56 min.

MY BARBARIAN

READ A BOOK, BABE
TURNING PAGES
ABOUT THE OLD DAYS
PICTURES LOOKED A LOT LIKE YOU
YOU LOST YOUR JOB AGAIN
FORGOT YOUR MANNERS
BURST INTO A RAGE A FLEW
ASK THE LIBRARIAN
WHO NEVER KNEW
'BOUT MY BARBARIAN

YOU SLEW A DRAGON
AND YOU IMAGINED
APPLICATIONS
TO A DESERT ISLAND SHORE
MEDIEVAL MORAL PLAYS
SATIRIC ESSAYS
CAN'T UNLOCK A BROKEN DOOR
AND YOU ARE CARRYING
A HEAVY SWORD
YOU'RE MY BARBARIAN

CHORUS:
MORNINGS ARE MADNESS
TRAFFIC IS BAD, THIS
CITY IS CRACKING
HORDES ARE ATTACKING
BEARS ARE ROARING
FALCONS ARE SOARING
SKULLS ARE GOBLETS
I'M ALWAYS FIGHTING CHRISTIANS
SUNSET IS HAZY
I MISS YOU MY CRAZY
WARRIOR, THE AGES
AND ALL OF THE SAGES
SAND
IN YOUR HAND

WHEN YOU WERE YOUNGER
PLAYED WITH MY BROTHER
QUEST TO UNCOVER
WOLF TRACKS IN THE GLOWING SNOW
AND THEN AT SCHOOL THAT DAY
YOU FREAKED AND WENT INSANE
HOWLING THROUGH YOUR BOOK REPORT
ARE YOU AN ALIEN?
YOU DON'T PLAY SPORTS
YOU'RE MY BARBARIAN

CHORUS

SAW A MOVIE
FLIPPING CHANNELS
ABOUT THE OLD DAYS
VILLAINS LOOKED A LOT LIKE YOU
BUT IN THE CANDLELIGHT
I WON'T PUT UP A FIGHT
PILLAGE ME AND LEAVE ME BRUISED
YOU DON'T WEAR UNDERWEAR
YOU TELL THE TRUTH
YOU'RE MY BARBARIAN

M. Gaines & A. Segade, Los Angeles, 2001

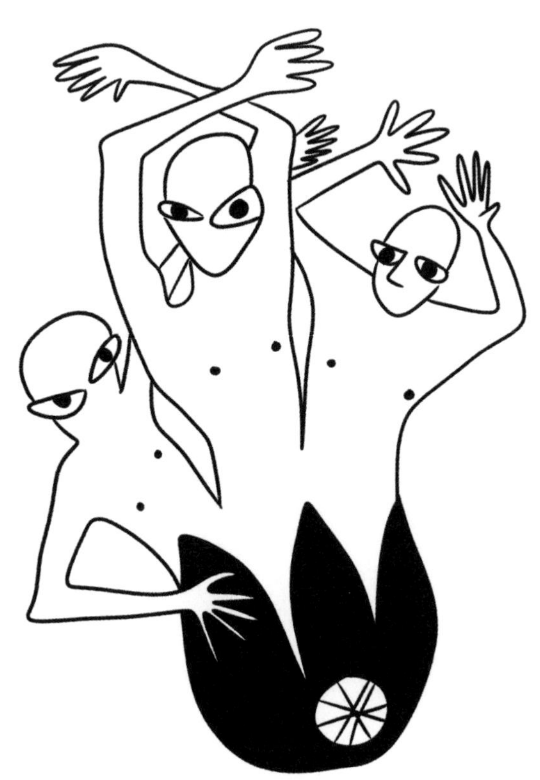

HYSTERA THREEWAY: MY BARBARIAN AND THE LABOR OF COLLECTIVE BEING

Joshua Chambers-Letson

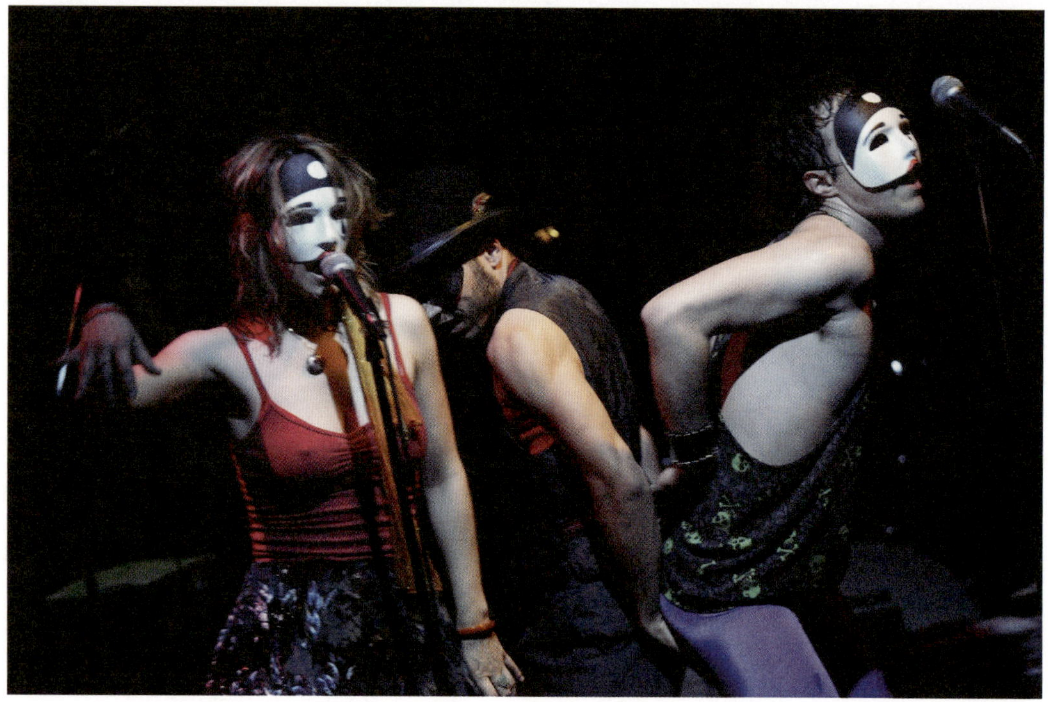

My Barbarian, *Purple Eyes*, 2004. Performance at Evidence Room Theater, Los Angeles

I.

When it is going well there can be a moment during group sex when the boundaries between participants blur. Selves and others are reorganized into a messy mesh of collective being. This is not to say that the self disappears or the distinctions fully fall away so much as that they loosen, withdraw, and are slightly suspended to make space for others. In that space a common consciousness can cohere. Decisions and choices are made (the mounting tension), not by any particular actor (the push and pull) but by the momentum of the collective (the build and crest, the release and undoing and redoing). Fingers and limbs, tongues and mouths, breasts and teeth and genitals, breath and sweat and spit, and all orders of fluid, flesh, and friction fold together as the interior and exterior are remade in, out, through, against, and above all *with* one another. Something new is born into being, but this being is provisional and contingent. Eventually the parties fall out or fold away. They collapse in a pile. Spent. The work of being with others can be exhausting.

Sex isn't the only place where collective being is produced, but it's a good place to start.[1] Sex can be hard work, but it has the potential to become what philosopher Jean-Luc Nancy describes as the "unworking of work."[2] Sex is both a form of collectivity and a mode of performance, and performance, like sex, is a generative womb for the birth of collective being. For the two decades they have been in a long-term relationship as collaborators, the art collective My Barbarian (Malik Gaines, Jade Gordon, and Alexandro Segade) has made the labor of collective being their work. Their work, in turn, has drawn on a long history of feminist and queer of color practices of being together in difference as they stage, and recruit their audiences into participating in, the labor of collective being.

The differences that cut across and through the collective inform the work. These differences include race (Gaines is Black, Gordon is white, and Segade is Latinx), sex and gender (Gaines and Segade are a queer couple, Gordon is a woman and a mother), and differential proximities to work security and economic precarity. Yet their practice functions in conscious opposition to the demands of neoliberal multiculturalism, where such differences are neutralized, instrumentalized, and absorbed through policy and tokenization. The labor of collective being performed by My Barbarian is a form of cooperative agitation and struggle that is itself a negotiation with difference. It finds its provenance in the historical struggles and fraught alliances forged between peoples of color; feminist, queer, and trans* liberation activists; and workers throughout history. It is an echo of W. E. B. Du Bois's description of the "dark proletariat" in 1935's *Black Reconstruction in America, 1860–1880*: a (not-yet-here) revolutionary class of Black, Asian, Latinx, and Indigenous workers forged by, and working together against, the interarticulated development of capital accumulation, white supremacy, and colonialisms across the world. It is also reflective of histories of queer and feminist agitation, as in the Black feminist labors of the Combahee River Collective; the knowledge materialized in Cherríe Moraga and Gloria Anzaldúa's 1981 anthology of writings by radical women of color, *This Bridge Called My Back*; José Esteban Muñoz's theories of queer of color and minoritarian performance; and the "intimacies of four continents" as described by Lisa Lowe.[3]

Participating in a My Barbarian performance can be like listening to a track from a group that excels at three-part harmonies: the trio play off of and support one another while reinforcing their different strengths with a kind of shimmering, collective flow that folds you in in the process. Having a conversation with them is a similar experience. "This has to do with our relationship, which is always about our differences as much as it is about being an interracial, intersexual family, and how that's shifted in time," Gaines said during a conversation with the group.[4] Segade begins to harmonize on this melody, describing the work as a "negotiation of differences and likeness" as they present mythologies and tropes that they know to be "provisional and rife with negative meanings and connotations that are harmful. We're still trying to work through them to find some kind of common ground—not just with ourselves but with the audience as well, knowing that this commons is happening in a very fraught situation." Gordon folds her voice into the chorus: "We're kind of working things out amongst ourselves and working things out with the world simultaneously. For the good of the collective, we've had to subsume ourselves into the collective a little bit. And that has been painful for each of us in our own way. Not only are we coming together as a collective to make something different than we could create individually, we've had to sacrifice some of our own identity in order for the collaboration to be possible."

They started performing in bars after meeting in Los Angeles in 1996, when, shortly after college, Gordon was introduced to Gaines and Segade by a friend. Gaines and Segade met in 1991; Segade was studying film and Gaines was training as a playwright.

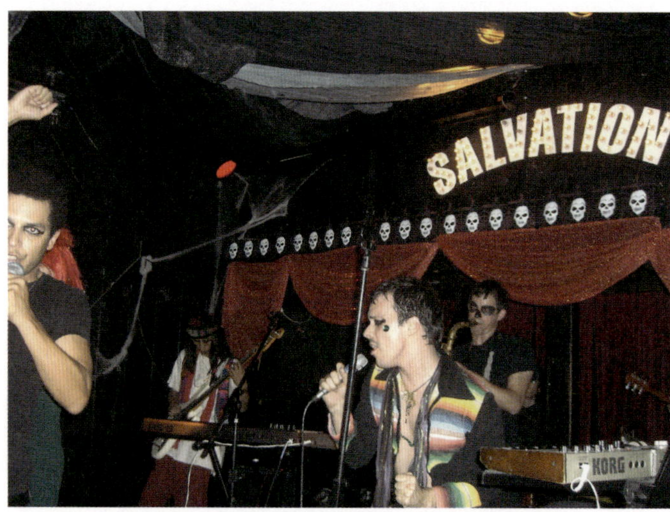

A.L. Steiner, *Untitled* (My Barbarian band performance at Silverlake Lounge, Los Angeles), 2007

Gordon came into the fold with a method-acting background, simultaneously studying and performing in theater, commercial TV, and independent films (as well as in one of Segade's student films). The economic conditions of theater and film production were prohibitive, so they formed a queer band as a gratifying and accessible means of making performance, dropping into the burgeoning band culture in LA's Silver Lake neighborhood, booking sets at the Silverlake Lounge and Spaceland. Working in the bar scene from 2000 to 2009 gave them relative autonomy over their work, so long as they centered music. Musicality is an enduring component of their practice and functions, formally, as a reflection of their interrogation of difference and collectivity. "Music," as Gaines wrote in his scholarly study of radical Black and queer performance, can be "used to create irresolvable formal differences, differences that allow critical comparisons to be made."[5]

During this period they were collaborating with and working alongside other members of LA's queer of color art undercommons, including luminaries like Vaginal Creme Davis and Jennifer Moon. By the middle of the decade they were increasingly performing and exhibiting in art spaces. Their early and seminal performance and video works such as *Unicorns LA* (2004), *Morgan Le Fay* (2004), *Gods of Canada* (2005), and *Pagan Rights* (2006) are a psychedelic fusion of their collective knowledge regarding performance histories and techniques. Classical Athenian theater's deployment of myth and mask conjoins with early modern and baroque technologies of parable and masquerade, Bertolt Brecht's techniques of theatrical estrangement in the service of political praxis, Augusto Boal's Theater of the Oppressed, and the earnest pleasures of pop and musical theater. They knowingly engage and activate feminist, queer, and BIPOC art histories and criticism, with influences and collaborators ranging from Davis and Muñoz to Jack Smith, Luce Irigaray, Lorraine O'Grady, Nao Bustamante, Glenn Ligon, Mary Kelly, and Eleanor Antin. They appropriate and queer popular performance acts like the Shangri-Las, the Supremes, or TLC.

These works stage engagements with mythical and historical pasts in a fashion that is ludic, campy, and playful, but this performs a pointed function. With the earnest critical ambivalence that is a signature trademark of the popular cultures of Gen X, My Barbarian drags up the past (sometimes literally dressing it in drag) to negotiate these contradictions. In so doing they undertake what Muñoz described as the group's "revisitation" of elided colonial and racial histories, a mode of queer utopianism that issues a critique of "the present for the ultimate purpose of imagining a future that is unimaginable in normative or straight [white, patriarchal, colonial] time."[6] By remembering *and* remaking the past, My Barbarian works within the register of what Lowe similarly describes as "the *past conditional temporality of the* 'what could have been.'"[7] Past conditional temporalities can be fabulated and strategically deployed "to reckon with the violence of affirmation and forgetting [attached to intimately entwined histories of racialization, colonization, and capital accumulation], in order to recognize that this particular violence continues to be reproduced in liberal humanist institutions, discourses, and practices today."[8] Recognition and reckoning lie at the heart of the labor of collective being within My Barbarian's practice.

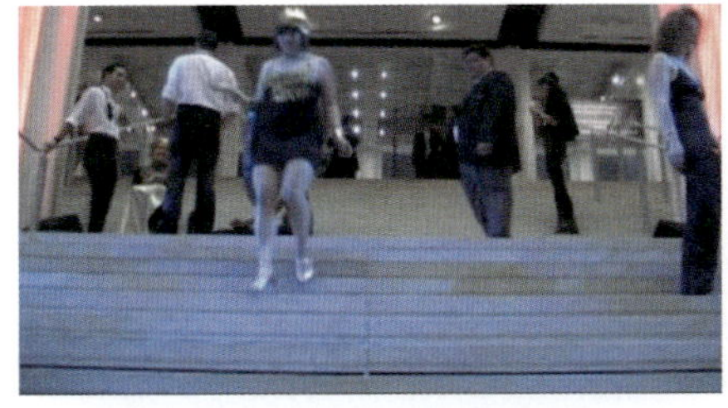
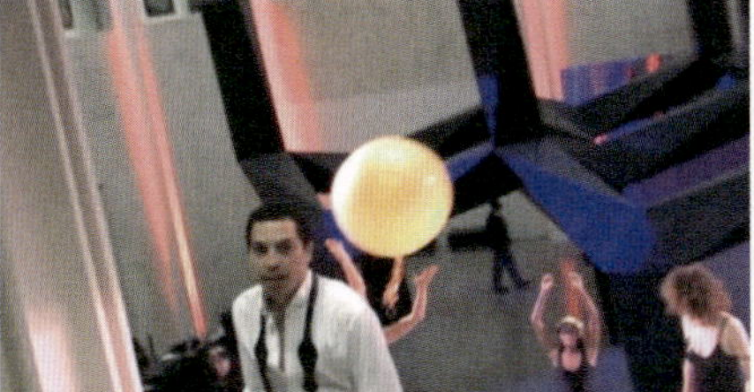
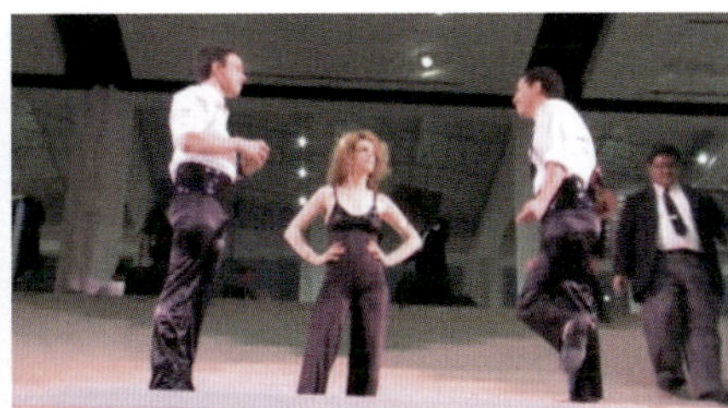
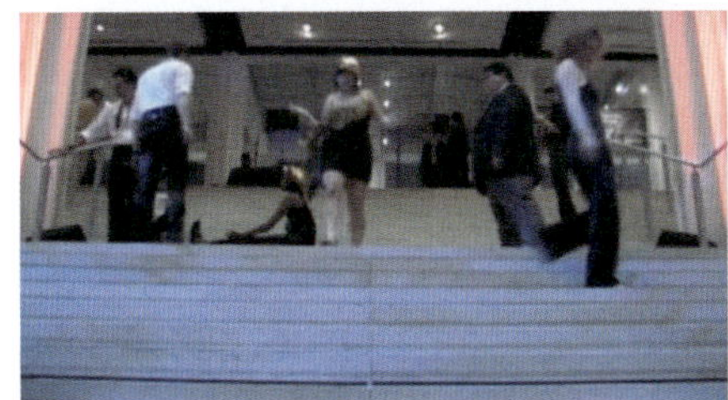
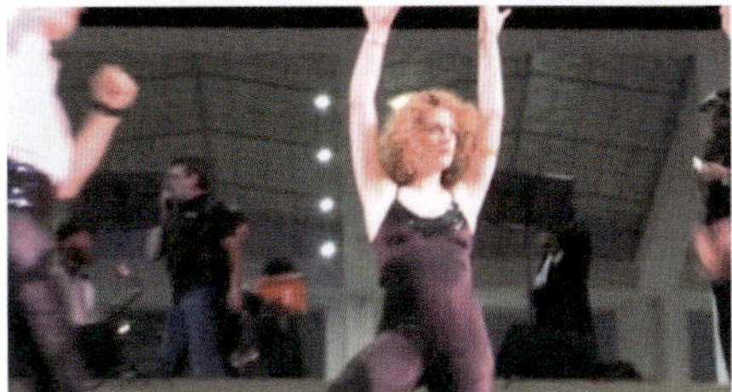
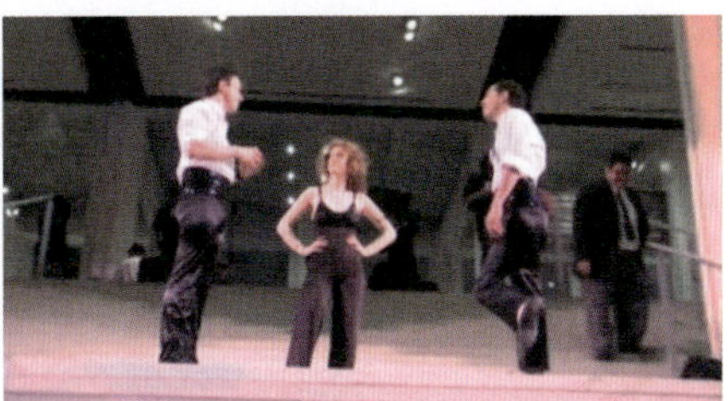

My Barbarian, *The Case of the Stairs*, 2008. Stills from performance documentation, Los Angeles County Museum of Art

II.

The more their work was incorporated into institutional settings, the more they pushed their practice to engage critically informed modes of institutional critique. This is evidenced in a series of works that include *The Case of the Stairs* (2008), *The Fourth Wall* (2009), *The Night Epi$ode* (2009), *Broke People's Baroque Peoples' Theater* (2009–, hereafter *Broke/Baroque*), *Double Agency* (2015), and *The Mother and Other Plays* (2013–14). All of these projects employ a sublime and stubborn theatricality in order to confront the contradictions underscoring My Barbarian's relationship to, and incorporation within, art institutions. They also interrogate the uneven, exploitative, racialized, and gendered divisions of labor that reproduce and are reproduced within such institutions.

Broke/Baroque critically appropriates the form of royal court performance, while *Double Agency* and *The Night Epi$ode* parody the dominant ideologies reflected in the institutional and curatorial logics that condition labor, culture, and commerce in the era of disaster capitalism.[9] *The Case of the Stairs* and *The Fourth Wall* highlight the exploitative divisions of labor within art institutions, which claim a public trust while principally serving a wealthy, white donor and patron class at the expense of a precarious and racialized workforce (artists, guards, and facilities and service staff). In early sequences from a three-channel film documenting *The Case of the Stairs*, My Barbarian prepares for a performance at the Los Angeles County Museum of Art, conversing with security guards and rehearsing with dancers and musicians to a diegetic soundtrack that underscores the nature of performance as labor: the facilities staff sweeping the performance space (a staircase), the caterers making kitchen cacophony, and their musical collaborators (wind ensemble LA Fog) tuning their instruments. When the tony patrons of the private party arrive, the collective's spectacular performance is drowned out as the wealthy, overwhelmingly white art patrons treat them with the same casual disregard with which they treat the service workers.

At the conclusion of *The Case of the Stairs* each member of the collective performs a monologue, ending with Segade's recitation of a passage from Michael Fried's famous screed against Minimalism. "Art degenerates as it approaches the condition of theater," Segade valiantly declares to a crowd that can't hear him and wouldn't be listening even if they could. "The concepts of quality and value are meaningful only within the individual arts. Theater corrupts. Theater perverts. What lies behind the arts is theater." Fried's critique rests upon and reifies the art world's (and Plato's, Cromwell's, or Jerry Falwell's) historically entrenched rejection of theatricality and performance.[10] The antitheatrical position often carries implicitly racist, sexist, transphobic, and homophobic valences insofar as queer, trans*, racialized, and femme affects are often derided as excessive or dramatic when defined against the impoverished minimalism of normative white, straight, cis, and male affect.[11] It is precisely by embracing the queerly "perverse" and "corrupt nature of theatricality" denounced by Fried that My Barbarian maintains a critically ambivalent, corrosive, and infiltrative position within the institution as they negotiate its impulse to incorporate the collective in a fashion that neutralizes the disruptions posed by their difference.

After their performance, Gordon brushes off the audience's inattention, playfully (if not bitterly) declaring, "I'm doing it for myself." Underscoring the fact that their intervention was never staged for the benefit of the institution or its donors, My Barbarian's mode of institutional critique does not entertain the fantasy that the institution can be revolutionized or radically transformed. *The Case of the Stairs* negotiates with the fraught conditions wrought by neoliberal and racial capitalism by taking up space and resources from within the institution in order to smuggle knowledge out of the museum.[12] In this sense they mobilize performance to embody what Anna Watkins Fisher describes as an artist's parasitical relationship to the institutions and systems that frame and forge their conditions of production.[13] Infiltrating, perverting, and parasitically absorbing institutional resources and space, My Barbarian puts these pilfered elements to work in the labor of forging queer collective being.

III.

The philosopher of critical utopianism Ernst Bloch described theater as a "rehearsal for the example": an anticipatory illumination of different worlds and different ways of being in the world together.[14] Theater's power, for Bloch, was its inherent reliance upon collectivity, the imagination, and the sensual, embodied pleasures that allow audience and performers alike to reflect upon and participate in the actual reorganization of their present circumstance. Just so, the failures and brutalities of historical communisms, as well as the vicious and racialized forms of authoritarian domination and extraction inherent to capitalist accumulation and liberal democracy (slavery, empire, and colonialism especially), force us to grapple with the limits of collectivity and its fascist, destructive, and patriarchal tendencies.

Hystera Theater (2008/2019), *The Mother and Other Plays*, and *Universal Declaration of Infantile Anxiety Situations Reflected in the Creative Impulse* (2013) explore forms of creative and collective being that decline submission to the law of the father. Negating Freud's suspect insistence that all group dynamics are conditioned by the father's phallic dominance over the family, these works contend instead with the generative, reproductive, and creative powers of the mother. As they do so, they emphasize the double valence of labor (work and birth) by recognizing the womb as a site of creativity and difference, just as it is a terrain for struggle, sacrifice, and potential subjection.

Hystera Theater engages Irigaray's feminist critique of Plato to explore the overlaps between collective creation, generation, the womb, the mother, sex, mimesis, masquerade, and the reproductive powers of theater.[15] Extending these concerns, *Universal Declaration* draws the second half of its title from an influential 1929 essay by psychoanalyst Melanie Klein. The essay posits creative and artistic practice as a means of working through emotional and social conflict.[16] In Klein's work, relations between mothers and their children serve as a primary template by which a person learns how to navigate such dynamics. In other words, the ideal Kleinian mother (and, by extension, analyst and artist) teaches a lesson about how to live with others and how to live with difficult and even destructive feelings. Like a performer, analyst, or teacher, the mother (for Klein) is tasked with the submission of her own body to this lesson. Mothering, in this sense, is a job. It is work. And work, in this world, always runs the risk of subjection for the worker.

The series of short films comprised in *Universal Declaration* focus on different aspects of "the mother," including sections centered on each of the artists' mothers. In the opening film, *Mary*, the collective explores the slippages between artist, mother, analyst, and teacher. Mary Kelly (who was Segade's teacher) steps into the role of the painter Mary Cassatt. She paints Gordon, who poses while holding her own child in her arms. Kelly later delivers a monologue, or lecture, in which she posits the mother as an alternative to the Oedipal order of patriarchy, in which group dynamics are governed by the submission of the many to the authority of the father. Kelly's mother is a figure who facilitates relations *between* siblings, teaching them a practice of being with others that is not destructive and dominating but is instead a communal project of negotiating with rivalry and difference.

Victoria attends to the ambivalences of motherhood as Gordon reads passages from her mother Victoria's diary describing her conflicted feelings about mothering during her daughter's early years. Klein suggested that a path to adapting to reality requires one to develop a capacity to feel ambivalence toward their mother. One can imagine that this ambivalence would work toward freeing the mother from the child's (and the world's) unsustainable demands that she be either a "good" or "bad" mother, potentially allowing her the freedom to be a complex being of her own accord. As Victoria interacts with a masked figure throughout the sequence, the relationship between mother and performer is once more underscored, as both are framed as teacher and worker. This conceit is further interrogated in *The Mother and Other Plays*, an adaptation of one of Bertolt Brecht's *lehrstücke* (teaching plays) where My Barbarian seductively recruits the audience into a lesson on the labor of collective being.[17]

The labor of collective being isn't a mere theoretical abstraction. It is the flesh and form of My Barbarian's collaboration in that it reflects the forms of collective practice that have blossomed as the state and the institutions of the prevailing order continue to fail and assault the commons. The labor of collective being is imminent within the practices of mutual aid and community cultivation that young activists and abolitionists enacted in the midst of the COVID-19 pandemic and the surging struggles for Black, Brown, Asian, and Indigenous life. It's the mothers taking their children by the hand and stepping out into the streets to work and agitate for an end to white supremacy and the carceral state. It's the young people distributing groceries in food deserts, handing out provisions and water at the marches, and practicing jail support in the demonstration's wake. It's the forms of care and community that feminists and femmes, Black, Latinx, Asian, Indigenous, trans*, and queer folk have always practiced and cultivated in the breach of these many years of loss and losing. Like the fleshy tangle of multiple lovers with which we began this essay, the labor of collective being is a constant, precarious, and ephemeral negotiation. It is hard and sometimes painful, but also sensuous and pleasurable work. The mounting tension. The push and pull. The build and crest. The release and undoing and redoing. In the difficult doing of these labors, a new kind of being, and being together, is being born.

"We have a lot of work to do."
—My Barbarian, *The Mother and Other Plays*

---

1 This is especially apt given Sigmund Freud's suggestion that all group dynamics are overdetermined by sexual (libidinal) drive. See Freud, *Group Psychology and the Analysis of the Ego*, trans. and ed. James Strachey (New York: Norton, 1959). It is worth noting that here Freud characterizes homosexuals as particularly inclined toward group sex: "It seems certain that homosexual love is far more compatible with group ties, even when it takes the shape of uninhibited sexual impulsions—a remarkable fact, the explanation of which might carry us far" (95).

2 The unworking of work occurs, for Nancy, in the realm of communication. See Jean-Luc Nancy, *The Inoperative Community*, ed. Peter Connor, trans. Connor et al. (Minneapolis: University of Minnesota Press, 1991), 31.

3 W. E. B. Du Bois, *Black Reconstruction in America, 1860–1880* (New York: Free Press, 1935), 16; Cherríe Moraga and Gloria Anzaldúa, *This Bridge Called My Back: Writings by Radical Women of Color*, 4th ed. (Albany, NY: SUNY Press, 2015); José Esteban Muñoz, *Disidentifications: Queers of Color and the Performance of Politics* (Minneapolis: University of Minnesota Press, 1999); Lisa Lowe, *The Intimacies of Four Continents* (Durham, NC: Duke University Press, 2015).

4 Quotes in this passage are edited from an interview with My Barbarian conducted by the author on March 19, 2021.

5 Malik Gaines, *Black Performance on the Outskirts of the Left: A History of the Impossible* (New York: NYU Press, 2017), 152.

6 José Esteban Muñoz, *Cruising Utopia* (New York: NYU Press, 2009), 178.

7 Lowe, *The Intimacies of Four Continents*, 40–41.

8 Ibid.

9 Naomi Klein, *The Shock Doctrine: The Rise of Disaster Capitalism* (London: Picador, 2008).

10 For an account of the antitheatrical tradition in Britain and the US (and its homophobic valences) see Alisa Solomon, "Great Sparkles of Lust: Homophobia and the Antitheatrical Tradition," in *The Queerest Art: Essays on Lesbian and Gay Theater*, ed. Alisa Solomon and Framji Minwalla (New York: NYU Press, 2002), 9–20.

11 On the racialization of affect, see José Esteban Muñoz, *The Sense of Brown*, ed. Joshua Chambers-Letson and Tavia Nyong'o (Durham, NC: Duke University Press, 2020).

12 See Fred Moten and Stefano Harney, *The Undercommons: Fugitive Planning & Black Study* (New York: Autonomedia, 2013).

13 Anna Watkins Fisher, *The Play in the System: The Art of Parasitical Resistance* (Durham, NC: Duke University Press, 2020).

14 Ernst Bloch, "The Stage Regarded as a Paradigmatic Institution and the Decision within It," in *The Utopian Function of Art and Literature*, trans. and ed. Jack Zipes and Frank Mecklenburg (Cambridge, MA: MIT Press, 1988), 227. See also Bloch, *The Principle of Hope*, vol. 1, trans. Neville Plaice, Stephen Plaice, and Paul Knight (Cambridge, MA: MIT Press, 1996).

15 Luce Irigaray, "Plato's Hystera," in *Speculum of the Other Woman*, trans. Gillian C. Gill (Ithaca, NY: Cornell University Press, 1974), 241–364

16 Melanie Klein, "Infantile Anxiety Situations Reflected in a Work of Art and in the Creative Impulse," in *The Collected Works of Melanie Klein*, vol. 1 (London: Karnac Books, 1975), 210–18. The themes I am describing here are also broadly explored throughout Klein's work and are infinitely more complex than my brief summary accounts for.

17 Ethan Philbrick provides an excellent account of *The Mother and Other Plays* along these lines. My essay owes a significant debt to his review, as it does to Tavia Nyong'o's and Shannon Jackson's work on My Barbarian. See Ethan Philbrick, "Performing a New Old Left: My Barbarian's *The Mother*," *women & performance* 26, no. 1 (2006): 111–14; Tavia Nyong'o, "In Finitude: Being with José, Being with Pedro," *Social Text 121* 32, no. 4 (Winter 2014): 71–85; and Shannon Jackson, "Just-in-Time: Performance and the Aesthetics of Precarity," *TDR: The Drama Review* 56, no. 45 (2012): 10–31.

"WE CAN WORSHIP ONE ANOTHER," OR, "THE ANTICIPATORY ILLUMINATION OF QUEER VIRTUOSITY"

Lia Gangitano

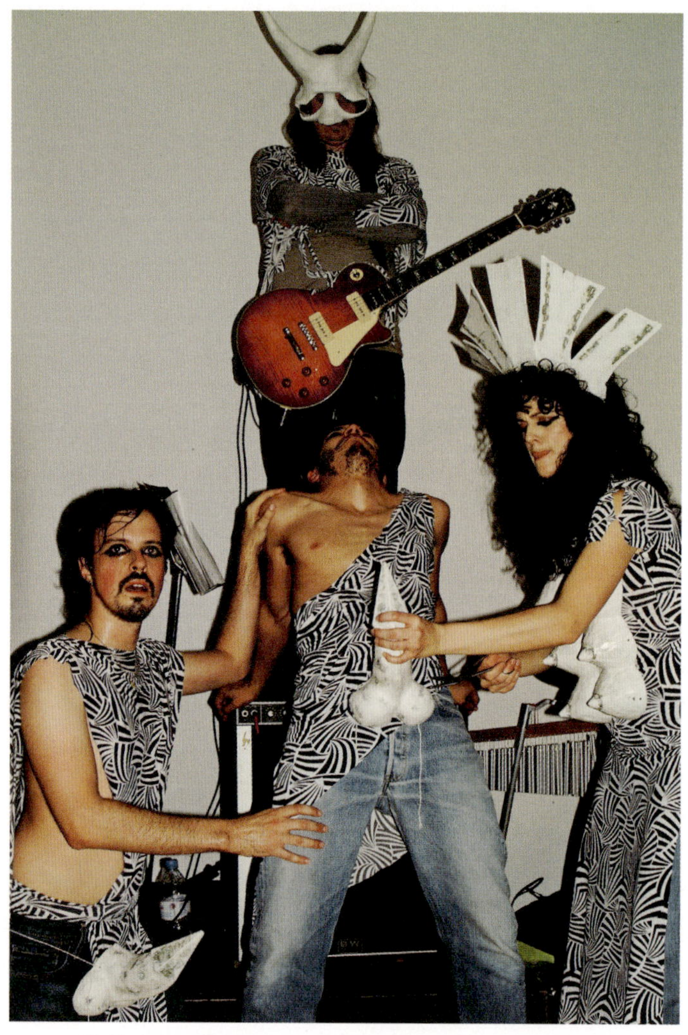

My Barbarian, *You Were Born Poor and Poor You Will Die*, 2005. Performance at *Performa 05*, Participant Inc., New York

[A] modality of queer virtuosity seems especially salient in the "show-core" harmonization of My Barbarian. The spirit of [Jack] Smith can be seen as an animating presence in the elaborate costumes and design of My Barbarian. The woodland frolicking of *Pagan Rights* can perhaps be seen as a contemporary version of Jack Smith's *Flaming Creatures* done as a musical. My Barbarian's interest in a mythic past, that of Arthurian legend, not unlike Jack Smith's investment in Atlantis, creates utopian deployments of the past in service of critiquing the present for the ultimate purpose of imagining a future that is unimaginable in normative or straight time. —José Esteban Muñoz[1]

According to early biographical statements, Alexandro Segade, Andy Ouchi, Jade Gordon, and Malik Gaines were born in '70s California and came together in the year 2000 in Los Angeles to form the art band My Barbarian, also forging collaborations and connections with a number of musicians and artists, including Scott Martin, Norwood Cheek, Giles Miller, Laura Schnitger, Pearl C. Hsiung, Mended Veil, Gillian Haratani (of Art Club 2000), and Jeff Ono. Their first full-length album, *Cloven Soft-Shoe*, was released in 2005; it was followed by *California Sweet & the 7 Pagan Rights* in 2006.[2] They performed *Pagan Rights*, a showcase of California-inspired vignettes, at seven venues throughout North America. During this time they also created self-directed video works addressing notably California-inflected themes, including *Unicorns LA* and *Morgan Le Fay* (both 2004). Wayne Baerwaldt, then director of the Power Plant, Toronto, and advisory board member of Participant Inc., New York, the alternative space I had founded in 2001 and continue to direct, emphatically insisted we extend an invitation to the group. The most expeditious opportunity to do so arose with the exhibition *Sugartown* in 2005, whose title paid homage to the 1999 Allison Anders and Kurt Voss film *Sugar Town*, starring Jade Gordon. I had met Gordon the previous year through Anders's daughter Tiffany Anders (on the occasion of the 1998 exhibition and publication *Beck & Al Hansen: Playing with Matches*, curated and edited by Baerwaldt). I was struck at that time by Gordon's ambivalence toward the genre of performance art, which was quite separate from her enthusiasm for an acting career that would come to include major roles in such legendary films as John Aes-Nihil's *Suddenly Last Summer* (2007), which also starred Vaginal Davis, Goddess Bunny, Lance Loud, and Bibbe Hansen.

As a lifelong East Coast dweller from the twentieth century, I am compelled to note that a cursory Google search for Aes-Nihil's *Suddenly Last Summer* pulls up "The Archives of Aesthetic-Nihilism," a website that declares itself "Home of the Manson Archives: the most extensive collection of Manson audio, video, photos, clippings & publications." So West Coast. In their radio play *Squirrel Radio Action* (2005), My Barbarian assumes the persona of an activist theater group of squirrels from the Angeles National Forest to examine "the apocalyptic sensibility that is endemic to Los Angeles." Sunny popular culture died with Charles Manson, it seems. An East/West (read: right/wrong) dichotomy informs my understanding of the group and their career, and I confess I tend to compare everything West Coast to its East Coast counterpart, sorry. Notably, several friends who were members of Art Club 2000 attended *Pagan Rights* at Participant, and Segade said of their transcontinental collegiality, "My Barbarian reads like an Art Club 2000 syllabus, but with added singing."[3]

Founded in 1992 (with a projected end date of the year 2000), Art Club 2000 was a collaboration between seven students at Cooper Union and American Fine Arts, Co. (AFA) founder Colin de Land, who exhibited their collective work during seven consecutive summers at AFA, beginning with the show *Commingle* in 1993. What started as a pedagogical, discursive process based on seminar-type meetings grew into what David Velasco later called "a potently glib, media-savvy collective," whose work was ultimately "'about' . . . institutional critique and the art world's fetishization of youth and contrived generations."[4] Practicing "garbology" and recognizing "corporate poetry" all around them, the group noted in a 2013 *Artforum* interview: "The impetus for . . . a lot of things Colin did . . . was his frustration with what people were getting away with, the status quo of the art world."[5]

In the mid '90s, Art Club 2000 member Danny McDonald, who was the archivist and co-director of AFA from 1993 to 2004, became known for his "conceptual and absurd costume jewelry line Mended Veil." Born and raised in California, McDonald defected to attend Cooper Union, but he shared My Barbarian's West Coast sensibility; the group incorporated works from his "Space Vampires" collection into their costumes, and McDonald designed numerous pieces with them in mind. Made to function and circulate in non-art retail contexts like Barney's, Colette, Paul Smith, and Ooga Booga, Mended Veil nevertheless spawned important artworks such as the "questionable beliefs" bracelet, with charms representing fairies, Santa

Claus, money, ghosts, aliens, astrology, Jesus, the myth of romantic love, and unicorns. McDonald credits Segade for introducing him to the Buffy Sainte-Marie song that inspired him to make jewelry.

The World Is Negative

> The city is not kind to men born in the 1970s. Trampled, bedraggled, punch-drunk, men of a certain age and weight walk into walls; they cannot see what is in front of them. . . . Someone is following them, they think. Someone is following them, they hope. But no one is following these men. . . . They gave us nothing, and nothing will be left of them when we are done with brunch. If these thoughts are yours, droning in your head like a ring tone, day after day, hour by hour, then you, my friend, are in your 30s, and you are having a Night Epi$ode. —My Barbarian[6]

Lingering upon cross-temporal affinities and *Suddenly Last Summer*, I will admit to a tendency to lean on some prior generational markers that span the US, coast to coast, and famously include those hailing from Clarksdale, Mississippi (Tennessee Williams), and Baltimore, Maryland (John Waters). In thinking about the work of East Coast forebears that altered my young adulthood, such as the films of Mark Morrisroe or the performances of Tabboo! (Stephen Tashjian), I imagine that their knowledge of books, plays, and lifestyles of this antecedent period (Williams, Edward Albee, Gore Vidal) provided a sense of fucked-up family that these young artists needed, even if those with whom they identified got eaten in the end.

Morrisroe's *Hello from Bertha* (1983), the film perhaps most aligned with his signature color photographs, is a tawdry drama about prostitution, delusion, and decline into death based on a Williams play. Toward the end of his life he expressed a desire to make a film based on another of Williams's plays, *In the Bar of a Tokyo Hotel* (1969). Perhaps he identified with both of its main characters: Miriam, a slutty, conniving woman trying to cash in on her former art star alcoholic husband; and Mark, a failing artist who convinced himself he invented color. Never leaving the hotel bar, Miriam tells the Barman: "I could absorb a pagoda in a minute."[7] Mark is frail, losing control, having, as Miriam enumerates, "gone through drip, fling, sopped, stained, saturated, scraped, ripped, cut, skeins of, mounds of heroically enduring color, but now he's arrived at a departure that's a real departure that I doubt he'll return from."[8] He dies in his hotel room. Miriam, almost sad, and entirely alone, admits, "He thought that he could create his own circle of light."[9]

Waters, another of Morrisroe's idols, recalled, "Tennessee Williams saved my life. As a twelve-year-old boy in suburban Baltimore, I would look up his name in the card catalogue at the library and it would read 'see Librarian.' I wanted these 'see Librarian' books."[10] Maybe Morrisroe thought Williams could save his life, too? Or perhaps he related to Williams's almost urgent need for recognition. *In the Bar of a Tokyo Hotel* includes a scene in which Mark, before dying, has a moment of clarity: "I've heard that finally on earth there'll be nothing but gigantic insects but now I know the last things, the imperishable things, are color and light."[11] By which he means his paintings?

Although searching for one's family tree in theater (and film) may be a widespread practice—in My Barbarian's case, through Bertolt Brecht, Rainer Werner Fassbinder, and William Shakespeare—subsequent generations of artists seeking visibility manifest this desire in very different ways from coast to coast. Some disregard the status given to the solitary "genius" artist altogether. Notably, Fassbinder did not really fashion himself as an artist, let alone an alternative one, but rather sought to make popular films specifically geared toward his own generation. His ensemble cast functioned much like a dysfunctional family whose hierarchies of love and alienation served as "radical self-critique," while also commenting on contemporary society in general. In *Beware of a Holy Whore*, "a group of people want to make a film and believe—or believe that they believe—they can change the world with their work."[12] Highly disillusioned by the potential futility of such a project, *Beware of a Holy Whore* is a stylish cautionary tale regarding the trappings of creative communities and their unrealizable dreams—a useful visualization of how prior oppositional movements might have come to unglamorous ends within a larger cultural arena that no longer found them entertaining. This all just reminds me of the paraphrased words of Los Angeles's own Vaginal Davis about her early art career: "I thought all artists needed to start a band."

Back to the summer of 2005. The band My Barbarian performed *Pagan Rights*, a seventy-five-minute "suite of rock-operatic mini-musicals that explore a California landscape," in what was ostensibly Participant's office workspace, for an enthusiastic crowd of New York fans. The first New York performance biennial, *Performa 05*, was already around the corner, so I extended Participant as a back-up venue, inviting them to perform again in

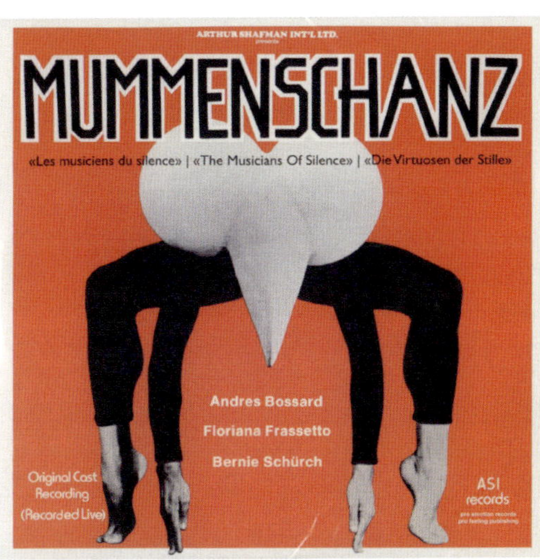

Cover of the Mummenschanz live album, 1977

the event that a better offer didn't come along. I was confident that it would, but when it didn't My Barbarian joined the line-up of a performance extravaganza that included Breyer P-Orridge, Luther Price and Katharine Finneran, Lovett/Codagnone, Rafael Sánchez, Derrick Adams, Julie Tolentino, Ron Athey and Juliana Snapper curated by Eileen Myles, Charles Atlas and Chris Peck, Suara Welitoff and Thalia Zedek, and of course, Davis. I guess we hadn't gotten the memo and thought the biennial was supposed to include a representative sample of the performance field at the time, so Participant, from our perspective, surveyed the moment as best we could.

In November 2005 the evolving ensemble known as My Barbarian performed in the gallery proper this time, premiering *You Were Born Poor and Poor You Will Die*, which converged performance, music, and sculpture in "a ritualistic incantation of class warfare." In this collaboration with artist Jeff Ono, they "don[ned] papier-mâché phalluses made of dollar bills and play[ed] percussion crafted out of loose change in chants and folk dances that . . . conjure[d] an Ancient World religion of human sacrifice that mirror[ed] the societal bloodletting of late-Capitalism." Perhaps Participant entered My Barbarian's trajectory already in a transitional period, from band and early showcore (appearing, for example, at curated club-like events like Ron Athey and Davis's Bricktops) to gallery-based work, from the "Campari context" (sponsored art entertainment events) and opening acts to the main event. I believe Campari also sponsored a panel discussion organized by Gaines and Segade on the topic "Castles and Caves: Spaces for Performance," in which Participant represented caves.

Time passed, and, while another New York City break for My Barbarian seemed imminent, economic decline in tandem with the city's at times provincial competitiveness with the Wrong Coast stood in the way. Participant engaged with My Barbarian in their first gallery-based exhibition in New York in the fall of 2009. *The Night Epi$ode* comprised a video installation that explored the genre of sci-fi television, linking narratives of supernatural anxiety with tales of economic collapse. The press release noted, "As a collective that works regularly with non-profit art institutions in an art world confronted by questions of sustainability, My Barbarian brings its own personal psychology to these uncanny images of economic dysfunction. The process for generating the work, all of which was made during the summer of 2009, was modeled after a fast form of television production, with the three members of the group writing, editing, performing, shooting, composing, costuming, and producing." This family-style process was mirrored in a sparse, dramatically lit installation whose props and furniture appear to have been inspired by Mummenschanz, an experimental theater troupe formed in Switzerland in the early 1970s that was known for their use of masks, props, light, and shadow.[13] Inspired by episodic TV shows from the 1950s to the 1980s, particularly Rod Serling's *Night Gallery* (1970–73), Gaines, Gordon, and Segade performed in six short video episodes that approach the financial crisis through the tropes of that genre. In one video, an unemployed woman loses her insurance and begins an affair with a being from another dimension. When her husband leaves her, she plans to marry the flickering light spirit in hopes of getting on the entity's insurance plan, only to discover that they are in fact a same-sex couple. Hosting the program is a seventh video (also the basis of the opening performance) in which three

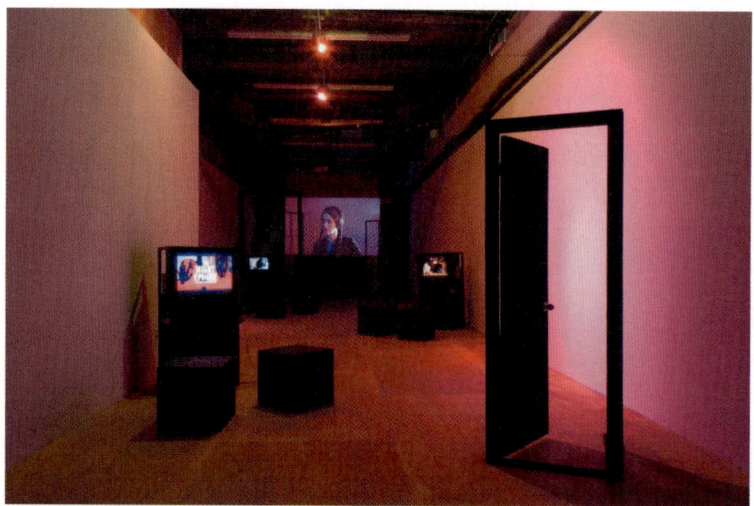

My Barbarian, *The Night Epi$ode*, 2009. Installation at Participant Inc., New York

"nightmare curators" are trapped in a curatorial meeting with "no exit from the aura of negativity that permeates the politics of exhibition."[14]

That Which Is Not Yet Here

It was in part the several years of engagement with My Barbarian that bonded me to the late queer performance theorist José Esteban Muñoz. We shared a certain family, mostly emanating from Davis, his first cover girl, and because of my work with My Barbarian he invited me to Madrid to speak on a panel about performance.[15] Jack Halberstam and Ms. Davis were there, Muñoz's family of friends on an academic vacation. The topic had unexpectedly shifted, I guess when I was mid-flight, from queer performance to "queer failure," which I kind of resented at the time, not knowing, exactly, what this concept meant just yet. Muñoz had been writing extensively about My Barbarian, initially under this heading of "queer failure," to which My Barbarian apparently responded, "but we're trying."[16] So Muñoz listened, through Paolo Virno, and went on to write in tandem about "queer virtuosity," thinking maybe they are the same thing: "I align queer failure with a certain mode of virtuosity that helps the spectator exit from the stale and static lifeworld dominated by the alienation, exploitation, and drudgery associated with capitalism or landlordism."[17]

In "The Blur and Breathe Books," a lecture given in honor of Muñoz, Fred Moten touches upon the blur, the slur, "aesthetic indiscretion" and "the materiality of shade," the charged space of public sex, and "a queer phenomenology of perception," or "a queer kind of loitering."[18] Moten considers alterity as an "already late-ness" or belatedness that aligns with Muñoz's analysis of Jack Smith's "investment in Atlantis," and, by comparison, with My Barbarian's "interest in a mythic past," as, for example, in their *Medieval Morality* (2004/2006), delineating a value system that is perhaps anachronistic, modeled on another time, past or future—it's hard to tell. New-ness is always haunted by the old, and necessitates longtime political imperatives to seek out tools to create—and make claims to describe—alternative worlds. In a subsequent lecture at the Museum of Modern Art, New York, "Blackness and Nonperformance," Moten also said that "performance studies is embarrassed of performance." However, Muñoz was not, and likened My Barbarian to "the ragtag queer collective hysteria that Smith staged in his legendary experimental films *Flaming Creatures* and *Normal Love*. Both the lone lunatic and the crazed collective stage a desire that I have called 'queer utopia.' Both modes of performance ask important questions of aesthetic practice, questions that attempt to visualize that which is not yet here."[19]

Muñoz invoked the films of Smith and performance generally as perhaps the one and only way art could be useful.[20] In describing Smith's critique of capitalism, or what he called "landlordism," Muñoz outlines Smith's aversion to private property: "Through his strange and moldy mode of address, Smith speaks of an economic system that is innately flawed, violently asymmetrical, and essentially exploitative. Smith's manifesto was utopian, not so much because he dreamed of Xanadu but, more nearly, because he performed alternate realities."[21] More specifically, Muñoz's reading of Smith also provides a cautionary tale for artists seeking strategies for "success." (Lutz Bacher once said, "I don't do strategy.") Discussing Smith's description of actress Yvonne De Carlo, the antithesis of his beloved B-movie star

Maria Montez, as a "walking career," he notes, "Those of us who attempt to dream utopia within . . . quotidian life must constantly overcome the disabling inertia generated by such agents of anti-utopianism. De Carlo's brand of careerism was . . . an ethos that limited the possibility of imagining a different time and place that was not organized by capitalism's injunctive to reproduce and be productive."[22]

Counterpublicity

> Disidentification's use-value is only accessible through the transformative politics that it enables subjects and groups to imagine. Counterpublics are not magically and automatically realized through disidentifications, but they are suggested, rehearsed, and articulated. Disidentifications are strategies that are called on by minoritarian subjects throughout their everyday life. —José Esteban Muñoz[23]

Disidentification, *world-making*, *optimism against exhaustion*, *minority performance*, *queer futurity*, *utopian force*, *radical attempt*, *belonging*—these were not just words in Muñoz's vocabulary, but a "not yet here" worth being here for. Just as Muñoz wrote with and for My Barbarian, My Barbarian performed Muñoz's writing. They are intertwined. It seems fitting that the performance *Counterpublicity*, based on a chapter of Muñoz's *Disidentifications: Queers of Color and the Performance of Politics* (1999) about Pedro Zamora from MTV's *The Real World*, occurred at the Whitney Museum of American Art, New York, where My Barbarian's "ephemera as evidence" is now gathering. Tavia Nyong'o, in his essay on the subject, highlights Muñoz's "prioritizing methexis over mimesis," "beyond the simply representational," as "a way of touching and being touched," and quotes Muñoz's manifesto: "'Methexis' is the aesthetic term that describes how the particular participates in a larger form; in Greek tragedy it literally means group sharing, accounting for the way in which an audience takes part in a drama, adding to it, augmenting it. Queer media must call for participation, vivification, and an expanded sense of a queer commons that is not quite present but altogether attainable."[24] As if this call to look beyond individual representation were written for and with My Barbarian, Nyong'o extrapolates from it that *Counterpublicity* "asks us to participate in both the potential and the uncertainty that claims to collectivity make."[25] I am reminded again of Mummenschanz, specifically their live album, which contains only the sounds recorded in the theater between their silent performances: gasps, laughter, and applause.

The title of this essay is drawn from the lyrics to My Barbarian's song "Pagan Rights," from the album *California Sweet & the 7 Pagan Rights* (2006), and the José Esteban Muñoz chapter title "After Jack: Queer Failure, Queer Virtuosity," in *Cruising Utopia: The Then and There of Queer Futurity* (New York: NYU Press, 2009), 177.

1 Muñoz, *Cruising Utopia*, 178.
2 Unattributed quotations and biographical details throughout this text come from early statements and promotional materials shared by My Barbarian in support of my research for this essay.
3 Alexandro Segade, My Barbarian interview with the author, April 2021.
4 David Velasco, "1000 Words: Art Club 2000," *Artforum* 51, no. 6 (February 2013): 219.
5 Ibid., 220.
6 My Barbarian, script for the Nightmare Curators, *The Night Epi$ode*, 2009.
7 Tennessee Williams, *In the Bar of a Tokyo Hotel,* in *Dragon Country* (New York: New Directions, 1970), 8.
8 Ibid., 41.
9 Ibid., 53.
10 John Waters, "The Kindness of a Stranger," *New York Times Review of Books*, November 19, 2006.
11 Williams, *In the Bar of a Tokyo Hotel*, 24.
12 Christian Braad Thomsen, "Self-Criticism," in *Fassbinder: The Life and Work of a Provocative Genius*, trans. Martin Chalmers (Minneapolis: University of Minnesota Press, 1991), 90.
13 Mummenschanz enjoyed a strange and commercially successful career, which included a three-year run on Broadway and appearances on *The Muppet Show* and *Sesame Street*. In 1992, founding member Andres Bossard died from AIDS-related illness.
14 The script for the Nightmare Curators recounts: "She made a piece in which she wrapped herself in a Wicker Man costume made of marijuana, which was illegal in her state at that time. She went to the capitol and burned herself alive. The legislature was supposed to become stoned from her burning body. It may have succeeded, there are varying accounts, and I am sifting through the documentation . . ."
15 "Presenting Performance," organized by José Esteban Muñoz, ARCO, Madrid, 2009.
16 Segade, My Barbarian interview with the author.
17 Muñoz, *Cruising Utopia*, 173.
18 Fred Moten, "The Blur and Breathe Books," lecture, Department of Performance Studies, New York University, February 24, 2016.
19 Muñoz, *Cruising Utopia*, 170. Moten's Museum of Modern Art lecture is available online at https://www.youtube.com/watch?v=G2leiFByllg.
20 In the preface to *Disidentifications: Queers of Color and the Performance of Politics*, (Minneapolis: University of Minnesota Press, 1999), Muñoz recounts Jack Smith's response to the question "Could art be useful?": "Ever since the glitter drifted over the burnout ruins of Plaster Lagoon, thousands of artists have pondered and dreamed of such a thing, yet, art must not be used any more as another elaborate means of fleeing from thinking because of the multiplying amount of information each person needs to process in order to come to any kind of decision on what kind of planet one wants to live on before business, religion, and government succeed in blowing it out of the solar system" (xi).
21 Muñoz, *Cruising Utopia*, 170.
22 Ibid., 172.
23 Muñoz, *Disidentifications*, 179.
24 Tavia Nyong'o, "In Finitude: Being with José, Being with Pedro," *Social Text 121*, 32, no. 4 (Winter 2014): 72.
25 Ibid., 83.

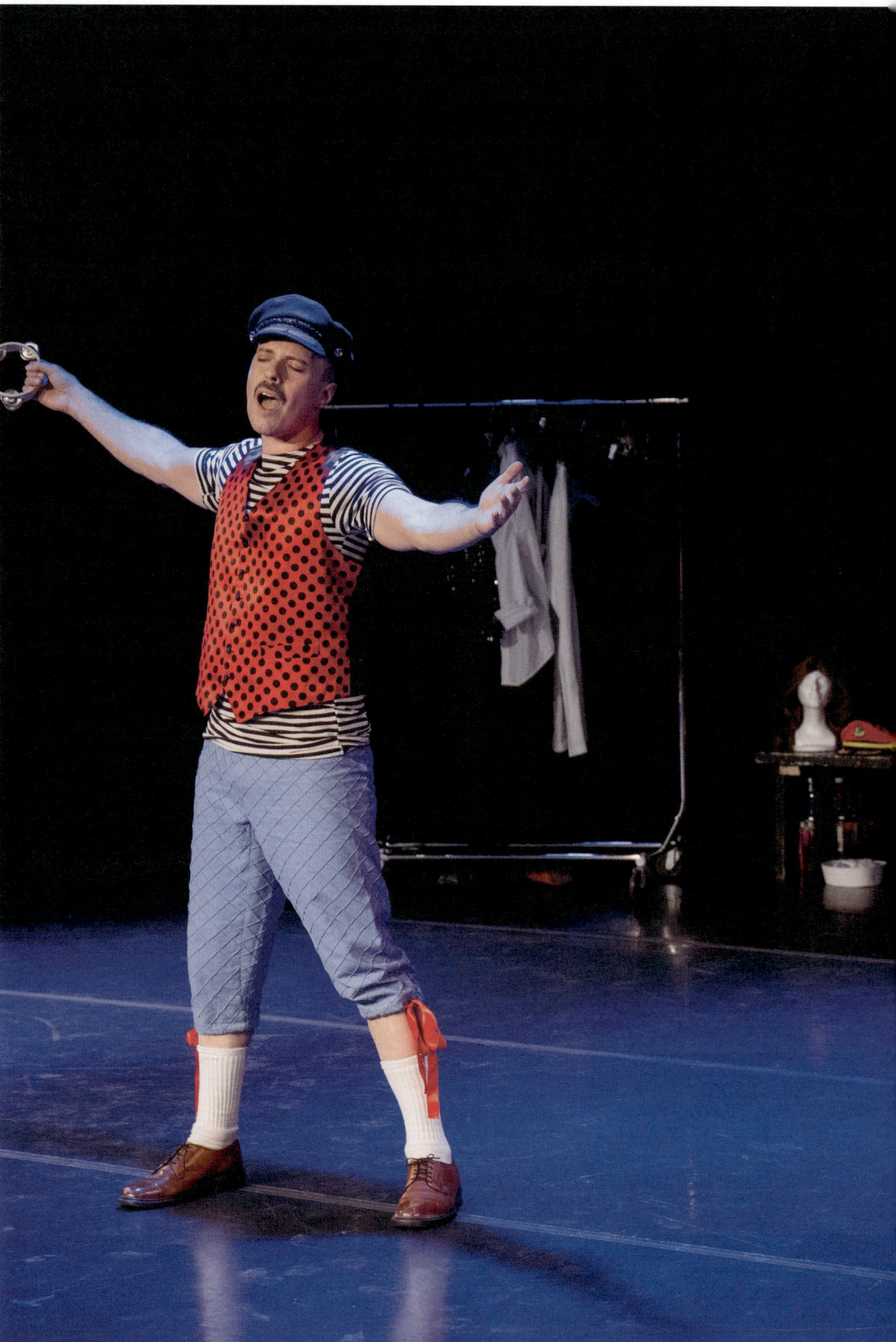

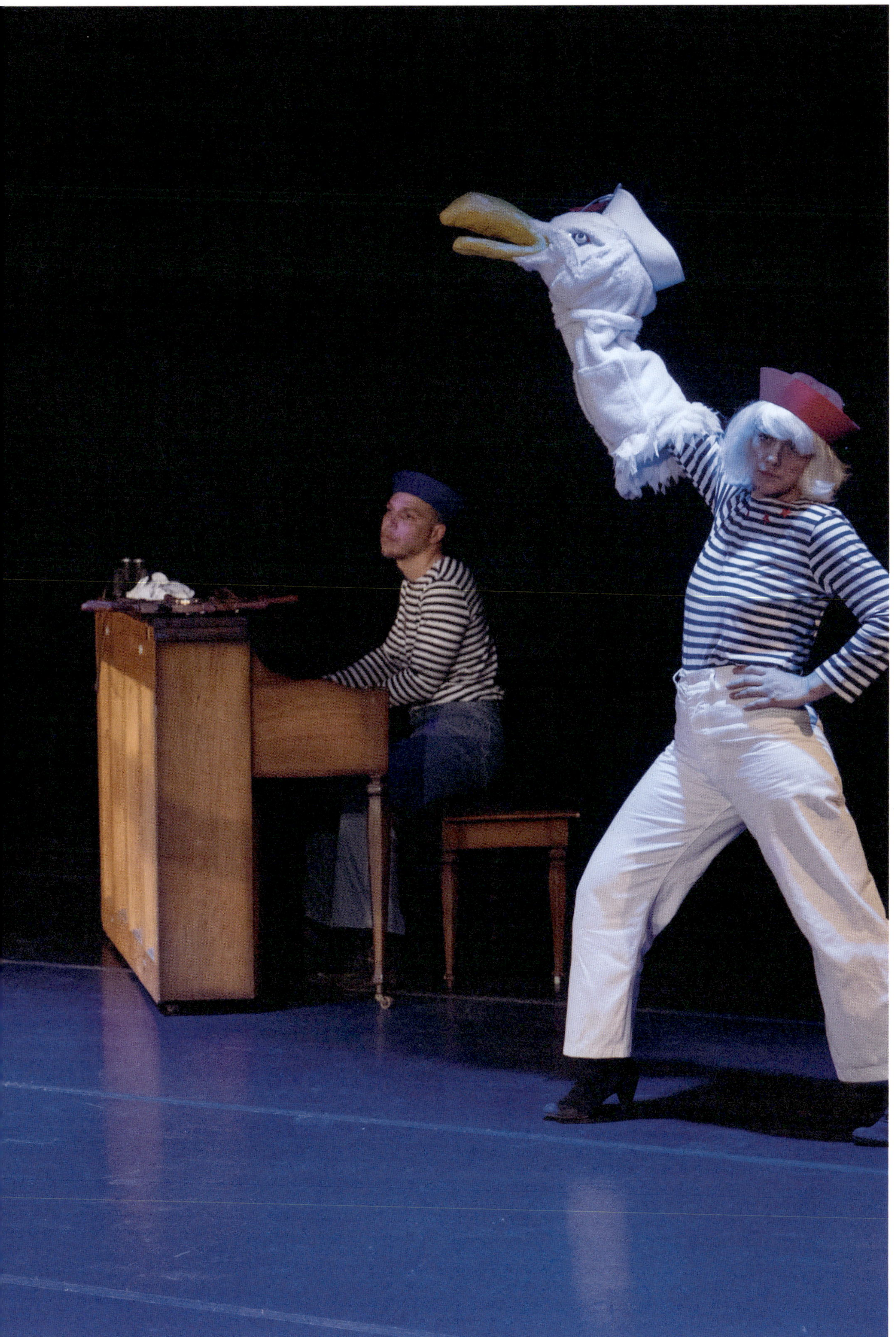

SELECTED PERFORMANCE AND EXHIBITION HISTORY

Projects are arranged alphabetically by title, with the associated performance and/or exhibition venues indicated in chronological order. Significant sub-projects are included in order of staging or presentation date below entries for the related primary projects. Page numbers reference illustrations in the visual chronology.

This listing reflects the information available at the time of publication.

○ Performance
● Exhibition
◑ Performance and Exhibition

Broke People's Baroque Peoples' Theater
pp. 106–11

● The College of Wooster's Art Museum, Wooster, OH, 2015
○ Whitney Museum of American Art, New York, 2015
● Diane Rosenstein Fine Arts, Los Angeles, 2014
○ Art Public, Art Basel Miami Beach, Art Public, 2012
◑ Human Resources, Los Angeles, 2012
○ Ball of Artists, Pacific Standard Time Performance and Public Art Festival, Greystone Mansion, Los Angeles, 2012
◑ San Francisco Museum of Modern Art, 2012
● Studio Museum in Harlem, New York, 2012
● Transformer Gallery, Washington, DC, 2012
● CANADA Gallery, New York, 2011
◑ The Kitchen, New York, 2011
○ San Diego Museum of Art, 2011
◑ Grand Arts, Kansas City, MO, and X Initiative, New York, 2009

Blood on the Cat's Neck
pp. 132–35

● Clifford Chance US LLP, New York, 2015
◑ Goethe-Institut New York, 2014

The Butterfly's Evil Spell
pp. 116–17
Collaboration with Lara Schnitger

● Anton Kern Gallery, New York, 2012

The Case of the Stairs
pp. 74–75

○ Los Angeles County Museum of Art, 2008. Performed with L.A. Fog, Hana van der Kolk, and Leilani Drakeford

California Sweet & the 7 Pagan Rights (Pagan Rights)
pp. 40–45

● PS1, Long Island City, NY, 2008
○ Socrates Sculpture Park, Long Island City, NY, 2008
◑ *California Biennial*, Orange County Museum of Art, Newport Beach, 2006
○ Torpedo, Oslo, Norway, 2006
○ Hammer Museum, Los Angeles, 2005
○ Participant Inc., New York, 2005
○ Drake Underground, Toronto, Canada, 2005
○ Evidence Room Theater, Los Angeles, 2005

Counterpublicity
pp. 128–31

● DePaul Art Museum, Chicago, 2017
● Clifford Chance US LLP, New York, 2015
○ Whitney Museum of American Art, New York, 2014
● Visual AIDS, Day Without Art, 2014

Dance Witches Dance
Collaboration with Lara Schnitger

◑ Luckman Gallery, Los Angeles, 2009
◑ Museum Het Domain, Sittard, the Netherlands, 2008

Double Agency
pp. 90–93

◑ Texas State Art Galleries, San Marcos, 2019
○ Los Angeles County Museum of Art, 2015. Performed with Robbie Acklen, Nao Bustamante, Jibz Cameron, and Adam Dugas

An Evening with My Barbarian

○ Museum of Modern Art, New York, 2012

Ecos de los Ecos de los Ecos
pp. 88–89

◑ Museo Experimental El Eco and Espacio Escultórico, UNAM, Mexico City, 2010. Performed with Las Reinas Chulas

Fairy Theatre at the Fisting Motel

○ *Platinum Oasis*, curated by Ron Athey and Vaginal Davis, Outfest 2002, Coral Sands Motel, Los Angeles, 2002

Forest Brothers & Sisters
pp. 86–87

◑ *Baltic Triennial 10*, Contemporary Art Center, Vilnius, Lithuania, 2009. Performed with Liūdni Slibinai (Vaidas Kublinskas, Aistė Lasytė, and Dominykas Vaitiekūnas)

Frenchboro, Maine
Collaboration with Candice Breitz and Glenn Ligon

○ Cohen Leslie and Brown, New York, 2001
○ The Palace, Los Angeles, 2001

Gods of Canada
pp. 58–61

Gods of Canada
● DeVos Art Museum, Marquette, MI, 2010
● Bard College, Center for Curatorial Studies, Annandale-on-Hudson, NY, 2006
○ The Power Plant, Toronto, Canada, 2005. Performed with Scott Martin and Andy Ouchi

Gods of Canada II: La Séparatisme Galactique
◑ Bíennale de Montréal, Canada, 2007

Honoring the Honorees in a World Without Honor

○ Foundation for Contemporary Arts, The Kitchen, New York, 2017

Hystera Theater
pp. 136–39

● Owens Art Gallery, Sackville, New Brunswick, Canada, 2019
● Studio Museum in Harlem, New York, 2009
◑ Art Basel Miami Beach, Art Positions, Steve Turner Contemporary, Miami, 2008. Performed with Jessica Espeleta

Medieval Morality
pp. 38–39

○ MAK Center for Art and Architecture, Schindler House, West Hollywood, 2004. Performed with Scott Martin and Andy Ouchi
○ Peres Projects, Berlin, 2006. Performed with Jan Hammer

Mountain People
pp. 62–63

○ Galleria Civica Trento, Trentino-South Tyrol, Italy, 2007

MB: The Mary Blair Story
pp. 36–37

○ NOW Festival, Roy and Edna Disney/CalArts Theater (REDCAT), Los Angeles, 2004. Performed with Norwood Cheek, Anh Do, Kim Humphries, Giles Miller, and Andy Ouchi

The Monkey Machine

○ Vaginal Davis's Bricktops, Los Angeles, 2004

Mythologic Mass
pp. 50–51

◑ Hyde Park Art Center and The Hideout, Chicago, 2006
○ Sweeney Art Gallery, University of California, Riverside, 2006
○ Stephen Weiss Studio, New York, 2006. Performed with Tim Koh and Giles Miller

The Night Epi$ode
pp. 76–79

The Night Epi$ode
● Institute of Contemporary Art, Philadelphia, 2010
● Hammer Museum, Los Angeles, 2010
● Participant Inc., New York, 2009

Death Panel Discussion
○ Hammer Museum, Los Angeles, 2011
○ Transformer Gallery, Washington, DC, 2010
○ Participant Inc., New York, 2009

Nightmarathon: Halloween Hextravaganza

○ Sundown Salon, Los Angeles, 2002

Non-Western
pp. 68–71

Non-Western
○ Contemporary Arts Forum, Santa Barbara, 2008
○ Estación, Tijuana, Mexico, 2008
○ Ground Zero, University of Southern California, Los Angeles, 2008
○ University of California, San Diego, and San Diego Museum of Art, 2008
○ La Noche en Blanco, El Matadero, Madrid, 2007
○ Steve Turner Contemporary, Los Angeles, 2007
○ *Wow and Now*, organized by José Muñoz, Nao Bustamante, and Karen Finley, Joe's Pub, New York, 2007

Hacia Una Postura Izquierdista (Toward a Leftist Positionality)
● Center for Contemporary Art, Tel Aviv, 2008
● Studio Museum in Harlem, New York, 2008
● Armory Center for the Arts, Pasadena, 2007

***Post-Living Ante-Action Theater* (PoLAAT)**
pp. 100–5

Post-Living Ante-Action Theater (PoLAAT)
● Museum of Contemporary Art, Miami, 2009
● DiverseWorks, Houston, 2009
● New Museum, New York, 2008

Intro: Pre-Paradise; Post-Party Dream State Caucus; Outro: Post-Apocalypse
○ New Museum, New York, 2016

My Barbarian: The Audience is Always Right
● New Museum, New York, 2016

Post-Living Ante-Action Theater: Pre-Apocalyptic Jam Band Dance-Soireé
○ Visual Art Center, University of Texas at Austin, 2016

Post-Living Ante-Action Theater: Together Forever?
◑ Yaffo 23, Jerusalem, 2013

Post-Living Ante-Action Theater: Born to Kill, Learn to Love
○ Institute of Contemporary Art, Philadelphia, 2012

Post-Living Ante-Action Theater: Post-Paradise, Sorry-Again
○ Roy and Edna Disney/CalArts Theater (REDCAT), Los Angeles, 2012

Post-Living Ante-Action Theater: PoLAAT Toronto
○ Rhubarb Festival, Toronto, Canada, 2011

Post-Living Ante-Action Theater: Todo El Dinero es Sueño
○ El Matadero, Madrid, 2010
○ ARCO, Madrid, 2010

Post-Living Ante-Action Theater: Club Remix
○ American Repertory Theater, Harvard University, Cambridge, MA, 2010

The Five Principles
◑ Museum of Contemporary Art, North Miami, 2009

Post-Living Ante-Action Theater: The Eleven Human Senses
○ Townhouse Gallery/Rawabet Theater, Cairo, 2008

Post-Living Ante-Action Theater: Post-Paradise, Never Say Sorry Again
○ Galleria Civica, Trento, Trentino-South Tyrol, Italy, 2008

Post-Living Ante-Action Theater: Post-Paradise, Sorry-Again
○ New Museum, New York, 2008
● Studio Museum in Harlem, New York, 2009

Purple Eyes

○ Spring Break Festival, Evidence Room Theater, Los Angeles, 2004. Performed with Norwood Cheek and Andy Ouchi

Retro-Active Self-Appropriation
pp. 84–85

○ San Francisco Museum of Modern Art, 2010

Rose Bird
pp. 94–95

● Whitney Museum of American Art, New York, 2023

Silver Minds
pp. 56–57

Silver Minds
○ Aspen Art Museum, 2006

Double Future (double feature with *You Were Born Poor and Poor You Will Die*)
○ Whitney Museum of American Art, New York, 2022
○ Roy and Edna Disney/CalArts Theater (REDCAT), Los Angeles, 2006. Performed with Scott Martin, Giles Miller, and Lynn Perko

Tourists from the Future
Collaboration with Megan Whitmarsh
○ Watermill Center, Water Mill, NY, 2011

Songbook

○ Whitney Museum of American Art, New York, 2021

Squirrel Radio Action
pp. 32–33

○ Commissioned by Pacific Drift, KPCC Southern California Public Radio, Pasadena, 2005. Performed with Andy Ouchi and Scott Martin

Suspension of Beliefs
pp. 114–15

● Steve Turner Contemporary, Los Angeles, 2010

Transparency
pp. 80–83

The Fourth Wall (Transparency)
- ○ Museum of Contemporary Art, Los Angeles, 2009. Performed with Hana van der Kolk

Transparency 2021
- ○ Whitney Museum of American Art, New York, 2021

Voyage of the White Widow
pp. 64–67

Voyage of the White Widow
- ● Anton Kern Gallery, New York, 2008
- ○ De Appel, Amsterdam, the Netherlands, 2007
- ○ *Performa 07*, Whitney Museum of American Art, New York, 2007

Bride of the White Widow
- ○ The Lightbox, Miami Dade College Museum of Art and Design, 2018

The Golden Age
- ● Studio Museum in Harlem, New York, 2009
- ● Center for Contemporary Art, Tel Aviv, 2008
- ● New Museum, New York, 2008
- ● Vox Populi, Philadelphia, 2007

Web of the Ultimate: A Séance

- ○ MAK Center for Art and Architecture, Schindler House, West Hollywood, 2004

Working Mother
pp. 118–27

Universal Declaration of Infantile Anxiety Situations Reflected in the Creative Impulse
- ● Gallery 400, University of Illinois, Chicago, 2014
- ● Vielmetter Los Angeles, 2013
- ○ Whitney Biennial, Whitney Museum of American Art, New York, 2014

The Mother and Other Plays
- ○ Vielmetter Los Angeles, 2013
- ○ Whitney Biennial, Whitney Museum of American Art, New York, 2014
- ○ Gallery 400, University of Illinois, Chicago, 2014

X-Mas Special

- ○ Performed at the homes of Allison Anders, Beck, Roddy Bottum, Luise Heath, Reneé Petropolous, Stephen Prina, and Kim Fisher, Los Angeles, 2001

You Were Born Poor and Poor You Will Die
pp. 46–49

You Were Born Poor and Poor You Will Die
- ○ California College of the Arts, San Francisco, 2005
- ○ *Performa 05*, Participant Inc., New York, 2005

Double Future (double feature with *Silver Minds*)
- ○ Whitney Museum of American Art, New York, 2022
- ○ Roy and Edna Disney/CalArts Theater (REDCAT), Los Angeles, 2006. Performed with Scott Martin, Giles Miller, and Lynn Perko

My Barbarian band performances, 2000–2009
pp. 28–31

- ○ Various venues, including: Spaceland, Silverlake Lounge, Knitting Factory, The Troubadour, and The Smell, Los Angeles; Hemlock Tavern, San Francisco; and The Passerby, New York. Performed with Norwood Cheek, Andy Ouchi, Scott Martin, Giles Miller, Amy Yao, and others

CHECKLIST OF THE EXHIBITION

As of September 17, 2021

Unless otherwise noted, all works are collection of the artists, courtesy Vielmetter Los Angeles.

Burning Flag, 2005/2021
from the performance series *Pagan Rights*
Textiles, sequins, and acrylic
75½ × 41 in. (191.8 × 104.1 cm)

Sorry 4 the Plague (Squirrel Radio Action), 2005
Permanent marker on foamboard
4 × 6 in. (10.2 × 15.2 cm)

Medieval Drawings, 2006
from the performance series *Medieval Morality*
Watercolor and marker on paper
8½ × 11 in. (21.6 × 27.9 cm) each

Red Monster, 2006
from the performance series *Pagan Rights*
Synthetic fur, plaster, and acrylic
34 × 10 × 13 in. (86.4 × 25.4 × 33 cm)

I Heart Mimesis, 2008
from the performance *Hystera Theater*
Linen, lace, and satin banner on wood dowel
86.5 × 56.5 in. (219.7 × 143.5 cm)
Courtesy the artists and Artist Pension Trust

Lifeboat Monster, 2009
from the installation *The Night Epi$ode*
Papier-mâché and acrylic
11 × 9 × 7 in. (28 × 22.9 × 17.8 cm)

Red Office Worker, 2009
from the installation *The Night Epi$ode*
Papier-mâché, acrylic, and wig hair
17 × 13 × 4 in. (43.2 × 33 × 10.2 cm)

From the performance *Ecos de los Ecos de los Ecos*

Bar Lesbico, 2010
Watercolor, marker, and acrylic on paper
16½ × 23⅛ in. (41.9 × 58.7 cm)

Three Figures, 2010
Watercolor, marker, and acrylic on paper
16½ × 23⅛ in. (41.9 × 58.7 cm)

Three Figures at the Espacio Escultórico, 2010
Watercolor, marker, and acrylic on paper
16½ × 23⅛ in. (41.9 × 58.7 cm)

From the performance series *Working Mother*

City of Tver, 2013
Oil stick on craft paper
18 × 24 in. (45.7 × 61 cm)

Factory (Suklinov Works), 2013
Oil stick on craft paper
18 × 24 in. (45.7 × 61 cm)

Home of the Teacher III, 2013
Oil stick on craft paper
18 × 24 in. (45.7 × 61 cm)

Household I, 2013
Oil stick on craft paper
18 × 24 in. (45.7 × 61 cm)

In Praise of Communism, 2013
Oil stick on craft paper
18 × 24 in. (45.7 × 61 cm)

Mask, 2013
Oil stick and charcoal on craft paper
118 × 24 in. (45.7 × 61 cm)

Mimic 1, 2013
Papier-mâché and oil stick
11½ × 6½ × 5 in. (29.2 × 16.5 × 12.7 cm)

Our Comrade, 2013
Oil stick on craft paper
18 × 24 in. (45.7 × 61 cm)

Printing Press II, 2013
Oil stick on craft paper
118 × 24 in. (45.7 × 61 cm)

Prison Guard, 2013
Papier-mâché
11¼ × 9 × 4½ in. (28 × 15.2 × 11.4 cm)
Collection of Robert and Anne Conn; courtesy Vielmetter Los Angeles

Shopper, 2013
Papier-mâché
10½ × 6¼ × 4½ in. (26.7 × 15.9 × 11.4 cm)
Collection of Robert and Anne Conn; courtesy Vielmetter Los Angeles

Unemployed Man, 2013
Papier-mâché
11¼ × 8 × 4½ in. (28.6 × 20.3 × 11.4 cm)
Collection of Robert and Anne Conn; courtesy Vielmetter Los Angeles

Your Son Has Been Shot, 2013
Oil stick on craft paper
18 × 24 in. (45.7 × 61 cm)

From the installation *Folk Play*

Death, 2014
Clay, felt, and acrylic
14½ × 16½ × 2½ in. (36.8 × 41.9 × 6.4 cm)

Heard-Hearted Barbara Allen, 2014
Clay, silk, thread, cardboard, sand, and acrylic
15½ × 5½ in. (39.4 × 14 cm)

Lady Margaret Coffin, 2014
Clay, felt, thread, and acrylic
14½ × 6 × 3 in. (36.8 × 15.2 × 7.6 cm)

Sir Tamlyn de Grey, 2014
Clay, polyester, silk, and acrylic
16 × 10¼ × 4 in. (40.6 × 26 × 10.2 cm)

Sweet William Wake, 2014
Clay, felt, and acrylic
18 × 8¼ × 3 in. (45.7 × 21 × 7.6 cm)

From the performance *Blood on the Cat's Neck*

Günther, 2014
Synthetic resin and acrylic
11½ × 7 × 4½ in. (29.2 × 17.8 × 11.4 cm)

Hanna, 2014
Synthetic resin and acrylic
9 × 7½ × 5 in. (22.9 × 19 × 12.7 cm)

Harry, 2014
Synthetic resin and acrylic
11½ × 7 × 4½ in. (29.2 × 17.8 × 11.4 cm)

Hedi (doll), 2015
Plastic, plaster, wire, and textiles
28½ × 10½ × 5½ in. (72.4 × 26.7 × 14 cm)
Collection of Beth Rudin DeWoody; courtesy Vielmetter Los Angeles

Margit and Kurt, 2015
Plastic, plaster, wire, and textiles, two parts
24 × 10 (61 × 25.4 cm) each
Collection of Carla Shen; courtesy Vielmetter Los Angeles

From the performance *Double Agency*

Masks of the World, AC 1994.203.1, 2015
Synthetic resin, fiberglass, plaster, papier-mâché, and acrylic
25 × 5 × 8 in. (63.5 × 12.7 × 20.3 cm)

Masks of the World, AC 1999.251.4, 2015
Synthetic resin, fiberglass, cardboard, wood, acrylic, raffia, and synthetic hair
19 × 13 × 5 in. (48.3 × 33 × 12.7 cm)

Masks of the World, M.71.73.247, 2015
Brass, acrylic, linen, and foam
9 × 10 × 1½ in. (22.9 × 25.4 × 3.8 cm)

Masks of the World, M.73.113.7, 2015
Terracotta, glue, mother of pearl, acrylic, and sand
11½ × 7 × 4 in. (29.2 × 17.8 × 10.2 cm)

Masks of the World, TR.4065.3, 2015
Synthetic resin, fiberglass, and acrylic
16 × 16½ × 2 in. (40.6 × 41.9 × 5.1 cm)

PoLAAT Mask #4 (Mandate to Participate), 2016
from the performance series *Post-Living Ante-Action Theater* (PoLAAT)
Synthetic resin and acrylic
13½ × 10¾ × 5¼ in. (34.3 × 27.3 × 13.3 cm)

My Barbarian, 2021
Three-channel video, color, sound, 120 min.

Standelabra 1 (4-Armed Bull Priestess), 2021
Collaboration with Jeff Ono
Steel with black matte paint with *Breastplate* (2005), *Phallus 1* (2005), *Phallus 2* (2005), *Gourd 1* (2005), *Gourd 2* (2005), *Mask (Panjandrum)* (2005), *You Were Born Poor* costume (2005–21), *Mask (Bull God)* (2005), and *Mask (Novitiate)* (2005)
Stand: 48 × 15 × 69 in. (122 × 38.1 × 175.3 cm)
Base: 18¼ × 18¼ × 1¼ in. (46.4 × 46.4 × 3.8 cm)

Standelabra 2 (Dancing Pagan), 2021
Steel with black matte paint with *Third Eye* mask (2006), *Pagan Rights* costume (2006–9), *Obama Pants* (2009), and *Head-kerchief* (2006)
Stand: 20¼ × 7 × 69 in. (50.8 × 17.8 × 175.3 cm)
Base: 18¼ × 18¼ × 1¼ in. (46.4 × 46.4 × 3.8 cm)

Standelabra 3 (3-Headed Oracle), 2021
Steel with black matte paint with *Shakuntala Du Bois* (2012), *Old Fairy* (2012), *Moon Goddess* (2012), *Gown by Alexandro* (2012–21), three wigs, and three porcelain busts
Stand: 46½ × 10 × 72¼ in. (118.1 × 25.4 × 183.5 cm)
Base: 18¼ × 18¼ × 1¼ in. (46.4 × 46.4 × 3.8 cm)

WHITNEY MUSEUM OF AMERICAN ART STAFF

Jehad Abu-Hamda
Hunter Adams
Stephanie Adams
Aimen Ali
Justin Allen
Adrienne Alston
William Amspacher
Sofa Answar
Jason Anzovino
Aaron Applebey
Marilou Aquino
Morgan Arenson
David Armacost
I.D. Aruede
Wendy Barbee-Lowell
William Beadle
Bernadette Beauchamp
Kate Behm
Michael Beiser
Harry Benjamin
Karen Bergman
Caitlin Bermingham
Pamela Besnard
Casey Betts
Danielle Bias
Ivy Blackman
Brian Block
Richard Bloes
Alexandra Bono
Austin Bowes
Rebecca Boxbaum
David Breslin
Colin Brooks
Algernon Brown
Carolina Brown
Lisa Brown
Douglas Burnham
Garfield Burton
Anne Byrd
Pablo Caines
Savannah Campbell
Margaret Cannie
Audrey Capria
Jane Carey
Amanda Carrasco
Aurian Carter
Sunil Chaddha
Morgan Chanon-Smith
David Chapman
Derrick Charles
Lokewantie Cheong
Mathieu Chester
Margaret Katherine Cheyne
Abby Chin-Martin
Jacqueline Chmura
Nerses Chorekchyan
Ramon Cintron
Ron Clark
Kimberly Conaty
Andrew Cone
Errol Coore
Brenna Cothran
Heather Cox
David Critides
Karishma Das
Lawrence DeBlasio
Monserrate DeLeon
Margo Delidow
Masseny Diakite
Nicholas DiLeonardi
Lauren DiLoreto
Mary Teresa DiSipio
Marisa Donovan
Louis DosReis
Lisa Dowd
Reagan Duplisea
Kasim Earl
Adrienne Edwards
David Enriquez Barroso
Joanna Epstein
Cesar Espinoza
Alvin Eubanks
Reid Farrington
Seth Fogelman
Jacqueline Foster
Toni France
Karissa Francis
Samuel Franks
Denis Frederick
Kyle Freeman
Annie French
Isaiah Frisbie
Kendall Galant
Judith Gallegos
Donald Garlington
Anthony Gennari
Ronnie George
Laura Gilbert
Jennifer Goldstein
Amber Gonzalez
Lucas Gonzalez
Jonathan Gorman
Caitlin Green
Hilary Greenbaum
Steven Grimaldi
Nicole Grullón
Alex Gudding
Marcela Guerrero
Peter Guss
Helena Guzik
Rita Hall
Tara Hart
Barbara Haskell
Andrew Hawkes
Benjamin Hawks
Maura Heffner
Araya Henry
Elizabeth Henschen
Lawrence Hernandez
Jennifer Heslin
Megan Heuer
Jonathan Heutmaker
Rujeko Hockley
Nicholas S. Holmes
Michael Honigsberg
Jacob Horn
Kossiwa Houngbedji
Gene Hua
Jared Huggins
Sarah Humphreville
Beth Huseman
Isobel Iles
Gina Im
Sarah Isenberg
Malcolm Jackson
Carlos Jacobo
Armando Jaramillo Garcia
Jesse Jenkins
Michael Jensen
Kevin Jijon Gochez
Alyssa Johnson
Anthony Johnson
Julia Johnson
Asia Jones
Joyce Joseph
Nancy Joyce
Nevin Kallepalli
Rory Keeley
Margaret Keiley
Grace Keir
Christopher Ketchie
Safwan Khan
Thomas Killie
Ramsay Kolber
Margaret Kross
Summer Krounbi
Sarah Kwok
Midrene Lamy
Melinda Lang
Sandy LaPorte
Martha LaRose
Erin Law
Cathy Lebowitz
Eunice Lee
Sang Lee
Jen Leventhal
Christopher Lew
Benjamin Lipnick
Ruth Lizardi Barreto
Kelley Loftus
Robert Lomblad
Kelly Long
Brianna Lowndes
Angie Lu
Jason Lutz
Douglas Madill
Claire Malloy
Carol Mancusi-Ungaro
Galina Mardilovich
Anna Martin
Madison Martin
Mia Matthias
Caitlin McKee
Caroline McKinley
James McKnight
Ni-Robi McNair
Christine Mellampe
Bridget Mendoza
Graham Miles
David Miller
Simon Moore
David Morales
Michael Moriah
Michael Morrissey
Victor Moscoso
Majida Mugharbel
Casey Mulholland
Elaine Muniz
Meer Musa
Micah Musheno
Rebecca Naegele
Daniel Nascimento
David Neary
Ruben Negron
Randy Nelson
Giulia Nicita
Carlos Noboa
Jaison O'Blenis
Lindsey O'Connor
Nelson Ortiz

Ahmed Osman
Nicky Ozir
Luis Padilla
Jean Pagano
Kimie Page
Jane Panetta
Connor Paradis
Max Parry-McDonell
Christiane Paul
Jessica Pepe
Roberto Perez
Jason Phillips
Laura Phipps
Sebastien Pierre
Evangelos Pikoulas
Lindsay Pollock
Carla Posner
Eliza Proctor
Laura Protzel
Vincent Punch
Christy Putnam
Emma Quaytman
Gary Quintero
Julie Rega
Caitlin Reid
Lindsay Reuter
Gracie Reyes
Gregory Reynolds
Omari Richards
Yevgeniy Riftin
Belen Rincon
Martin Riofrio
Felix Rivera
Melissa Robles
Enrique Rocha
Mario Rodriguez
Gabriel Rojas
Clara Rojas-Sebesta
Julia Rome
Justin Romeo
Paul Romo
Sara Romo
Antonio Rosa
Chris Rosas Vargas
Charlotte Rosenberg
Joshua Rosenblatt
Amy Roth
Scott Rothkopf
Karsani Rusdi
Angelina Salerno
Laura Salomon
Leonel Sanchez
Awa Sanogo
Vincent Santiago
Ximena Santiago
Bermet Sargazakova
Lisa Saunders
Cristina Scorza
Peter Scott
Shawnace Seegars
Monica Sekaquaptewa
David Selimoski
Jason Senquiz
Dumitru Sersea
Joseph Shepherd
Leslie Sheridan
Elisabeth Sherman
Sofía Silva
Dyeemah Simmons
Matthew Skopek
Roxanne Smith
Joel Snyder
Michele Snyder
Elizabeth Soland
Barbi Spieler
Mark Steigelman
Minerva Stella
Jennifer MacNair Stitt
Emilie Sullivan
Denis Suspitsyn
Elisabeth Sussman
Daryl Szak Prasso
Arthur Tang
Melanie Taylor
Joseph Teliha
Ellen Tepfer
Latasha Thomas
Zoe Tippl
Charles Tisch
Ana Torres-Hurtado
Ambika Trasi
Stacey Traunfeld
Julius Treadway
Beth Turk
Lauren Turner
Matthew Vega
Eric Vermilion
Nancy Viglione
Cynthia Vogt
Eva von Schweinitz
Farris Wahbeh
Adam D. Weinberg
Erika Wentworth
Clemence White
Sherronda Williams
Marcia Witter
Corinne Worthington
Lori Wright-Huertas
Mengjiao Ally Xing
June Yoon
Lauren Young
Raul Zbengheci
Sefkia Zekiroski

As of August 3, 2021

INDEX

PHOTOGRAPHY CREDITS

In reproducing the images contained in this publication, the publisher obtained the permission of rights holders whenever necessary and possible. Reasonable efforts have been made to credit the copyright holders, photographers, and sources; if there are any errors or omissions, please contact the Whitney Museum of American Art so that corrections can be made in any subsequent edition.

Except as noted, photography of works by My Barbarian is courtesy the artists. All works by My Barbarian © 2021 My Barbarian.

p. 12: Jeff McLane. p. 15, right: Courtesy Eleanor Antin and Ronald Feldman Gallery, New York. p. 16: Fayette Hauser. p. 17: © 1974, Harry Gamboa Jr. p. 18: image © Albert Sanchez. pp. 26–27: Patterson Beckwith. pp. 36–37: Amy Bessone, image © 2021 Artists Rights Society (ARS), New York/ADAGP, Paris. p. 39: Jeff McLane. p. 41: Eve Fowler. p. 44: Jeff McLane. p. 46 (all): Rosalie Knox. pp. 48–49 (all): Patterson Beckwith. pp. 50–51: Rosalie Knox. p. 63 (all): Hugo Muñoz. p. 66: images courtesy the Museum of Art and Design at Miami Dade College. p. 67: image © Paula Court, courtesy PERFORMA. pp. 68–69: images courtesy Armory Center for the Arts, Pasadena, CA. pp. 72–73: Rosalie Knox. p. 74, top: photograph by Alexandra Wyman/WireImage. p. 76, top and bottom: Rosalie Knox. p. 80: images courtesy Museum of Contemporary Art (MOCA), Los Angeles. p. 81, top: Rosalie Knox; bottom: Aandrea Stang. p. 82: Photograph courtesy the Museum of Contemporary Art (MOCA), Los Angeles. pp. 84–85: Charles Villyard, courtesy the San Francisco Museum of Modern Art. p. 88, bottom: Jeff McLane. p. 89, top: Jeff McLane. p. 93: Robbie Acklen. pp. 94–95: stills courtesy My Barbarian and Telefantasy Productions. pp. 102–3: El Matadero and ARCO Madrid photographs by Becky Snodgrass; Galleria Civica, Trento, Italy, photographs by Hugo Muñoz; New Museum, New York, photographs courtesy the New Museum. pp. 104–5: images courtesy the New Museum, New York. p. 111, center: Rosalie Knox. p. 113: Sam Horine. pp. 114–15: Maxine Olson. p. 118–19: Robert Wedemeyer. p. 121: Jason Mandella. pp. 122–23: Robert Wedemeyer. pp. 132–33 (all): Jacobia Dahm. p. 135: Jacobia Dahm. p. 136: images courtesy Steve Turner. p. 141: Courtesy the Mummenschanz Foundation. p. 142: image courtesy Evidence Room Theater. p. 144: image © A.L. Steiner. p. 148: image courtesy Participant Inc. p. 152: Alan Weiner. pp. 154–55: image courtesy the Museum of Art and Design at Miami Dade College.

This catalogue was produced on the occasion of the exhibition *My Barbarian*, organized by Adrienne Edwards, Engell Speyer Family Curator and Director of Curatorial Affairs, with Mia Matthias, curatorial assistant, Whitney Museum of American Art, New York.

Whitney Museum of American Art, New York, October 29, 2021–February 27, 2022

Institute of Contemporary Arts, Los Angeles, September 2022–January 2023

The exhibition is sponsored by

NORDSTROM

Generous support is provided by Judy Hart Angelo; the John R. Eckel, Jr. Foundation; and the Whitney's National Committee.

Support is also provided by the Marshall Weinberg Fund for Performance, endowed in honor of his parents, Anna and Harold Weinberg, who taught him the meaning of giving.

Whitney Museum of American Art
99 Gansevoort Street
New York, NY 10014
whitney.org

Distributed by
Yale University Press
302 Temple Street
P.O. Box 209040
New Haven, CT 06520-9040
yalebooks.com/art

This publication was produced by the publications department at the Whitney Museum of American Art, New York: Beth A. Huseman, director of publications; Jennifer MacNair Stitt, editor; Beth Turk, editor; and Jacob Horn, editorial coordinator.

Project manager
Jacob Horn

Editor
Amanda Glesmann

Design
Joseph Logan and Katy Nelson, assisted by Erica Getto

Production
Nerissa Dominguez Vales and Sue Medlicott, The Production Department

Proofreader
Sarah Wolberg

Indexer
David Luljak

Separations
Altaimage, New York

Printing and binding
Ofset Yapımevi, Istanbul, Turkey

Typeset in Scto Grotesk, designed by Lauri Toikka and Florian Schick

Printed on 140gsm Magno Natural and 170gsm Magno Satin

Printed and bound in Turkey

10 9 8 7 6 5 4 3 2 1

Cataloging-in-publication data is on file with the Library of Congress
ISBN 978-0-300-26012-0

Cover artwork and illustrations on pages 1, 20, 141, and 168 by Alexandro Segade

Pages 6–7: *Broke People's Baroque Peoples' Theater*, 2011. Studio photograph. Pages 154–55: *Bride of the White Widow*, 2018. Performance photograph, The Light Box, Miami

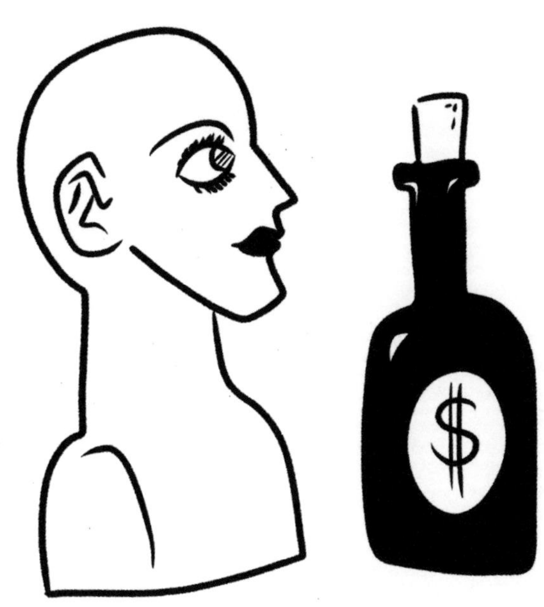